THE COMPLETE ENCYCLOPEDIA OF

HOME REPAIR

JULIAN WORTHINGTON
& BOB PENNYCOOK

CHARTWELL
BOOKS, INC.

CHARTWELL BOOKS, INC.
A Division of
BOOK SALES, INC.
110 Enterprise Avenue
Secaucus, New Jersey 07094

Original British edition published 1984 by
Orbis Publishing Limited, London

under licence from
Whinfrey Strachan Limited
315 Oxford Street
London   W1R 1AJ

Acknowledgements

Photographs: Jon Bouchier, Simon Butcher, Carrier Canada Limited,
Clay Brick Association, Paul Forrester, Jern Grischotti, Keith Morris,
Karen Norquay, Ian O'Leary, Portland Cement Association of
Canada, John Routledge and Roger Tuff.

Artists: Roger Courthold Associates, Drury Lane Studios,
Bernard Fallon, Nick Farmer, Tony Hannaford, Trevor
Lawrence, Linden Artists, David Pope, Peter Robinson, Mike
Saunders, Ian Stephen, Will Stephen, Craig Warwick, Brian
Watson, Gary Watson and David Worth.

Cover Design: First Image

Printed and bound in Italy

ISBN 1-55521-019-8

CONTENTS

INTRODUCTION

To appreciate your home fully and get the most out of it, you will need to look after it. This not only involves maintaining the overall appearance, both inside and out, but also making sure that all the systems are working properly.

It is an often painful fact of life that problems occur at the most inconvenient times — and this is as true in the home as anywhere. So a basic knowledge of home repair will come in very handy when you are faced with an emergency.

Even when the job that needs doing is not that urgent, the fact that you are in a position to handle it yourself will certainly save you money — and maybe time as well.

The Complete Encyclopedia of Home Repair is invaluable in either situation, for the information it provides will ensure that, whatever the job, you will get it right. And, of course, this is just as important as being able to do it yourself, since there is little point in carrying out work or making a repair if it is not done correctly. In this case, the problem is almost certain to occur again — and this time it may cost you a lot more to put it right.

You must pay particular attention to planning and preparation. The golden rule in any situation is to stop and think about what needs to be done. Are you clear in your mind exactly how to tackle the work? Have you considered all the possible problems you are likely to encounter? Have you got the right tools to hand? Have you bought all the materials you need?

All these may seem obvious, but it is surprising how often people rush into the work without giving it proper consideration and either hit a snag halfway through or end up with a sub-standard result.

Never rush into a job, particularly if it is one you are tackling for the first time. By taking a little longer to plan and prepare thoroughly, you will save time and effort in the end. Bear in mind what it would cost to do the job again.

Never neglect safety. Although a job may appear simple, there could be unseen hazards in using worn or damaged tools. For this reason you should always look after your tools, store them carefully and treat them with respect. This way they will not only do the job you want them to do — and correctly — but they will also last a lot longer.

If you are working at a height, make sure you are standing on a secure base. This applies just as much when reaching for the ceiling as when working outside from the top of a ladder.

There are certain basic precautions that must be taken when working on the domestic systems. With electricity it is essential that you switch off the power or isolate the relevant circuit when handling electrical fittings and connections. On the plumbing system, make sure you have turned off the supply and drained the relevant part of the system before starting any repair, maintenance or installation work.

If there are young children in the house, keep them well away from the work area and never leave tools lying around for them to play with. Pets, too, should be kept away while you are working.

The guideline should always be — think before you act. It is far easier and safer to get the job right from the start than to have to iron out problems later.

The Complete Encyclopedia of Home Repair gives you the information you need to plan and prepare for each job, and its step-by-step guide to techniques will help ensure you get it right. In achieving the best results each time, you will have the satisfaction of knowing that each job you do is a job well done.

CHAPTER 1
Painting

PAINTING WOOD

Painting is the most popular way of decorating and protecting much of the wood in our homes. As with so many do-it-yourself jobs, getting a good finish depends on your skill. Here's how to paint wood perfectly.

Wood is used extensively in every part of our homes — from roof trusses to baseboards. Structural lumber is usually left rough and unfinished, while joinery — windows, doors, staircases, door casings and so on — is usually decorated in some way. Wood has just one drawback; as a natural material it's prone to deterioration and even decay unless it's protected. Painting wood is one way of combining decoration and pro-

tection, and the popularity of paint is a testimony to its effectiveness. Properly applied and well looked after, it gives wood a highly attractive appearance and also provides excellent protection against dampness, dirt, mold, insect attack, and general wear and tear.

Of course, paint isn't the only finish you can choose for wood. If its color and grain pattern are worth displaying, you can use

PREPARING WOOD FOR PAINT

1 Before you can apply the paint, you must fill any cracks or holes with wood filler (applied with a putty knife) and leave to dry.

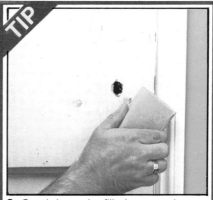

2 Sand down the filled areas using medium-grade sandpaper. Wrap the abrasive around a sanding block or wood offcut so it's easier to use.

3 Where paint has been chipped off, sand down the area and apply an ordinary wood primer to the bare wood using a small paintbrush.

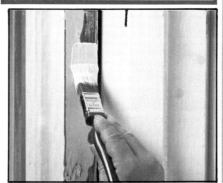

4 When the surface of the wood is smooth, apply undercoat (as the maker recommends) and leave to dry before you put on the top coat.

Ready Reference

PAINT TYPES
Paints for wood can be:

● **solvent-based gloss** (the 'oil' paints of the days before the advent of synthetic resins), which can be used indoors or outdoors

● **solvent-based satin** (also called eggshell or silk), intended for indoor use.

Both are fairly slow-drying, have a strong smell and have to be cleaned from equipment with turpentine, kerosene or mineral spirits.

● **water-based satin and gloss** (latex) don't give a finish as hardwearing as that of a solvent-based paint but are quicker drying and have less smell. Clean equipment with hot or cold water and soap or detergent.

PREPARING PAINT

1 *Remove the lid from the paint can using the edge of a knife as a lever – don't use a screwdriver or you'll damage the lip of the lid.*

2 *Stir the paint (if recommended by the maker) using an offcut of wood, with a turning, lifting motion, or use an electric drill attachment.*

3 *Decant some paint into a pail, which you'll find easier to carry than a heavy can. Top up the pail from the can as you work.*

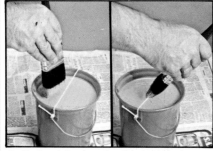

4 *To load the brush, dip the bristles into the paint to one-third of their length and wipe off excess on a string tied across the can rim.*

oils, stains or varnishes to enhance the overall effect and protect the surface. But as most of the wood used in our houses is chosen more for performance and price rather than looks, bland and uninteresting softwoods are generally the order of the day for everything from windows and door frames to staircases, baseboards and door casings. And painting them offers a number of distinct advantages.

Firstly, paint covers a multitude of sins — knots and other blemishes in the wood surface, poorly made joints patched up with filler, dents and scratches caused by the rough and tumble of everyday life — and does it in almost every color of the spectrum. Secondly, paint provides a surface that's hard-wearing and easy to keep clean — an important point for many interior surfaces in the home. And thirdly, paint is easy to apply . . . and to keep on applying. In fact, re-decorating existing paintwork accounts for the greater part of all paint bought.

What woods can be painted?

In theory you can paint any wood under the sun. In practice, paint (solvent-based or emulsion, see *Ready Reference*) is usually applied only to softwoods — spruce, pine and the like — and to man-made boards such as plywood, hardboard and chipboard. Hardwoods and boards finished with hardwood veneers can be painted, but are usually given a clear or tinted finish to enhance their attractive color and grain pattern.

Paint systems

If you're decorating new wood, there's more to it than putting on a coat of your chosen paint. It would just soak in where the wood was porous and give a very uneven color — certainly without the smooth gloss finish expected. It wouldn't stick to the wood very well, nor would it form the continuous surface film needed for full protection. All in all, not very satisfactory. So what is needed is a paint system which consists of built-up layers, each one designed to serve a particular purpose.

The first in the system is a primer (sometimes called a primer/sealer) which stops the paint soaking into porous areas and provides a good key between the bare wood and the paint film. Next, you want another 'layer' — the undercoat — to help build up the paint film and at the same time to obliterate the color of the primer, so that the top coat which you apply last of all is perfectly smooth and uniform in color. With latex, an undercoat is not always used and instead several coats of primer or two top coats are applied with the same result.

HOW TO APPLY PAIN

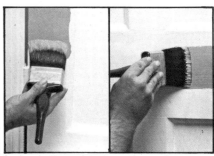

1 *Apply the paint along the grain.*

4 *Now you must 'feather' the paint with very light brush strokes along the grain to give a smooth finish that's free from brush marks.*

The general rule to obey when choosing primer, undercoat and top coat is to stick with the same base types in one paint system, particularly out of doors and on surfaces subjected to heavy wear and tear (staircases and baseboards, for example). On other indoor woodwork you can combine primers and top coats of different types.

If the wood you are painting has been treated with a preservative to prevent decay (likely only on exterior woodwork), an ordinary primer won't take well. Instead, use an aluminum wood primer — not to be confused with aluminum paint — which is recommended for use on all hardwoods too. Oily woods such as teak must be degreased with mineral spirits and allowed to dry before the primer is applied.

As far as man-made boards are concerned, chipboard is best primed with a solvent-based wood primer to seal its comparatively porous surface. Hardboard is even more porous, and here a stabilizing primer (a product more usually used on absorbent or powdery masonry surfaces) is the best product to use. Plywood and chipboard should be primed as for softwood. There's one other

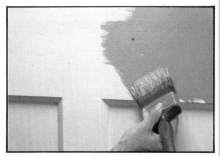

2 Still working with the grain and without reloading the brush, paint another strip alongside the first one and blend the two together.

3 Reload the brush and apply strokes back and forth across the grain over the area you've just painted to ensure full, even coverage.

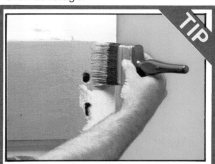

TIP

5 Paint an area adjoining the first in the same way, blending the two sections together by about 50mm (2in) and feather as before.

6 Brush towards edges, not parallel with them or onto them, as the paint will be scraped onto the adjacent face, forming a ridge.

WHAT CAN GO WRONG WITH PAINT

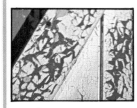

Left: Lifting and flaking occurs if paint is applied over a surface that is damp or powdery.

Right: Crazing is caused when paint is applied over a previous coat that was not completely dry.

Left: Blistering occurs when damp or resin is trapped beneath the paint film and is drawn out by heat.

Right: Cratering results from rain or condensation droplets falling onto the wet paint surface.

Left: Running, sagging or 'curtaining' happens when paint is applied too thickly on vertical surfaces.

Right: Wrinkling or shrivelling can occur on horizontal surfaces if paint is applied too thickly.

Ready Reference

HOW MUCH PAINT?

Large areas — in all cases coverage per litre (1½ pints) depends on the wood's porosity and the painter's technique:
Wood primer 9-15 sq metres (95-160 sq ft)
Aluminum primer 16 sq metres (170 sq ft)
Primer/undercoat 11 sq metres (120 sq ft)
Undercoat 11 sq metres (120 sq ft)
Gloss or satin 17 sq metres (180 sq ft)
Latex 15 sq metres (160 sq ft)

Small areas — add up all the lengths of wood to be painted. One sq metre (1 sq yd) is equivalent to:
● 16m (52 ft) of glazing bars
● 10-13m (33-43 ft) of window frame
● 6m (20 ft) of sill
● 10m (33 ft) of narrow baseboard
● 3-6m (10-20 ft) of deep baseboard

CHOOSING BRUSHES

The best brushes have a generous filling of long bristles and are an even, tapered shape. Cheaper brushes have short, thin bristles and big wooden filler strips to pack them out. The ideal sizes for wood are:
● 25mm (1in) or 50mm (2in) for panel doors, baseboards
● 50mm (2in) or 75mm (3in) for flush doors, baseboards, large areas
● 25mm (1in) cutting-in brush for window glazing bars
● 12mm (½in), 25mm (1in) or cheap paintbox brush for spot priming, applying knotting sealer

Alternative to brushes
Paint pads are more widely used on walls than on woodwork, but the crevice or sash paint pad will do the same job as a cutting-in brush. It should be cleaned with mineral spirits or hot water and detergent (paint solvents might dissolve the adhesive between the mohair pile and foam).

TIP: PREPARING A BRUSH

Before using a new (or stored) brush, work the bristles against the palm of your hand to remove dust and loose hairs.

thing you need to know. If the wood you want to paint has knots in it, you should brush a special sealer called knotting sealer over them to stop the resin oozing up through the paint film and spoiling its looks. If the knots are 'live' — exuding sticky yellowish resin — use a blow-torch to draw out the resin and scrape it off before applying sealer.

Paint on paint

You'll often want to paint wood that has already been painted. How you tackle this depends on the state of the existing paintwork. If it's flaking off and is in generally poor condition, you will have to remove the entire paint system — primer, undercoat and top coat — by burning off with a blow-torch, applying a chemical paint stripper or rubbing with an abrasive. You then treat the stripped wood as already described for new wood.

Where the paintwork is in good condition, you simply have to clean it and sand it down lightly to provide a key for the new paint and to remove any small bits that got stuck in the surface when it was last painted. Then you can apply fresh top coat over the surface; the paint system is already there. You may, of course, need two top coats if you add a light color to a dark one to stop the color beneath from showing through.

If the paintwork is basically sound but needs localized attention, you can scrape or sand these damaged areas back to bare wood and 'spot-treat' them with primer and undercoat to bring the patch up to the level of the surrounding paintwork, ready for a final top coat over the entire surface.

Painting large areas

Though the same principle applies to wood as it does to any other large surface area — ie, you divide it into manageable sections and complete one before moving on to another — if you're using an oil-based gloss paint you have to make sure that the completed area hasn't dried to such an extent that you cannot blend in the new. On the rare occasion that you might want to paint a whole wall of wood you should make the section no wider than a couple of brush widths and work from ceiling to floor.

With emulsions there isn't the same problem, for although they are quick drying, the nature of the paint is such that brush marks don't show.

You might think that a wide brush is the best for a large area but the constant flexing action of the wrist in moving the brush up and down will tire you out fast. Holding a brush is an art in itself and aches are the first indication that you're doing it wrongly. A thin brush should be held by the handle like a pencil, while a wider brush should be held with the fingers and thumb gripping the brush just above the bristles.

You'll find a variety of paint brushes on sale — some are designed to be 'throwaway' (good if you only have one or two jobs to do), others will stand you in good stead for years. But remember before using a new brush to brush the bristles back and forth against the palm of your hand — this is called 'flirting' and will dislodge any dust or loose hairs that could spoil your paintwork.

It is wise to decant the paint to save you moving a heavy can from place to place — a plastic pail would be ideal. Plastic ones are easier to keep clean than metal ones.

Never be tempted to dip the bristles too far into the paint and always scrape off excess from both sides. Paint has the habit of building up inside the brush and if this happens on overhead work, you risk it running down the handle and onto your arm.

ORDER OF PAINTING

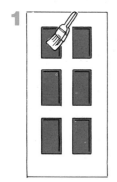 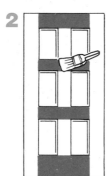 

Panel doors: *tackle any mouldings first, then the recessed panels, horizontal members, vertical members and lastly the edges.*

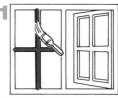  

Casement windows: *start with any glazing bars, then paint the opening casement itself (the hinge edge is the only one which should match the inside); lastly paint the frame.*

 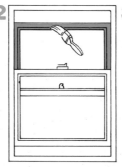 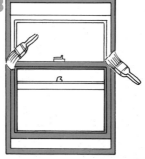

Sash windows: *paint the inside top and bottom and a little way up and down the sides of the frame first. Then paint the bottom of the outer sash. Move the sashes and do the rest of the outer sash, the inner sash and finally the frame.*

Painting small areas

These tend to be the fiddly woodwork on windows, around doors and lengths of stairs or baseboards — and the hardest bit about all of them is working out how much paint you'll need (see *Ready Reference*).

Special shaped or narrow brushes can make painting these areas easier — for example, they prevent you 'straddling' angles in wood (like you find on moldings) which damages the bristles in the middle of the brush. With windows and panelled doors you should also follow an order of working to avoid causing overlap marks on the parts you've already painted.

Fiddly or not, they are the jobs you have to do first if you are putting up wallcoverings (if you're painting a room, the walls should be done before the woodwork) so that the drops can be placed against finished edges. If you want to touch up the paint without changing the wallpaper, it's best to use a paint shield.

Getting ready to paint

Ideally, before painting doors and windows you should remove all the 'furniture' — handles, fingerplates, keyholes, hooks etc — so you can move the brush freely without interruption. You should also take time to read the manufacturer's instructions on the can. If, for example, they tell you to stir the paint, then stir it for this is the only way of distributing the particles which have settled.

If you open a can of oil paint and find a layer of solvent on the top, you should stir it in, then leave it to become jelly-like again before painting.

All your brushes should be dry — this is something to remember if you are painting over several days and have put them to soak overnight in turpentine or another brush cleaner. If you don't get rid of all the traces of the liquid, it will mess up your paintwork.

They should be rinsed, then brushed on newspaper till the strokes leave no sign.

Cleaning up

When you've finished painting, clean your brushes thoroughly, concentrating on the roots where paint accumulates and will harden. They should be hung up, bristles down, till dry, then wrapped in aluminum foil for storage. Don't ever store them damp for they can be ruined by mildew.

If there's only a small amount of paint left, you can either decant it for storage into a dark glass screw-topped jar so you can use it to touch up damaged spots — it's important to choose a suitable sized jar so there's very little air space. Air and dust are both potential paint spoilers, and there are two ways to keep them out if you're storing the can. Either put a circle of aluminum foil over the paint surface before putting the lid on securely, or — and this is the best way if the lid is distorted — put on the lid and then invert the can to spread the paint around the inner rim to form an airtight seal. Set it back the right way for storage.

If despite these safeguards a skin forms on the paint (usually over months of storage) you have to cut around the edge of it with a sharp knife and carefully lift it off.

PAINTING WINDOWS

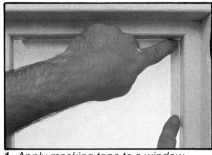

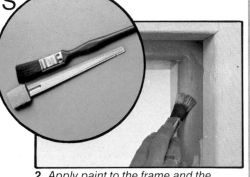

1 Apply masking tape to a window pane to prevent paint getting onto the glass – leave 3mm (¹/₈in) of glass exposed so the paint forms a seal.

2 Apply paint to the frame and the glazing bars using a small brush, or (inset) a cutting-in brush or a sash paint pad.

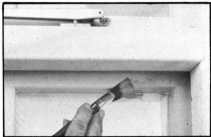

3 Apply the paint along the grain; remove the tape when the paint is almost dry – if it dries completely you might peel it off with the tape.

4 An alternative way of keeping paint off the glass is to use a paint shield or offcut of plywood but, again, leave a paint margin on the glass.

PAINTING WALLS AND CEILINGS

The quickest and cheapest way to transform a room is to paint the walls and ceiling. But, for a successful result, you have to prepare the surfaces properly and use the correct painting techniques.

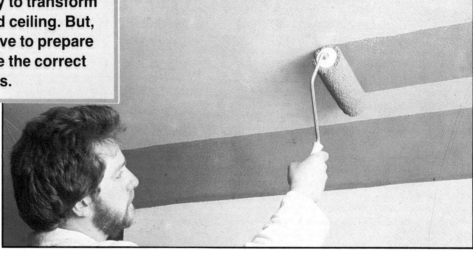

Dulux Russet over Dulux Cameo

Paint is the most popular material used to protect and decorate walls and ceilings in the home. Whereas many people hesitate before hanging wallpaper or sticking more permanent wall and ceiling coverings in place, few would worry about wielding a paint brush for the first time.

One of the chief advantages of painting a room is that it doesn't take much time; large areas can be given two or even three coats of latex paint in a day. The paints now available are hardwearing. They are easy to apply by brush, roller or pad and can be safely washed at frequent intervals to keep them looking fresh.

Any drawbacks are usually caused by faults in the wall or ceiling surface, rather than by the paints. A standard paint alone cannot cover up defects in the same way that some other wallcoverings can, so a surface which is to be painted usually needs more careful preparation than one which is to be papered.

Some walls and ceilings are plastered and this type of surface, when in sound condition, is ideal as a base for latex and other paints. However, it is not the only surface finish you are likely to come across in a house.

Previous occupiers of the house may well have covered the walls with a decorative paper and even painted on top of that. At the very worst there may be several layers of paper and paint, making it very difficult to achieve a smooth paint surface. In this situation it is invariably better to strip the surface completely down to the wallboard and to start again from scratch.

This does not mean that no paper should be overpainted. Certain types such as plain white relief wallcoverings and woodchips are intended to be so treated, and actually look 'softer' after one or two redecorations. In short, most wall or ceiling surfaces you are likely to encounter will be paintable. All you have to do is select the right paint for the job and get the surface into as good a condition as possible.

Choosing paints
Latex paints are the most commonly used types of paint for painting walls and ceilings. They are easy to apply and come in a wide range of colors. You will usually have a choice of three finishes: matt, silk, or gloss.

There are also textured paints which are increasing in popularity, particularly for ceiling use. These are latex paints with added 'body' so they can be applied more thickly and then given a decorative textured finish.

Oil-based eggshell paints can be used where a more durable surface is needed or where you want to use the same color on both walls and woodwork. Oil-based gloss paint is used occasionally also on walls and ceilings, particularly in humid rooms like kitchens and bathrooms.

You should choose paint carefully. The fact that one make is half the price of another may indicate that it has only half the covering power and you would therefore need to apply two coats of the cheaper paint. Also, if you're using white paint, you may find that one brand is noticeably 'whiter' than another.

Tools and equipment
Few specialized tools are needed for wall and ceiling paintwork. If you are content to work with only a brush, you will require two sizes: one larger one for the bulk of the work, and a smaller brush for working into corners. It is worth decanting quantities of paint into a roller tray, which is easier to carry around than large heavy cans.

Rollers make the job of painting large areas of wall or ceiling much quicker and also help to achieve a better finish. But you will still need a small brush for working into corners and for dealing with coving, cornices etc.

To prepare a new fibre roller for painting, soak it in soapy water for 2 to 3 hours to get rid of any loose bits of fibre, then roll it out on the wall to dry it off. One point to remember: if you intend using latex eggshell paint, it's best not to use a roller as this tends to show up as a stippled effect on the silk surface.

Large paint pads will also enable you to cover big expanses of wall or ceiling very quickly. You can use a brush or a small paint pad for work in corners.

Apart from these paint application tools you'll need a variety of other items for preparing the surfaces so they're ready for the paint. The walls must be cleaned, so you'll need washing-down equipment: sponges, cloths, detergent, and a bucket or two of water.

You'll need filler for cracks and a putty knife about 75mm (3in) wide. When any filler is dry it will need to be sanded down, so have some sandpaper ready for wrapping around a cork sanding block. A scraper will also be needed if old wallpaper has to be stripped from the walls.

Finally, because of the height of the walls and ceiling, you'll need access equipment, such as a stepladder, to enable you to reach them safely and comfortably.

Preparing the surface
No painting will be successful until the

PAINTING THE CEILING WITH A ROLLER

1 Use a brush to paint a strip about 50mm wide round the outside edge of the ceiling; a roller cannot reach right into angles or corners.

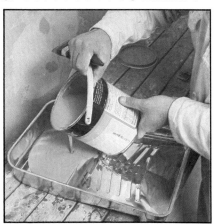

2 Pour paint into the roller tray; don't put in too much at a time or you risk overloading the roller and splashing paint out of the tray.

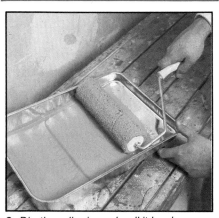

3 Dip the roller in and pull it back so there is paint at the shallow end of the tray. Push the roller back and forth in the paint at the shallow end.

4 Run the roller over the ceiling so there is a band of paint next to the strip of paint you have brushed along the edge of the ceiling.

5 Reverse the roller's direction so you join up the two strips of paint into one band. Then finish off by running the roller over the band.

6 Now start the next section by running the roller alongside the completed band. Work your way round the ceiling in bands.

Ready Reference

LINING WALL SURFACES

You can use lining paper to do the same job for paint as it does for wallpapers, covering minor cracks and defects on the wall or ceiling and providing a smooth surface for painting.

TIP: SEAL STRONG COLORS

Wallcoverings with strong colors, and particularly those tinted with metallic inks, will almost certainly show through the new paint. To prevent this, they should be stripped off, or sealed with special aluminum spirit-based sealer.

FILLING HAIRLINE CRACKS

You may not be able to push enough filler into hairline cracks to ensure a good bond:
● it is often better to open the crack up further with the edge of an old chisel or screwdriver so the filler can penetrate more deeply and key better to both sides of the crack
● when using a textured vinyl paint there is no need to fill hairline cracks, but cracks wider then 1mm (1/32in) should be filled.

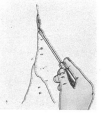

DEALING WITH FITTINGS

Protect electrical fittings so paint or water can't enter them during cleaning and decorating:
● ideally, power to these fittings should be cut off and the fittings removed
● if items cannot be removed, use masking tape to protect them.

SELECTING PAINTS

When choosing paints, remember that:
● latex paints are quicker to apply, dry more quickly and lack the smell of resin- or oil-based paints. They are also cheaper and can be easily cleaned off painting equipment with water
● a silk or gloss finish will tend to highlight surface irregularities more than a matt finish
● textured paints are suitable for use on surfaces which are in poor condition, since they will cover defects which a standard latex paint cannot.

PAINTING THE WALL WITH A BRUSH

1 *Use a small brush to cut in at the wall and ceiling join and in corners. With a larger brush paint the wall in bands. First, brush across the wall.*

2 *Move the brush across the wall in the opposite direction. The bands of paint should be about 1m wide and you should be working downwards.*

3 *When you are working at the top of the wall your next strokes should be downwards to complete the area you have covered with crossways strokes.*

4 *At the bottom two-thirds of the wall continue working in crossways strokes, but this time finish off each section by brushing upwards.*

USING PAINT PADS

1 *Thin the paint a little (with water for latex, turps for oil-based ones). Cut in with a small brush or pad and use a larger pad to paint in bands.*

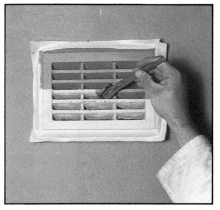

2 *For precise work you can use a small pad like this. Ensure that you cover areas you don't want painted with masking tape.*

surface beneath has been properly prepared. Unless wallpaper is of a type intended for painting, it is usually better to strip it off, and walls which have been stripped of their previous wallcoverings need a thorough washing to remove all traces of old paste. Make sure the floor is protected against debris by covering it with a dust sheet or sheets of old newspaper. Latex painted walls also need washing to remove surface dirt. In both cases, use warm water with a little household detergent added. Then rinse with clean water.

If you decide to leave the wallpaper on the walls you will have to wash it down before you paint. Take care to avoid overwetting the paper, particularly at joins. When the surface is dry, check the seams; if any have lifted, stick them down with a ready-mixed paste.

Ceilings should be washed in small areas at a time and rinsed thoroughly before you move onto another section systematically.

If the surfaces are left in perfect condition, they can be painted as soon as they are dry.

It's possible that walls or ceilings may have been painted with distemper, which may only become apparent after you have removed the existing wallcovering. Unless it is the washable type, you will have to remove it completely since latex paint will not adhere well to it. Use hot water, detergent and a scrubbing brush to soften and get rid of the coating; this is hard work, but you could use a steam stripper to speed up the process.

With all the surface cleaned, the next job is to fill any cracks and repair defects such as indentations caused perhaps by knocks or the blade of a carelessly handled wallpaper scraper (see *Ready Reference*).

Whenever a filler has been used, it should be left to dry and then sanded down flush with the wall surface, and the resulting dust should be brushed away.

If the plaster is in bad condition and obviously covered in cracks, you should consider covering it completely with lining paper, woodchip or other relief wallcovering before painting it. The paper will provide a good base for redecoration, and will save a great deal of preparation time. However, this can only be done if the plaster itself is still bonded securely to the wall. If it is coming away in chunks or sounds hollow behind the cracks, then the wall should be replastered.

Cracks which have developed around door and window frames are best filled with a flexible sealant, which will be unaffected by movement of the frames. Acrylic-based sealants are available for this purpose and they can be easily overpainted.

After all the preparation work has been completed, clean the room well so that when you begin painting you do not stir up

PAINTING PROCEDURE

Paint the ceiling first in 1m (1yd)-wide bands (1 & 2). Paint around a ceiling cap (3), then complete the rest of that band (4). On walls work downwards (1). At a window, paint along the top band (2) and repeat the process at the bottom (3). Work from right to left unless you are left-handed.

dust and have to work around numerous bits and pieces scattered over the floor space.

Re-lay dust sheets and set up your access equipment before even opening the first can of paint. Make sure your brushes or rollers are clean and ready for use.

Painting sequences

If possible, do all your painting in daylight hours. Artificial light is less easy to work by and can lead to small areas being missed.

Painting is always done from the highest point downwards, so ceilings are the first areas to be tackled. The whole ceiling will be painted in bands across the room no wider than you can easily reach without stretching on your stepladder or platform. This generally means that at any one time you will probably be painting a band no wider than 1m (1yd) and less than 2m (2yd) long unless you are using scaffolding boards to support you.

You start at the edges first and then work into the main body of the room.

Linking one section to another is seldom difficult with latex paint and is simply a matter of blending the paint from the new section back into the previous one.

Walls are treated similarly, starting at the top and working downwards in sections about 1m (1yd) wide, cutting in at the ceiling and at return walls.

Painting tips

The number of coats required will depend on the previous color and condition of the surface and the type of paint. If another coat has to be applied, be sure that the previous one is fully dry first. With modern latex paint it may be that because the paint is water-based it will cause the paper underneath to swell and bubble; however, you shouldn't worry about this because as the water in the paint dries out, the paper and paste behind the paint surface will begin to flatten again.

If the paper is badly hung with a lack of adhesive at the edge, seams may lift as the paint dries. They will have to be stuck down in the same way as if they had lifted during washing. Careful preparation would prevent this problem anyway.

APPLYING TEXTURED FINISHES

Textured finishes which you can paint on walls or ceilings are an inexpensive way of covering up poor surfaces. They also give you the chance to exercise your ingenuity in creating relief patterns on them.

Textured wall and ceiling finishes can provide a relatively quick form of decoration. You don't, for example, need to apply more than one coat. And, unlike relief wallcoverings (another type of product commonly used to obtain a textured wall or ceiling surface), you don't have to go through the process of pasting, soaking, cutting, hanging and trimming; you simply spread the finishes on the surface with a paint brush or roller.

One of the advantages of using a 'texture' on walls is that it will tend to mask the effect of any general unevenness in the surface. Similarly, ready-mixed textures are often marketed specifically as a solution to the problem of improving the appearance of old ceilings. They are very suitable for this and can save a lot of tedious repair work.

However, there is no need to think of textures just as a cover-up. You may simply prefer a textured surface to a flat, smooth one. If you use patterning tools, the range of textured effects you can achieve is practically endless, depending only on your skill and imagination.

Choosing textured finishes

One of the factors which will influence your choice of finish is, obviously, how much you are prepared to pay. The traditional compound which you buy in powder form to mix with water is the cheapest type, but, like ordinary plaster, is rather porous and needs to be painted over. Even so, the cost of coverage, including overpainting, is very reasonable. Ready-mixed types are rather more expensive but you don't normally need to paint over them, and some brands offer a reasonable range of colors.

The traditional powder type, thickly painted on a wall or ceiling, has a slow setting time, which makes it ideal for creating a decorative impression with a patterning tool. Ready-mixed products can also be given a textured finish in the same way as the powdery type, but doing so will tend to vary the thickness of the finish so that overpainting might be necessary. (If you just paint them on without carrying out any follow-up patterning treatment, you will be left with a ran-

dom textured effect.) Some of the textured products suitable for exterior use can also be patterned with tools; check the manufacturer's instructions for guidance here.

Tools and equipment

Apart from the texture finish itself, and paint if you're going to overpaint, you will need a brush or roller to apply the finish. The most suitable type of brush is a 200mm (8in) one. The type of roller you use will affect the pattern created and special rollers are available to create certain effects (see step-by-step photographs). Sometimes you paint the material on first with an ordinary roller (or a brush) and then work it over with a patterning roller; follow the manufacturer's instructions for the type of roller you will need.

If you are dealing with a ceiling you will need some form of access equipment; two stepladders with a plank resting between them will usually suffice. Textured finishes, especially when applied with a roller, tend to spray and spatter about, so it's best to have goggles and a mask to protect your eyes and mouth when you are looking up; also, don't forget to protect your hair. In addition, whether you're painting walls or ceiling, you'll need a dust sheet or some other form of protective covering for the floor.

You may also require a plumb bob and line

(see *Ready Reference*, page 19) and any equipment required for filling cracks or joints such as a caulking tool, jointing tape knife, putty knife, filler and so on.

Where you intend to texture the surface after painting on the finish, you will also need your patterning tool(s). These can be store-bought or home-made; you can even use equipment which was chiefly designed for other purposes which you may decide will create the pattern you want. Apart from patterning rollers, the store-bought tools available include combs (some of which can give special effects within the combed patterns such as 'rose' and 'flower'), stipple brushes and pads and special 'swirl' brushes. You can also buy a tool called a 'lacer' to dull any sharp ridges; however, a plastic straight edge or the blade of a putty knife is a suitable alternative.

Preparing the surface

Textured finishes can be applied to bare or painted surfaces but the surface must be sound and, in some cases, treated. You should not, for example, think of textured finishes as a means of covering up walls which really need replastering or a ceiling which should be replaced.

All porous surfaces should first be treated with a stabilizing primer recommended by

SEALING JOINTS

1 *To seal a joint between boards, first use a caulking tool to apply cellulose filler (or a thicker mix of texture compound) along it.*

2 *Use a special taping knife to press a length of jointing tape into the filler so it's securely embedded and free of air bubbles.*

3 *Spread on another layer of filling material, again using the caulking tool, but this time so the filler covers the jointing tape.*

4 *Use a damp sponge to wipe away surplus filler and to feather the edges so the joint surface becomes flush with the plasterboard.*

Ready Reference

TOOLS TO USE

You can buy various tools designed for patterning textured finishes. They include combs, patterned rollers, various types of brushes and a 'lacing' tool for smoothing high points.

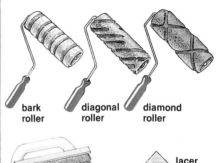

bark roller   **diagonal roller**   **diamond roller**

swirl brush   **lacer**   **comb**

MAKE YOUR OWN COMB

You can make a comb with a wooden handle and a rigid plastic blade (cut, for example, from an old ice-cream carton). Cut your own designs out of the plastic.

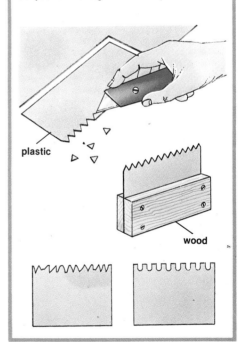

plastic   **wood**

---

the manufacturer of the finish so that the setting of the texture material is not spoilt by suction. Surfaces requiring such treatment include brick, concrete, plaster and some types of wallboards.

Texture finishes can be used to hide very fine hairline cracks and are usually marketed for their flexible ability to cope with normal movement so cracks don't reopen. However, none of them can cover cracks or joints of more than 1.5mm (1/16in) with any guarantee that these will remain covered up. You will have to caulk the cracks or joints with texture compound (perhaps thickened with a little ordinary filler). Ideally, joints between boards of any kind should also have a layer of jointing tape over them between layers of whatever types of filler you are using (see step-by-step photographs). Make sure you feather the edges of the filling material so there is no ridge when the texture covers it.

Painted surfaces should be clean, sound and sanded lightly to provide a key for the finish. Low-quality latex paint may not hold the texture; test by pressing adhesive tape on a small area first and remove any painted surface that has a tendency to delaminate when the tape is peeled off. If the surface has been painted in a dark color, it's best to paint over it in a light color first before you apply the texture.

You will have to remove wallpaper or light tiles such as polystyrene tiles. You can, however, safely apply a textured finish over ceramic tiles provided they are clean, the gaps are filled and they are primed with a coat of PVA adhesive, diluted according to the manufacturer's instructions.

Do check that lath-and-plaster ceilings are strong enough to support the extra weight of the textured coating. If they are showing any signs of sagging, lift a floor-

MAKING TEXTURED PATTERNS

Textured materials can be applied by brush or roller. If you are applying this type of finish to walls, it's best, if possible, to work in an upwards direction to minimize the amount of material which gets sprayed over you and the floor. Apply the finish to the wall in bands and apply it thickly so the texture will stand out. You can roll it on with an ordinary roller (see left) which will give a stipple effect and then leave the surface to dry as it is. Alternatively, you may prefer to go ahead and use other tools to create other kinds of textured effects.

board in the room or attic above and check that the laths are still nailed firmly to the joists, and the plaster is well keyed to the laths.

Where there are nails or screws which will be embedded in the texture material, you should paint them over with gloss paint to prevent them from rusting.

You will have to prime wood-faced wallboards if they are absorbent and it's best to treat wood-effect plastic boards with PVA adhesive in the same way as ceramic tiles. In the case of thin wallboards there is a risk that movement will cause the texture material to crack, so test them for flexibility and remove them if necessary.

Applying textured finishes

It's best to apply a textured finish thickly; remember you will only be applying one coat and the thicker the coat the more protection it will provide for the wall or ceiling surface. Also, if you intend using a patterning tool, working on a deep, even coat of texture will give the best results. Apply the finish in bands across the room until the entire wall or ceiling is covered.

Exterior textures are normally applied with a natural bristle brush, though on smooth surfaces where you want a coarser texture you can use a roller. Whenever possible, you should work in the shade. If you are painting near drainpipes, you should tape newspaper around the pipes to protect the area you wish to avoid painting. Similarly, use masking tape to protect window frames (outdoors and inside) and also window reveals, light fittings, ventilator grilles and so on. If it does get on any of the areas, wipe it off with a damp rag immediately.

Using patterning tools

The drying time for textured finishes varies from 12 to 24 hours, though the working time for patterning can be much lower, depending on atmospheric conditions. You will normally have at least 4 hours to complete your patterning, but it would make sense to complete one wall or ceiling at a time as far as possible. If in doubt, study the manufacturer's instructions for the particular product you are using.

A random pattern will usually be quicker to achieve than a regular one where you will have to take care in matching up the pattern. In the latter case, it may be better to spread the texture on in strips and pattern each strip as you go rather than covering the whole wall or ceiling and then patterning it.

Finishing off

After patterning, it is normal practice to 'lace' the pattern (to dull any sharp ridges) just as the material begins to dry. Even after it has dried you may still need to remove sharp points; use the blade of a putty knife to knock them back, or, if you want to go to the trouble, wrap fine sandpaper around a sanding block and sand them down. If you don't remove sharp ridges and points, the surface may cut someone who leans against it or brittle parts may break off.

Textured finishes can usually be covered with either a latex or oil-based paint but check the manufacturer's recommendations.

Cleaning and maintenance

Most texture finishes are designed to last, which is just as well as it's a messy, time-consuming and difficult job to remove them. Maintenance will normally consist of redecorating them with a coat of paint when they show signs of wear or hard-to-remove dirt or stains. Surfaces should be kept clean: to do so, apply warm soapy water with a paint brush to loosen dirt and dust.

3 *A specially designed, grooved 'bark' effect roller is being run over the textured material to produce a bark pattern on a wall surface.*

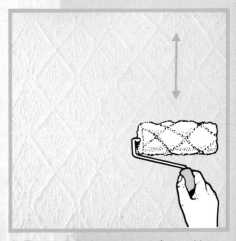

6 *This diamond pattern was formed by a purpose-designed roller. With a regular pattern like this you should check that the pattern rows match.*

1 *A straightforward and at the same time striking effect can be produced by running a purpose-designed diagonal roller up and down across the surface.*

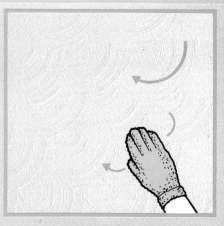

2 *A wide variety of tools can be used to form patterns on texture materials; here a coarse nylon glove produced a swirled effect.*

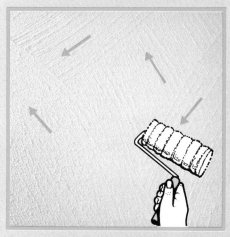

4 *Here a 'bark' effect roller was again used but this time in a random sweeping motion to create a curved criss-cross variation of the basic pattern.*

5 *The fine stipple effect (left) was made using an ordinary roller; the coarser stipple (right) by dabbing with a sponge wrapped in plastic.*

7 *Another design: the background pattern was produced by running a 'bark' roller over the surface; a sponge was then used to make circles on this.*

8 *This criss-cross pattern of alternate facing 'squares' could be created using a comb but here a serrated scraper was used instead.*

Ready Reference

TYPES OF FINISH

There are various types of textured finishes available. They include:
● the traditional type, which is a powder compound, generally available only in white, which you mix with water; it needs to be painted afterwards
● textured 'paints', which are ready-mixed products containing similar light aggregates and binders to the traditional type but also plasticized like modern paints; they come in a range of colors and usually don't have to be painted over (though you can if you wish)
● textured paints and coverings suitable for exterior use.

HOW FAR WILL THEY GO?

Powder compounds will cover about 2.5sq m per kg (12sq ft per lb) of unmixed powder. Ready-mix materials will cover 2 to 2.5sq m (22 to 27sq ft) per litre.

BEWARE ASBESTOS

Traditional compound powder textures sometimes contain asbestos (check the manufacturer's instructions); such types should be mixed in well-ventilated conditions to protect you against a potential health risk.

THE RIGHT TEMPERATURE

Texture finishes can be affected by extremes in temperature so:
● don't apply ready-mix products to a ceiling which incorporates a heating system
● don't carry out application when the temperature is below 5°C (40°F) or above 40°C (100°F) or when the temperature is likely to exceed these limits before the material is dry.
  You can apply a traditional compound type of texture over 'hot' surfaces such as heated ceilings and chimney breasts, but you should first seal the surface with a good quality alkali-resisting primer.
  Don't apply either type in freezing conditions.

CREATING REGULAR PATTERNS

If you are creating a regular pattern which requires matching, use a plumb bob and line to mark guidelines on the walls (or to snap chalked lines on the ceiling); paint and pattern in bands between the straight lines.

TIP: REMOVE MASKING QUICKLY

If you have used tape or newspaper to protect window frames, pipes or fittings, remove it before the texture dries; it may be difficult to remove later when the texture has set.

EXTERIOR PAINTING preparation

Whether you like it or not, preparing the outside of your house before painting it is a job that has to be done. If you provide a sound surface the paint will last much longer.

If your house is in good order and has been decorated regularly, then the paintwork may need no more than a quick wash down and a light sanding before it's ready for repainting. But if your house is in a rather worse state than this, take some time now to make a really good job of the preparation and you'll have a much easier time in the future. The preparation may seem rather time-consuming, but don't be tempted to miss out any of the steps. Properly applied, paint will protect your house for several years, but it won't stick to an unsound surface.

The most convenient order of working is to start at the top of the house and work down, and to do all the preparation before you start to paint so that dust and grit won't fall on wet paint. When working at a height, make sure the ladder or platform is firm and secure.

Gutters and downpipes
Gutters manage to trap a surprising quantity of dirt and old leaves, so clear this out first. It's a good idea to check that the gutter is at a regular slope towards the nearest downpipe. You can easily check this by pouring a bucket of water into one end and seeing if it all drains away. If puddles form, you'll need to unscrew some of the gutter brackets and adjust the level of the gutter until the water flows away freely. Check all the joints for leaks and if you do find any, seal them with a mastic compound applied with a gun.

Plastic gutters need little maintenance, and they don't need painting. But if you want to change their color, simply clean them thoroughly and wipe them over with a rag dipped in mineral spirits or turps to remove any grease spots before starting to paint. There's no need for a primer or undercoat, but you may need two top coats for even coverage.

Metal gutters and pipes need more attention as all rust has to be removed. Scrape off flaking paint first, then use a wire brush and sandpaper to remove the rust. A wire brush attachment on an electric drill would make the cleaning easier (but wear a mask and goggles while using one). You can buy an anti-rust chemical from paint shops which is useful for badly rusted metalwork. It works by

turning iron oxide (rust) into phosphate of iron which is inert and can be painted over. In any case, prime all bare metal immediately with either a red lead primer or a zinc chromate metal primer. Metal primers contain a rust-inhibitor which protects the metal against further corrosion, so don't miss them out. If the gutters and pipes are in good condition with no sign of rust, simply wash them down and sand the surface lightly to key it ready for repainting.

Fascias and soffits
Fascias and soffits run along the top of a wall just below the roof. Fascias support the guttering below pitched roofs and edge flat ones, while soffits are fitted beneath the roof overhang on gable ends. Because they are so high up, don't worry too much about their appearance; the main consideration is protection as they are in such an exposed position. Clean out well behind the gutters as damp leaves or even bird's nests can be lodged there. Then, using a wide scraper, remove all loose flaking paint, sand down the whole board surface and prime the bare patches. Fill holes and cracks with an exterior-grade filler or waterproof compound and smooth it level while still damp using a putty knife. You can prime the filler when it's dry.

Walls
The main surface materials and finishes used on the outside of your house are brick, stone, wood and render.

Walls of brick and stone, especially when

weathered, have a beauty all of their own and don't really need painting. But the surface can become cracked and dirty and a coat of paint will cover up repairs that don't match the original surface, and protect the wall from further damage. Examine the pointing and, if it has deteriorated, rake out the damaged parts and re-point with fresh mortar. Use a mixture of about 1 part cement to 4 parts fine sand, or buy a bag of ready-mixed mortar. Use a small trowel and try to match the original pointing in the surrounding brickwork. Don't worry about hairline cracks as these will easily be covered by the paint. The white crystalline deposit which sometimes appears on brickwork is known as efflorescence. It is caused by water-soluble salts in the brick being brought to the surface, and should be brushed off with a dry brush. Don't try to wash it off as this will only make it worse.

The main types of render are plain, roughcast and pebbledash. Plain render can be applied to give a smooth finish or a textured 'Tyrolean' finish, for example. Roughcast consists of pebbles mixed with mortar before application, and with pebbledash the pebbles are thrown on while the mortar is still wet. Pebbledash deteriorates more quickly than the other types of render as, over the years, differences in rates of expansion between each pebble and the surrounding mortar may result in small surface cracks causing the pebbles to become loose and fall out. Paint will bind in the pebbles and protect small cracks.

PREPARING THE WALLS

1 *Before painting an exterior wall, brush it down well to remove any loose material. Start at the top and use a fairly stiff brush.*

2 *Kill mold and algae with a solution of 1 part bleach to 4 parts water. Leave for two days, then wash down and brush off.*

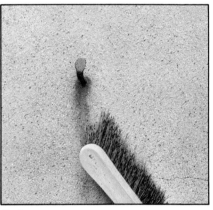

3 *Rusty metal and leaky gutters can easily cause stains, so cure the leaks and clean and prime all metal first. Sterilize the stain and brush down.*

4 *Holes in the wall are often created when old downpipe brackets are removed. Brush them out well and damp the surface with a little water.*

5 *Fill the hole with a sand and cement mixture using a small trowel. Small bags of ready-mixed mortar are ideal for jobs of this size.*

6 *If the wall is powdery or highly porous, or if a cement-based paint has been used previously, seal the surface with a stabilizing primer.*

Ready Reference

CHOOSE THE RIGHT PRIMER

Different materials require different primers; be sure to choose the right type.

Wood

softwood & hardwood	wood primer or acrylic primer
resinous wood	aluminum wood primer

Metal

iron and steel	calcium plumbate primer, zinc chromate primer or red lead primer
galvanized iron (new)	calcium plumbate primer
(old)	calcium plumbate or zinc chromate primer
aluminum	zinc chromate primer
brass, copper and lead	none necessary: allow new lead to weather

Masonry etc

brick, stone, concrete & render	stabilizing primer, alkali-resisting primer, acrylic primer

Other materials

asbestos	stabilizing primer, alkali-resisting primer or acrylic primer
bitumen-coated wood	aluminum wood primer
bitumen-coated metal	aluminum spirit-based sealer

PROPERTIES AND COVERAGE

Where there is a choice of suitable primers, it's often helpful to know something more about each type. For instance, many primers are toxic and you should choose a non-toxic one if you're painting anything in a child's room.
● Acrylic primer — white or pastel shades, water-based, quick drying, non-toxic.
● Alkali-resisting primer — needs two coats on very porous surfaces, non-toxic.
● Aluminum wood primer — dull metallic gray, self-knotting, non-toxic.
● Calcium plumbate primer — off-white, rust inhibiting, toxic.
● Lead-free wood primer — white or pink, non-toxic.
● Red lead primer — bright red, rust inhibiting, only for exterior use, toxic.
● Lead-based wood primer — white or pink, only for exterior use, toxic.
● Zinc chromate primer — yellow, rust inhibiting, non-toxic.

PREPARING THE WOODWORK

1 Start preparing the woodwork by scraping off all the loose flaking paint. Large areas of unsound paint are better if stripped completely.

2 Sand and prime all the bare wood, taking care to work the primer well into cracks and any exposed end grain, then leave the surface to dry.

3 Where joints have opened up, scrape off the paint and rake out the gap with a knife or shavehook. Clean out all the loose debris.

4 Small cracks can be filled with putty, but larger cracks and holes should be filled with exterior-grade filler.

5 Gaps often appear between the window frame and the wall. Fill these with caulking to provide a continuous water-tight seal.

6 Make sure the groove underneath the window sill is clear of paint, then thoroughly sand down the whole of the window frame.

REPLACING OLD PUTTY

1 Old, damaged putty must be raked out. Scrape old paint from the glass, and clean the glass with mineral spirit to remove any grease spots.

2 Work the putty in your hands until it has an even consistency. If it's too oily, roll it on newspaper first. Press it firmly into the gap.

3 Smooth the new putty level with the old using a putty knife, then run a soft brush over it to make a water-tight seal with the glass.

TREATING KNOTS

1 *Active knots like this ooze out a sticky resin which quickly breaks through the paint surface, leaving a sticky and unsightly mess.*

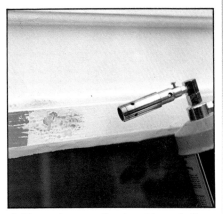

2 *The paint must first be stripped off to expose the knot. Use any method of stripping, and scrape the paint off with a shavehook or scraper.*

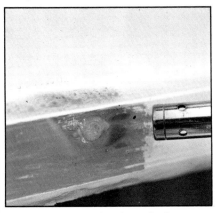

3 *Use a blow-torch to heat the knot until the resin bubbles out. Scrape off the resin and repeat until no more of it appears.*

4 *Sand the knot with fine sandpaper, then wipe over the area with sealer applied with a soft cloth. Prime the wood when it has dried.*

it will seal a porous surface and stop paint from being sucked in too much. The stabilizer also helps to waterproof the wall and you can paint it on as an extra layer of protection whether it's really necessary or not. Most stabilizers are colorless, but off-white stabilizer/primers are available and this would be a good choice if you were planning to paint your house in a light color, as it could save one coat of the finishing color. These off-white stabilizers, however, are not recommended for use on surfaces painted with a cement-based paint.

Stabilizers must be painted on a dry wall and should be left to dry for 24 hours before painting on the top coat. Don't paint if rain is expected. Clean your brush in mineral spirits or turps as soon as you stop work.

Wood cladding

If the cladding or siding is bare and you want to leave the natural wood surface showing, it should be treated with a water-repellent wood preservative to give protection against dampness penetration and decay. The preservative is available clear or pigmented with various colors.

If the wood has been varnished, scrape off the old varnish and sand down well, following the grain of the wood. Fill cracks and holes with plastic wood or a tinted filler to match the color of the wood.

If you wish to paint the surface, you'll have to wait a year or so for the water-repellent agents in the preservative to disperse before priming with an aluminum wood primer.

Woodwork

If the paintwork on the windows is in good condition, all you need do is give them a wash and a light sanding. If the paint is cracked and flaking, a little more preparation is needed. To check if the paint surface needs stripping, lay on a piece of sticky tape and see if it lifts off any paint. Occasional chipped or blistered portions can be scraped off and cut back to a firm edge. As long as the edge is feathered smooth with sandpaper, it shouldn't show too much. If previous coatings are too thick for this treatment, build up the surface with filler until it is just proud of the surrounding paint, then sand level when it's dry. Don't allow the filler to extend too far over the edge of the damage or it'll be difficult to sand it smooth.

There comes a time, however, when the condition of the old coating has become so bad that complete stripping is advisable.

A blow-torch or an electric hot air stripper are the quickest tools to use. Start at the bottom softening the paint, and follow up immediately with a scraper. Hold the scraper at an angle so the hot paint doesn't fall on your hand, and don't hold it above the flame or it may become too hot to hold. Try not to concentrate the flame too long on one part or you're likely to scorch the wood, though

When repairing any of these surfaces, try and achieve the same finish as the original, or as near as you can, so that when it's repainted the repair won't be too noticeable. Stop up cracks with mortar, using a mix of 1 part cement to 5 parts sand. Chip away very wide cracks until you reach a firm edge, then undercut this to provide a good key for the new mortar. Dampen the surface, then stop up with a trowel. Use a float if the surface is plain, or texture the surface to match the surrounding area. Where the rendering is pebbledash, throw on pebbles with a small trowel while the mortar is still wet, then press them into the mortar lightly with a flat piece of wood.

Mold and stains

If there's any sign of mold or algae on the wall, treat this next. Mix up a solution of 1 part household bleach to 4 parts water and paint this on the affected area. Be generous with the solution and cover the area well.

Leave for 48 hours for the bleach to kill off all the growth, then wash off thoroughly and brush down with a stiff brush.

Rusty gutters, pipes and metal fittings can all cause stains if rusty water drips down the wall. So cure any leaks first and clean and prime all metal to ensure there's no trace of rust. Mold and algae thrive on damp walls; even if you can't actually see any growth on a damp patch, there may be some spores lurking there, so you should make absolutely sure that you sterilize all stains with the bleach solution just to make sure.

Dusty or chalky walls

All walls, whether dusty or not, should be brushed down thoroughly to remove any loose material. But if, after brushing, the wall is still dusty or chalky, if a cement-based paint was used previously to decorate it, or if the wall is porous, you'll have to brush on a stabilizing solution. This will bind together loose particles to allow the paint to stick, and

PREPARING METAL

1 Metal pipes and gutters are often in a very bad state of repair and need a lot of preparation. Scrape off all the old flaking paint first.

2 Brush well with a wire brush to remove all traces of rust. Badly rusted pipes should be treated with an anti-rust chemical.

TIP

3 Hold a board or a piece of card behind the pipe to keep paint off the wall, and paint on a metal primer, covering every bit of bare metal.

4 A small paint pad on a long handle is a useful tool for painting behind pipes, especially when they are very close to the wall.

New doors and windows

New wooden windows and doors may already have a coat of primer applied at the factory, but it's best not to rely on this for complete protection. Knots, for instance, will rarely have been properly treated, and the primer film will have been damaged here and there in transit. So sand down the whole surface, treat any knots with sealer and apply another coat of wood primer overall. It may be advisable to paint doors while they're lying flat; certainly it's vital to paint the top and bottom edges before you hang them in place. It's very important to paint the bottom as rain and snow can easily penetrate unpainted wood causing it to swell and rot. Paint also protects the wood against attack from woodworm.

Metal and plastic windows

Metal doors and windows should be treated in the same way as metal pipes and gutters. So sand them down and make sure all rust is removed before priming. Aluminum frames can be left unpainted, but if you do want to paint them you must first remove any surface oxidation which shows as a fine white deposit. Use a scraper or wire brush, but go very gently and try not to scratch. Prime with a zinc chromate primer. Plastic window frames should not be painted.

Galvanized iron and asbestos

You're likely to find galvanized iron used as corrugated iron roofing, gutters and downpipes. The zinc coating on galvanized iron is to some extent 'sacrificial', so that if a small patch becomes damaged, the surrounding zinc will, in time, spread over to cover the damage. But this weakens the coating and an application of paint will prolong its life. If the galvanizing is new and bright, simply clean it with a rag dipped in mineral spirits or turps to remove any grease, and apply a calcium plumbate primer. If it's old and gray-looking, first remove any existing paint by rubbing lightly with a wire brush, trying not to scratch the surface. Then clean with mineral spirits or turps and apply zinc chromate primer.

Asbestos may have been used for guttering, fascia boards, as walls on out-buildings and as corrugated sheeting for roofs. Asbestos is a very dangerous material and for this reason great care should be taken when dealing with it. It'll probably need cleaning before painting and the only safe way is to wet it thoroughly first and scrub it down with a scrubbing brush. Be sure to wear rubber gloves and a face mask. Leave it to dry, then prime it with a stabilizing primer, an alkali-resisting primer, or simply a coat of thinned-down latex paint. Asbestos is very porous, so always paint both sides of any asbestos sheet to prevent dampness penetrating from the back.

this rarely matters on exterior woodwork which will be over-painted again. Always be extremely careful when using a blow-torch, and keep a bucket of water or sand nearby in case something does catch fire. A chemical paint stripper is the best method to use near glass in case the glass cracks under the heat of a blow-torch.

Knots, putty and holes

Check the woodwork for any live knots which are oozing out resin. If you find any, strip off the paint over them and then play a blow-torch or electric hot air stripper over them to burn out the resin. Sand lightly and treat with sealer, then prime when dry.

You should also check the putty fillet round each pane of glass, and if any has disintegrated, rake it out with an old knife. Then sand and prime the wood and bed in new putty using a putty knife. Use linseed oil putty

on wood and metal glazing or all purpose putty on metal-framed windows. Smooth the putty with a damp cloth and leave it for about a week before painting.

Rake out any cracks in the wood and cut back wood which is starting to rot. If a large amount of wood is rotten — usually along the bottom edge of a sash window — a larger repair is needed. This could involve replacing a section or all of the window. Prime the bare wood, working the primer well into cracks and end grain as this is where the weather gets in. Small cracks can be filled with putty, but larger ones should be filled with exterior filler. Sand level when dry and spot-prime. Gaps between the window frame and the wall should be filled with a flexible, waterproof, caulking compound applied with a special gun.

Finally, sand down the whole of the woodwork to make it ready for repainting.

EXTERIOR PAINTING
completing the job

The first two parts of this article described how to prepare the outside of your house to make it ready for repainting. This last part shows you the best way to paint the walls, pipes, windows and doors to give a professional look to your home.

I f you have completed all the cleaning, repairs and preparation on the outside of your house, and if the weather has been dry for the past couple of days and looks settled for a while, you are now ready to start painting. Tackle the painting in more or less the same order as the preparation, starting at the top and working downwards.

Gutters, fascias and soffits

If you have plastic gutters and want to paint them, simply apply a thin coat of gloss paint to the outside surface. This is the only case outside where paint is used purely for decoration rather than protection. Iron gutters can be painted on the inside with a bituminous paint as this will provide a waterproof coating and protect the iron. Paint the outside of gutters and downpipes with the usual gloss paint system. You'll need a small paint pad or crevice brush to get into the narrow gaps at the back of gutters and pipes. Protect the fascia with a piece of board held behind the guttering. Don't miss out these awkward bits as this is where the rust will start up again.

TEXTURED WALLS

1 Use a 'dust pan' brush for painting rough-textured finishes such as pebbledash or a randomly textured finish.

2 Paint brickwork with a well-loaded old brush. Small cracks are bridged by the paint, but larger cracks have to be filled first with exterior filler.

3 Alternatively, use a roller on brick to give a thicker coat of paint and a slightly textured finish. Special rollers give even deeper textures.

Fascias and soffits are so exposed that it's best to give them an extra coat of gloss. You'll need your crevice brush or paint pad again to paint behind the gutters.

Walls

There is a wide range of paints available for exterior walls, and full information is usually available from suppliers. As for tools, a 100mm (4in) brush is the easiest size to handle; anything larger would put too much strain on the wrist. An alternative is a long-pile roller which has the advantage of being much quicker to use — about three times quicker than a brush. An extra long-pile roller is needed for roughcast or pebbledash; choose one with a pile 32mm (1¼in) deep, or use a dust pan brush instead. Use a cheap disposable brush or roller for cement paints as they are almost impossible to clean afterwards.

A large plastic bucket or paint tray is essential when working up a ladder. Stir the paint thoroughly first, then pour some into the bucket until it's about one third full. If you're using a roller, use a special roller tray with a large paint reservoir, or else stand a short plank in the bucket to allow you to load the roller evenly.

Application

Start at the top of the wall and paint a strip across the house. Work from right to left if you're right-handed, and left to right if you're left-handed. Be sure to secure the ladder to prevent it slipping and allow a three-rung overlap at the top.

Use a brush to cut in under the eaves or fascia boards and to paint round obstacles, then fill in the larger areas with a brush or roller. Paint an area only as large as you can comfortably manage and don't lean out too far, your hips should remain between the ladder's stiles at all times.

If you have an awkward area which is too far away to reach, push a broom handle into the hollow handle of the roller, or buy a special extension handle. Protect pipes by wrapping them in newspaper, and mask any other items you don't want to paint. Leave an uneven edge at the bottom of each patch so the join won't be too noticeable, then move the ladder to the left (or right) and paint another strip alongside the first. The principle is always to keep working to the longest wet edge so the joins won't show. When you've done the top series of strips, lower the ladder

and paint another series across the middle. Lower the ladder again or work from the ground to do another series along the bottom. Working across the house like this means you have to alter the ladder height the least number of times.

Woodwork

You can choose either a latex or a solvent-based paint for the exterior woodwork.

The sequence of painting all woodwork — windows, doors and frames — is determined by the method of construction. In nearly all cases the rails (horizontal bars) are tenoned into mortises cut into the stiles (uprights). Therefore, you should paint the rails and cross bars first, then deal with the stiles.

By painting in this way, any overlaps of paint from the rails and bars are covered up and leave a neater finish. An even edge on the glass is best achieved freehand, but if you doubt the steadiness of your touch, use a paint guard or masking tape. Bring the paint onto the glass for up to 3mm (⅛in) to protect the edge of the putty. If you are using masking tape, remove it shortly after painting round each pane; the paint may be peeled off if it is left to harden completely before the tape is removed.

When a visitor calls at your house, he'll stand face to face with your front door and have nothing to do but examine it while he awaits your answer. So it's here you should put in your best work. Remove all the door furniture such as knobs, knockers, locks, keyhole covers and letterbox. Prepare the woodwork carefully and wipe it down with a tackrag (a soft cloth impregnated with a sticky varnish) to collect any remaining dust. Tackrags are obtainable from any good paint shop. Use a perfectly clean brush, preferably one that has been used before so that no loose bristles will come adrift. Wedge the door ajar and cover the floor with a dust cloth or old newspapers. Use paint which doesn't need straining, and pour about 50mm (2in) into a small container or paint pail.

All coats of paint should follow the grain of the wood. Don't attempt to cross-hatch – that is, apply a primer in one direction, undercoat at right angles and finishing coat in the direction of the primer. If you do, you'll get a criss-cross effect when the paint dries which produces a poor finish.

Deal with the door frame first (the top, then the sides) so that any splashes can be wiped off an unpainted surface immediately. Then do the door itself, following the sequence of painting shown on page 29 Don't put too thick a coat on the inner edge of the door frame because although gloss paint dries fairly quickly, it won't oxidize (ie, thoroughly harden) for about a week. So in

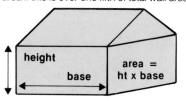
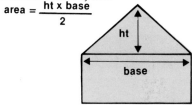

PAINTING WALLS

1 A roller is much quicker to use than a brush, but make sure you have a large enough bucket to dip the roller in. Fill this about ⅓ full.

2 Cut a short plank of wood to the same width as the roller and put it in the bucket so you can load the roller evenly by pressing against it.

3 When painting the house wall, start at the top right hand corner (if you are right-handed) and use a brush to cut in round the edges.

4 Using the roller, cover a strip on your right-hand side. Don't lean over too far and only make the strip as long as you can easily manage.

5 Move the ladder to the left and paint another strip by the first, without overlapping too much. Touch in round obstacles with a brush.

6 Using the brush again, carefully paint round the window. Try to leave a neat edge with the woodwork and wipe off any splashes with a damp cloth.

7 Continue painting a strip at a time from right to left, then lower the ladder and paint a further series of strips until the wall is covered.

8 Protect pipes by wrapping old newspaper round them and securing it with adhesive tape. Use a brush to paint the wall behind the pipes.

9 Be very careful when painting the bottom edge of the wall, and don't load the brush too thickly or paint will run onto the sidewalk.

Ready Reference

HOW MUCH GLOSS PAINT?

The coverage of a litre (1½ pints) of gloss paint depends on several factors, including the smoothness of the surface and whether it is interrupted by edges and moldings. Also, a lot depends on the painter's technique. However, as a general guide, for one litre (1½ pints) of paint:
● gloss covers 17m² (180sq ft)

CALCULATING AREAS

It would be very difficult to calculate the area of every bit of wood and metal you wanted to paint. But you need to make a rough estimate so you'll know how much paint to buy. The following examples are intended as a rough guide and they should give you an idea of how much paint you'll need, assuming you're using **gloss** and you give everything **two coats of paint**.
● a panelled front door will take ⅓ litre (½ pint)
● a flush door will take about ⅕ litre (⅓ pint)

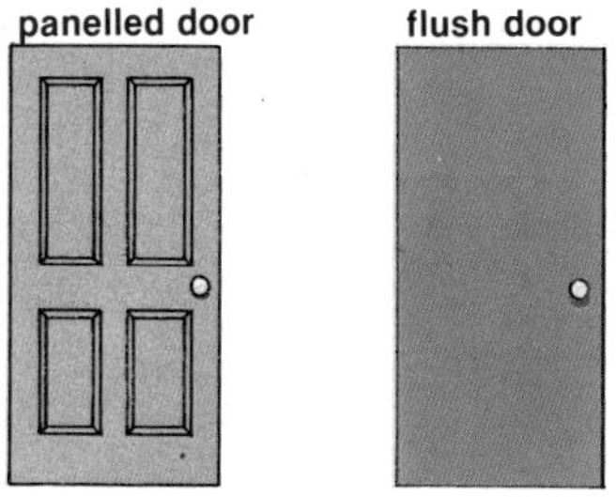

panelled door	flush door
3 doors/litre	**5 doors/litre**

● a sash window, about 2x1m (6ft 6in x 3ft 3in) with an ornate frame will take about ⅙ litre (¼ pint)
● a modern picture window of the same size with a plain frame will take only ⅛ litre (⅕ pint)

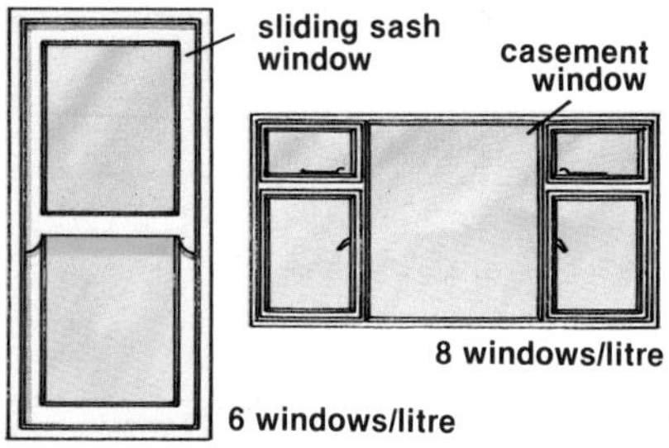

sliding sash window

casement window

8 windows/litre

6 windows/litre

● to find the area of a downpipe, simply measure round the pipe and multiply by the height, then add a little for clips and brackets. For two coats of paint, one litre (1½ pints) will cover 18m (60ft) of 150mm (6in) diameter pipe and 27m (90ft) of 100mm (4in) pipe.

PAINTING WINDOWS

1 *Start to apply undercoat at the top of the window. Prop the window open, tape up the stay and paint the frame rebates first.*

2 *Paint the rebates next. If you get paint on the inside surface, wipe it off immediately with a cloth dipped in mineral spirits or turps.*

3 *Close the window slightly and paint the area along the hinged edge. You may need to use a narrow brush (called a fitch) to reach this part.*

4 *A neat paint line on the glass is best achieved free-hand, but if you find this too difficult, use a paint shield or apply masking tape.*

5 *The general order of painting is to do the cross bars (rails) first, followed by the uprights (stiles) and then the window sill.*

6 *When the undercoat is dry, sand it down with a fine grade sandpaper, then apply the top coat in the same order as the undercoat.*

PAINTING SEQUENCES

Windows and panelled doors are tricky areas to paint properly but you shouldn't have any trouble if you follow the correct sequence of painting shown here.

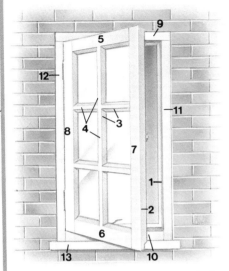

Start with the rebate on the frame (1), then paint the outside edge of the window (2). Do the putty (3) next, followed by the glazing bars (4) and the rails and stiles (5 to 8). Paint the frame (9 to 13) last.

Wedge the door ajar and paint the frame (1 to 3), the hinged edge of the frame and door. Do moldings and panels next (4 to 13) followed by the muntins (14, 15) the rails (16 to 19) and finally the stiles (20, 21).

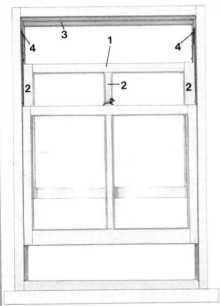

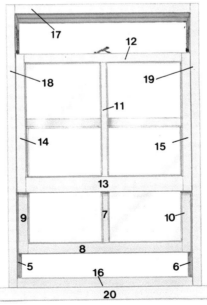

Sliding sash windows need to be painted in two stages. Pull down the top sash and paint the top rail of the inside sash (1) and the sides as far as you can go (2). Do the runners at the top of the frame (3) and a short way down the outer runner(4). Almost close the windows, then paint the bottom runners (5,6), and the remainder

of the bottom sash to meet the other paint (7 to 10). Paint the whole of the top sash including the bottom edge (11 to 15) and finally the window frame (16 to 20). This view shows the interior of the window: for the exterior the sequence is identical except of course, that you start with the top sash.

that period, when you close the door, paint may 'set-off' from the frame onto the door, producing a vertical streak an inch or so from the door's edge. A good idea to prevent this is to insert a thin strip of plastic sheeting around the door's edge after the paint has become touch dry, and leave it until the paint has thoroughly hardened.

Siding
Siding and wood cladding can be left in their natural state as long as you treat them with a wood preservative, and you can use wood stains to enhance or change their color. If you prefer a glossy finish, use a suitable external varnish such as an oil-resin varnish (marine varnish), rather than a polyurethane varnish which can prove brittle and difficult to over-coat in future. If you wish to paint the wood, you'll have to apply one coat of wood primer, followed by an undercoat and two finishing coats of gloss.

Galvanized iron and asbestos
Because it is waterproof, bituminous paint is best for galvanized or asbestos roofs. In addition to the customary black, it can be obtained in shades of red, green or brown to simulate or match tiles. These colors are more expensive than black and may have to be ordered specially from a builders' merchant. Bitumen soon loses its gloss and its surface tends to craze under a hot sun. But that doesn't matter as roofs are not usually visible.

Paint the walls of asbestos out-buildings with outdoor-grade emulsion in a color to match the rest of the house. Thin the first coat to allow for the porosity of the asbestos and follow this with a normal second coat. Apply emulsion on the interior surface as well to minimize moisture absorption. Galvanized iron on vertical surfaces should be painted with gloss paint.

When painting corrugated surfaces, give the high parts a preliminary touch-up with paint, leave it to dry and then paint the whole lot. If you apply paint all over in one go it will tend to flow from high to low parts, giving an uneven coating.

STRIPPING WOOD

Wood has a natural beauty, but it's often a beauty concealed by layers and layers of paint. Doors, window frames, even baseboards and door casings can all become attractive features in themselves when stripped back to reveal the wood. Even if you prefer to repaint, using the right techniques to strip off the old will give the best possible surface on which to work.

Stripping wood of old paint or layers of ancient varnish isn't the easiest of jobs. It's usually only done because you're after a natural finish, or because the painted surface has degenerated to such an extent that further coats of paint simply can't produce a smooth finish. Either way, once wood has been stripped back to its natural state, it then has to be sealed again — to protect it from moisture which can cause cracking, warping and ultimately decay. Both varnishes and paints act as sealants, giving a durable finish. But which one you choose might depend on the wood itself — and you won't know what that's like until you've stripped it. If you're unsure of its quality, it's advisable to strip a test area first.

Some of the wood used in houses is of a grade that was never intended for a clear finish — large ugly knots, cracks, splits or even an unattractive grain are some of the signs. In cases like this it is probably better to treat the problems (eg, applying a special liquid sealer to make the knots tight and prevent them from 'bleeding'; filling cracks and splits to give a flush surface) and then paint to seal.

If you are set on having the wood on show and don't want to paint it — because it wouldn't fit in with a color scheme or make the feature you want — you can give it a better appearance and extra protection with stain or colored varnish.

Stripping with abrasives

For dry stripping there are several different kinds of powered sanders available, all of which use abrasive papers of some kind to strip the surface off wood. On large areas, such as floors, it is best to use a purpose-made power sander which you can rent. A drill with a sanding attachment, however, is useful for getting small areas smooth after paint has been removed by other methods.

One such attachment is a 'disc sander' and is quite tricky to use effectively without scoring the wood surface. Hold it at a slight angle to the wood and present only half the disc to the surface. Work in short bursts and keep the disc moving over the surface — if it stays too long in one place it can damage the wood.

A 'drum sander' attachment has a belt of abrasive paper stuck round the edge of a cylinder of foam, and if used along the grain only is rather easier to handle than a disc

USING SCRAPERS

1 A triangular shavehook needs two hands when paint is thick. Hold the blade at an angle to the wood so it doesn't cause gouges.

2 A combination shavehook has round, straight and pointed edges to help remove paint and varnish from moldings around windows and doors.

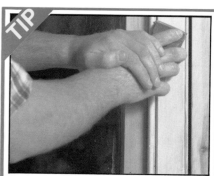

3 A special hook scraper has a sharp replaceable blade suitable both for scraping paint off flat surfaces and for getting into awkward crevices.

sander. Whichever type is chosen, a fine grade abrasive should be used for finishing stripped wood.

Orbital sanders (which are also known as finishing sanders) usually come as self-powered tools — although attachments are available for some drills. These have a much milder action and as long as the spread of wood isn't interrupted by moldings they smooth well and are useful for rubbing down between coats. These sanders are rectangular and should be moved over the surface in line with the grain. Make sure you choose the right type of sander, depending on the work at hand.

For sanding by hand — hard work, but much better for finishing — there are many grades of sandpaper from the coarse to the very fine. On flat surfaces it's best to wrap the paper round a small block of wood. As an alternative to sandpaper, there's also steel wool, which is most useful when you're trying to smooth down an intricate molding. Always sand backwards and forwards *with the grain of the wood,* not across it. Scratches across the grain will always be highlighted by a clear finish. To remove remaining bits of paint use medium grade sandpaper; for finishing, a fine grade is better. Renew the sandpaper frequently as the

paint will clog the surface, although a useful tip is to try cleaning clogged paper with a wire brush. It'll work once or twice, but after that the abrasive surface is usually lost. Alternatively pull the sheet backwards and forwards, abrasive side uppermost, over a table edge to dislodge paint particles.

A useful tool for cleaning paint from corners and moldings is a hand scraper with replaceable blades. These 'hook' scrapers are also used for 'smoothing' and often need two hands — they slightly raise the surface of a clear run of wood, giving an attractive finish under a clear seal. Use with the grain.

Heat stripping

Heat stripping is the quickest way to remove paint or varnish, but it needs a lot of expertise if you are to avoid charring the wood. So it is best reserved for stripping out of doors where a less-than-perfect surface will be less noticeable. A gas blow-torch is used along with metal scrapers to lift the finish off the wood while it's still warm. Blow-torches with gas canister attachments are light to use and a flame spreader nozzle makes the job easier (it can be bought separately).

Where there's no glass, it's a two-handed operation. Light the blow-torch and hold it a

Ready Reference

WHICH TOOLS?

Wide bladed scraper: useful for scraping off large areas of old paint loosened with a blow-torch or chemical strippers.

Triangular shavehook: useful for both flat surfaces and crevices. Take care not to gouge surface of wood.

Combination shavehook: because it has both straight and rounded blades, as well as a point, this is the most versatile scraper for awkward areas.

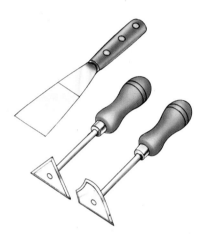

Steel wool: especially useful for tricky corners. Use medium grade (no 2) wool, and keep turning it inside out so all the cutting surfaces of the steel are used.

TIP: PICK THE RIGHT ABRASIVE

● Silicon carbide abrasive papers are less likely to clog up than sandpaper. They can also be used wet or dry.

DIFFICULT SURFACES

Where old paintwork is very thick, stripping may require repeated efforts.
● with a blow-torch, heat the paint until it bubbles up and scrape off as much as possible before softening and scraping the next layer
● when the wood is exposed and only stubborn bits of paint remain, use chemical stripper or sand by hand
● with chemical strippers, allow the first application to bubble up and then stipple on fresh stripper with a brush — working it well into the unstripped surface — before scraping off. If necessary repeat until the wood is fairly clean
● to remove stubborn bits, use steel wool and a small dab of stripper.

HEAT STRIPPING

1 *Play the blow-torch onto the paint and when it begins to bubble, start to scrape. Protect floor and sills with a sheet of non-flammable material.*

2 *When stripping paint near windows one hand must hold protection for glass. When paint hardens again, return the flame to the area.*

3 *Working overhead can be tricky if using a blow-torch. Protect your hands with gloves, your eyes with safety goggles and cover surfaces below.*

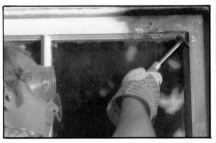

4 *To strip paint overhead, remove torch (be careful where it points), blow out flames and scrape quickly. As the paint loses heat it hardens.*

little way from the surface. Move it back and forth, going nearer and withdrawing, till the paint starts to wrinkle and blister. Now begin to scrape – be careful where you point the flame at this stage or you may damage other surfaces. As soon as the paint is hard to move return the flame to the area. Wear gloves to save your hands from being burnt by the falling paint, and cover areas below where you are working with a sheet of non-flammable material to catch the scrapings. In awkward areas, especially overhead, you should wear protective goggles for safety's sake.

Chemical stripping

Chemical strippers are probably the easiest way to strip wood. Available in liquid, gel and paste forms, their methods of application and removal vary, so always remember to read the manufacturer's instructions before you begin. Though all of them will remove paint and varnish, if you are dealing with a large area of wood they can work out to be very expensive – they're also very messy.

Liquid and gel strippers, decanted if necessary into a more convenient-sized container (read the instructions as to whether it can be heavy gauge plastic or should be glass or metal), are stippled onto the surface with a brush and left till the paint bubbles

before scraping. Usually these strippers will work through only 1 layer of paint at a time so several applications can be necessary. If stripping a chair or table, stand the legs in old paint cans or jam jars so that any stripper which runs down the legs can be recycled. Artist's brushes rather than paint brushes are useful when applying these strippers to moldings or beading in windows and No 2 steel wool is useful for removing it.

After liquids or gels have been used, the surface must be cleaned down with mineral spirits or water (it depends on the stripper used) to remove any trace of chemical and must be left till completely dry before any stain or seal is applied.

Pastes are mostly water soluble and manufacturers stress important conditions for using them safely (eg, not in direct sun, in well ventilated rooms, the wearing of protective gloves, etc). Bought in tubs ready-mixed or in powder form to be made up, they are spread in thick (3-6mm) layers over the wood which must then be covered with strips of polyethylene (good way of using up plastic bags) or a special 'blanket' (supplied with the tub) which adheres — when you press it — to the paste. They have to be left for between 2 and 8 hours after which the paste can be scrubbed off (with a firm brush) or washed down. Frequent changes of water

are needed; follow manufacturer's advice about additives (eg, vinegar). Pastes are particularly effective with extraordinarily stubborn paint or varnish in very awkward places (eg, windows, bannisters etc); or where using a scraper might damage old wood. Some pastes are unsuitable for certain types of wood and can stain it — so read instructions carefully. Washing down should not be done, for example, with valuable furniture for this can raise the grain of the wood.

Bleaching

If the wood is discolored once stripped (either from the stripper used or from some other source) you can try and achieve an overall color with bleach — the household type, used diluted 1:3 with water to begin with and more concentrated if necessary, or better still a wood bleach.

Clean the surface of the stripped wood with paint thinner and steel wool and leave for 15 minutes to dry. Cover areas you don't want bleached with plastic, then brush bleach on generously. Work it into the wood *with the grain* using medium steel wool.

CHEMICAL STRIPPING

1 *Liquid strippers are stippled onto wood with a brush. First pour the liquid into a smaller container — but remember it will dissolve light plastic.*

2 *When paint is bubbling use a scraper to remove it. Work upwards and be careful not to gouge the wood with the blade.*

3 *Several applications of liquid may be needed as chemicals often only eat through one layer at a time. Use gloves to protect your hands.*

4 *After all paint has been stripped off, wipe the wood down with mineral spirits or water so that the chemicals are neutralized.*

5 *A good way to deal with moldings is to apply a thick layer of stripping paste. This needs to be covered while it works, but is very effective.*

6 *After leaving for the specified time (can be several hours) wash the paste off with sponge or a scrubbing brush, changing the water often.*

CHAPTER 2
Papering

PAPERING WALL
the basics

No other wall covering can quite so dramatically alter the look and feeling of a room as wallpaper. Correctly hung paper makes the walls sharp and fresh, and to achieve this finish there are important things to know. What do you do if the walls are out of true? Where's the best place to start? How do you prevent bubbles and creases? The answers are here.

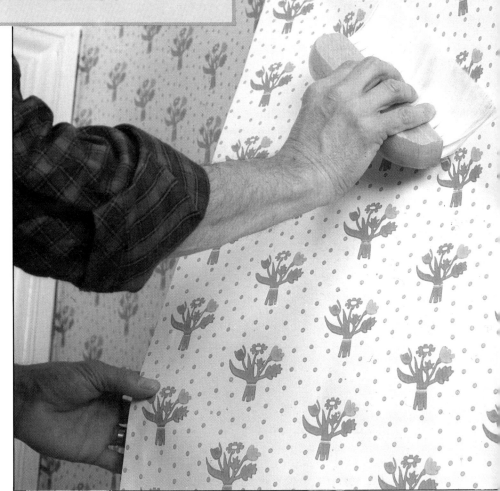

Wallpapering isn't so much an art, it's more a matter of attention to detail. And perhaps the first mistake that's made by many people is expecting too much of their walls. Rarely are walls perfectly flat, perfectly vertical and at right angles to each other. So the first and most crucial part of hanging wallpaper is to prepare the walls properly. Obviously you can't change their basic character – if they're not entirely flat or vertical, you're stuck with them – but you can make sure that the surface is suitably prepared so that the new paper will stick.

This means that any old wallpaper really should come off before you do anything else. Papering on top of old wall coverings won't *always* lead to disaster, but it will quite often simply because the new adhesive will tend to loosen the old. The result will be bubbles at best and peeling at worst.

Adhesives
Always use the correct adhesive for the wall-covering and follow the manufacturer's instructions for mixing. Using the wrong paste can result in the paper not sticking, mold growth or discoloration of the paper.

A cellulose-based adhesive is used for all standard wallcoverings. There are two types, ordinary and heavy-duty which relates to the weight of the paper being hung. Heavy-duty pastes are for heavyweight wallcoverings. Certain brands of paste are suitable for all types of wallcoverings – less water being used for mixing when hanging heavy papers.

Since vinyls and washable wallcoverings are impervious, mold could attack the paste unless it contains a fungicide. Fungicidal paste is also needed if the wall has previously been treated against mold or if there is any sign of dampness.

Some wallcoverings (like vinyl wallcoverings and foil wallcoverings) require a specially thick adhesive which is pasted onto the wall. Follow manufacturer's instructions.

Ready-pasted papers are exactly that and require no extra adhesive – although it's useful to have a tube of latex glue handy for finishing off corners and joints which mightn't

have stuck. (The same applies to all washable wallpapers).

Glue *size* (a watered down adhesive) is brushed over the walls before papering to seal them and prevent the paste from soaking in to the wall. It also ensures all-over adhesion and makes sliding the paper into place easier.

Although size can be bought, most wallpaper pastes will make size when mixed with the amount of water stated in the instructions.

If you buy a size and the wallcovering you are using needs an adhesive containing fungicide, make sure that the size you buy also contains a fungicide. Use an old brush to

apply and a damp cloth to clean off any that runs on to paintwork. It can be difficult to remove after it has dried. Sizing can be done several days or an hour before.

Where to begin
The traditional rule is to start next to the window and work away from it, but that is really a hangover from the days when paper was overlapped and shadows showed up joins. Today, papers butt up, so light isn't the problem. But as inaccuracies can occur with slight loss of pattern, you have to be able to make this as inconspicuous as possible. In

an average room, the corner nearest the door is the best starting point. Any loss of pattern will then end up behind you as you enter the room. In a room with a chimney breast, hang the first drop in the center and work outwards from both sides of the drop.

Problem areas in a house (recesses, arches, stairwells) are dealt with later in this chapter.

Measuring and cutting

Measure the height of the wall you want to paper using a steel tape measure and cut a piece of paper from the roll to this length, allowing an extra 50mm (2in) top and bottom for trimming. This allowance is needed for pattern matching, and to ensure a neat finish at baseboard and ceiling.

Lay the first drop — that's the name given to each length of paper — pattern side up on the table and unroll the paper from which the second drop is to be cut next to it. Move this along until the patterns match, then cut the second drop using the other end of the first as a guide. Subsequent lengths of paper are cut in exactly the same way, with each matching the drop that preceded it.

Remember some wallpapers have patterns that are a straight match across the width, while others have what is called a drop pattern that rises as it extends across the width. With drop match papers the second length will begin half a pattern repeat further along the roll. Length 3 will match length 1, length 4 will match length 2 and so on.

For things to run smoothly, you should establish a work routine when paper hanging. Cut all the wall drops first (so you only have to measure once) and cut bits for papering above windows and doors as you come to them. If you paste say 3 drops, the first will have had its required booking time

HOW TO CUT AND PASTE

1 Mark the pasting table with lines at 150mm (6in) and 300mm (1ft) intervals. Measure wall drop and use guidelines to cut your first length.

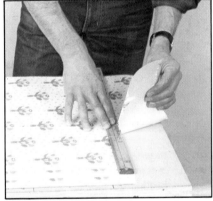

2 Use the first length as a guide for the other drops, matching the pattern carefully. Tear off the waste against a wooden rule.

3 Lay all the drops pattern down, overhanging the far edge of the table. Pull the first drop to the near edge and paste it from center to edges.

4 Fold pasted end, paste the rest and fold in. Now fold up the whole drop and leave it to soak. The top of the longer fold always goes to the top of the wall.

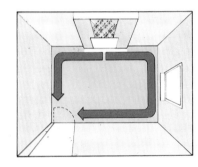
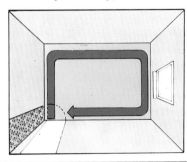

PAPER HANGING TECHNIQUES

1 Place chosen pattern on ceiling line with waste above. Align side edge with the plumb line and turn waste onto adjacent wall. Brush up to ceiling first, then corners and edges, and then down. Open out short fold last.

2 Mark cutting line for waste at ceiling and baseboard with a pencil — ends of scissors won't fit creases neatly and can give a thick line, which causes you to cut the paper inaccurately, an uneven look giving.

3 To cut waste, pull short length of paper away from wall so pencil line catches the light. Cut using full length of blades — hurried, short cuts can make the edges jagged. Brush paper back on wall so that it is perfectly flat.

4 Reduce waste on adjacent wall to 6mm (¼in) to lessen bulk when paper overlaps from other direction.

5 Continue along wall matching the pattern horizontally. Press drop onto wall so long edges butt.

6 As each drop is hung, brush up first, then to edges and finally down to remove any trapped air.

7 To turn a corner, measure between hung paper and corner at the top, middle and bottom of wall. Add 6mm (¼in) to widest width, then use this measurement to cut the pasted and folded drop into two. Set aside offcut for new wall.

8 Hang drop to complete wall, brushing the waste round the corner. Drop a plumb line and mark the line the width of offcut from the corner. Check this measurement at the top, middle and bottom of wall. If the same, hang offcut.

9 If corner is out of true, offcut and wall measurements will differ. To disguise pattern loss, hang the offcut so waste laps onto completed wall. Brush into corner, run pencil down crease line and cut waste.

(with medium weight paper) by the time the third is pasted and folded and is ready to be hung. With heavy papers paste, fold and book 6 drops at a time as extra booking time is needed.

Avoiding bubbles

The purpose behind booking time (apart from making paper supple enough to handle) is to give it time to expand to its natural limit. On the width this can be 6mm-12mm (¼in-½in) and the average wall-size drop will gain 24mm (1in) on the length — this explains why you have more to cut as waste than you started with.

If you haven't given paper the time it needs, it will expand on the walls – but its spread will be contained by adjoining drops and so you get bubbles in the central part.

Book medium weight papers for 3-4 minutes, heavy weights for about 10. Ready-pasted papers don't need too long a booking, but to ensure they get wet all over, roll drops loosely and press into water till they are completely covered.

Pasting and soaking

Position the paper with its top edge at the right-hand end of the table (or at the other end if you're left handed). Paste it carefully to ensure that all parts, the edges especially, are well covered. Work from the center outwards in herring-bone style using the width of the brush to cover the drop in sweeps, first to the nearest edge, then the other — excess paste here will go onto second drop, not the table. Cover two-thirds of the drop, then fold the top edge in so paste is to paste. Move the drop along the table and paste the remainder, folding bottom edge in paste to paste. Because the first folded part is longer than the other, this will remind you which is

the top. Fold the drop up and put aside to book while you paste the others.

This technique will give you a manageable parcel of paper to hang no matter what length the drop – but always remember to make the first fold longer – this is the one offered to the ceiling line. If in doubt mark the top edge lightly with a pencil cross.

Hanging pasted paper

Wallpaper must be hung absolutely vertical if it is to look right, so always work to a vertical line (see *Ready Reference*).

Position your step ladder as close as possible to where you want to work, and climb it with the first length of paper under or over your arm. Open out the long fold and offer the top edge up, placing the pattern as you want it at the ceiling with waste above. Align the side edge of the drop with your vertical guide line, allowing the other side edge to turn onto the adjacent wall if starting at a corner. Smooth the paper onto the wall with the paperhanging brush, using the bristle ends to form a crease between wall and ceiling, and at corners. When brushing paper into place, always work up first then to the join, then to the side edge, then down. This will remove trapped air.

As soon as the paper is holding in place, work down the wall, brushing the rest of the drop in position, opening out the bottom fold when you reach it. Again use the bristle ends to form a good crease where paper meets the baseboard.

The next step is to trim off the waste paper at the top and bottom. Run a lead pencil along the crease between the ceiling or baseboard and the wall — the blades or points of scissors will make a line that's too thick for accurate cutting. Gently peel paper away from the wall and cut carefully along the line with your scissors. Finally brush the paper back in place.

Hanging the second drop is done as the

Ready Reference

HANGING TO A VERTICAL

For perfect results wallcoverings must be hung absolutely vertical. You can't trust the corners of rooms to be perfectly true so you must
● mark a vertical line on the wall against which the first length can be aligned
● mark a similar line on the next wall every time you turn a corner

Mark line on first wall 25mm (1in) less than a roll's width from the corner, using a plumb bob and line
● hold the line at the top of the wall and allow the bob to come to rest just above baseboard level
● mark the string's position at three points on the wall with a pencil
● join up the marks using a long straight edge as a ruler

PAPERHANGING TOOLS

Plumb bob and line: for establishing a true vertical. Any small weight attached to a string will do.
Pasting brush: it's thicker than a paint brush and about 150mm (6in) wide. A paint brush will do as a substitute.
Paperhanger's scissors: for trimming on or off the wall. Long-bladed household scissors can be used instead.
Paperhanging brush: for smoothing paper onto walls and into angles. Use a sponge on washable and vinyl papers.
Seam roller: for ensuring good adhesion along seams (not used with embossed papers). A cloth-wrapped finger does almost as well.
Pasting table: for pasting lengths prior to hanging, it's slightly wider than a standard roll width. Any table over about 1.8 metres (6ft) long can be used.

Estimator

Calculate rolls needed by measuring perimeter of the room and height from baseboard to ceiling.

MEASUREMENTS FOR SINGLE STANDARD ROLLS 7 yds × 20½''

Distance around room in feet	8 ft. high	9 ft. high	10 ft. high
36	9	10	11
40	10	11	13
44	11	12	14
48	12	14	15
52	13	15	16
56	14	16	17
60	15	17	19
64	16	18	20
68	17	19	21
72	18	21	22

MEASUREMENTS FOR SINGLE EURO ROLLS (METRIC) 5.5 yds × 20½''

Distance around room in feet	8 ft. high	9 ft. high	10 ft. high
36	12	14	16
40	14	16	18
44	16	16	20
48	16	20	20
52	16	20	20
56	20	22	24
60	20	24	26
64	22	24	28
68	24	26	28
72	24	28	30

The number of rolls needed can be greatly affected by the frequency of pattern repeat. With a large pattern repeat, buy an extra roll.

first except that you have to butt it up against the edge of the first length, matching the pattern across the two. The secret here is not to try and do it all in one go. Get the paper onto the wall at the right place at the ceiling join but just a little way away from the first length. Now press against the paper with the palms of your hands and slide it into place. Using well-soaked paper on a wall that's been sized makes this easy, but if you're using a thin wallpaper press gently as it could tear. Butt the paper up after pattern matching and brush into place.

When trimming waste from drops other than the first, cut from where the lengths butt to ensure even ceiling and baseboard lines.

Hanging ready-pasted wallpaper

With these you won't need pasting table, bucket and pasting brush but you will need a special light plastic trough made for the purpose. Put it below where the first drop is to be hung and fill with water – covering the floor with layers of newspaper will soak up accidental spillages. Don't try to lift the trough; slide it along the floor as the work progresses.

Cut each drop so patterns are matching, then roll the first one loosely from the bottom up with the pattern inside. Place it in the trough and press it down so water can reach all the parts covered with paste. Leave for the required soaking time (check manufacturers' instructions but, it's usually between 30 seconds and 2 minutes), then pick the drop up by the two top corners and take it to the ceiling line. Press onto the wall using an absorbent sponge to mop up and push out air bubbles. Press firmly on the edges with the sponge or a seam roller, then trim waste.

COPING WITH WALL FITTINGS ... AND CREASES

Few walls present a perfectly clear surface for paperhanging. Almost all will contain such small obstacles as light switches and receptacles, while some may carry wall-mounted fittings such as curtain tracks and adjustable shelving. Small obstacles can be papered round with some careful trimming, but larger obstacles are best taken down from the wall and replaced when you have finished decorating. That way you will get a really professional finish.

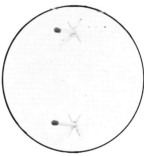

1 *Use matchsticks, pushed head out into wall plugs, to show where wall fittings have been taken down.*

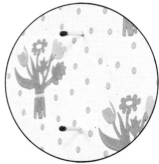

2 *Brush paper firmly over match heads so they pierce it. With hanging complete remove matches and replace fittings.*

1 *To cut around light switches, mark center of plate, insert scissor tips and cut out towards plate corners.*

2 *Crease tongues of paper against edges of plate, lift away from wall, trim along line and brush back into place.*

3 *With washable and vinyl papers push a strip of rigid plastic against plate edges and trim with a sharp knife.*

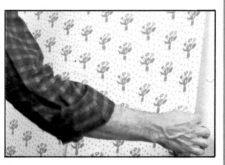

1 *Creases are a common fault where the wall is out of true or if you haven't brushed the paper out properly.*

2 *To remove the crease, peel the paper from the wall to a point above the crease – to the ceiling if necessary.*

3 *Brush the paper back into position – across towards the butt join, then to the other edge and down to the bottom.*

[PAPERING] A STAIRWELL

Even if the walls are flat, papering a stairwell presents problems. The awkward angles, height of the walls and long lengths of wallcovering make for special difficulties of access and handling, but you'll find that these can be overcome.

Hanging wallpaper in an ordinary room is not too difficult. But with stairwells there are awkward corners and long lengths to cope with.

Gaining access

The chief problem in wallpapering a stairwell is that of gaining access to the walls you are papering. This is because of the height of the walls and the awkward angles involved.

It is essential to have a safe working platform and to set this up in the right way to suit the layout of the stairwell and the way the stairs rise. You can rent special platforms for decorating the stair/hall area, or use the components of a tower platform. Alternatively, you can use ladders and steps linked with scaffold boards (see page 41).

A particularly useful item of equipment is a hop-up, a small platform which you can make yourself (see *Ready Reference*).

Preparation

Before you start decorating, remove the handrail and any other wall-mounted obstacles so you can get at the wall. Then prepare the walls properly so the new wallcovering will stick. Always remove any old wallcovering; some will peel off, although with most types you will have to soak and scrape them off.

Once the walls are stripped, you can work out where to begin hanging. You should position the longest drop of wallcovering first, and to establish where this will be, measure the height of each wall in the stairwell. (You will need a long tape and someone to help you when you are measuring the wall in a stairwell.) Then, starting as close as possible to this point but about 50mm (2in) away from any obstacles — such as a door or window opening — take a roll of the wallcovering you are going to use and move it along the wall to estimate where succeeding widths will fall. If, according to your calculations, there will be a join between lengths within 50mm (2in) of an external corner (at another window opening, for example), change your starting point slightly and measure again so you avoid this. Then mark off where this first drop will be hung.

When you have established where you will hang the first drop, use a plumbline to work over a true vertical at this point. Coat the line with chalk, pin it to the top of the wall and allow it to hang. Then, at the baseboard, hold the plumb bob with one hand, pluck the string with the other and let it snap back against the wall to leave a vertical chalk line on the wall. Alternatively, instead of coating the plumb line with chalk, fix it in place, allowing it to hang down, and then place a long straight-edge so the edge is exactly against the line, and use it as your guide to draw a true vertical line down the wall. Remember to plumb a new line every time you turn a corner.

Hanging the wallcovering

The decorating sequence is the same as for any other area — see the techniques already covered. If the wall is bare plaster, start by applying size to the wall to prevent the paste soaking in. Then measure and cut the wallcovering to length, remembering to allow for the angle of the baseboard if applicable, paste it and allow it to soak. If you are using a ready-pasted wallcovering, place your water trough in the hall or on the landing, not on the stairs where you are likely to knock it over. Wallcoverings hung by the paste-the-wall

Ready Reference

SAFETY FIRST IN STAIRWELLS

Falls from ladders and steps cause many deaths and injuries in the home. To prevent the risk of an accident
● make sure ladders and steps can't slip by resting their feet against a piece of wood screwed or nailed to the floor or tread on which they are standing
● always secure boards to whatever they are resting on – with rope, or bolts dropped through pre-drilled holes
● never trust a handrail to support your weight or that of a board.

MAKE A HOP-UP

As part of your access equipment, make a hop-up from 150mm × 25mm (6in × 1in) lumber nailed or screwed together. It should be about 460mm (18in) high and 760mm (30in) wide.

PREPARATION

1 To prepare the wall surface you will have to remove the existing wallcovering. In this case it is vinyl which is easy to remove; it is simply peeled off.

2 Before you remove lining paper it's worth cutting along the paper at ceiling level or you may find you tear off the ceiling paper with the lining paper.

3 When working at a high level make sure that the ladders and scaffold boards you are working from are firmly secured and well supported to ensure safety.

4 To remove paper from the wall when preparing to hang a new wallcovering, soak it thoroughly with a damp sponge. Leave for a while, then soak again.

5 Use a scraper to take the paper off the wall and scrape off old flaking paint at the same time. Wash the wall down to remove any remaining bits.

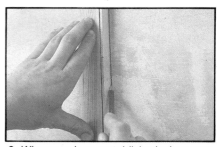

6 When you have established where you will hang the first length, use a plumbline to make sure you get a true vertical and mark a pencil line on the wall.

HANGING THE WALLCOVERING

1 Place the first drop up against the wall, using the line you have drawn as a guideline to get it straight. Get someone to help you hold the long drop.

2 Use a soft-bristled wallpaper-hanging brush to smooth the covering into place. Leave an overlap at the top and bottom for trimming when the drop is fixed.

3 Hang subsequent lengths of wallcovering so they butt join and so the pattern matches. Trim each piece; a scraper will help as a guide.

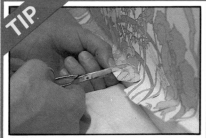

4 Where there is a curve cut into the overlap so the paper will fit round the curve easily without puckering.

5 You can then trim off the overlap in the same way as at a door surround, using a scraper to help guide the knife as you trim along the bottom edge.

6 For convenient paper hanging you will have to remove a wall handrail. This can be replaced when the wallcovering is fixed and the adhesive completely dry.

SAFE WORKING PLATFORMS

1 stairs with quarter landing

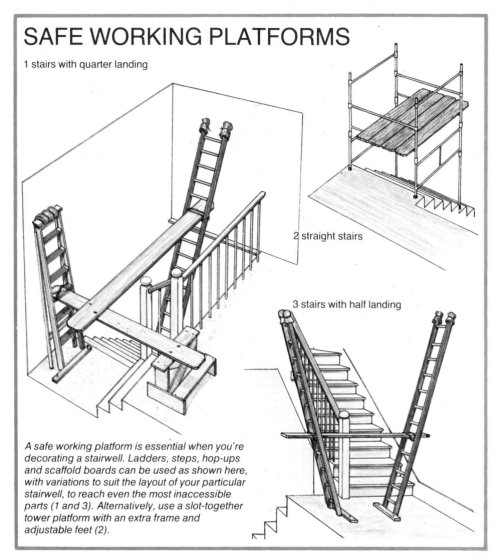

2 straight stairs

3 stairs with half landing

A safe working platform is essential when you're decorating a stairwell. Ladders, steps, hop-ups and scaffold boards can be used as shown here, with variations to suit the layout of your particular stairwell, to reach even the most inaccessible parts (1 and 3). Alternatively, use a slot-together tower platform with an extra frame and adjustable feet (2).

technique are particularly easy to hang in stairwells, because you are handling lengths of dry wallcovering.

Because the lengths of paper for the wall at the side of the stairs will all be of a different size – caused by the rise of the stairs – it is better to cut and paste one length at a time, unlike straightforward rooms where you can cut and paste several lengths at a time.

Hang the first and longest length of wallpaper, using the vertical line you have marked on the wall as a guideline to get it straight. Then work round the stairwell from this length, making sure the pattern matches as you go along.

If your staircase is curved at the bottom the wallcovering is likely to pucker as it fits around the curve. To prevent this, you can snip into the overlap at the foot of the wall at intervals so the paper is more flexible in its fit.

Coping with long drops

A problem unique to stairwells is the length of paper you are handling – often as much as 4.5m (15ft) long. Apply paste liberally so it is less likely to dry out before you have fixed the bottom of the length. (It's worth keeping a small amount of adhesive ready to apply where the adhesive has dried out before the wallcovering is fixed.) Fold the pasted paper in concertinas (see *Ready Reference*) and then gather up the folds and drape the folded-up length over your arm to carry it.

Because the weight of the paper may cause it to stretch or tear as you are hanging it, try to get someone to help you take the weight. Where there is no one available to help, you will have to sit on your scaffold board, or other form of support, and allow the bottom of the drop to unfold gently to baseboard level. Then you can take the top up to the ceiling and start brushing it into the correct place. Remember too, that when you are trimming along the bottom of a length of wallcovering that meets the staircase baseboard, you will be trimming at an angle rather than horizontally as at the foot of a wall in a room.

Ready Reference

CARRYING LONG LENGTHS

To make it easier to carry a long length of wallcovering, fold it in concertinas and then drape it over your arm.

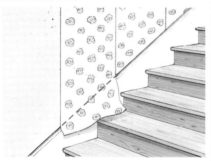

BEWARE ANGLED BASEBOARD

When measuring up, remember that lengths meeting the stairs baseboard must be measured along their longer edge, not their shorter one.

EQUAL BOOKING TIME

To minimize the risk of stretching
● allow the same amount of booking time between pasting and hanging on each length
● if you do find the paper has stretched, match the pattern as best you can at eye level, where bad matching would be most noticeable.

YOU'LL NEED HELP

It's best not to try hanging long lengths of paper by yourself; the weight of the paper may cause it to stretch or tear. Get someone to take the weight and unfold the paper as you work down the wall.

TIP: TRIM NARROW PIECES DRY

Where long narrow strips are needed, measure up and trim the drop approximately to size before pasting. This is easier to handle than having large waste pieces covered in paste flapping around.

OVERLAPS WITH VINYL

Vinyl will not stick to vinyl where you are using ordinary paste. If an overlap is unavoidable use a special vinyl overlap adhesive.

PAPERING AWKWARD AREAS

The techniques for papering round tricky areas like corners and reveals are quite basic. But care and patience is required if you are going to get really professional results from your paperhanging.

Although the major part of wallpapering, hanging straight lengths is fairly quick and straightforward. The tricky areas – corners, doorways and so on – which call for careful measuring, cutting and pattern matching are the bits that slow the job down. There's no worse eye-sore than a lop-sided pattern at a corner; but if you use the right techniques you can avoid this problem.

You have to accept in advance that the continuity of a pattern will be lost in corners and similar places; even a professional decorator can't avoid this. However, he has the ability to match the pattern as closely as possible so that the discontinuity is not noticeable, and this is what you have to emulate.

Things would, of course, be a lot simpler if all corners were perfectly square, but this is rarely the case. When you wallpaper a room for the first time you are likely to discover that all those angles that appeared to be true are anything but.

You can, however, help to overcome the problem of careful pattern matching at corners by choosing a paper with the right design (see *Ready Reference*). The most difficult of the lot to hang are those with a regular small and simple repeat motif. The loss of pattern continuity will be easy to spot if even slight errors are made. The same is often true of large, repeat designs. With either of these types, a lot more time will be involved and it could take a couple of hours to hang a few strips around a single window reveal.

Sloping ceiling lines are another problem area and certain patterns will show it up clearly. You can understand the nuisance of a sloping ceiling by imagining a pattern with, say, regular rows of horizontal roses. Although the first length on the wall may be hung correctly to leave a neat row of roses along the ceiling line the trouble is that as subsequent lengths are hung and the pattern is matched, you will see less and less of that top row of roses as the ceiling slopes down. And, conversely, if the ceiling line slopes upwards, you will start to see a new row of roses appearing above. So, despite the fact that each length has been hung

vertically, the sloping ceiling will make the job look thoroughly unsightly.

Internal and external corners

Before you begin papering round a corner, you must hang the last full length before the corner. Your corner measurement will be done from one edge of this length. You can use a steel tape or boxwood rule to measure the gap to the corner (see *Ready Reference*) and then cut the piece required to fill it, plus a margin which is carried round onto the new wall. Since it's likely that the walls will be out of square and that the margin taken round the corner will not be exactly equal all the way down, it's obvious you would have a terrible job hanging the matching offcut strip to give a neat butt join.

For this reason you must hang the matching offcut which goes on the 'new' wall to a true vertical and then brush it over the margin you've turned onto this wall. You should aim to match the pattern at the corner as closely as possible. Since the paper overlaps, the match will not be perfect, but this is unavoidable and will not, in any case be noticeable as the overlap is tucked into or round the corner out of sight (see *Ready Reference*).

Papering round window reveals

Unless you intend to paper just one or two walls in a room you will eventually have to cope with papering round a window. Pattern matching is the problem here, but you should find cutting the paper to fit above and

below a window is not too difficult provided you work in a logical order (see box opposite). But you may have to be prepared for lots of scissor work when you cut out strips of paper for the two sides and top of the reveal to ensure the pattern matches the paper on the facing wall. (It's worth getting into the habit of marking some sort of code on the back of each piece of paper before it's cut up so you will be able to find matching pieces quickly.)

Make sure that you don't end up with a seam on the edge of the reveal, where it will be exposed to knocks and liable to lift. Before you begin work on the window wall, take a roll of wallcovering and estimate how many widths will fit between the window and the nearest corner. If it looks as though you will be left with a join within about 25mm (1in) of the window opening you should alter your starting point slightly so that, when you come to the window, the seam will have moved away from the edge of the reveal.

Where the lengths of paper are positioned on the window wall obviously depends on the position of the window, its size and the width of the wallpaper. But the ideal situation occurs when the last full length before you reach the window leaves a width of wall, plus window reveal, that measures just less than the width of the wallpaper. You can then hang the next length so its upper part goes on the wall above the window, the lower part on the wall below it and (after making two scissor cuts) turn the middle part to cover the side of the window reveal. The edge of

PAPERING ROUND A WINDOW

Top: Fill the narrow gap left on the underside of the reveal with a small offcut.
Above: The papering sequence; piece 7 fills the gap left on the reveal by piece 6.

TIP: CHOOSE PATTERNS CAREFULLY

In rooms full of awkward corners and recesses, pick a paper with a random, busy design which the eye doesn't try to follow. This will help disguise the fact that a corner is out of square, or a ceiling is sloping.

MEASURING AT CORNERS

When you are measuring for the width of paper required to fill a corner gap:
● measure from the last full fixed length to the corner at the top, middle and bottom of the gap
● take the largest measurement; for an internal corner add 12mm (1/2in) and for an external corner 25mm (1in) to give you the width to cut from the next length
● the offcut left is used on the 'new wall' and overlaps the 12mm (1/2in) or 25mm (1in) strip turned round the corner.

TIP: TURN NARROW STRIPS

Never try to take a lot of paper round a corner. If you do, you will end up with it badly creased into the angle of the corner, and the part that is taken onto the 'new wall' will be completely askew.

AVOID OBVIOUS JOINS

On an external corner the overlap of the edges of the two strips of paper which cover the corner should be positioned where they will be least obvious (eg, on a chimney breast it is better to make the overlap on the side wall rather than have it on the wall facing into the room).

PAPERING ROUND A DOORWAY

Ideally, you'll use the minimum of paper if you center a full-width strip of paper over the door opening. Where the door is close to a corner, fit a narrow strip above the doorway. Pattern discontinuity will be least noticed in between two full strips.

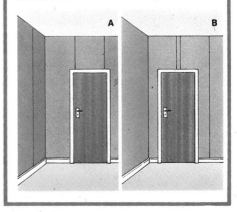

the middle part can then be creased and trimmed so it fits neatly up against the window frame.

Go on to hang short lengths of wallpaper above the window, cutting them so their lower parts can be taken on to the underside of the top window reveal, and again trim them so they fit neatly up against the window frame. When you reach a point where the reveal on the opposite side of the window is less than the width of the wallpaper away from the last edge hung, you should stop and repeat the papering process below the window between the sill and baseboard, trimming as you go.

You can then hang the next full length in the same way as the one you hung on the first side of the window. You should, first, however, hang a plumbline over the pieces in place above the top and bottom of the window then hang the full length to the plumbline, trimming any slight overlap on the new length if necessary. (By doing this, you will ensure that the lengths to be hung on the rest of the wall will be truly vertical.)

Often, however, the position of the last full length at the window will fall so that the paper does not cover the reveal at the side of the window, and in this case you will have to cut matching strips to fill the gap. Similarly, you

will have to cut strips to fill the gaps on the underside of the reveal at the top of the window.

Dormer windows

In attics and loft rooms there will be sloping ceilings and dormer windows with which you will have to contend. If you decide to paper rather than paint the sloping ceiling, then you treat it in the same way as you would a vertical wall; there are no unusual problems involved, other than the peculiar working angle. Remember, too, that if you choose the wrong type of paper the irregular pattern-matching could give unfortunate results.

Paper the wall alongside the window and then round the window itself, moving on to the wall below the other side of the sloping ceiling (see step-by-step photographs). Finally, you can paper the dormer cheeks.

Chimney breasts and fireplace surrounds

Special rules apply to chimney breasts. For a start, since they are a focal point in the room, any pattern must be centralized. The design of the paper will affect where you begin to hang the wallpaper. Where one length of paper contains a complete motif, you can simply measure and mark off the central point of the chimney breast and use a plumb-

PAPERING AN INTERNAL CORNER

1 *Hang the last full length before the corner. Then measure the gap (see Ready Reference) to determine the width to be cut from the next length.*

2 *Cut from the next length a piece which will overlap 12mm (1/2in) round the corner. Then paste and fix it in position so it fills the corner gap.*

3 *Measure the width of the matching offcut strip of paper and use a plumbline to mark a guideline on the wall this distance from the corner.*

4 *Hang the offcut so its cut edge overlaps the matching edge of the first corner piece and its 'good' edge aligns with the vertical guideline.*

FLUSH WINDOWS

1 *Fix the last full length of paper before the window and pull the excess across. Cut round the sill and fix the paper beneath it.*

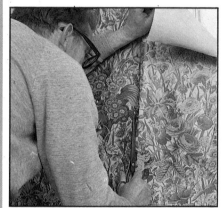

2 *You can then trim off the excess paper which runs alongside the window. Now press and brush the pasted paper into position.*

3 *Work along the wall underneath the window, fixing, creasing and trimming as you go. Afterwards you can fix the paper on the other side of the window.*

line at this point to help you draw a vertical line down the center. You can then begin hanging the wallpaper by aligning the first length with this line.

On the other hand, if it is the type of paper where two lengths, when aligned, form a motif, you will first have to estimate the number of widths which will fit across the chimney breast and then draw a line as a guide for hanging the first length of paper so the combined motif will, in fact, be centralized.

Your order of work should be from the center (or near center) outwards and you will then have to turn the paper round the corners at the sides so you form an overlap join with the paper which will be applied to the sides of the chimney breast. Follow the usual techniques for measuring and papering round external corners, remembering not to take too much paper round the corner.

When it comes to fireplace surrounds, there are so many varying kinds of mantels and surrounds that only general guidance can be given. Usually the technique is to brush the paper down on to the top part of the wall and then cut it to fit along the back edge of the mantel. You can then cut the lower half to fit the contours of the surround. If it's a complicated outline, then you'll have to gradually work downwards, using a small pair of sharp scissors, pressing the paper into each shape, withdrawing it to snip along the crease line, then brushing it back into place.

If there is only a small distance between the edge of the mantel and the corner, it's a lot easier if you hang the paper down to the mantel and then make a neat, horizontal cut line in the paper. You can then hang the lower half separately and join the two halves to disguise the cut line.

PAPERING ROUND A DORMER

1 Where the dormer cheek meets the junction of the wall and ceiling, draw a line at right angles to the wall on the ceiling by the dormer cheek.

2 Draw a vertical line at right angles to the first line on the dormer cheek. You can then fix the first length of paper in place on the dormer cheek.

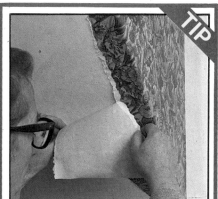

3 Work along towards the window, trimming as you go. Gently tear along the overlap to feather its edge so you won't get a bulky join later.

4 At the window, crease along the side of the frame by running the edge of the scissors along it. You can then carefully trim along the creased line.

5 Return to the small gap which needs to be filled at the narrow end of the dormer cheek; fix this piece in position, crease and trim.

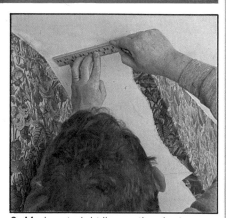

6 Mark a straight line on the sloping ceiling to serve as a guideline for fixing the first length of paper on the underside of the dormer cheek.

7 Cut a piece of paper so it reaches from the point you have marked up to the window and brush it into position ensuring that it covers the feathered edges of the overlap.

8 At the junction of the wall and ceiling you will have to cut round awkward angles. You can then go ahead and brush the paper into its final position.

9 Finally, you can brush the strip of paper which fills the gap between the wall and the underside of the dormer cheek into position to finish off the dormer area neatly.

PAPERING CEILINGS

One way to cover up a ceiling with cracks or other imperfections is to use lining paper or a textured wallcovering and then paint over it. But a good alternative is to make a special feature of the ceiling by using decorative paper.

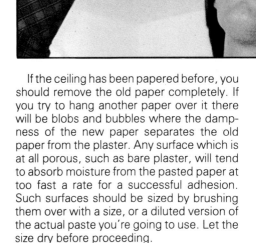

Papering ceilings can be a rather daunting prospect, even to the experienced home decorator. In fact, once you have mastered the basic technique of paperhanging, ceilings are quite straightforward and you are likely to be presented with far fewer problems than on walls. There will be no windows, few (if any) corners and not so many obstacles with which you have to deal.

If you intend to paint the ceiling it's usually best to hang a lining paper or a textured paper first to hide the inevitable blemishes of a plaster ceiling. Or you might decide to choose a fine decorative paper and make a feature of the ceiling with it. Most of the papers that are suitable for walls can also be used for ceilings.

But before you opt for papering, it makes sense to consider the alternative: if the sole objective is to get a textured surface which will cover up cracks and bumps, you can do it just as well with a textured paint. However, if you want a smooth ceiling or a decorative surface of distinction then papering is for you.

The equipment you'll need
You will need the same equipment as for papering walls, with the addition of a safe working platform that spans the width of the room (see *Ready Reference*). You should check with your supplier that the paper of your choice is suitable for ceilings (some heavier types may not be) and ask him to provide a suitably strong adhesive, including fungicide if it is a washable vinyl paper. Such papers are extremely suitable for high humidity environments like bathrooms and kitchens.

Preparing the surface
The surface to which you fix the paper must be clean and sound. This means washing down existing paintwork with detergent and then sanding it with a fine abrasive paper or pad to provide a key for the adhesive. Distempered ceilings, often found in old houses, must be scrubbed to remove the distemper, or the paper will not stick.

If the ceiling has been papered before, you should remove the old paper completely. If you try to hang another paper over it there will be blobs and bubbles where the dampness of the new paper separates the old paper from the plaster. Any surface which is at all porous, such as bare plaster, will tend to absorb moisture from the pasted paper at too fast a rate for a successful adhesion. Such surfaces should be sized by brushing them over with a size, or a diluted version of the actual paste you're going to use. Let the size dry before proceeding.

New gypsum board, often used in modern construction, needs painting with a primer/sealer before decoration. It is also wise to fix a layer of lining paper before your main decorative paper if you are hanging heavyweight or fabric wallcoverings.

Decorating perfectionists always recommend using lining paper anyway, whatever the surface. There is no doubt it does improve the final appearance, particularly on older surfaces or with thinner papers. Lining paper comes in different thicknesses or 'weights' and you should consult your supplier about a suitable grade.

One last preparation tip: don't leave cracks and dents in ceilings for the paper to cover. Fill them and sand them smooth, particularly at joints between gypsum boards, and at the wall/ceiling angle. Think of your paper as a surface that needs a good smooth base, not as a cover-up for a hideous mess.

Planning the job
Consult the estimator panel (see *Ready Reference*) to gauge the approximate number of rolls you will need; also think about the pattern of your intended paper. Can you cope with a complex drop pattern on a ceiling, or would you be better off with a straight match? A bold paper that looks fine on walls might be a bit overpowering above your head. Is your ceiling good enough for a plainish paper, or do you need texture to draw the eye away from the ravages of time that appear in all old lath-and-plaster ceilings?

Modern papers are designed for the strips to be butted against each other, not overlapped. This means the traditional pattern of working away from, but parallel to, the main source of natural light is not essential. You will generally find it easier working across the narrowest dimension of the room. Well-applied paper will tend not to show the joins too much anyway, particularly if the pattern draws the eye.

All ceiling papering starts from a line which is strung or marked across the ceiling 10mm (⅜in) less than the width of the paper away from the wall. The 10mm (⅜in) on the length of paper which runs next to the wall allows for the walls being out of square and its overlap is trimmed off at the wall and ceiling junction. You can chalk a line and snap it against the ceiling between two tacks to make a mark, or just pin it temporarily in place and butt the first strip of paper against it.

MARKING UP AND PASTING

1 Measure in from the width of the paper minus 10mm (³/₈in), to allow for an overlap at the wall, and mark this distance on the ceiling.

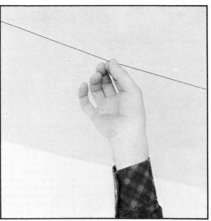

2 Make another mark at the opposite end, the same distance from the wall. Use a chalked line to link the marks, then snap the line onto the ceiling.

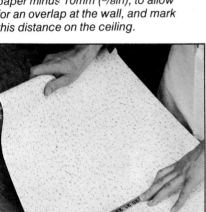

3 Cut or tear the lengths of paper. You should allow 100mm (4in) excess on each piece to give an overlap of 50mm (2in) for trimming at each end.

4 Apply paste to the back of the paper and fold it into concertina folds as you go. Paste enough lengths to allow adequate booking time.

TIP

5 Take the last fold in the length to meet the first, short, fold so the edges meet without paste getting on the front of the paper.

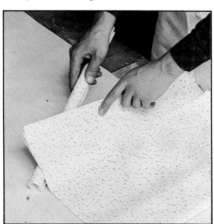

6 Slip a spare roll of paper under the folded-up length; this will serve as a support for the paper so you can carry and hold it easily.

Ready Reference

ESTIMATOR

Distance around room	Number of rolls
	(approximate)
10-12m (33-39ft)	9
12-14m (39-46ft)	11
14-18m (46-59ft)	14
18-20m (59-66ft)	16
20-22m (66-72ft)	18

For Eurorolls add two rolls.

TIP: WHISK YOUR PASTE

To speed up the process of mixing paste, use a kitchen whisk to beat up the mix.

A SAFE WORKING PLATFORM

Set up two stepladders and a solid plank, at a height where you can comfortably touch the ceiling with the palm of your hand.

TIP: HAVE TOOLS AT HAND

Have the necessary tools with you (in the pocket of an apron or overall) when you're on the working platform to save you scrambling up and down more than you need.

PREVENT WASTAGE

If you are pattern matching, paper in the direction which will save long bits of waste paper left over after cutting the lengths.

LINING PAPER

If you are hanging lining paper, remember that it should be hung at right angles to the paper which goes over it.

PAPERING TECHNIQUE

With the concertina-folded paper supported by the spare roll held in your left hand (if you are right-handed; vice versa if you are left-handed) pull one fold out taut and then brush it into place, working outwards from the center to avoid trapped air bubbles. Repeat with the other folds.

TIP: TRIM CEILING CAPS

Don't be tempted to remove the cover of a ceiling cap to trim the paper round it; inaccurate cutting may mean there are gaps when the cover is replaced. Instead:
● trim round the fitting with the cover in place leaving a slight overlap (see step-by-step photographs)
● remove the cover and press the overlap into place.

FINAL TRIMMING

When the last piece of paper has been hung you may need to spend some time on final trimming if the walls and ceiling do not meet squarely and evenly.

HANGING STRAIGHT LENGTHS

1 Hang the first length on the 'room' side of the chalk line, not next to the wall. Brush the paper into place gently but firmly.

2 Brush the ends carefully into the angles where walls and ceiling meet, and trim. Then hang the next length alongside the wall.

3 The lengths should be butt-jointed. Use a seam roller to ensure well-stuck edges by running it gently over the length of the seam.

4 Trim off the overlap at the ends and side (if necessary) of each length of paper. Use a scraper as a guide for the knife for accurate cutting.

5 Wipe off any excess adhesive where the overlap has been before it dries, or it will leave ugly marks on the wall surface.

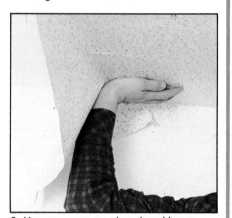

6 You can now go ahead and hang the next length on the other side of the first piece hung. Continue until you have covered the entire ceiling.

It makes sense to get all the lengths measured and cut out in advance, and pasted up in batches of twos or threes (depending on your speed of working) to give adequate booking time for the type of paper you are hanging; check the manufacturer's instructions on this point. Cut all the strips, including those which will be trimmed for chimney breasts, to full room dimensions plus 100mm (4in) excess for trimming.

The concertina fold

The secret of successful ceiling papering is the correct folding technique, as you paste, so that the paper can be transferred to and laid out against the ceiling surface in a smooth manner. Each fold of the concertina should be 300mm (1ft) wide approximately, apart from the first, which can be shorter (see step-by-step photographs). It's worth practising folding with dry paper first.

Hanging the paper

Assemble the working platform securely at the correct height across the whole length of the room, beneath the area where the first strip is to be pasted. Before you get up there with a fold of wet, pasted paper, make sure you have the tools you will need at hand.

The last-to-be-pasted section of each length is first to go on the ceiling; tease off this first section and brush it into place. Continue to unfold the concertina in sections, brushing it down as you go and checking it is straight against the guideline.

Trimming and seam rolling

When you trim, you should make sure the paper butts exactly up to covings, but allow a 5-10mm (¼-⅜in) overlap down to the surface of the walls you intend to paper later. Except with embossed papers, you should roll the butt joints between strips with a seam roller.

Light fittings or shades should always be removed, leaving just the wire hanging down. Turn the power off, to ensure safety.

If a chimney breast falls parallel to the run of the paper, you will need your scissors handy to take out an approximate piece as you work along the platform. It's worth anticipating this before you get up there; mark a rough line on the paper at the approximate position of the chimney breast. Cut out the chimney breast piece, leaving an excess of about 15mm (⅝in) for detailed trimming when the whole strip is in place.

If the strip ends at a chimney breast there are less problems. Remove any vast unwanted sections as you work and trim to fit later. External corners are dealt with by making a V-cut so that one flap of the paper can be folded down the inside alcove edge of the chimney breast (or trimmed there if you are working to a coving).

PAPERING AROUND OBSTACLES

1 *If there is a ceiling cap, use a knife or scissors to make a little slit in the paper so it fits round the cap; don't cut too deep.*

2 *Hang the next length so it butts up against the previous one; at the cap take the paper over the top of the obstacle.*

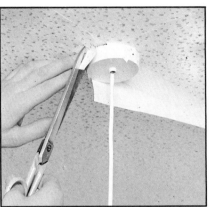

3 *Again, make slits in the paper so it fits round the cap; this will allow you to brush the rest of the length of paper in place.*

4 *When the paper is in place, trim round the cap. Place the edge of a scraper between the knife and ceiling so there's a slight overlap.*

TIP

5 *Turn off the power, remove the cap cover and press the overlap into place. When the cover is replaced it will conceal the cut edges completely.*

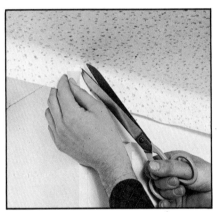

6 *Where the paper meets an alcove, make a slit in the paper in line with one corner of the alcove and then in line with the other.*

7 *You can then brush the paper into place in the normal fashion so it fits neatly into the gap between the two corners. Trim the overlap along the wall leading to the alcove.*

8 *Fix the next length so it butts up against the previous one. Adhesive may ooze out when seams are rolled; so long as the paper is colorfast, you can remove it with a damp sponge.*

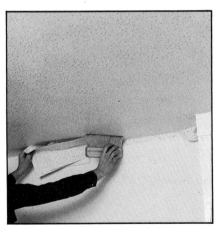

9 *Measure up and cut the last narrow piece, allowing for an overlap of about 25mm (1in) at the wall and ceiling junction. Paste and brush it into place; trim to complete the job.*

CHAPTER 3
Tiling and Flooring

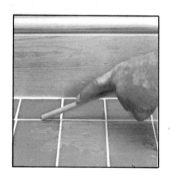 

CERAMIC TILES for small areas

Ceramic tiles are easy-clean, hygienic and hard wearing. By starting with a small area in your home where these qualities are needed – like splashbacks or worktops – you'll not only grasp the basics but also gain confidence to tackle bigger things.

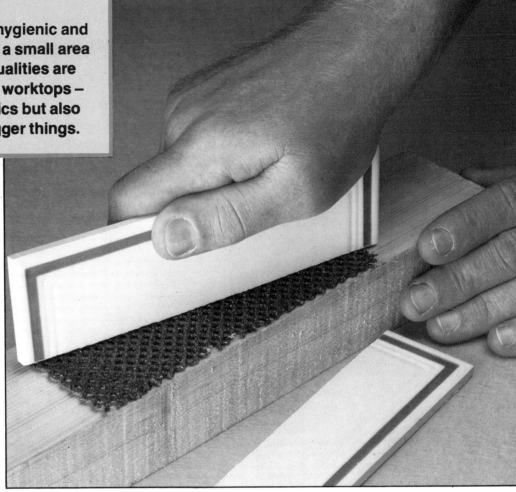

Modern ceramic tiles are thin slabs of clay, decorated on one side with colored glazes. These are baked on to give the tile a hard, glassy surface resistant to water, heat and almost all household chemicals. The clay from which tiles are made, which is known as the biscuit, varies and you need to know the differences before you choose the tile to use. The thinnest ones with a pale colored biscuit are good on all vertical surfaces (including doors where extra weight puts stress on the hinges).

If the biscuit is reddish/brown it has been high baked (vitrified). The thicker and darker colored it is the more strength the tile has — floor tiles, for example, are usually big in size as well as thick in biscuit.

Work surfaces need tiles that are strong to withstand weights of heavy pots, while splashbacks and bathroom surfaces can take lighter, thinner ones.

Types of tiles
Within each range of tiles there are usually three types. *Spacer* tiles have small projections on each edge called lugs which butt up to the neighboring tile and provide the correct space for grouting (with these it is very hard to vary the width of the grouting). *Border* tiles are squared off on all sides but are glazed on two adjacent edges — these give a neat finish to outer corners and top or side edges. *Universal or continental* tiles have no lugs and are square on all edges. All three can be used successfully in small areas, but do remember that if tiles do not have lugs you have to include grouting space in your calculations — the thinnest tiles need to be spaced by nothing more than torn-up pieces of cardboard, 6mm (¼in) tiles are best with a matchstick width in between.

Tiles are sold by the sq metre, sq yd, boxed in 25s or 50s, or can be bought individually. Boxed tiles usually advise on adhesive and grout needed for specific areas. When buying, if there's no written information available always check that the tile is suitable.

How to plan the layout
When tiling small areas you don't have much space to maneuver. The idea in all tiling is to create a symmetrical effect, using whole tiles or, if any have to be cut, making them equal.

Knowing about the different sizes of tiles helps in the planning. For example, if you know the width and height or depth of the surface you intend to tile, you can divide this by the known size of tiles until you find the one that gives the right number of whole tiles. Remember that the width of grouting has to be added to the measurement with non-lugged tiles – and except with the very thinnest tiles this can be slightly widened if it saves cutting a tile.

If you're prepared to incorporate cut tiles into the planning remember:
● on the width of the tiled area, place equal cut tiles at each end
● on the height, place cut tiles at the top edge
● on the depth (eg, window-recesses) put cut tiles at back edge
● frame a fitting by placing cut tiles at each side and the top

A mix of patterned or textured with plain tiles is best done first on graph paper. This will help you see where you want the pattern to fall.

Fixings should be made in the grouting lines where possible. Some tile ranges have soap dishes, towel racks, etc attached to tiles so they can be incorporated in a scheme, but if these don't suit your purposes, you can drill the tiles to screw in your own fitting.

A working plan
All tiles should be fixed level and square so it's important to establish the horizontal and vertical with a spirit level. Draw in the lines with pencil. If you plan to tile where there is no support (eg, on either side of a basin or sink) lightly pin a length of 50 × 25mm (2 × 1in) wood below the tiling line — the wood will prevent the tiles slipping.

On doors you may have to consider adding a wood surround to keep the tiles secure as they will be subjected to movement (also see section on *Adhesives* below).

Adhesives and grouting
The choice of both of these depends on where the tiles are to be fixed. In a watery situation (eg, a shower cubicle or a steamy kitchen) it is important to use a waterproof variety of both, even though you might have

Ready Reference

TILE SHAPES AND SIZES

Ceramic tiles for walls are usually square or oblong in shape. The commonest sizes are shown below. The smaller sizes are usually 4mm (5/32in) thick, while larger tiles may be 6mm (1/4in) or more in thickness.

▼200x200mm   6x6in▼

100x100mm▲

▲ 4¼ x 4¼in   50x50mm▲

HOW MANY TILES?

Square or oblong areas
● measure lengths and width of the area
● divide each measurement by the size of tile you're using, rounding up to the next whole number if you get a fraction
● multiply the two figures to give the number of tiles needed

Awkwardly-shaped areas
● divide area into convenient squares or oblongs
● work out each one as above adding up the area totals to give the final figures

Patterns using two or more different tiles
● sketch out design on graph paper, one square for each tile (two for oblong tiles); use colors to mark where different tiles fall
● count up totals needed of each pattern, counting part tiles as whole ones

Add 10% to your final tile counts to allow for breakages

ADHESIVE/GROUT

For each square metre of tiling allow:
● 1.5kg (about 3lb) of adhesive
● 150g (9oz) of grout

TIP: AVOID NARROW STRIPS

Less than about 25mm/1in wide is very difficult to cut. When planning, if you see narrow strips are going to occur you can:
● replan the rows to use one less whole tile with two wider cut pieces at either end
● or increase the grouting space slightly between every tile in the row

HOW TO HANG TILES

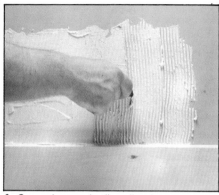

1 *Spread ceramic tile adhesive to cover 1 sq metre (1 sq yd) then 'comb' with notched spreader. To support tiles where no other support exists, pin a horizontal 1 × 2 to the wall.*

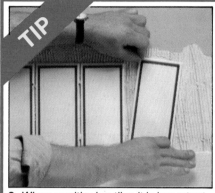

2 *When positioning tiles it is important to twist them slightly to bed them. Don't slide them as this forces adhesive between joints.*

3 *Form even grouting spaces between tiles without lugs with pieces of matchstick. Or you can use torn-up cardboard from the tile packaging or similar if you want only a narrow grouting space.*

4 *Remove matchsticks or card after all tiles are hung, and grout 12-24 hours later. Press grout into the spaces using a small sponge or squeegee, making sure no voids are left in either vertical or horizontal spaces.*

5 *After 10 minutes, wipe off excess grouting with soft cloth. Use fine dowelling (sand the end to round it) to even up and smooth the lines. Fill any voids that appear with fresh grout to prevent water penetration.*

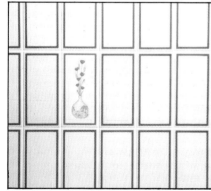

6 *When grouting is dry, polish the tiles with a soft cloth so the area is smooth. All the surface needs now is an occasional wipe-down although non-waterproof grout may tend to discolor as time goes by.*

to wait for 4-5 days before exposing the tile surface to use.

All ceramic tile adhesives are like thin putty and can be bought ready mixed in tubs or in powder form to be made up with water. They are what is known as thin-bed adhesives in that they are designed to be applied in a thin layer on a flat even surface. The spread is controlled by a notched comb (usually provided by the manufacturer but cheap to buy where you bought the tiles) to make furrows of a specified depth. When the tiles are pressed on with a slight twist, the adhesive evenly grips the back of the biscuit.

Special latex-based adhesives (usually, two-part products which have to be mixed before using) have much more flexibility and are good for tiles where there is any movement (eg, on doors).

Spread the adhesive on an area no more than 1 sq metre (1 sq yd) at a time, or it will lose its gripping power before you have time to place the tiles. If you remove a tile, before refixing comb the adhesive again.

Grout gives the final finish to the tiled area, filling the spaces between the tiles and preventing moisture getting behind them and affecting the adhesive. Grouting can be done 12-24 hours after the last tile has been pressed into place. Grout can be standard or waterproof (with added acrylic), and both are like a cellulose filler when made up.

If you only make up one lot of grouting, you can color it with special grouting tints — but remember that it's hard to make other batches match the color. Waterproof grouting cannot always take these tints.

Press grout between the tiles with a sponge or squeegee and wipe off excess with a damp sponge. Even up the grouting by drawing a pencil-like piece of wood (eg dowelling) along each row first vertically, then horizontally. Do this within 10 minutes of grouting so it is not completely dry.

Leave the tiles for 24 hours before polishing with a clean dry cloth. Wash clean only if a slight bloom remains.

Tiles should never be fixed with tight joints for any movement of the wall or fittings will cause the tiles to crack. Similarly where tiles meet baths, basins, sinks etc, flexibility is needed – and grout that dries rigid cannot provide it. These gaps must be filled with a silicone rubber sealant

Techniques with tiles
To cut tiles, lightly score the glaze with a tile cutter to break the surface. Place the tile glazed side up with the scored line over matchsticks and firmly but gently press the tile down on each side. If using a pencil press on one side, hold the other. Smooth the cut edge with a file. Very small adjustments are best done by filing the edge of the whole tile.

CUTTING TILES

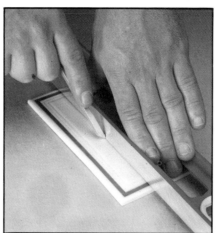
1 Before a tile will break, the glaze must be scored — on the edges as well as surface. Use a carbide-tipped cutter against a straight-edge.

2 Another type of cutter has 'jaws' which clasp the tile during breaking. (It also has a small 'wheel' for scoring through the glaze on the tile).

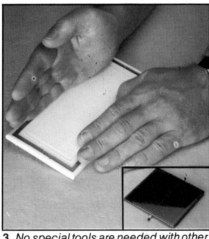
3 No special tools are needed with other tile-breaking methods. For medium thick tiles use a pencil, for thin tiles use matchsticks.

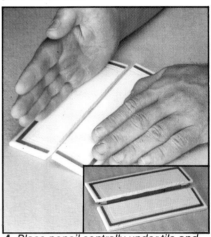
4 Place pencil centrally under tile and score line, hold one side and press firmly on other. With thin tiles, press lightly both sides.

To remove a narrow strip of tile, score the line heavily by drawing the tile cutter across the tile more firmly several times in the same place. Then use pincers to 'nibble' the waste away in small pieces and smooth the edge. Glaze on broken tiles is as sharp as glass, so be careful not to cut yourself.

Templates for awkwardly shaped tiles are not difficult to make. Cut the shape in card, place on a tile and score a line freehand with the tile cutter. Any straight score marks can be deepened afterwards, using a straight edge for support. Then nibble away the waste with pincers. If there's a large amount to be cut away, score the waste part to divide it into sections, then nibble away. A good tip is to do this on a soft or padded surface so the tile doesn't break in the wrong place.

Suitable surfaces
The ideal surface for tiling is one that's perfectly flat, dry and firm. Small irregularities will be covered up, but any major hollows, bumps or flaking, need to be made good.

Plastered walls: these are perfect for tiling, but wait a month after any new plastering to allow the wall to dry out completely. Unless the surface has been previously painted, apply a coat of plaster primer to prevent the liquid in the tile adhesive from being absorbed too quickly.

Plasterboard: again, ideal for tiling as long as it's firmly fixed and adjacent boards cannot shift. (If they did the joints would probably crack). To prepare the surface, remove all dust, wipe down with mineral spirits to re-

Ready Reference

TOOLS FOR TILING

Tile cutter: essential for scoring glaze of tiles before breaking them. Score only once (the second time you may waver from the line and cause an uneven break).

Pincers: these are used for nibbling away small portions of tile, after scoring a line with the cutter. Ordinary pincers are fine for most jobs, but special tile nibblers are available.

Special cutter: combines a cutting edge (usually a small cutting wheel) with jaws which snap the tile along the scored line.

Tile file: an abrasive mesh, used as a file to 'shave' off small amounts.

TIP: TO DRILL A TILE

● make a cross of masking tape and mark the point where you want the hole
● drill after adhesive and grouting have set using lowest speed or a hand drill with masonry bit — too much speed at the start will craze the tile
● once through the glaze, drill in the normal way

● cut tile into two along line corresponding with center point of pipe; offer up each half to the pipe
● mark freehand semi-circles on tile to match edge of pipe; score line with tile cutter and nibble away waste with pincers

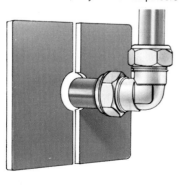

SHAPING TILES

5 *Edges of broken tiles need to be smoothed off — use a special tile file mounted on wood, a wood file or rub against rough concrete.*

7 *On a soft surface, use pincers to take tiny nibbles out of the tile. If you're over enthusiastic you'll break off more than you intended.*

6 *To cut an awkward shape, make a card template. Place it on the tile and score glaze on the surface and edges with the tile cutter.*

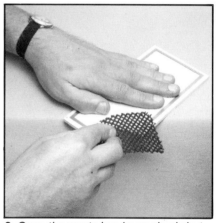

8 *Once the waste has been slowly but surely nibbled away, smooth up the edge. Files are also useful when a whole tile needs a slight trimming.*

move grease, then treat with primer.

Paint: old latex paint needs to be cleaned thoroughly with detergent to remove all traces of dust and grease. Gloss paint needs to be cleaned thoroughly; remove any flaking paint then roughen up whole surface with a coarse abrasive to provide a good key for the adhesive.

Wallpaper: DO NOT tile directly onto wallpaper, as this can be pulled away from the wall by the adhesive. Strip it off completely.

Wood and Chipboard: perfect for tiling as long as it is flat and adjacent boards cannot shift. Treat with an ordinary wood primer.

Laminates: joins and small, minor blemishes in the surface can be covered up so long as the entire sheet is soundly fixed and absolutely flat. Its smooth face must be roughened with coarse abrasive to provide a key for the tile adhesive.

Old ceramic tiles: the thin biscuit ceramic tiles are excellent for tiling over as they add little to the wall's thickness and won't protrude beyond existing fittings. Loose and cracked tiles will have to be removed. Scrape out the grouting surrounding the tile using an old, thin screwdriver or something similar, then, beginning in the center and working outwards, remove the tile using a club hammer and cold chisel.

Small sections or mis-shapen pieces (as around a new fixture) can be built up level with neighboring tiles with cellulose filler.

The area should then be sealed with plaster primer or latex paint to finish the surface.

CERAMIC TILING WALL TO WALL

Ceramic tiles are an ideal decorating material for they make a room look good for years and require virtually no maintenance. But covering several walls with tiles is a large-scale job which needs a methodical and careful approach if you are to achieve the best results.

Jem Grischotti   Tiles: Rustica Roberta pattern   Flooring: GAF terra cotta cushion vinyl Coburg

The all-in-one look that wall-to-wall tiling can give has to be planned carefully to avoid expensive and time consuming mistakes. How to do this may depend on whether you want to include special patterns in the design, but following certain rules will give a desirable symmetry to the look.

One of the hardest tasks will probably be choosing the tiles for there's a vast array of shapes, sizes and colors available. Having picked out the ones you want though, don't buy until you've done the planning — for the plans of each wall should tell you whether the pattern will work in the room or would be lost in the cutting or amid the fittings.

Plans on paper also give you an instant method of working out how many tiles to buy (counting each cut one as a whole, and adding 2-5% for unintended breakage) including the number which will need to be border (two glazed edges) or mitered (on square or rectangular universal tiles) for the top row of half-tiled walls or external corners. Buy all the tiles at once, but do check each carton to make sure there's no variation in the color (this can occur during the firing of different batches).

Planning on paper

The best possible way to start planning for a large expanse of tiling is not on the wall, but on paper. Graph paper is ideal, particularly if you intend including a mix of plain and patterned tiles, or a large motif that needs building up. Of course, advance planning is also essential if you're tiling round major features like windows, doors, mirrors, shower cubicles and so on.

You need separate pieces of graph paper for each wall you intend tiling. Allow the large squares on the paper to represent your tiles — one for a square tile of any size, two for a rectangular tile; this will give you a scale to work to. Now mark up sheets of tracing paper with your actual wall sizes using the scale dictated by the tile size on the graph paper. Measure and outline on the see-through paper the exact position and in-scale dimensions of all fixtures and fittings (see the planning pictures on page 56).

At this stage, the objective is to decide how to achieve the best symmetrical layout for your tiles — the 'ideal' is to have either whole or equal-size cut tiles on each side of a fixture.

First you have to mark in the central guide lines. For instance, on *walls with a window* draw a line from the sill center to the floor, and from the center of the top of the window to the ceiling. If there are *two windows,* also draw in the central line from floor to ceiling between them. Mark the center point above a *door* to the ceiling and also indicate the horizontal line at the top of the door. In the same way draw in a central line from the top of a *basin or vanity unit* to the ceiling.

For all these lines use a colored pen for you have to be aware of them when deciding where whole tiles should be positioned. But they're only the starting point — other potential problems have to be looked at too.

Place the see-through paper over the tile sizes on the graph paper so you can see how the tiles will fall in relation to the guide lines. Now take into account the following important points:

● The first row above the lowest level — either the floor, the baseboard or a wall-to-wall fitting — should be whole tiles. If necessary, change this to prevent a thin strip being cut at the ceiling.

● Check where tiles come in relation to fittings. If very thin strips (less than 38mm/1½in) or narrow 'L' shapes would need to be cut, move the top sheet slightly up, down, left or right till the tiles are of a cuttable size — areas to watch are around windows, doors and where one wall meets another.

Placing patterns

When you are satisfied that you have a symmetrical and workable arrangement you can tape the top sheet in the right position on the graph paper, then start to plan where you're going to position your patterned tiles. Use pencil this time in case you change your mind and want to make adjustments. These are the points to watch:

● Don't place single motif patterns at internal corners where they would have to be cut — you won't find it easy to match up the remaining piece on the adjacent wall.

Ready Reference

TILING SEQUENCES

You can use the 'step' method, or build 'pyramids'. Here are the sequences for different bonds.

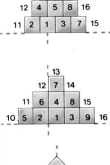

Running bond staggers the tiles. Place the first one centrally on your vertical line.

Jack-on-Jack has the joints lined up. Work either side of your vertical line.

Diamond bond puts plain or outlined tiles at an angle. Place the first centrally on the vertical, fill in 'triangles' last.

● If the pattern builds up vertically and horizontally over four or more tiles, 'center' the pattern on the wall so that cuts are equal at both ends. If pattern loss can't be avoided with designs of this type, at least it can be kept to internal corners.

● Whole tiles should be used on both faces of external corners.

Now butt each of the wall plans up to the other to make sure that the patterns relate both vertically and horizontally.

Planning on the wall

When there are no complicated tiling patterns involved and walls are free of interruptions such as windows, it's often easier to do the planning directly on the wall itself. Here, the simple objective is to place the tiles symmetrically between the corners. And to do this, all you need is a tiling gauge which you can make.

A tiling gauge is like a long ruler, except that it's marked off in tile widths. Use a long, straight piece of wood ideally about 25mm square (1in square) and remember to include the grouting gap between tiles as you rule off the gauge. If you're using rectangular tiles, mark the widths on one side, the lengths on the other.

Holding the gauge against the walls — first vertically, then horizontally — tells you instantly where the whole tiles will fit in and where cut tiles will be needed. But first you must find the center of each wall. Measure the width — doing this at three places will also tell you if the corners are vertical (hang a plumb line or use a spirit level to make absolutely sure) — and halve it to find the center point. Use the tiling gauge to mark this vertical center line with a pencil, then hold the gauge against it. Move it up or down until you have at least a whole tile's width above the floor or baseboard — this can be adjusted slightly if it avoids a thin piece of tile at ceiling height — then mark off the tile widths on the vertical line itself.

Now hold the tiling gauge horizontally, and move it to left or right of the vertical line if thin pieces of tile would have to be cut near windows or fittings, or to make cut tiles at both ends of the wall equal. Following this adjustment, mark the wall and draw in a new vertical line if necessary. The wall can now be marked horizontally with tile widths. Keeping to the same horizontal, mark up adjacent walls in the same way.

At corners, whether internal or external, don't assume they're either square, vertical or even. An internal corner is the worst place to start your tiling for this very reason, but it doesn't matter if you position cut tiles there. On external corners use the tiling gauge to work inwards in whole tile widths.

You can also use the tiling gauge to check that your graph plan is accurate, and make any necessary adjustments.

Putting up guides

Once you have determined that your plan is correct, fix a length of perfectly straight 1 × 2 across the full width of the wall — use a spirit level to ensure that the wood is horizontal. Use masonry nails to fix it in place but do not drive them fully home as they will have to be removed later. If using screws, the wall should be plugged. The 1 × 2 provides the base for your tiling and it's important that its position is correct.

If more than one wall is being tiled, continue to fix the strips around the room at the same height, using the spirit level to check the horizontal. The last one you fix should tie up perfectly with the first. If there are gaps, at the door for example, check that the level either side is the same, by using a straightedge and spirit level to bridge the gap.

Once the horizontal guides are fixed, fix a vertical guide to give yourself the starting point for the first tile. Use a spirit level or plumb line to make sure it's positioned accurately.

Fixing tiles

Begin tiling from the horizontal base upwards, checking as you work that the tiles are going up accurately both vertically and horizontally. Work on an area of approximately 1 sq metre (1 sq yd) at a time, spreading the adhesive and fixing all the whole tiles using card or matchsticks as spacers as necessary. Make sure no excess adhesive is left on the surface of the tiles.

Next, deal with any tiles that need to be cut. You may find the gap into which they fit is too narrow to operate the adhesive spreader properly. In this case spread the adhesive onto the back of the tiles.

When all the tiling above the base strip has been completed wait for 8-12 hours, before removing the wood, and completing the tiling. Take care when removing the base strip that the tiles above are not disturbed — the adhesive is unlikely to be fully set.

Dealing with corners

Your original planning should have indicated how many border or mitred tiles you will need for tiling external corners or for the top line of tiles on a half-tiled wall. You will find external corners, those which project into the room, in virtually all tiling situations — around boxed-in pipework, or around a window or door reveal, or in an L-shaped room.

Where you are using universal tiles at an

PLANNING TILE LAYOUT ON PAPER

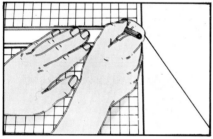

1 *On graph paper with large squares, let each square represent one whole square tile. Strengthen the grid lines with colored pen if necessary.*

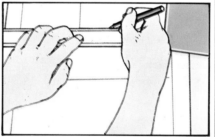

2 *On tracing paper, draw the outline of each wall to be tiled, and mark in doors and windows. Use the scale 1 square = the actual tile size.*

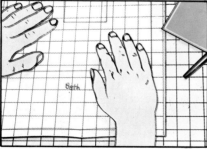

3 *Place tracing paper over graph paper and move it around till you get the most manageable size cut tiles, especially near fixtures, ceiling and floor.*

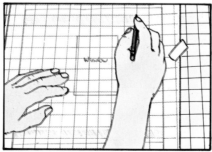

4 *Tape the top sheet in place, then mark the pattern in with pencil. Do each wall the same so that the alignment of the horizontal is correct.*

Jem Grischotti

external corner, start at the corner with a whole tile — it should project by the depth of the mitre so that the mitre on the other face neatly butts up against it with a fine space for grouting in between.

With window reveals the correct method is to tile up the wall to sill level, cutting tiles if necessary. Fit whole tiles either side of the reveal, then again cut tiles to fill the space between those whole ones and the window frame. Attach whole border or mitred tiles to the sill so they butt up against the wall tiles. If using square-edged tiles the ones on the sill should cover the edges of those on the wall so the grouting line is not on the sill surface. If the sill is narrower than a whole tile, cut the excess from the back — not the front. If the sill is deeper than a whole tile, put cut tiles near the window with the cut edge against the frame. Continually check the accurate lining up of tiles with a spirit level.

Some vertical external corners are not as precisely straight and vertical as they should be and this can lead to problems of tile alignment. The use of a thick-bed adhesive will help to straighten out some irregularities where a corner goes inwards (a thin-bed helps where the wall leans outwards). Buying a 'flexible' adhesive will give you both qualities. As a general rule it is

PLANNING ON THE WALL

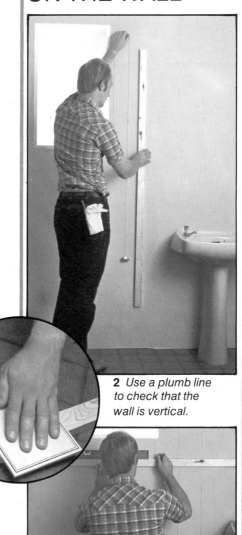

1 (inset) Mark the tiling gauge in tile widths (and lengths if they are rectangular).

2 Use a plumb line to check that the wall is vertical.

3 Draw verticals down the wall, marking off the exact tile widths to give an accurate guide.

4 Check each horizontal with a spirit level, then mark tile positions from floor to ceiling.

5 Place horizontal support at least a tile's width above floor or a fitting using masonry nails or screws.

6 Fix vertical support and begin to tile where the 1 × 2s meet. Spread adhesive to cover 1 sq metre (1 sq yd).

Jem Grischotti

Ready Reference

TACKLING TILING PROBLEMS

Whenever a fitting, a door or window interrupts the clean run of a wall, it becomes the focal point of the wall. So you have to plan for symmetry around the features. Here are some guidelines:

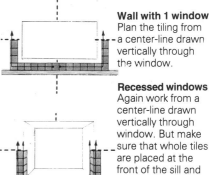

Wall with 1 window
Plan the tiling from a center-line drawn vertically through the window.

Recessed windows
Again work from a center-line drawn vertically through window. But make sure that whole tiles are placed at the front of the sill and the sides of the reveals. Place cut tiles closest to the window frame.

Wall with two windows
Unless the space between the two windows is exactly equal to a number of whole tiles, plan your tiling to start from a center-line drawn between the two.

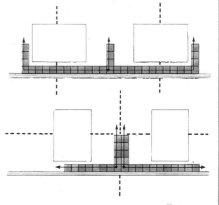

Wall with door
If the door is placed fairly centrally in the wall, plan your tiling from a center-line drawn vertically through the door. If, however, the door is very close to a side wall, the large expanse of wall is a more prominent focal point. So plan the tiling to start one tile's width from the frame. If the frame is not exactly vertical, you'll be able to cut tiles to fit in the remaining space.

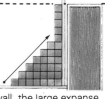

MAKE YOUR OWN TILE BREAKER

1 *Use an offcut wider than the tile as the base. Use 3mm (⅛in) ply for the top and sides.*

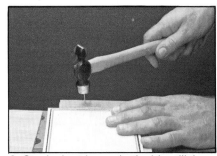

2 *Stack ply strips on both sides till the same height as the tile, then pin. Nail on the top piece.*

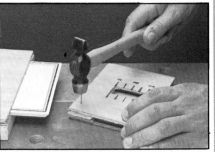

3 *The breaking part needs to be as wide and deep as the tile, with the opening on the top a half tile long.*

4 *Score the glaze on the top and edges with a carbide-tipped cutter. Put the tile into the main part.*

5 *Slip on the breaking part so the score line is between the two. Hold one side while you press the other.*

6 *The tile breaks cleanly. This aid costs nothing and will save you time when tiling a large expanse.*

TILING CORNERS

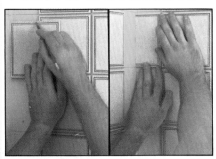

1 *At an internal corner, mark amount to be cut at top and bottom. Break the tile, then fit in position.*

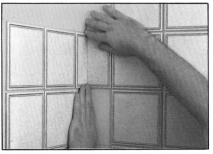

2 *File the remainder until it fits the adjacent area with enough space left for a fine line of grout.*

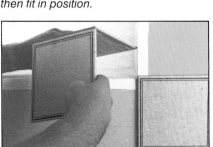

3 *On a window sill, use a whole tile at the front and make sure that it overlaps the one on the wall-face underneath.*

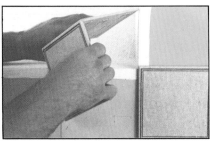

4 *Mitred edges of universal tiles and glazed edges of border tiles give a better finish to external corners.*

better to concentrate on lining up your border or mitred tiles perfectly vertically with only minute 'steps' between tiles, then bedding spacer or ordinary tiles behind to correspond with the line. Don't forget that if you do have to create a very slight stepped effect, you can reduce the uneven effect between the corner tiles and others by pressing in extra grouting later.

Internal corners seldom cause serious problems as cut tiles can be shaped to suit fluctuations from the truly vertical. Don't assume when cutting tiles for a corner that all will be the same size — the chances are that they will vary considerably and should be measured and cut individually. Another point: don't butt tiles up against each other so they touch — leave space for the grouting which will give the necessary flexibility should there be any wall movement.

Tiling around electrical fittings

When tiling around electrical fittings it is better to disconnect the electricity and remove the wall plate completely so that you can tile right up to the edge of the wall box. This is much neater and easier than trying to cut tiles to fit around the perimeter of the plate. Cut tiles as described in the illustrations on pages 53 and 54 and fit them in the normal way with the plate being replaced on top, completely covering the cut edges of the tiles. This same principle applies to anything easily removable. The fewer objects you have to tile around the better, so before starting any tiling get to work with a screwdriver.

You have the greatest control over the end result if at the planning stage you work out where you want to place fittings such as towel racks and soap dishes, shelves and the like. Some tile ranges offer them attached so it's only a matter of fitting them in as you put the tiles up.

Tiling non-rigid surfaces
On surfaces which are not totally rigid or which are subject to movement, vibration or the odd shock, tiles should not be attached using adhesive which dries hard as most standard and waterproof types do. Instead use adhesives which retain some flexibility. These may be cement-based types with a latex rubber content, or acrylic adhesives. You may have to surround a non-rigid surface with wooden lipping to protect the tiles.

TILING AROUND FIXTURES

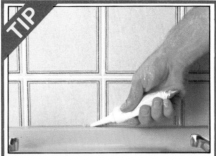

1 *At awkward corners use card to make a tile-size template. Place it on the tile and score the shape, then gently nibble out the waste with pincers — the smaller the bits the better.*

2 *Where basins, baths, kitchen sinks or laundry tubs meet tiles, seal the join with silicone caulking to keep out water. Caulking comes in various colors to match fixtures.*

3 *After the adhesive has had time to set, the tiles are grouted both to protect them and to enhance their shape and color.*
Accessories can be bought already attached to tiles, can be screw mounted after drilling the tile, or if lightweight can be stuck on to tiles with adhesive pads.

Ready Reference

CHECK FREQUENTLY
● the vertical (with a plumb line)
● the horizontal (with spirit level)
● that tiles don't project beyond each other

TIP: MAKING TEMPLATES
Cut the card tile-size then make diagonal snips into the edge to be shaped. These pieces will be forced out of the way and an accurate cutting line can be drawn.

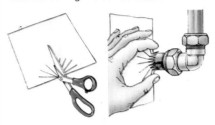

ADHESIVE AND GROUT
You need 1 litre (1½ pints) of adhesive and 0.25kg (½lb) of grout per sq metre (a little less for 1 sq yd), but for large areas buy in bulk.

WHEN GROUTING
● don't press mixture in with your fingers (it can abrade and irritate your skin)
● do wear light flexible gloves
● don't leave excess on tiles till dry
● do grout or caulk between tiles and window or door frames
● don't forget to grout edges of universal tiles if run finishes halfway up the wall
● use an old toothbrush to get grout into awkward places

TIP: GROUTING WALLS
On a large expanse, it's less tiring to use a rubber float to push grout between tiles – work upwards, then across; remove excess diagonally.

TILING SHOWERS
● use water resistant or waterproof adhesive and grout
● tile at least 1 row above shower head
● on ceiling use large drawing or upholstery pins to hold tiles till adhesive dries
● do floor and ceiling before walls
● don't expose tiles to water for 1 week

DE ORATING WALLS WITH CORK

Cork in tile, panel or sheet form provides an easy-to-fix wallcovering which is highly decorative and warm to the touch. It will also add to your peace and quiet by insulating against noise.

You may decide to decorate one or more walls of a room in your house with cork simply because you like the look of it. But there are practical advantages in doing this as well. You will also be providing extra insulation as, apart from its decorative qualities, cork deadens sound, is warm to the touch and keeps heat in and cold out. Also, it doesn't cause condensation and will absorb a certain amount of moisture. It can be quite hardwearing, taking its share of knocks and bumps without bruising, and many of the ranges of cork tiles, panels, sheets and rolls available are treated to be fully washable and steam-proof.

Where to use cork

Because of its highly decorative quality and natural texture, cork usually looks best as a feature wall, or forming a focal point on a chimney breast, or in an alcove, or behind some display shelves. But because of its insulating quality it is ideal on the inside of walls which face away from the sun, particularly if a headboard or seating is placed next to them. Cork tiles on a ceiling can help reduce noise and also add warmth; in children's rooms, teenage bedsitting rooms, family living rooms, hobby areas, even the kitchen, a panel of cork can also provide a place to pin pictures, posters and memos. Pre-sealed cork is practical for kitchens and bathrooms so long as it does not come in direct contact with the bath, sink or basin edge (you can isolate it with a row of ceramic tiles). It can also be used to face doors, cover window seats and ottomans, or cover screens and bath panels — so long as you select the right product.

Types of cork

Cork for walls comes in several different types. Some are made by pressing the cork into layers, or mixing cork chippings with a binder, and then cutting it into sheets, tiles or panels of various sizes, thicknesses and textures. Sometimes, to get a rougher homespun look, the actual bark of the cork tree is peeled, mounted on a backing and sold for decorative purposes. The backing may be colored, and if the cork is slivered thinly

enough, this backing will show through, giving a hint of color to the cork. This type may be sold as panels or sheets.

Another attractive cork wallcovering is made by shaving the cork so thinly that it is almost transparent and because of the natural uneven texture, the effect is like hand-crocheted lace. This is then mounted onto a foil backing which glints through the layer of cork. This type is usually sold in sheets or by the roll, as wallpaper.

A new development is a wallcork which is laminated to crêpe paper so it is extremely flexible and can be bent round curved surfaces. This type comes in a natural finish, which can be painted, and also in several colors. It is sold by the linear metre (yard) off the roll.

Most wallcorks are presealed, either waxed or treated with a sealant, which makes them washable; some come unsealed including some of the heavily textured types and the very open granular tiles.

Buying and planning

Cork tiles, panels and sheet come in various sizes. When you have decided on the type you want to use you will have to work out how much you will need to order from your supplier. Remember the cardinal rule that you should always order more than will be exactly required to cover the wall, to allow for any mistakes, accidents or errors when you are putting the cork up.

You may decide to fix tiles or panels in a particular pattern, for example, so they create a diamond or herringbone design. If so, it's best to work out the design on paper

first; then, after you've prepared the surface, you can square up the wall and mark the position of each tile or panel on it. (Remember you can also create interesting effects by using light and dark tiles to form a checkerboard pattern or to form a border or 'framed' effect; but you shouldn't need to mark up the wall for this.)

Preparing the surface

As with any other form of decoration, cork must be hung on a properly prepared surface. If you are going to cover a wall with cork which has already been decorated you should strip off old wallpaper, scrape off any flaking paint and fill any deep holes; cut and re-plaster any crumbling 'live' areas. If the plaster is porous, prime with PVA primer diluted 1:5 with water.

Gloss or matt-painted walls can be keyed by rubbing over them with sandpaper to roughen the surface, but as the paint can sometimes cause the adhesive to break down, most cork suppliers recommend lining a painted wall with heavy lining paper before fixing the cork in position. Follow the instructions supplied with the particular product you intend using. If you are going to use lining paper, remember to cross-line the walls, that is, hang the paper horizontally just as you would before hanging a good quality wallpaper or fabric wallcovering to avoid the risk of joins coinciding.

If you are hanging sheet cork wallcovering and using a heavy-duty wallpaper paste to fix it, it may be necessary to prime the wall surface first with a coat of size or diluted wallpaper paste.

FIXING THE FIRST TILE

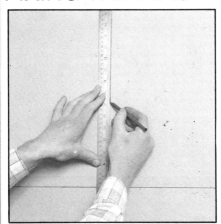

1 Work out how the tile pattern will fall on the wall by drawing central horizontal and vertical lines. Adjust these to avoid awkward cuts.

2 Starting at the center, spread adhesive in one of the angles formed by the lines. (With contact adhesive apply it to the back of the tile as well.)

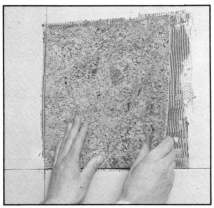

3 Cover an area slightly larger than a tile, then align the first tile using the horizontal and vertical lines as a guide to the exact position.

4 Press the tile into place flat against the wall, taking care not to let it slip out of line as you do this. It's crucial you get the tile correctly positioned.

5 Roll the tile with a wallpaper seam roller to get a better bond particularly at the edges. Be careful not to get adhesive on the roller.

6 If any adhesive gets onto the face of the tile wipe it off with a damp cloth before it sets. With some adhesives you may need to use turpentine.

Ready Reference

CHOOSING THE RIGHT CORK

Cork swells when it gets wet and could become distorted and start peeling off the wall. It therefore makes sense to
● use a pre-sealed type for kitchens, bathrooms and areas where you are going to have to wipe off sticky finger marks, or
● use a type of cork which can be sealed after hanging in these areas.

TIP: CONCEAL CUT TILES

When you are planning the layout of the tiles you are going to use on a wall, aim to place cut tiles where they won't draw attention. For example:
● it's best to have cut tiles at the baseboard rather than at the ceiling
● on a chimney breast, butt cut tiles up to the junction between the chimney breast and wall rather than to the outer corner of the chimney breast.

TIP: MAKE DEMOUNTABLE PANELS

Because of the adhesive used to fix them, cork tiles can be difficult to remove once they are up; if you try to scrape them off you may either have large lumps of cork left stuck to the wall or large holes left in the plaster. To help you make it easier to have a change of decor later:
● fix the cork to panels of plasterboard, hardboard, partition board, chipboard, plywood or other dry lining
● fix the panels to furring strips which are screwed to the wall; these can be unscrewed and removed when you choose

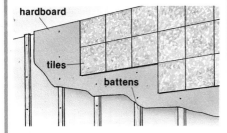

hardboard

tiles

battens

TILES IN HOT SPOTS

If you are fixing cork tiles to a chimney breast where a fire will be used, behind a radiator or other 'hot spot', it is best to put adhesive down the edges of the tiles as well as on the back to make extra sure of a secure bond.

PREVENT FIRE RISK

Many adhesives suitable for use with cork are highly inflammable. Therefore, when using them, make sure all pilot lights are switched off and turn off any electric or gas fires. Don't smoke or work near a naked light, and provide adequate ventilation.

FIXING OTHER TILES

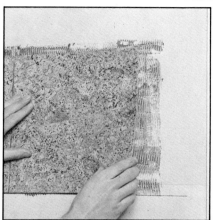

1 *Apply more adhesive then butt the second tile into place using hand pressure and a roller. Then continue to fix all the whole tiles.*

3 *Butt another tile up against the corner so that it overlaps the tile to be cut; use this as a guide to mark off a cutting line with chalk or pencil.*

5 *Coat the exposed wall with adhesive and fix the cut tile in the same way you've fixed the whole tiles. Continue marking up, cutting and fixing the tiles.*

2 *Where the tile has to be cut, for example, to fit at the edge of a chimney breast, you should first place it over the last whole tile in the row.*

4 *To cut the tile, place it on a firm surface then use a sharp knife to cut along the marked line. Use a straightedge as a guide.*

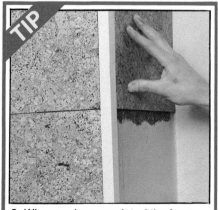

6 *When you've completed the front of a chimney breast you can tile the sides. Work so the cut edges go into the junction with the wall.*

Tools and equipment

You are already likely to have most of the tools and equipment required for covering walls with cork, particularly if you have hung some other type of wallcovering before. You will need a sharp knife to trim the cork, a straightedge, a notched adhesive spreader (sometimes supplied with the adhesive) or a pasting brush, a plumbline and chalk or pencil, a T-square or set square, a wallpaper seam roller and (for sheet cork) a wallpaper hanger's roller (which is wider than a seam roller). You will also require a tape measure and, to cut bark-type cork, a fine-toothed tenon saw. A pasting table (or some other suitable surface) may be needed; put this in a good light so you can see that the back surface of the tile or sheet (where these are pasted on the back rather than pasting the wall for fixing) is completely covered. As you'll be working at a height for part of the fixing process you'll need a stepladder. Make sure this is in sound condition so it will provide you with safe, secure access.

Fixing the cork

When you are fixing cork tiles or panels, as with all tiling, the setting-out is vitally important. The tiles should always be centered on a focal point or wall, so you end up with cut tiles or panels of equal width in the corners or at the edge of a chimney breast. Once you have established your central point and squared up the wall for the first line of tiles, tiling should be quite straightforward; the tiles are fixed with contact adhesive applied to the back of the tile and the wall or with an adhesive which is applied to the wall only.

Sheet cork is hung in different ways (see *Ready Reference*). The crucial thing here is to hang the lengths of cork to a true vertical and to plan the layout so cork which has to be cut to fit in width will come at the corners where any unevenness (due to the walls being out of square) will be least likely to be noticed.

Finishing touches and maintenance

If you put up cork tiles, panels, or sheet cork which are not sealed you can seal them with a transparent polyurethane varnish (a matt finish looks best). Dust the surface thoroughly and apply two or three coats of varnish; you may find a spray-on type is easier to apply than one which you brush on but this is only economical if you don't have too large an area to cover.

Most wall corks (whether sealed or unsealed) can be cleaned by dusting them down (use a cloth or the soft brush attachment on your vacuum cleaner). Most of the sealed corks and the crêpe-backed cork can be wiped with a damp cloth. The paper and foil-backed corks may not be wipable, so check before you buy, and don't hang them in a place where they will get dirty quickly.

HANGING SHEET CORK

1 Use a plumb line to mark off a guide line for fixing the first length. It should be less than the width of the cork sheet away from the corner.

2 Mark off more lines the width of the cork sheet apart along the wall. You can then apply the adhesive; in this case with a notched spreader.

3 Trim the first length to size at the ends and then fix it in place; work down the wall and use a wide roller to help you smooth the cork in place.

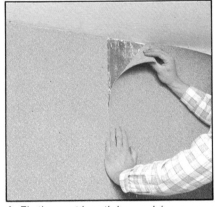

4 Fix the next length by applying adhesive and then butting the cork up against the first length. Continue to fix cork lengths along the wall.

5 At a corner, measure the width at several places down the wall. Transfer these measurements to the cork and cut it to fit exactly.

6 Fix the corner length in place. It should have been cut to fit an out of square wall. The other adjacent (cut) corner length butts up to it.

Ready Reference

FINISHING RAW EDGES

It you will get a 'raw' edge down the side where you are fixing tiles to the face of a chimney breast only or where thick, soft types of tiles will meet at an exposed corner, protect the tile edges with a wooden lipping or molding. For this you:
● attach the lipping (of the same thickness as the tiles) with pins or adhesive down each vertical angle before you start tiling
● tile up to the liping as if it were an internal angle
● stain the lipping the same color as the tiles so it will be barely noticeable or coat it with clear varnish to make it more of a feature in the decorative scheme.

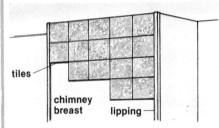

tiles

chimney breast   lipping

TIP: REMOVE EXCESS ADHESIVE

If you inadvertently get adhesive on the front of the cork you may be able to remove it by rubbing with your finger when the adhesive is partly set. If it dries before you notice it, rub it gently with a cloth moistened with turpentine. You may need to reseal or touch up the surface with wax polish when the cork is dry in order to hide the marks.

FIXING CORK SHEET

Cork in sheet form can be fixed in various ways. When you are fixing it, remember that
● with some types you use a special cork adhesive, applied to the wall
● with others you apply a heavy-duty wallpaper adhesive to the back of the cork or to the wall (check with the manufacturer's instructions)
● unlike wallpaper, which you trim after fixing, each length of cork should be cut exactly to fit before you hang it
● the joins between the lengths of cork shouldn't be rolled with a seam roller, as this will simply make the joins more obvious and spoil the overall look.

BARK-TEXTURED CORK

It's a pity to seal a really heavily textured bark cork, as part of its appeal lies in the matt, almost crumbly surface. Another point is that this type of cork should not be hung where it gets constantly knocked or touched, nor used as a noticeboard or pinboard or it will show signs of wear.

LAYING CERAMIC FLOOR TILES

You can lay ceramic tiles to provide a floor surface which is particularly resistant to wear and tear. If you follow a few basic rules you shouldn't find it too difficult a task and you could at the same time turn the floor into a decorative feature.

C eramic floor tiles provide a floor-covering which is attractive, extremely hard-wearing and easy to maintain and keep clean. The wide variety of tiles available means you should easily find a pattern which suits your color scheme.

Floor tiles are usually thicker than ceramic wall tiles (they are generally at least 9mm/⅜in thick), very much stronger and have a tough hardwearing surface to withstand knocks as well as wear from the passage of feet.

The backs of the tiles have a brownish appearance caused by the extra firing – done at a higher temperature than for wall tiles, which are often almost white on the back.

Types of tiles

Square tiles are commonest, in sizes from 150 x 150mm (6 x 6in) to 250 x 250mm (10 x 10in). Besides square tiles you can choose oblong ones in several sizes, hexagons or other interlocking shapes. Surfaces are usually glazed but are seldom as shiny as those of wall tiles or scratch marks would inevitably become apparent as grit was trampled in. So most floor tiles are semi-glazed; others have a matt, or unglazed finish.

Patterned ceramic tiles are quite frequently designed in such a way that several tiles can be laid next to one another to complete a larger design. The commonest is built up by laying four identical tiles in a square, each tile being turned at 90° to its neighbors. The full impact will only be achieved if a sufficiently large area of floor is being tiled.

Patterned and plain tiles can also successfully be intermixed to create unusual designs, but it is essential that the tiles are all supplied by the same manufacturer, and ideally come from compatible ranges, to ensure uniformity of thickness and size.

Some manufacturers supply floor tiles designed to coordinate with wall tiles, and in addition make matching panels to act as baseboards between wall and floor tiles.

Types of adhesives

There are several types of adhesives for laying floor tiles. Some come ready-mixed, others in powder form to be mixed with water. A number are waterproof and where the floor will

be subjected to frequent soakings (as, for example, in a shower cubicle) or heavy condensation you will need to use one which is water-resistant. Usually the adhesive does not become waterproof until it has set completely, which means that you can clean tools with water and do not require a special cleaner.

On a solid floor with underfloor heating you should use an adhesive which is also heat-resistant or the adhesive will fail and the tiles will lift necessitating continual re-fixing.

A cement-based floor tile adhesive is suitable for use on good, level concrete whereas a suspended wooden sub-floor will need an adhesive with some degree of flexibility built in. Combined cement/rubber adhesives are available for this purpose but even these should not be used on suspended wooden floors which are subject to a lot of movement – you will have to add a covering of man-made boards to provide a more stable surface before fixing the tiles.

Manufacturers' instructions give guidance as to the type of adhesive suited to a particular situation and you should study these carefully before making your choice. You should also follow their recommendations as to the thickness of adhesive bed required; most

resin-based ready-mixed adhesives are used as thin beds (3 to 6mm/⅛ to ¼in), while cement-based powder adhesives may be laid up to 12mm (½in) thick. Usually a spreader is supplied with the adhesive to make applying it a straightforward job.

Planning

As when tiling a wall, it is well worth planning your layout on paper first, particularly if you intend using a complicated design. For rectangular or square tiles make a scale drawing on graph paper; for hexagons or other specially-shaped tiles, draw the shapes to scale on tracing paper, to act as an overlay to a scale floor plan of the room. From your scale drawings you can see if the layout you have in mind is going to work. It will help you set out an attractive design and it will also enable you to work out the number of tiles you will require.

Mark on your plan the position of fixtures such as a toilet, wash or sink stand, cupboards or pipes to indicate where cutting will be required — where necessary adjust your plan so you will not have to cut pieces which are too narrow for convenient cutting.

Similarly, your layout should be designed so you avoid having to cut narrow pieces of tile to

MARKING UP

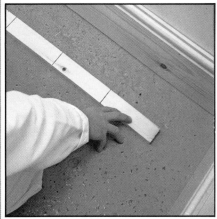

1 *Choose the corner at which you wish to start tiling, and use a tiling gauge to find out how many whole tiles will fit alongside one wall.*

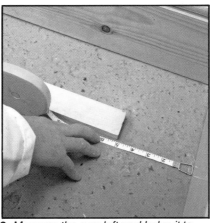

2 *Measure the gap left and halve it to give the width of the cut pieces for each end. Allow one less whole tile in the row to avoid very narrow cut pieces.*

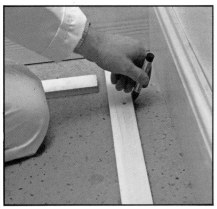

3 *Measure in the width of one cut piece, plus grouting gaps, from the adjacent wall. Mark a line to show where one edge of the first whole tile will be placed.*

4 *Repeat the measuring process along the adjacent wall to establish the position of the other edge of the first whole tile. Mark this line on the floor too.*

5 *Lay a 1 × 2 on the line drawn in **4** and nail it to the floor alongside the first wall to act as a guide for laying the first complete row of tiles.*

6 *Pin a second 1 × 2 alongside the other wall, its edge on the line drawn in **3**, and check that the two 1 × 2s are at right angles to each other.*

THE RIGHT TILES
Always check that the tiles you buy are suitable for use on floors.
● floor tiles are usually 6mm (¼in) or more thick and have brown backs
● some are flat-backed, others have projecting studs.

TILE SHAPES
Most floor tiles are square or oblong. Common sizes, and the number of each needed to cover 1 sq metre (11 sq ft), are:
● 150 x 150mm (6 x 6in)   : 44
● 200 x 200mm (8 x 8in)   : 25
● 250 x 250mm (10 x 10in) : 16
● 300 x 300mm (12 x 8in)   : 17
Hexagons usually measure 150mm (6in) between opposite edges. You need 50 per sq m (11 sq ft).

ADHESIVES AND GROUT
● use a *thin-bed* (3mm/⅛in) adhesive for *flat-backed tiles* – you'll need about 3.5kg (8lb) per sq metre (11 sq ft)
● use a *thick-bed* (6-12mm/¼-½in) adhesive for *tiles with studs* or if the floor is uneven – you'll need double the above quantities
● allow 1.2kg (2½lb) of *grout* per sq metre (11 sq ft) for joints 6mm (¼in) wide.

TILING SPACING
● space tiles that build up to form a larger pattern about 2mm apart. With plain tiles a wider gap looks better. Use a tile on edge as a spacer

● dry-lay a row of tiles along each wall to see how wide an edge piece you will need at each end of the row.

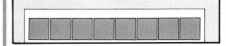

● avoid having to cut thin edge pieces by laying one whole tile less in each row.

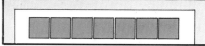

TILE GAUGE TO MAKE
Use a straight 1830mm (6ft) long 1 × 2 and mark its length with tile width and grouting space.

TIP: BUYING TILES
Add on a few extra tiles to allow for breakages during laying and replacements in the future.

LAYING TILES

1 *In the corner framed by the two 1 × 2s, spread enough tiling adhesive with a notched spreader to cover an area of about 1 sq m (11 sq ft).*

2 *Lay the first tile in position in the angle between the two 1 × 2s, pushing it tightly up against them, and bed it into place with firm hand pressure.*

3 *Continue laying tiles along the first row, butting them against the 1 × 2 to keep the edge straight. Use a cardboard spacer to create even gaps.*

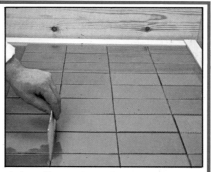

4 *Lay tiles until you have reached the edge of the adhesive, using the spacer as before. Carry on area by area until all whole tiles are laid.*

fit around the perimeter of the room. Floor tiles, being so much tougher, are less easy to cut than wall tiles and attempting to obtain narrow strips is likely to cost you several broken tiles.

Where you are not using a complicated design you can plan your layout directly on the floor. For this you will need a tiling gauge (see *Ready Reference*).

Preparing the floor surface

Surfaces to be tiled should be dry, flat, stable, clean and free from grease, dirt and unsound material. A flat, dry, level concrete floor can be tiled without any special preparation. If, however, there are small depressions in the concrete, these should be filled with a mortar mix of three parts sharp sand and one part cement. A more uneven floor should be screeded with a self-levelling flooring compound.

The screed should be left for two weeks to allow it to dry thoroughly before fixing tiles. If the floor is a new concrete one, it should be left for a minimum of four weeks to allow all moisture to disperse before you begin covering it with tiles.

Existing ceramic floor tiles, quarry tiles or terrazzo surfaces can be tiled over. They should be checked to ensure that there are no loose or hollow-sounding areas. Any defective sections must be made good before you lay new tiles on top.

You can tile on suspended wooden floors, but it is important that the floor should be made as rigid and firm as possible. To achieve this, cover the floorboards with a layer of water-resistant resin-bonded plywood at least 12mm (½in) thick. Alternatively, you can use chipboard of the same thickness.

Before laying tiles over wood floors, cover the surface thoroughly with a priming coat — either a special priming agent from the adhesive manufacturer, or else diluted PVA building adhesive.

Finding the starting point

The first whole tile you lay will determine where all the other tiles are laid, so it is important that you get this positioning correct. Choose the corner in which you wish to start tiling and, laying your tile gauge parallel to one of the walls, measure how

many whole tiles will fit along that side of the room. There will almost certainly be a gap left over. Measure this gap, and divide the answer by two to find the width of the cut tiles that will fill the gap at each end of the row. (These should be of equal size.)

If these cut tiles turn out to be less than one quarter of a tile-width across (and therefore tricky to cut), reduce the number of whole tiles in the row by one. The effect of this is to increase the width of each cut tile by half a tile – much easier to cut.

Return to the corner and with your tile gauge parallel to the wall along which you have been measuring, move it so the end of the gauge is the width of one cut tile away from the adjacent wall. Mark this position off on the floor – it indicates where one edge of the first whole tile in that row will fall.

Repeat this same measuring process along the adjacent wall to establish the positioning of the row at right angles to the one you've just set out; you will then be able to mark off where the other edge of this same first tile will fall, and so fix its position precisely. Once that is done, every other tile's position is fixed right across the floor.

You can then place this first tile in position. Mark off and cut the boundary tiles between it and the corner. Remember to allow for the width of the grouting gap when measuring each cut tile.

Each cut tile should be measured individually because the wall may not be perfectly straight. You may then go ahead with laying whole tiles, starting from your original corner.

Laying tiles

In the corner area spread adhesive evenly on the floor over an area of about 1 sq m (11 sq ft) — it is important to work on only a small area at a time, otherwise the adhesive may have begun to dry out by the time you reach it. With a gentle, twisting motion, place the first tile in the corner, and use light hand pressure to bed it firmly in the adhesive. Place the second tile alongside the first, using the same gentle pressure, and placing spacers of cardboard or hardboard between the tiles if they don't have spacer lugs. Continue laying tiles, building up a rectangular area, until you have reached the edge of the adhesive bed.

Use a spirit level to check that the tiles are level; if any are too low, lever them off the bed as quickly as possible with a wide-bladed trowel, add adhesive and re-set them, pressing them down gently.

With the first square yard of tiles laid, you can spread another layer of adhesive over a further area, and lay the next area of tiles.

As you lay the tiles, it is worth checking every now and again that adequate contact with the adhesive is being made and that there are no voids beneath the tiles – any gaps or

FITTING BORDER TILES

1 *Mark the width of each border tile in turn, using the spacer to allow for the necessary grouting gap. Kneel on a board so you don't disturb the whole tiles.*

2 *Score across the tile surface at the mark with a tile cutter. Press firmly so its tip cuts the glaze cleanly; scoring again may cause a ragged edge.*

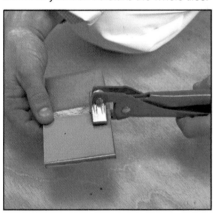

3 *Use a tile breaker with V-shaped jaws to break the tile along the scored line. Floor tiles are usually too thick to break over a straight-edge.*

4 *Butter adhesive onto the back of the cut piece, and press it into position. Use the spacer to form an even grouting gap at either side of the cut piece.*

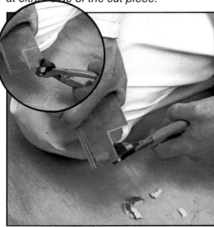

5 *Finally mark and cut the piece of tile to fit in the corner of the room, lay it and leave the newly tiled floor for 48 hours to allow the adhesive to set.*

6 *To cut an L-shaped piece of tile, score the surface carefully and nibble away the waste with tile pincers. Work from the corner (inset) in to the score lines.*

Ready Reference

TIP: CUTTING FLOOR TILES

Because of the high-baked clay back, floor tiles can be hard to snap by hand. Save time and breakages by buying a tile cutter with angled jaws, or rent a special floor tile cutter from a tool rental shop.

TIP: ALLOW 48 HOURS SETTING

● don't walk on the floor for at least 48 hours after tiling
● where access is essential, lay plywood or chipboard sheets over the tiles to spread the load
● avoid washing the floor until the grout and adhesive have set completely (1 to 2 weeks).

DON'T FORGET DOORS

Tiling will raise the floor level. Remove inward-opening doors from their hinges before starting tiling or they will not open when tiling reaches the doorway.

● measure the depth of tile plus adhesive laid
● plane the door bottom down by this amount
● fit a sloping hardwood strip across the door threshold

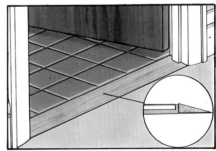

TIP: TILES FOR WET AREAS

Unglazed tiles are less slippery than glazed but ones with a textured surface reduce the chance of accidents in bath and shower rooms.

GROUTING TILES

1 When the adhesive has set, you can grout the joints. Use a sponge or a rubber squeegee to force the grout into all the gaps.

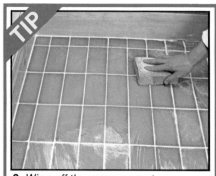

2 Wipe off the excess grout as you work with a damp sponge; if you allow it to set hard it will be very difficult to remove later.

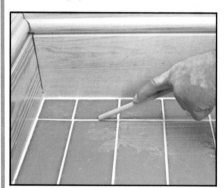

3 Use a piece of thin dowel with a rounded end to smooth off the joints. Don't be tempted to use a finger as grout could irritate your skin.

4 Leave the grout to set for the recommended time, and then polish the surface all over with a clean, dry cloth to remove the last traces of grout.

PREPARING FLOOR

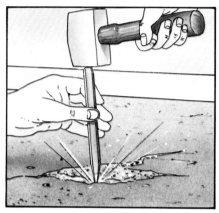

Clean out the small depressions and cracks to be filled with a club hammer and chisel. Beware of flying chippings.

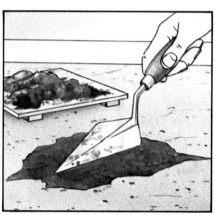

Use a trowel to fill in the depressions with mortar and to level off to provide a suitable surface for the tiles.

hollows under the tiles will become weak points later on.

You can proceed with the tiling in 1 sq m (yd) sections until all the tiles are in place, then leave them for at least 48 hours. The tiles must not be walked on during this time so that any risk of them being knocked out of place or bedded too deeply is avoided. If you have to walk on the tiles, lay a sheet of plywood or chipboard over them first to spread the load. When 48 hours — or longer; check the manufacturer's instructions — are up, you can remove the spacers. Check with the adhesive manufacturer's instructions to see whether you need to allow extra time after this before you begin grouting.

Cutting tiles

You will have to cut each tile individually since you will almost certainly find variations around the room. Place the tile which is going to be cut against the wall and on top of the adjacent whole tile. Mark it off for cutting.

Using a straight edge as a guide, score the tile surface and edges with a scribing tool. You *can* use a hand tile cutter to cut and

break the tile along the scoreline; but it's probably worthwhile renting a special floor tile cutter to make the job easier.

To cut a tile to give an L-shape you will need to use tile nips to nibble away at the waste area. You can use a tile file, carborundum stone or coarse sandpaper to smooth off the rough edge. For curved shapes (eg, to fit round a toilet pedestal), you will need to make a template and again use tile nips to nibble away at the tile.

Grouting the tiles

Mix the grout according to the manufacturer's instructions; make up only a small amount at a time and, as with adhesive, work in areas of 1 sq metre (11 sq ft). Apply it with the straight edge of a rubber float, or a sponge or squeegee, making sure the joints are properly filled. Pack the grout firmly into the joints and smooth off using a small rounded stick – don't try using a finger as the grout is likely to irritate your skin.

It's best to remove excess grout (and adhesive) as soon as possible. If it sets it will be difficult to remove.

Filling cracks and hollows

If you have a concrete floor which is flat, dry and level you can go ahead and lay tiles without further preparation. Often, however, the floor is not level or there are cracks and small hollows on the surface. Indentations should be filled with mortar (a 3:1 sand:cement mix is suitable) mixed to a creamy but not too runny consistency. For mortar with a good bond add some PVA bonding solution to the mix. Cut back the holes to a clean shape and brush out any loose material so it doesn't mix in with the mortar making it difficult to get a smooth surface. You can also coat the holes with a PVA bonding solution to help the mortar adhere.

SURFACES FOR TILING

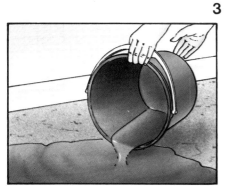

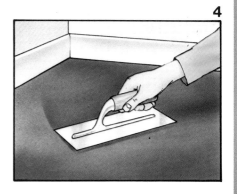

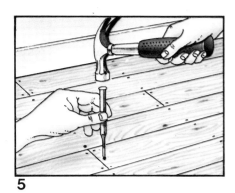

Levelling a concrete floor

A concrete floor which is out of true can be levelled using a self-levelling flooring compound so it is suitable for tiling. For the compound to form a smooth, even surface, it should only be applied to a floor which is clean and free from dust, oil, grit or grease, so you should first sweep the floor and then scrub it thoroughly (1). You may find you have to use a cleaner to remove stubborn greasy patches. The compound comes in powder form and you will have to mix it according to the manufacturer's instructions so it forms a runny paste (2).

If you try covering the entire floor in one operation, it's likely the compound will set into large pools which are difficult to join up. It's better to work in small areas; you can delineate your working area by forming a bay using wood strips. Pour the compound onto the floor (3) and then spread it out as evenly as possible using a steel float (4), any marks from the float will disappear quickly. The compound will set within a couple of hours. If you want extra thickness you can apply a second coat once the first is hard.

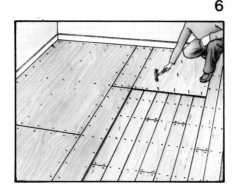

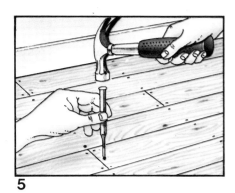

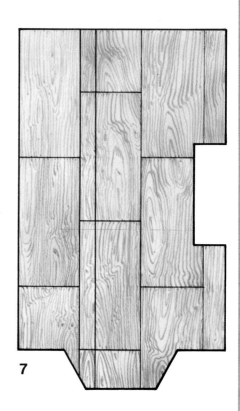

Laying plywood over a wood floor

A floor which is subject to movement will disrupt tiles laid over it so if you intend tiling over a suspended wooden floor you will first have to make the surface as firm as possible by covering it with a layer of man-made boards. Water-resistant resin-bonded plywood is a suitable material as it will resist penetration by the damp adhesive you will be spreading over it and you will avoid the problem of rotting boards. The boards should be at least 12mm (1/2in) thick. To prepare the floor to take the plywood you should punch any protruding nails below the surface (5) at the same time checking that the floorboards are firmly secured. You can then go ahead and fix the sheets of plywood to the floor (6) using nails spaced at 225mm (9in) intervals across the middle of the sheets and at 150mm (6in) intervals round their perimeter. You will have to cut the boards to shape round any recess or alcove(7), and where there is a pipe run, fix narrow strips of plywood over the pipes to make access to them easier. Make sure you stagger the joints; this will prevent any floor movement causing the tiles to break up in a run across the floor.

LAYING CORK TILES

Cork tiles will provide you with a floor surface which is warm, wears well and is quiet to walk on. In addition, they are the easiest of tiles to lay.

You can use cork floor tiles in bathrooms, kitchens, dining rooms and children's rooms; anywhere, in fact, where any other resilient floorcovering (eg, vinyl sheet or tiles, or thermoplastic tiles) could be used. They are warmer and quieter than most other floorcoverings and tend not to 'draw the feet', unlike, for example, ceramic tiles, which are very tiring if you have to stand round on them for long periods. They will look particularly elegant if they are softened with rugs or rush matting and blend equally well with modern or traditional style furniture and décor.

Ordinary cork tiles are made from granulated cork, compressed and baked into blocks; the natural resins in the grain bond the particles together, though sometimes synthetic resins are added to improve wearing and other qualities. The tiles are cut from these blocks so they are 5mm (¼in) or more thick. 'Patterned' cork tiles (see below) are made by alternating wafer-thin cork veneers with thicker layers of insulating cork and sealing with a protective PVC surface.

Types of tiles

Cork tiles have an attractive natural look; usually they are a rich honey-gold, although there are some darker browns and smoky tones. Dyed cork tiles are available in many different colors ranging from subtle shades to strident primary colors. There are also 'patterned' tiles which have an interesting textured, rather than a heavily patterned look; these come in natural colors as well as red, soft green and rich dark smoky brown: the color tends to 'glow' through the top surface of cork. One design gives a subtle miniature checkerboard effect. Other tiles come with designs (such as geometric patterns) imprinted on them.

For floors that are likely to get the occasional flood or where spills and 'accidents' are inevitable, such as in kitchens, bathrooms and children's rooms, it is wiser to use pre-sealed types of tiles (see *Ready Reference*). The cheaper seal-it-yourself types are, however, perfectly adequate for living rooms, bedsitting rooms and halls.

Preparing the surface

As with other types of tiles and resilient floorcoverings the subfloor surface on which you lay cork tiles must be smooth, clean and free from lumps, bumps, protruding nails, tacks or screws. Where floorboards are uneven, it's best to cover them up with flooring-grade chipboard, plywood or flooring quality hardboard, either nailed or screwed down securely. Remember to stagger the sheets of chipboard or other material to avoid continuous joins. Then, if there is any floor movement it will not disturb the tiles fixed on top and cause them to lift or be moved out of alignment.

There must also be adequate ventilation underneath a wooden subfloor. Poor ventilation can cause condensation which could lead to the rotting of the floorboards and the floorcovering above them. If the floor is laid at ground level, or directly to joists or battens on ground level concrete, you should protect the cork from moisture penetration by covering the wood with bituminous felt paper before laying hardboard or plywood. The paper should be fixed with bituminous adhesive; and you should allow a 50mm (2in) overlap at joins and edges.

Solid subfloors, such as concrete or cement and sand screeds, should be thoroughly dry. Make sure the floor incorporates an effective damp-proof membrane before laying the tiles: this can

ESTABLISHING THE STARTING POINT

1 *Find the center points of two opposite walls. Stretch a string line between them, chalk it and snap a line across the floor.*

2 *Repeat the procedure, but this time between the other two walls. Where the two lines intersect is the exact center of the floor.*

3 *Dry-lay a row of tiles along the longest line from the center point to one wall. Adjust the other line if necessary (see* Ready Reference*).*

4 *Lay a row of tiles along the other line from the center point and again adjust to avoid wastage or very narrow strips at the edges.*

is irregularly shaped, divide it into rectangles and measure each one separately. If you take these measurements to your supplier, he should be able to help you calculate the quantity of tiles you will require. Or, as many tiles are sold ready-boxed with a guide to quantities printed on the box, you can study the guide to work out the number of tiles you'll need.

If you plan to buy tiles of contrasting colors, and to form a border pattern, or to lay them so you get a checkerboard effect, you should plan out the design on squared paper first. Divide up the floor area so each square represents a tile, and color the squares in different colors to represent the different colors of the tiles so you can judge the effect. You can then calculate the quantity needed by reference to your plan.

Laying tiles
Whichever type of tile you are laying, it is best to work at room temperature, so don't switch off the central heating. Leave the tiles in the room overnight to condition them.

Make sure you have enough tiles and adhesive on the spot; you don't want to have to stop work halfway through the job and go out and buy extra. Collect together the necessary tools: measure, chalk and string, pencils and ruler or straight edge, notched trowel or spreader, sharp knife, cloth and mineral spirit. If you are using the seal-later type of tile, you will need a sander and brush or roller plus sealer.

As with other types of tiles, cork tiles look best if they are centered on the middle of the room and any narrow or awkwardly shaped tiles come at the edges. So you'll have to establish your starting point (see *Ready Reference*) at the center of the room. You can then begin laying whole tiles, working from the center outwards. It's best to work on a quarter of the floor at a time; when all four quarters of whole tiles are laid, you can cut and fix the border tiles. If you are using adhesive, you may have to spread only about one square metre (1 square yard) at a time before it is ready to take the tiles. In other cases it will be best to cover a larger area with adhesive, so you don't have to wait too long to bed the tiles, increasing the length of time it will take to complete the job. Since the length of time needed before the adhesive is ready to take the tiles does vary depending on the type of adhesive, you should follow the manufacturer's instructions.

If tiles have to be cut to fit around obstacles such as door casings, toilet bases, or wash stands you can use a scribing block to mark the outline you require. Make up a paper template or use a special tracing tool (which has little needles which retract to fit the shape) if the shape is particularly complicated.

be in polyethelene sheet form, a cold-poured bitumen solution, or a hot pitch or bitumen solution. If the subfloor is porous or flaky and tends to be very dusty, you can use a latex floor-levelling compound to cover it. This is also practical for very uneven floors. The solution is poured on, left to find its own level and then allowed to dry out before the final floorcovering is laid.

Other floors, such as quarry or ceramic tiles, can have cork laid on top, but they have to be degreased, dewaxed and keyed by rubbing them with steel wool; once again, a floor-levelling compound may be necessary. With flagstones laid directly on the ground there could be dampness or condensation problems; it may be best to take up the existing floor and re-lay it, probably a job for a professional to do. Alternatively, the floor could be covered with a layer of rock asphalt at least 16mm (5/8in) thick, but you will need

to call in professional help for this. (Always seek expert advice if you are worried about the state of the subfloor; the expense incurred will be worth it to get successful results when you are laying the final floorcovering.)

If there is already a linoleum, vinyl sheet, tile or other resilient floorcovering on the floor, you are advised to take this up, then resurface or rescreed it if necessary; alternatively, use a floor-levelling damp-resistant latex powder mix, or an epoxy surface membrane. If it is not possible to remove the old floorcovering, you should use a floor cleaner to degrease and dewax it and then key the surface by rubbing over it with steel wool.

Planning
Measure the room, at floor level, using a steel tape or wooden measure; don't use a cloth tape as these stretch in use. If the room

Ready Reference

MARKING OUT

For a balanced look, aim to cut your edge tiles to equal size on both sides of the room. To do this, establish the center point of the floor, using chalked string lines:
● if, when you've dry-laid a row of tiles from the center point out to the wall, a gap remains of more than half a tile-width at the wall end (A), adjust your chalked line half a tile-width off-center (B); this will save undue wastage later when you are cutting the perimeter tiles.

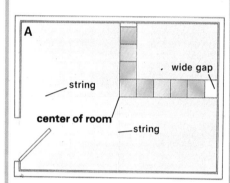

A

string

wide gap

center of room

string

B

narrow gap

move string about 75mm (3in) across

new string line

● if, however, by moving the chalked line you are left with very narrow perimeter strips (less than 75mm/3in wide) leave the center of the floor as your starting point; there will be wastage but narrow cut perimeter tiles won't look very good and should be avoided if possible
● when marking out, avoid narrow strips at door thresholds where they will be subjected to a lot of wear
● adjust your starting point so you don't end up with narrow strips round a feature of the room, such as a chimney breast.

CHECK UNSEALED TILES

Be sure to lay unsealed tiles the right way up. They have a smooth top surface and a bottom surface which is rougher to provide a key for the adhesive. You can judge which surface is which by running your fingers over the tile.

LAYING WHOLE TILES

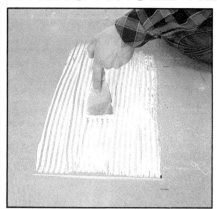

1 Use a notched spreader to apply adhesive to a quarter of the floor area, using the marked lines as a guide to the area to be covered.

3 Lay a row of tiles following the guidelines, treading each tile down gently but firmly to make sure it is securely bedded.

2 Place the first whole tile in the center right angle which has been coated with adhesive. Check that it aligns with the guidelines.

4 Work across the floor until that quarter is covered with whole tiles. Then lay tiles on the other quarters of the floor area.

For some awkward shapes (eg, fitting tiles around an L-shape or in an alcove) you can mark out the pieces to be cut by placing a whole tile or tile offcut up against the baseboard and the tiles which are already in place and draw the required shape on it. Cork tiles are very simple to cut: all you need is a sharp knife and a straight edge to guide it; there is no risk of breakages as there may be with other tiles which are more difficult to cut, such as ceramic types.

Sealing tiles

If your tiles are the seal-after-laying type, you will have to sand the floor carefully, using a powered sander, to ensure the surface and joins are smooth. Dust carefully; you can wipe the tiles with a slightly damp cloth to remove excess dust but take care not to saturate the tiles. Leave them to dry and then seal them, using a brush or roller to apply the sealer.

If you attach your applicator to a long handle, you can avoid bending or crawling on all fours; work from the furthermost corner, backwards to the door. Leave each coat to dry thoroughly, before applying the next one. There will always be more than one coat of sealer but the exact number will depend on the type of wear to which the floor will be subjected (see Ready Reference).

Ideally, you should leave the sealer to dry for a few days before you walk on the floor, but if you have to use the room, seal half the room at a time. Cover the unsealed part with brown paper so it can be walked on without damaging or marking the cork. When the sealed part is completely dry, you can seal the other half.

Don't wash a new cork floor for at least 48 hours after laying and sealing; ideally it should be left for at least five days. It's worth

LAYING BORDER TILES

1 *To cut border tiles accurately to size, place the whole tile to be cut exactly on top of the last whole tile in a particular row.*

2 *Place a second tile over it, this time butting it up against the baseboard. Use its edge as a guide to scribe a line on the first tile.*

3 *Remove the tile to be cut and make a deeper mark. The tile should then break through cleanly when gentle pressure is applied.*

4 *Place the cut border tile in position against the baseboard. You may need to apply extra adhesive to its back to ensure secure fixing.*

TILING AN L-SHAPE

1 *As when cutting other border tiles, use a tile as a guide to scribe the outline of one side of the L onto the tile to be cut.*

2 *Move the tile to be cut and the guide tile to the other side of the L and use the same method to scribe its outline for cutting.*

3 *Remove the loose tiles, cut through the back of the tile along the scribed lines and then fix the tile in position so it aligns with the whole tiles.*

putting up with grubby marks for a few days rather than running the risk of moisture penetrating the flooring and reducing its useful life.

Care and maintenance

Once pre-sealed tiles are laid, or the unsealed type has been properly sealed, it will probably be unnecessary to do more than wipe over the floor with a damp mop or cloth to keep it clean. To remove grease or dirt, add a few drops of liquid detergent to the washing water; wipe over again with a cloth rinsed in clean water to remove any traces of detergent. If there are some particularly stubborn marks, made, for instance, by rubber-soled shoes, or paint or varnish spots, you should be able to remove them by rubbing gently with a little turpentine on a damp cloth.

An important point to remember when you

are cleaning your cork floor is that you must take care not to overdampen the floor or the tiles may lift. Also, never use strong abrasive cleaners as these can damage the PVC wear layer.

If you like a fairly glossy surface or are worried about scratches on the floor, you can use an emulsion wax polish on top of the sealed tiles. However, never use a wax floor polish as the surface could become too slippery.

Sometimes a tile can become damaged. If the area which needs repair is small (a cigarette burn hole, for instance) you can fill it with shavings from a cork out of a bottle and reseal the tile. For more extensive damage, you should remove the tile carefully and replace it with a spare one; reseal if this tile is an unsealed type with the number of coats of sealer required to give it adequate protection.

Ready Reference

TIP: STORE TILES FLAT

If you take tiles out of their box, weight them down to keep them flat when you are storing them.

GLUING TILES

Gluing methods and adhesives vary. Some adhesives should be applied to both the back of the tiles and floor, others to the floor only; follow the manufacturer's instructions. Remember:
● pre-sealed tiles are always glued with adhesive
● unsealed tiles are often fixed by driving in 5 headless nails, one at each corner and one in the center, a technique which may be combined with adhesive (the nail holes can be filled, if necessary, and will then be covered up by the sealer).

REMOVE EXCESS ADHESIVE

As you lay the tiles, wipe off any adhesive from the front of the tiles with a soft cloth which has been dipped in mineral spirits.

CUTTING AROUND PIPES

To cut a tile so it fits round a pipe, make a cardboard template of the shape required and trace the shape onto the tile. Then cut a slit from the hole made for the pipe to the baseboard; this line will be almost invisible when the tile is fixed in place.

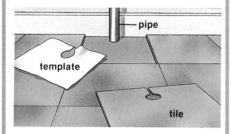

SEAL TILES PROPERLY

Cork is porous and fairly absorbent, so proper sealing is essential; if the tiles get wet, they swell and lift and have to be trimmed and re-stuck. For unsealed tiles, several coats of sealer will be necessary for real protection:
● in areas of ordinary wear, apply two or three coats of sealer
● in heavy wear areas you will need to apply 4 or 5 coats.

TRIM DOORS

To allow doors to open freely after the cork floor has been laid you may have to trim along the bottom of the door to give adequate clearance.

LAYING TILES IN AN ALCOVE

1 *Place a tile over the glued tiles with its corner butting up against the baseboard and make a mark on the 'wrong' side at the correct distance.*

2 *Repeat this procedure, this time to make a mark on the adjacent edge. Transfer the marks to the front of the tile and draw a line between them.*

3 *Cut along the drawn line to give the required shape and then place the cut tile in position so it aligns properly with the whole tiles.*

4 *Use the same techniques to cut the next tile. If there is a pipe against the wall, butt the tile up to it and mark where it's to be cut.*

5 *Cut the triangular-shaped piece required to fill the gap between the two larger shaped pieces and fix this in position so that it butts right up against the baseboard.*

6 *To complete the job, cut the corner piece to shape and glue it in place. For economy, you can cut these smaller shaped pieces from any tiled offcuts which you may have available.*

LAYING SHEET VINYL

Vinyl provides a tough, easy-to-clean floor surface which is ideal in kitchens, bathrooms and other areas of the house where floors are likely to be subjected to heavy wear or spillages. It's also straightforward to lay.

Vinyl flooring was developed in the 1960s and revolutionized the smooth (and resilient) flooring market. At first it was a thin and rather unyielding material. But it was something which could be laid fairly easily by the do-it-yourself enthusiast; and this was a breakthrough because its predecessor, linoleum, had had to be professionally laid. Since then, vinyl flooring has been greatly improved and there are now several different types available.

Types of vinyl
The cheapest type of vinyl is known as a 'flexible print' and has a clear wear layer on top, with the printed pattern sandwiched between this and the backing. Then there are the cushioned vinyls, which are more bouncy underfoot and have a soft inner bubbly layer between the wear layer and the backing. They are often embossed to give them a texture, which is particularly successful when the embossing enhances the design, as with simulated cork or ceramic tile patterns. Finally, the most expensive type is solid flexible vinyl, made by suspending colored vinyl chips in transparent vinyl to create color and design which goes right through the material and consequently wears longer.

All three types come in a wide variety of colors and designs ranging from geometric and floral patterns to simulated cork, wood block, parquet, ceramic tiles, slate and brick. Some ranges include special glossy no-wax surfaces. Also, there is a special 'lay-flat' type which does not have to be stuck down, except on very heavy wear areas or at doorways. Some vinyls can be folded without cracking, but as with carpets, a good guide to durability is price: the more expensive the flooring, the longer-lasting it is likely to be.

Buying vinyl
To work out the amount of vinyl you'll need, measure up the floor using a metal tape; note down the measurements and then double-check them. Draw a scale plan of the room on squared paper, marking in all the obstacles, door openings and so on.

Take the measurements and plan to your supplier, who will help you to work out quantities. Remember to allow for walls which are not quite true and for trimming the overlap (see *Ready Reference*).

Whatever the type, vinyl is available in standard sheet widths (see *Ready Reference* again). Choose one in a wide width for use on a floor where you do not want to have a seam. (A wide sheet can be difficult to lay so make sure you have someone to help you – If you are going to lay sheets of a narrower width which will have to be joined, remember to allow for pattern matching when buying.

Check the manufacturer's instructions for fixing and order the correct adhesive and other sundries. Make sure you get the right amount; there is nothing worse than running out of adhesive halfway through the job.

A roll of vinyl is usually 30 to 40m (100 to 130ft) long and the retailer will cut off the length you want, re-rolling it for you. Take the roll of vinyl home and leave it, loosely rolled, in the room where it is to be laid for about 48 hours. This will allow it to become acclimatized and it should then be easier to lay. Do not stand it on edge as this can crack the material and take care not to damage the ends when you are transporting or storing the roll.

Preparing the sub-floor
Vinyl must be laid on a sound, reasonably smooth and even sub-floor if the best results

Ready Reference

SHEET SIZES
Sheet vinyl usually comes in three different widths: 2m (6ft), 3m (9ft) and 4m (12ft).

SUITABLE SURFACES
Vinyl can be laid over concrete, wood or tiles. Don't attempt to lay it over old vinyl, linoleum or cork; these should be removed or covered with hardboard.

PREPARING A WOOD FLOOR
To prepare a bumpy wood floor for laying vinyl, cover it with large sheets of flooring-grade chipboard or hardboard. Stagger the joints between sheets.

If you are using hardboard, place the shiny side down as the rough side provides a better grip for the vinyl.

staggered joints   **hardboard**

LAYING HARDBOARD SHEETS

1 Fix sheets of hardboard, rough side up, by nailing them to the old floor surface. The nails should be spaced about 100-150mm apart.

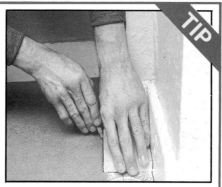

2 Where part of the wall protrudes, use a scribing block to provide a guide when marking off the contour of the wall on the hardboard.

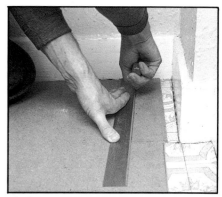

3 Cut along the line you have marked on the hardboard, using a sharp knife and a straight edge to guide the knife.

FITTING AND FIXING VINYL

1 Lay the flooring out fully across the room; with a large width such as this you will probably need help to get it roughly into position.

2 Make diagonal cuts at each corner, taking care not to cut too deep, to make accurate positioning much easier.

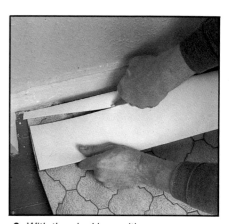

3 With the vinyl in position, use a sharp knife to trim off the excess, starting at the longest straight wall. Remember to allow an overlap.

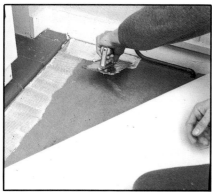

5 With the excess trimmed away from the longest straight wall and the adjacent wall, pull back the vinyl and spread adhesive on the floor.

6 Push the vinyl down onto the adhesive making sure it is firmly stuck down. Smooth out the surface as you go so there are no air bubbles.

7 Trim off the overlap on the edges where the vinyl has been stuck down. Continue fitting, fixing and trimming round the rest of the room.

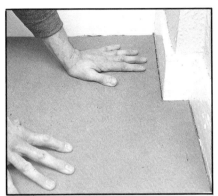

4 *After you have cut out the required shape, push the hardboard into place, making sure it butts up against the bottom edge of the baseboard.*

4 *At a doorway, cut into the corners (see* Ready Reference) *and again trim off the excess, allowing for an overlap for later, final trimming.*

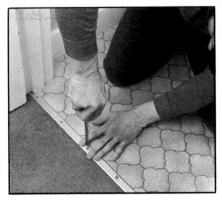

8 *At the entrance to a room, fasten down the fixed vinyl with a threshold strip to cover the join between the vinyl and the carpet.*

are to be achieved and the flooring is to give adequate wear. The floor must also be free from dirt, polish, bits of plaster or splashes of paint, but above all it must be damp proof, so deal with this first.

The floor may have to be rescreeded or old floorboards taken up and replaced. But whatever is needed must be done before laying the new flooring. A cover-up job will never be satisfactory and the new material will start to perish from the back.

Remember that screeding a floor will raise its level and so doors will almost certainly have to be taken off their hinges and trimmed at the bottom to accommodate the new floor level.

Where the existing floor covering does not provide a suitable surface for laying vinyl, you will have to remove it. You can remove old vinyl by stripping it off from the backing, then soaking any remaining material in cold water, detergent and household ammonia before scraping it off with a paint scraper.

With a wooden sub-floor you should remove any protruding tacks, nails or screws, or punch them down level with the floor.

Any rough or protruding boards should be planed smooth and wide gaps between boards filled with fillets of wood; small holes or gaps can be filled with plastic wood. If the floor is very bumpy, it can be covered with man-made boards.

Fitting seamed lengths

Measure for the first length of vinyl along the longest unobstructed wall unless this brings a seam into the wrong position (see *Ready Reference*). After measuring you can cut the first length from the roll.

Butt the edge of the vinyl right up to the baseboard at one end of the room, tucking the overlap underneath the baseboard if possible so you don't have to trim this edge. Then cut the material off across the width, allowing for an overlap at the other end, at doorways and obstacles.

To fit the first doorway you will have to cut slits at the door jambs and then ease the vinyl around the door recess and supports, cutting off a little at a time, until you get a perfect fit.

Next, either tuck the overlap of the vinyl under the baseboard which runs along the length of the room if you can, or trim along the wall or baseboard, allowing for a good (but not too tight) fit. Smooth down the flooring as you work along its length and then cut the vinyl to fit at the other end.

If the wall is uneven, you will have to scribe' its contour onto the vinyl. You pull the vinyl slightly away from the wall and then run a wooden block, in conjunction with a pencil,

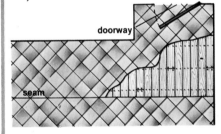

LAYING VINYL IN A RECESS

1 With the vinyl fixed in place at the straightest edges of the room, deal with awkward areas like a recess. First trim at the corners.

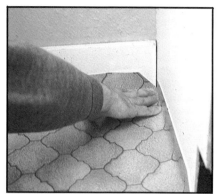

2 Turn back the vinyl and spread a band of adhesive round the edges of the recess. You can then push the floorcovering firmly into position.

3 To complete the job, use a sharp knife to trim off the overlap. Again, make sure there are no bubbles by smoothing the vinyl down.

along the wall so its profile is marked on the vinyl. To cut along this line you can use a knife and straight edge (with the straight edge on the vinyl which will be used), or if the line is very wobbly, use scissors.

With the first length fitted, you can then place the next length of vinyl parallel to the first, matching the pattern exactly, and cut off the required length, again allowing for extra overlap at the ends and sides. Some people cut all the required lengths first before fitting, but if the room is not perfectly square and several widths are being used, there could be a mismatch.

If the two sheets overlap, the excess will have to be trimmed away. Place one on top of the other, aligning the design carefully, and cut through the two sheets together at the overlap, using a knife and straight edge. Remove the trimmings and then adjust the second sheet to fit doors, baseboards and so on, trimming where necessary.

Where there are more than two sheets, repeat the fitting procedure, making sure the pattern matches.

If you are renewing the baseboards, to get a perfect fit you can fit the material first and put the baseboard on after the vinyl is laid. Remember, though, that this may make it difficult to take up the floorcovering when you need (or want) to change it.

Fitting extra-wide flooring

The technique is largely the same as for fitting strips of vinyl except there will not be any seams to stick, or pattern matching to do. You should start by laying the flooring out fully – you will probably need help for this – and try to find a long straight wall against which the first edge can be laid. Then make diagonal cuts at each corner to allow the flooring to be positioned roughly, with the

excess material 'climbing up' the baseboard or wall. Trim away the excess, leaving a 50 to 75mm (2 to 3in) overlap all round. Scribe the first wall, if necessary, then trim and ease the flooring back into its exact position. Deal with corners, projections, and obstacles as you work your way round the room, leaving the same overlap; finally trim to a perfect fit.

Fixing vinyl

How you fix vinyl will depend on the type; always follow the manufacturer's instructions. As vinyl can shrink it's wise to stick it down immediately before or after trimming it. To stick the edges you should first turn them back and apply a 75mm (3in) wide band of adhesive to the sub-floor, using a serrated scraper in a criss-cross motion, and then press the vinyl into position immediately. This will usually be at doorways, round the edges of the room, or round obstacles. Where heavy equipment will be pulled across the floor regularly (a washing machine for example) it is worth ·sticking down the entire area.

At the seams, you should make the width of the spread adhesive generous — 150 to 200mm (6 to 8in). Again, turn back the edges, apply the band of adhesive to the sub-floor and press the vinyl back into position immediately. Wipe away any adhesive which seeps through the seam or round the edges of the vinyl immediately, as this can discolor the flooring if it hardens.

At the entrance to rooms, particularly in heavy traffic areas, or if you have used the 'lay-flat' type of vinyl, you can fasten down the vinyl with a ready-made threshold strip. These come in metal, wood or plastic and are also used to cover joins between two different materials, such as vinyl and carpet.

Cleaning and maintenance

Once you have laid your floor you will need to look after it. Always wipe up any spills immediately, particularly hot fat and grease. It is also wise to protect the surface from indentation by putting heavy pieces of furniture on a piece of hardboard, or standing legs and castors in castor cups.

Some of the more expensive vinyls have a built-in gloss, so they do not need polishing. This type can be mopped with a damp cloth.

Never use a harsh abrasive cleaner on any type of vinyl floor as this could damage the surface layer. The glossy surface should not wear away, but if it does become dull in heavy traffic areas, it can be recoated with a special paint-on liquid provided by the manufacturer.

The less glossy vinyls will need regular sweeping or vacuuming and mopping. It also makes sense to use a clear acrylic polish, applied very sparingly according to the manufacturer's instructions and then buffed gently. Wash occasionally with warm water and a mild liquid detergent, and don't apply lots of coats of wax, or you will get a thick discolored build-up, which spoils the look of the floor; 2-4 coats over a 12-month period is plenty. Always let the floor dry thoroughly before walking on it, after it has been washed or polished.

Once several coats of wax have built up, you will have to strip off the polish and start again. To do this, add a cupful of household ammonia to a bucket of cold water, to which a little detergent has been added. Scrub the floor with this, taking care not to saturate it too much. When the old surface begins to break down, wipe it with an old soft cloth, rinse thoroughly with warm, clean water and dry before applying a new protective coating.

CUTTING AROUND OBSTACLES

The best way to get a neat floor when fitting vinyl around obstacles such as bathroom fittings is to make a template of paper or cardboard which is slightly larger (by about 25mm/1in) than the obstacle. Place one sheet of paper up against the basin pedestal, toilet base or whatever, and tear it around so you have half the obstacle's shape on it. Then repeat the procedure with another sheet of paper for the other half.

Fit the template around the obstacle and use a scribing block and pencil to give the exact profile. Then lay the pattern over the flooring and use the block and pencil to reverse the procedure and transfer the exact outline onto the vinyl by running it around the inside of the line. You can then cut and fit; you will have to make a slit in the edge of the vinyl in some cases to get a snug fit at the baseboard. Carefully trim away any excess material around the obstacle once the flooring is placed in position. Fix the vinyl according to the manufacturer's instructions.

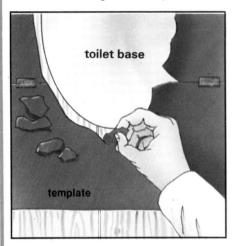

Making a template

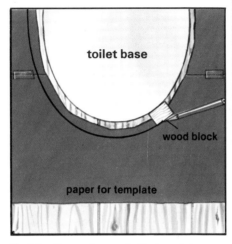

Scribing the contour onto the template

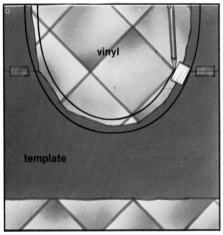

Scribing the contour onto the vinyl

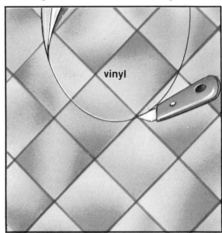

Cutting the vinyl

If you wipe up spills at once you should not get any stains on vinyl flooring, but sometimes they become marked from tar or grit trodden into the house; some types of shoe can leave black scuff marks, and cigarette burns are not unknown.

If normal cleaning doesn't remove marks, rub them very gently with a very fine grade steel wool, used dry. Take care not to rub too much of the surface layer away. Wipe with a damp cloth, and reseal/polish the area if necessary. Some grease marks can be removed with white vinegar, others with mineral spirit. Always, however, wipe the area immediately with clean water.

Any badly discolored or damaged area may have to be patched, so save any offcuts of sufficient size for this purpose.

Ready Reference

FITTING CORNERS
To fit vinyl:
● at internal corners, gently push the vinyl into the corner and cut away the excess, diagonally across the corner, until it fits. Cut a little at a time and pare the edge carefully
● at external corners, press the vinyl into the corner, pull up the excess and cut to allow the vinyl to fall into place round the corner; then trim the excess.

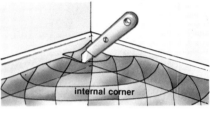

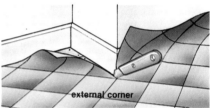

FIXING METHODS
Sheet vinyl can be fixed either by sticking it down all over or only at the edges and seams. Check the manufacturer's instructions.

'Lay-flat' vinyls do not have to be stuck down but they must be firmly fixed at doorways by gluing, or another method. Double-sided tape may be used to secure seams.

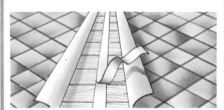

TIP: SMOOTH OUT BUMPS
If there are any bumps in the vinyl after you have laid it fill a pillowcase with sand and drag this round the floor to iron them out.

TIP: HIDING GAPS
If you have an unsightly gap between the baseboard and the floor, because the walls are very uneven or your vinyl has shrunk, you can pin painted quarter round to the baseboard to hide the gap.

LAYING VINYL FLOOR TILES

Vinyl tiles are supple, easy to handle and don't take much time to lay. They come in many colors and designs so you should have no trouble finding tiles of the type you want.

Vinyl tiles are ideal for use on kitchen and bathroom floors because they are waterproof and resistant to oil, grease and most domestic chemicals. They have the advantage over vinyl sheet flooring in that they are easier to handle, and also, if you make any mistakes when cutting, they will be confined to individual tiles. So if you have a room where you will have to carry out quite a lot of intricate cutting to make the floorcovering fit round obstacles or awkwardly shaped areas, it would be well worth considering laying tiles rather than sheet material.

The tiles come in a wide variety of patterns and colors, with a smooth gloss finish or a range of sculptured and embossed designs. They can be bought with or without a cushioned backing. Cushioned tiles are softer and warmer underfoot, but more expensive than uncushioned tiles. However, even among tiles without a cushioned backing there is a wide variation in price. The cost of a tile is usually a fair indication of its quality, so, in general, the more expensive the tile the longer it will last. You don't need to be greatly concerned about this: even the cheapest tiles can have a life of twenty years in average domestic use, and long before then you will probably wish to remove or cover up the tiles. (On average floorcoverings are changed every seven years.) So your choice of tiles will probably be based simply on the fact that you like the color or pattern and feel it will fit in well with the rest of the decorative scheme in the room.

Preparing the surface

The floor surface on which you intend to lay vinyl tiles should be free of dust and dirt, so you should go over it first of all with a vacuum cleaner. Then check that the subfloor is in sound condition.

If it is a wood floor, you will have to repair any damaged boards, and if the floor has been treated in whole or in part with stains and polishes, these will stop the tile adhesive from adhering properly, and will have to be removed with a floor cleaner. There may be gaps between the boards and they could possibly be warped and curling at the edges. You can cure these faults by lining the floor

with hardboard without adding much to the cost of the job or the time it takes to do it. First inspect the floor; punch home any protruding nails and countersink any screws. Replace missing nails. Where a board squeaks because it is loose, screws will hold it in place more securely then nails.

Hardboard sheets 1220mm (4ft) square will be a manageable size for this type of work. To condition them, brush water at the rate of ½ litre (2/3 pint) per 1220mm (4ft) square sheet onto the reverse side of the sheets. Then leave them for 48 hours stacked flat back to back in the room where they will be laid so they will become accustomed to its conditions. When fixed they will dry out further and tighten up to present a perfectly flat subfloor.

You can begin fixing the hardboard in one corner of the room. It's not necessary to scribe it to fit irregularities at the walls; small gaps here and there at the edges of the boards will not affect the final look of the floor.

Fix the sheets in place with nails at 150mm (6in) intervals round the edges and 225mm (9in) apart across the middle of the sheets. Begin nailing in the center of a convenient edge and work sideways and forwards so the sheet is smoothed down in place. Where there are water pipes below the floor use nails which will not come out on the underside of the floorboards.

The sheets should normally be fixed with their smooth side down so the adhesive will grip more securely; also the nail heads will be concealed in the mesh.

Nail down the first sheet and work along the wall. When you come to the end of a row of sheets, you will have to cut a sheet to fit. Don't throw the waste away; use it to start the next row so the joins between sheets will not coincide. When you come to the far side of the room you will have to cut the sheets to width. Again, don't worry about scribing them to fit the exact contours of the wall.

On a solid floor, check to see if there are any holes or cracks and whether it is truly level and smooth. Fill in holes and small cracks with a sand/cement mortar. Large cracks could indicate a structural fault and, if in doubt, you should call in an expert. To level an uneven floor, use a self-levelling compound, applying it according to the manufacturer's instructions.

When dealing with a direct-to-earth floor you will have to establish whether it is dry or not. There's no point in attempting to lay the tiles on a damp floor: you will get problems with adhesion and in time the tiles themselves will curl and lift.

One difficulty is that dampness in a floor is not always immediately apparent, especially if there is no floorcovering. (If the floor has a sheet covering you should lift up a corner of the covering and inspect beneath for any signs of dampness.) A slight amount of dampness can rise up through floors of quarry tiles or concrete and evaporate in a room without being noticed.

To test for dampness, you can heat up a plate of metal over a blow-torch, or heat a brick in the oven for about an hour, then

LAYING SELF-ADHESIVE TILES

1 *Sponge primer over the floor and leave it to dry for 24 hours. It will help the tiles to form a secure bond when they are fixed in place.*

2 *Snap two chalk lines which bisect at the floor's center. Dry-lay a row of tiles along one line to find out the width of the cut border tiles.*

3 *Adjust the first (center) tile if the cut tiles will be too narrow. Fix the tiles in place by peeling off the backing and pressing them down.*

4 *With the first row in place, continue fixing the tiles, working in sections, until all the whole tiles are laid. You can then lay the cut border tiles.*

5 *Place a tile over the last whole tile in a row and another one over it butted against the wall to use as a guide to mark the cutting line.*

6 *Leave the backing paper on when cutting the tile with a sharp knife. Remove the paper and press the cut border tile in place.*

Ready Reference

TILE SIZES
Vinyl tiles are sold in packs sufficient to cover about 50 square feet. The most common size tile is 300mm (12in) square.

FIXING TILES
Some tiles are self-adhesive; you simply pull off a backing paper, then press the tile down in place. Others require adhesive; this should be special vinyl flooring adhesive.

TIP: MAKE A TRAMMEL
A simple device called a trammel can help you find the center of a room. Take a 1 × 3 about 900mm (3ft) long and drive a nail through the wood near each end.

FINDING THE CENTER OF THE ROOM
In an irregularly shaped room you can find the room's center in this way:
● strike a chalk line to form a base line, parallel to and 75mm (3in) away from the wall with the door
● place the center of your trammel on the center of the base line (A) and use the trammel to mark points B and C on the chalk line
● with one nail of the trammel placed in turn on points B and C, scribe two arcs, meeting at D
● find the center of the line through A and D to give the center point of the room (E), then draw a line across and at right angles to it using the same technique.

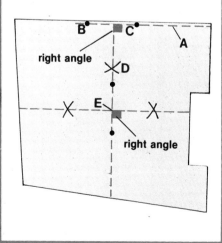

TILING AN L-SHAPE

1 *At an external corner, place the tile to be cut over the last whole tile in one of the rows of tiles which adjoin at the corner.*

2 *Place another tile over the tile to be cut, but butted up against the baseboard, and use it as a guide to mark the cutting line.*

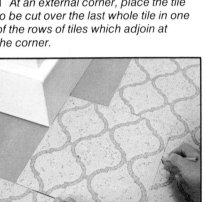

3 *Place the tile to be cut over the last whole tile in the other row leading to the corner. Use another tile as a guide for marking off.*

4 *Cut the tile along the marked lines with the backing paper on. Test if the cut tile fits, then peel off the paper and fix it in place.*

TILING AROUND A DOOR CASING

1 *Make a template of the area around the casing. Always test a template out: put it in place before using it on the tile to be cut.*

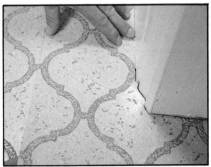

2 *When the template fits, use it to mark out the required shape on the tile. Cut the tile, remove the backing paper and press it in place.*

place it on the floor. If a damp patch appears on the floor or moisture gathers under the metal or brick, this indicates that dampness is present. Another test is to place a sheet of glass on the floor, seal its edges with putty, then leave it for a few days. If moisture appears underneath it is again a sign of dampness. These methods are, however, rather hit-and-miss and it may be worth calling in an expert to give a true diagnosis.

Curing a damp floor is a major undertaking which may involve digging up the existing floor and laying a new one with proper precautions taken against dampness. You should seek professional advice here.

Existing sheet floorcoverings should be removed before you start laying vinyl tiles. You can, however, lay them over existing vinyl tiles provided these are in sound condition and are securely fixed. If they are not, you will have to remove them before you fix the new tiles. To lever them up, use a paint scraper, or even a garden spade (the long handle will give you plenty of leverage).

Marking up
You should start laying tiles from the middle of the floor. To find the center of a room which is a reasonably regular shape, you should take one wall and, ignoring any bays, alcoves or projections, measure and mark its center. Go to the wall opposite and do the same. Between these two center points you should snap a chalked line. Snap a second chalk line from the middle of the other two walls: the point where the lines meet is the center of the floor.

If you are going to tile an irregularly shaped room, you should strike a chalk line, to form a base line, parallel to and 75mm (3in) away from a wall which has a doorway in it. You can then strike a line at right angles to the base line, and stretching to the wall on the other side. The center of this line will be the center point of the room; draw a line through this center point parallel to the base line. (Instead of using a large square to help you draw the lines at true right angles, you can use what's known as a trammel; see *Ready Reference*.)

Laying the tiles
When you come to lay the tiles, the first one is all-important. There are four possible positions for it. It can go centrally on the center point; neatly inside one of the angles where the center lines cross; centrally on one line and butting up to the second, or centrally on the second line and butting up to the first.

You should choose the position that gives you the widest border of cut tiles round the room. Very narrow cut strips at the edges will tend to give an unbalanced look, especially if you are laying the tiles in a dual color or checkerboard pattern. So set out the tiles dry

TILING AROUND A TOILET

1 *Butt a paper template, which is the same size as a tile, against the base of the toilet and mark off the shape of the toilet on the template.*

2 *Cut the template to shape, then test to see if it fits exactly around the toilet base and between the base and the whole laid tiles.*

3 *Place the template over a whole loose tile (check the tile is the right way round for pattern matching) and mark off the cutting line.*

4 *Use a sharp knife to cut the tile to shape following the marked line. You can then remove the backing paper and fix the tile.*

TIP

5 *Aim to get the tile position right first time. Tiles can be taken up and restuck, but will lose some of their adhesive in the process.*

6 *Continue to make templates and fix shaped tiles round the curved toilet base. You can then fix the cut border tiles next to the walls.*

(that is, not stuck down) to find out which position for the first tile gives you borders with the largest cut tiles. In a regularly shaped room this will be quite straightforward; a couple of dry runs should make things clear. In an awkwardly shaped room, especially if it has a lot of alcoves or projections, you will have to make several of these practice runs. When you've decided on your final starting position, draw round the outline of the first tile to be placed.

When you've stuck down your first tile you can begin laying the rest. If you are laying tiles which require adhesive, you should apply this to as large an area as you can cope with in one go; possibly a square metre (square yard). Butt all the tiles accurately up against each other, and check that they are precisely aligned. Then apply firm hand (or foot) pressure to bed them firmly in place.

It's normal practice to stick down all the full tiles, known as the 'field', leaving a border of cut tiles to be fitted round the edges.

If you are laying self-adhesive tiles, you simply peel off the backing paper and press each tile into place. Where you have to cut tiles, don't peel off the backing until the cutting-to-size is completed. Should a tile be misplaced, lift it quickly and relay it correctly; the adhesive 'grabs' quickly and later attempts to lift the tile will probably tear it.

Cutting tiles

Vinyl tiles can be quite easily cut using a sharp knife and a straightedge. For an intricate shape make a template first.

Border tiles can be marked up for cutting in the usual way; that is, you take the tile to be cut, place it on the last complete tile in the row, place another tile over the first one but jammed hard against the wall and use this tile as a guide for marking off the cutting line

on the first tile (see step-by-step photographs). The main thing wrong with this method is that it can leave a narrow border in which it is difficult to apply adhesive, with the consequent risk that the border tiles will not adhere properly.

Another method, which avoids this problem, is to lay the field except for the last full tile in each row. Then take a tile and place it against the last full tile in the field. Place another tile on top of the first one and jammed against the wall. Use this second tile as a guide to cut through the first (and it will itself become the last full tile fixed in the relevant row).

The two tiles can temporarily be placed on top of the field, adjacent to the position they will occupy, while you cut the rest of the border. When you come to stick the border tiles down you will have plenty of room in which to wield your adhesive spreader and ensure adequate coverage.

CHAPTER 4
Repairing

MAKING GOOD
walls and ceilings

If you're making a lot of alterations to your house, you'll probably pull out cupboards, partitions, remove trim and strip off old wallcoverings. Don't worry if you cause some damage, since you can quite easily put it right.

No matter what sort of decorating you intend to do, the surface you're covering must be sound. If you paint, paper or tile over cracks or loose plaster you're wasting your time. The professionals call this preparation 'making good' — and the reason is obvious. Without time spent here the end result will be less attractive, won't last very long, and you won't be getting value for the money you've spent on decorating materials. Making good takes time, but it is never wasted. Here is a guide for the sort of problems you'll face in making good walls and ceilings ready for decorating.

Cracks

There are two types of cracks in walls to watch for. A structural one will be large, deep, and often wider at one end than the other — this has been caused by settling and you should seek the advice of a professional before any attempt is made to repair it. The second type is usually just a crack in the surface covering of the wall — the plaster, for instance — and because it's only super-ficial it can be easily repaired.

For such superficial cracks in plaster, first detach all loose material with the edge of a stripping knife and brush out thoroughly. If more plaster than you bargained for comes away, the plaster must have been weak — in which case, treat as large holes. Fill hairline and small cracks with cellulose filler, bought as powder and mixed with water to a thick

creamy paste (mix only small quantities to avoid waste). Smooth it on with a putty knife and sand it down when dry.

In wood, cracks and opened grain can again be filled with cellulose filler — but it will show up rather than blend. If the wood is going to be painted, this probably won't matter. But if you're going to finish the wood with a clear varnish, plastic wood or filler should be used to ensure the best possible finish.

Gouges

These are superficial marks caused by a badly-used shavehook or stripping knife (held at the wrong angle or because it slipped) or an electric abrasive tool which during the smoothing created ridges in the surrounding plaster. Fill as in cracks with cellulose filler, making it slightly proud of the surface. Leave it to dry hard and then sand

flush with medium sandpaper. Gouges in wood should be treated in exactly the same way as cracks.

Holes

Small holes are often left when old screws and nails are removed or if wires have been chased in — for these the remedy is simple. Large holes, however caused, can require a lot more attention especially if they're deep as well as wide (eg, if a partition has been removed leaving gaps in walls or ceilings).

It can boil down to a question of cost — cellulose filler bought in the quantity required for a large hole will be more expensive than a small bag of plaster. Plaster, however, has its own problems — it's difficult to mix properly, sets very fast and takes some skill to get it to stick to the wall in the first place. In small areas there are ways around this (see page 88 for *Ready*

STRIPPING WALL COVERINGS

● Brush wallpaper with a solution of warm water and detergent or a stripper. Leave for about 5 minutes to allow the water to soak through to the old paste. Ease the stripping knife under the paper at a join and lift the paper off and away. This will prevent gouges in the plaster.

● If the paper clings stubbornly, soak it again but add a handful of wallpaper paste to the water. This will help the water soak in.

● Vinyl wallcoverings are removed simply by lifting the plastic coating at the

bottom edge of the drop, then pulling it upwards and off in a complete sheet. Strip off the thin paper backing if it is damaged by soaking as above.

● Washable or gloss painted heavy wallcoverings will resist water. If you can get a scraper behind the paper at a join or at the top, spray water containing some wallpaper paste in with a plant sprayer. Leave for a few minutes, then move the scraper backwards and forwards between the wall and the paper. Or you can break down the surface. Use either a wire brush or a serrated scraper.

Reference on plaster and fillers).

Very large holes need to be treated in the same way as plastering a wall — you start with an 'undercoat' plaster (it's much coarser than a 'finishing' plaster) to fill to about 6mm (¼in) from the surface, and this provides a key for two coats of finishing plaster which is applied with a float. As it dries it has to be 'polished' by applying water and smoothing with the float. Because of the speed at which plaster dries, this can be a difficult skill to master and telltale ridges may remain where the plaster has dried before the polishing began. Experience will overcome this problem.

Large or small holes in a plastered wall first have to be thoroughly cleaned out. Chip out all loose material and undercut the edges with a knife, then brush out thoroughly to remove all the dust.

If the wall is block or brick underneath, and the hole is no more than 100mm (4in) in diameter, then use a small trowel and build up the surface with thin layers of filler.

With a wall constructed of laths (thin strips of wood) and plaster, you first have to expose the laths, removing all loose plaster in the same way as above. But you won't be able to undercut the edges so easily, so you have to make sure that the filling goes between the slats. If the slats are damaged then treat as drywall. Otherwise, build up the filler in layers.

Always overfill a large hole, and to get it flush use a board (long enough to bridge it) in a sawing action to reduce excess or redistribute it till the required level is reached. Finally smooth the finished surface with a knife or trowel, and sand down when dry with sandpaper or an orbital sander.

If holes aren't too large but are deep, an alternative method is to press in balls of wet newspaper, then skim a layer of plaster or cellulose filler over the top.

If there's a hole or holes where walls meet to make an external corner, nail a board vertically along the edge of one wall and fill the hole on the other as described above. When this patch is dry, remove the board and repeat on the other wall. If the damage to an exposed corner is extensive, or if it is particularly vulnerable, greater reinforce-

SURFACE CRACKS

1 *These tiny cracks usually occur in plaster and are superficial. Use the edge of a stripping knife to remove any loose material along its length.*

2 *Brush out the crack thoroughly so there's no dust left. In a small carton mix some cellulose filler to a creamy paste with water.*

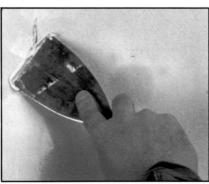

3 *Use a filling knife to press the filler onto the wall surface over the tiny cracks. Leave the filler slightly proud as it will shrink a little.*

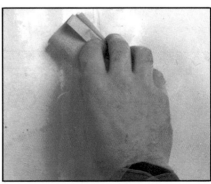

4 *When the filler has dried (it will lose the gray look and turn white) use sandpaper wrapped round a wood block to make the surface flush.*

HOLES IN DRYWALL

1 With large holes in ceilings or walls use a utility knife and straight edge to cut back the drywall to the nearest joists or studs on each side.

2 The new piece of drywall should fit the hole fairly neatly. Press it in and fix to joists or studs on either side using drywall nails.

3 Use a steel trowel to press drywall compound well into gaps. Then smooth the whole area keeping the top of the trowel angled away from the wall.

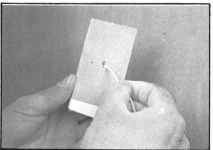

4 For small holes, cut a piece of drywall a little larger than the hole (but small enough for you to get it through) and drill a hole in the middle.

TIP

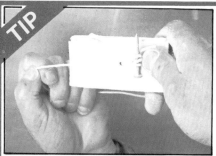

5 Feed a short length of string through the hole, then tie a nail to one end — this will keep the string secure and prevent it being pulled out later.

6 Dab freshly mixed compound onto both ends of the piece of drywall, then guide it into the hole. Pull on the string to position it in the hole.

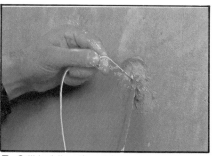

7 Still holding the string, press compound into the hole then use a trowel to remove the excess so that it's not quite flush with the surface.

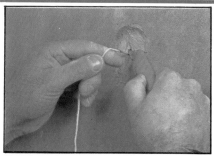

8 When the compound is hard cut off the length of string with a utility knife. After the cut is made there should be no sign of the string.

9 Apply a thin finishing coat of compound to the surface.

ment may be desirable. Cut back the plaster as described under weak plaster to beyond the limit of the damage and square off to neaten edges. Then fix an expanded metal corner-piece to the underlying wall with dabs of plaster and plaster over it using the board technique. Internal corners are a bit trickier. There are two methods. Either fill one side, smooth with board, then leave to dry before doing the other. Or fill both and when semi-dry, smooth down with an angle trowel.

For small holes in drywall use drywall compound. Edges of larger holes should be cleaned up with a utility knife and can be covered with a patch of drywall tape stuck in place with dabs of compound. Or you can use an offcut of drywall (see the photographs above). When secure, gently fill over using a creamy mixture of drywall compound and allow to dry. Finally sand smooth.

Large holes in drywall must be patched with drywall offcuts. To nail in position it will

be necessary to cut a hole big enough to expose the nearest wooden supports (in a wall these are called 'studs', in a ceiling 'joists'). On a ceiling, if you can get at it from above, the hole can be cut square and boarded along each side, the boards being nailed to the joists. Use 30mm (1³⁄₁₆in) or 40mm (1¹⁄₂in) drywall nails to fix the drywall in place, then fill in gaps as above.

Holes in wood are best filled with wood, and if the hole is circular, use a piece of

WHICH FILLER IS WHICH?

Cellulose fillers: these are based on plaster with added cellulose resins to improve flexibility, adhesion and reduce drying time.
● remains workable for up to 1 hour
● it will shrink, so cracks should be overfilled and sanded back
● expensive to use in large quantities
● dries white.

Drywall compound: like ordinary cellulose fillers, but with added ingredients to improve performance and sold in plastic tubs.
● quick-drying in thin layers (thick layers may take up to 24 hours)
● less likely to shrink or slump
● waterproof, so can be used in wet areas or outdoors
● relatively expensive to use in large quantities.

Plaster: this is made from gypsum (calcium sulphate) and numerous different types are available.
● relatively inexpensive for large repairs
● very quick setting (less than 30mins)
● may shrink in deep cracks or thick layers
● dries gray or pink.

Brush-on skim plaster, specially-formulated and ready-mixed, is designed to be brushed on and smoothed with a spreader instead of a float.
● remains workable for up to 4 hours
● doesn't shrink or crack
● more expensive than plain plaster
● dries white

Wood fillers are resin-based ready-mixed fillers designed for wood that's going to be varnished.
● sets quickly with little shrinkage
● dries wood-color but can take stain.

Caulking is a rubber or acrylic-basic sealant that can be used for gaps between walls and woodwork where slight movement would crack ordinary fillers.
● remains flexible without shrinking
● can be painted
● available in different colors.

SEALING GAPS

1 *Gaps between woodwork and walls can be filled with a flexible sealant. The nozzle is directed into the space with the help of a caulking gun.*

2 *For a smooth finish, lightly sprinkle the sealant with water then run down the corner with a dowel or moistened finger. It can be painted 24 hours later.*

dowelling glued in place with PVA adhesive. With some holes, you can achieve the same result with a wedge — hammered into place, and then planed off for a flush finish. Alternatively, use plastic wood or filler and sand the finish down when dry. If knots are loose and very dry, they should be cut out and the hole filled with a small piece of dowelling, glued in place.

Gaps
Where gaps occur between woodwork and walls (eg, near windows, casings and base-boards), a flexible sealant will fill them. Bought as 'cartridges', they have a nozzle which can be directed straight into the gap. A 'gun' attachment gives even more control and is especially useful in awkward places. The sealant can be painted 24 hours later. Cellulose filler can also be used for gaps but take care to get it smooth. If the gaps are particularly deep partly fill them with strips of folded newspaper and apply flexible sealer over the top. If they're wide, use thin wood to fill and wood filler to finish, then sand down when dry.

Gaps in plaster cornices (the shaped molding where walls meet ceilings) occur when a framework (eg, an old cupboard) has been pulled away. Clean up the gap and apply liberal quantities of cellulose filler. When the filler is 'stiff' but not hard, take a profile comb (you can make this yourself from a piece of card cut to the same 'profile' or shape as the coving) and run it along from the existing coving onto the filler. When the match is perfect, allow the filler to dry and then gently smooth with the folded edge of a sheet of sandpaper.

Weak plaster
Old plaster may be loose against its backing and will move when you press it. If th's is the case in any more than small areas, then

complete replacement may be necessary. Unsound plaster will sound hollow when you tap it gently with your knuckles.

The extent of the weak area should be found by tapping, then lines drawn around it with a pencil. Using a club hammer and a bolster, gently chip out the weak area starting at the outside edges of the patch and working inwards (cover the floor below to catch the mess). If you don't start at the edges of the weak areas and work inwards, you may end up removing half the wall. When the patch has been removed you should fill as in holes. With larger areas you may need a professional plasterer. If the weakness was caused by dampness, the underlying wall should also be treated with a suitable waterproof sealant before repairing.

Mold
This may be found in steamy conditions which encourage its growth or where condensation is a problem (eg, in kitchens and bathrooms). Mold appears as gray, green or black spots or patches, and first should be treated with a fungicidal solution. Alternatively you can use a three parts water to one part household bleach solution. The wall should be dry before redecoration. If the problem persists, then you'll have to tackle the underlying cause — which may be dampness penetrating the wall from outside or from below, or lack of insulation and ventilation which causes persistent condensation.

Old adhesives
Where ceramic tiles have been removed tile cement may remain fixed to the wall. In some situations — if you're retiling, for instance — this won't matter because as long as the surface is fairly flat any new adhesive will stick perfectly well. In the case of polystyrene tiles on a ceiling there may be dabs of adhesive left when you remove them and

REPAIRING HOLES

1 Mark straight guide lines slightly beyond the weak area. Use a bolster and club hammer to cut back to the brick, block or laths underneath.

2 Brushing out any dust and then dampening the surface with a little water helps the plaster stick and stops it drying too quickly.

3 Apply a plaster backing coat to the hole — use either a coarse type which sets slowly or 'brush-on' plaster.

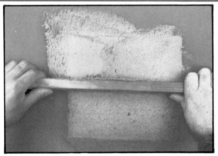

4 To level, use a board with a side-to-side sawing action. As the plaster hardens, cut it back with a trowel so it's not quite flush with the wall surface.

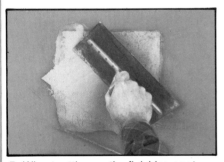

5 When putting on the finishing coat, scoop plaster from the hawk onto the trowel, then angle the bottom edge of the trowel in to the wall.

6 Keep the trowel moving at all times. Smooth upwards, then from side to side. To 'polish' flick on drops of water, and move the trowel in a circular motion.

CORNERS

1 Repairing corners is a two-stage job. Brush out the damaged area, then fix a board on one side. To ease removal, don't drive the nails fully home.

2 Use the edge of the trowel to fill in the hole with traditional quick setting compound. When it's dry move the board to the other side.

3 Fill in the rest of the hole. Leave to dry, then remove the board. Gently smooth the new edge to match the old.

---

the surface has to be cleaned off. The only answer to this is an arduous, bit by bit, removal of each dab. (In places, plaster may come away with the tile or adhesive in which case treat as holes in plaster.) Gently ease the adhesive or cement away from the surface using a stripping knife and a mallet. Then sand the area smooth before decorating. If cork tiles have been taken down, any adhesive remaining will have to be sanded off with an orbital sander — another time-consuming but essential job — if you're decorating with paint or wallpaper.

Paint problems

If the paint on plaster, drywall or wood has flaked, blistered or bubbled, scrape off the damaged area with a scraper or a coarse abrasive until a sound paint edge is reached. Wash down the exposed surface, allow to dry and prime before repainting.

If paint on wood repeatedly blisters or discolors, this could mean that there's a knot there that's giving out resin. Use a blowtorch to burn off the discolored part then play the flame gently on it to draw the resin out. Scrape this off, sand the surface and wipe off

all traces of dust, then apply two coats of 'knotting' sealer (available from most hardware shops) to the patch. It must be dry before painting.

Crazing is another common problem, visible as very fine hair-like cracks in a painted surface. On a plastered wall it's often caused by applying the paint before the plaster is completely dry. On wood it may be because the paint underneath the top coat had not completely dried. The remedy is to scrape off the surface and repaint (see also pages 30-32).

REGLAZING A WINDOW

Windows may be a vital barrier against the elements but they're also quite fragile and can be broken easily. When this happens the glass has to be replaced. It's not a complicated job and few specialist tools are required – it does, however, need a degree of care.

Windows may be all shapes and sizes but basically all have a main frame containing one or more fixed or opening frames. The glass is held in a rebate – a narrow 'shelf' – on the outer face of the window, and is kept in place with either angular metal nails called sprigs (on wooden frames) or wire clips (on metal frames). These are then covered with putty, a pliable material which hardens when exposed to the air and provides a waterproof bedding for the glass (see *Ready Reference*).

The technique for reglazing a window depends mainly on what the window frame is made from – and wooden ones are by far the most common.

Removing the glass
Obviously, this has to be done carefully. If necessary, tap the old pane with a hammer until it is sufficiently broken to let you pull out most of the pieces by hand – you should wear thick gloves for protection. Any tiny fragments embedded in the putty can be tugged out with pincers, but don't worry if they refuse to budge. They can wait until the putty is removed.

Preparing the frame
The professional glazier uses a tool called a hacking knife to chop out the old putty. It's an inexpensive tool to buy. If you have an old chisel, you could use this in conjunction with a mallet. If the putty is very old it can be quite stubborn, so take care not to damage the window frame. On multi-paned windows, you should also avoid using so much force that surrounding panes crack.

As soon as the rebate is clear, brush it out. Rub it down with medium grade sandpaper until it is clean and smooth, then give it a coat of ordinary wood primer — not paint because this will prevent the putty drying.

PREPARING A WOODEN FRAME

1 Tap out most of the broken glass with a hammer, then remove the remaining splinters by hand – but wear thick gloves for protection.

2 Chop out the old putty from the rebate using a hacking knife. Tap it with a hammer if necessary. Be careful not to damage the window frame.

3 Pull out the old glazing sprigs with a pair of pincers. If the sprigs aren't damaged you can re-use when fitting the new pane of glass.

Buying new glass

It's important to choose the right type of glass, but don't try to cut it to size yourself. Your local glazier will do a much better job, and is less likely to break the pane in the process. There's also no financial advantage to doing the job yourself for you'll be left with unusable off-cuts. And don't think you can use up that odd piece of glass you may have lying about. Old glass does not cut well at all, and tends to break in the wrong place even when you've scored it with a carbide-tipped glasscutter.

So measure the width and height of the rebate into which the glass must fit; double check the measurements to be sure, and order the glass to be cut 3mm (1/8in) smaller on each dimension. This allows for any slight inaccuracy in your measurements, and avoids the risk of the glass cracking due to expansion or contraction of the frame. If you need patterned glass, make a note of which way the pattern runs.

The fixing process

First you must line the rebate with putty. You can either take a ball of putty in the palm of your hand and squeeze it out between thumb and forefinger using your thumb to press it in; or you can roll the putty into finger-thick sausages and press these into place. Wet your hands before handling putty to prevent it sticking to your fingers, and knead it until it is pliable and any surface oils are thoroughly mixed in.

Next, press the pane into the puttied rebate with the palms of your hands, so that putty oozes out, around and behind the glass. Apply pressure around the edges rather than in the center of the pane and check that, when you've finished, the glass is separated from the frame on the inside by a bed of putty which is 2mm to 3mm (up to 1/8 in) thick.

Now for the unnerving part, nailing the glass in place. It's best to use glazing sprigs,

but you could make do with 19mm (3/4in) panel pins that have had their heads nipped off with pliers. You'll need at least two per side, spaced no more than 230mm (9in) apart, and you must be sure to drive them squarely into the wood so they don't pinch and crack the glass. When you've finished, just over 6mm (1/4in) of pin should be showing.

The final stage is to fill the rest of the rebate with a triangular fillet of putty that neatly covers the pins. Apply the putty in the same way as when lining the rebate, and use a putty knife to do the shaping, mitering the corners of the fillet as neatly as possible. Wet the knife blade to prevent the putty sticking to it as you draw it over the fillet.

Clean off the excess putty — including any that oozed out inside the pane earlier — and allow to dry hard before painting.

When you need to reglaze a window that isn't at ground level, you'll have to work from a ladder. Obviously you'll have to be organized when working at a height. Tap out most of the glass first from inside — and make sure there's no one standing below as you do so. Put all the tools and equipment in a bucket which you can hang on a hook attached to the ladder at the top. Don't try to carry the glass — it's best to get someone to pass it through the window.

Modern windows

Conventional steel-framed windows are reglazed in almost the same way as wooden ones, except that the glass is fixed with wire clips fitting into holes in the frame, rather than with glazing sprigs. Remove these and re-use them to fix the new pane – along with the right type of putty – after priming with a metal primer.

Because putty needs paint to protect it, and because modern aluminum and plastic windows aren't meant to be painted, a different method is used to hold the glass. Normally, it's a variation on the rubber gasket system used to keep the windows fixed in a car.

Just how easy these windows are to reglaze depends on the design; different manufacturers have their own systems and unless it is obvious how the glass fits in, all you can do is ask the window manufacturer for his advice. In some cases, he will prefer to do the repair himself.

Replacing double glazing

There are few problems where secondary double glazing is involved. This system uses a completely separate window frame to hold the extra pane of glass. All you do is treat each element of the system as a single glazed window. One complication you may come up against is where a do-it-yourself

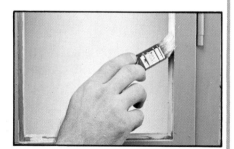

4 *Clean the rebate using medium-grade sandpaper, then remove any dust and prime the rebate with a narrow paintbrush.*

PUTTING IN NEW GLASS

1 *When the primer is dry line the rebate with putty. Hold the putty in the palm of your hand and squeeze it out between your forefinger and thumb.*

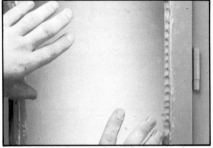

2 *Position a new pane of glass in the rebate. Press it in place gently from the sides to avoid pressure on the center, which could shatter the glass.*

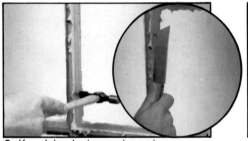

3 *Knock in glazing sprigs using a cross-pein hammer or (inset) the back of a hacking knife. Slide the tool across the surface of the glass.*

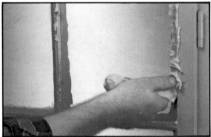

4 *When all the glazing sprigs have been inserted, apply putty to the rebate to cover the edges of the glass. Press it into the angle with your thumb.*

5 *Shape the putty fillet into a slope using the straight edge of a putty knife. The slope shouldn't extend beyond the rebate line on the inside of the frame.*

6 *When you've shaped the putty into a slope, miter each corner with the square edge of a putty knife, laying the blade on lightly to smooth out any ridges.*

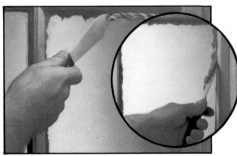

7 *Trim off any surplus putty – from the surface of the glass and (inset) from the inside face of the pane – by running the putty knife along the rebate.*

8 *Leave the putty to dry for about two weeks, then prime, undercoat and top coat. Allow the paint to extend 2 or 3mm (⅛in) onto the glass surface.*

Cross-pein hammer Stanley Tools

double glazing kit has been used. In this case the extra 'frame' may be no more than plastic channelling clipped over the edge of the glass, so it's more a case of remaking this frame than reglazing it.

Replacing double glazing where both panes are mounted in the same frame is more involved, and how you approach it depends on whether factory-made sealed units or two ordinary panes of glass have been used.

In the latter case, you merely fix two new panes in the same way as if reglazing an ordinary window. Just be sure you don't get marks on the panes facing into the double glazing's air gap – you can't clean them off once the second pane is in place.

Factory-made sealed units are also sometimes fitted like a single pane of glass but, more often, you'll have a modern gasket system to contend with. In any case, the most important thing is to order the new sealed units to exactly the right size. They cannot be trimmed if you make a mistake.

Dealing with leaded lights

Strictly speaking, to reglaze a leaded light, you must remove the putty and glazing sprigs from the main window frame and lift out the entire glass and lead latticework, so it can be worked on flat. You may, however, get away with working in situ if you get a helper to hold a sheet of hardboard or something similar against the other side of the pane, to keep it flat while you carry out the repair.

Whichever approach you adopt, you must lever away the lip of lead (called the 'came') holding the glass in place by using an old chisel. Cut the lead near the corners of the pane with a knife to make this easier. Remove the broken glass, clean out the putty from the channel in the lead, apply new putty and then fit the new pane — this should be cut to fit the dimensions of the rebate exactly. Finally, smooth back the lead with the handle of the chisel to hold it in place. To finish, make good the knife cuts with solder, or with a plastic repair compound.

Why glass?

You may be wondering why nobody has come up with a glass or glass substitute that never breaks. Well, they have. Leaving aside bullet-proof glass and the like, there are a host of plastic glazing materials on the market ranging from the familiar acrylic to compounds with complicated chemical names. But they all have two major drawbacks — they are comparatively expensive to buy, and they scratch so easily that they lose their transparency.

Jem Grischotti

REPLACING GUTTERING

The chances are you won't realise there is anything wrong with your home's guttering until it leaks. Note where the water is coming from and, once the rain has stopped, get up a ladder and see what's wrong

The gutters on your home are supposed to capture all the rain falling on the roof and channel it to one or more downpipes. In turn these downpipes take the water into the main drain, a storm drain, or to a soakaway in your garden.

This efficient removal of rainwater is important to keep your outside walls sound. Any missing, damaged, or blocked guttering will result in water cascading down the face of your wall, leading to dampness, and eventually mortar and brick decay. You may be able to repair it; or you may be faced with having to replace whole sections or the complete system.

Gutters are available in steel, aluminum, vinyl, copper and wood. Steel gutters come both galvanized and with a white baked-on enamel coat. Although it's one of the lowest priced eavestrough systems, steel gutters have a short lifespan. The galvanized steel system needs regular painting to keep it looking good. Aluminum gutters are available in a variety of colors, can be cut easily, are lightweight compared to the metal systems and are therefore easier to handle. They are corrosion resistant and need little upkeep. Although you can paint this type of gutter, the baked-on finish is durable, eliminating the need for painting. On the negative side, aluminum gutters aren't as strong as the steel ones and they will dent with light force. Vinyl gutters provide a maintenance-free eavestrough system. Seams are solvent welded and there's little chance for corrosion. Copper gutters need to have soldered joints and leaks could develop at these joints. Other than the possibility of leaks, there's little need for maintenance of this type of system. Copper is corrosion resistant and will develop a green patina over time if left unpainted. Wood gutters need to be painted frequently. They must be allowed to dry out before being painted and the interior surfaces must be sanded. Two coats of asphalt roof paint are applied to the interior while exterior house paint is used on the outside surfaces.

Blockages

You should check why a blockage has occurred in the first place. This may be due to sagging, or poor installation preventing a free run for the water. Or the blockage may be combined with a faulty joint which may be possible to repair. But if galvanized guttering is at all cracked it needs replacing.

If your gutter overflows during heavy rain, the chances are that it's blocked with leaves.

PREPARING FOR WORK

1 *Access is always a problem when working on guttering – a convenient garage roof made this job a lot easier. Scaffold towers are useful on high roofs.*

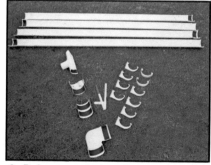

2 *Before you start work assemble all the components you will need. You can check them off against the existing guttering.*

REMOVING OLD GUTTERING

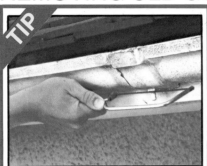

1 *Gutter sections are usually bolted together and these bolts won't come out easily. Saw through the nut.*

2 *When the nut has been detached try to hammer the bolt out but don't use too much force as the gutter itself may crack and collapse dangerously.*

3 *You may need to use a hammer and chisel to get the joints moving. Loosen the joints before unscrewing the gutter sections.*

4 *Galvanized guttering is supported by brackets or screws depending on its profile. You can lift it off brackets, or in this case unscrew it.*

5 *Start to take down the guttering at the point closest to the down pipe – it should come free quite easily even if it's attached directly to the pipe.*

6 *Detach and lift off each succeeding section in turn.*

7 *Always carry pieces of guttering down to the ground, never throw them down.*

8 *Thoroughly brush down the fascia board to remove dirt and cobwebs, then fill any holes using a filler suitable for outside work.*

9 *If the fascia board has not been painted, use this opportunity to do the work. Sand down first and then apply primer and topcoats.*

You can use an old dustpan brush to clean it out, scraping the debris into piles and scooping them out with gloved hands. But prevent any bits from getting into the down-pipe or this may get blocked as well.

Coping with sags

If a section of guttering has sagged, making it lower than the top of the downpipe, the water will not drain away properly. And you will be able to see this from puddles of water collecting in the guttering itself. You must decide whether to raise the sagging section, or lower the mouth of the downpipe to bring everything back into line. If you flex galvanized guttering more than about 25mm (1in) you'll break the seal on the joints, causing a leak. So choose the option that involves moving the guttering least.

In order to reset the guttering to the correct gradient you'll need to fix a piece of string taut between two nails hammered into the fascia board. You can then use this as a guide as you reposition each gutter support in turn.

Leaking joints

Joints in galvanized gutters are made by overlapping the two lengths of gutter, and bolting them together with a layer of sealant in between to form a watertight seal. As this sealant begins to deteriorate with age, the joint starts to leak.

To make the repair, first remove the bolt holding the joint together. Often this is too rusty to undo, so hacksaw off the bolt between the nut and the guttering, or drill out the rest of the bolt. Lever the joint apart with an old chisel, and scrape away all the old sealant. Clean up the joint with a wire brush, then apply a finger-thick sausage of new sealant and bolt the sections back together using a new nut and bolt and a couple of washers. Scrape off any sealant that has oozed out before giving the repair a coat of asphalt-based paint on the inside of the gutter.

Dealing with rust

If one bit of guttering has rusted right through, it won't be long before the rest follows suit, so you may as well save yourself a lot of trouble and replace it all. If meanwhile you want a temporary repair, there are several suitable repair kits on the market. They consist of a sort of wide metal sticky tape which you apply inside the guttering and over the holes with asphalt adhesive.

Choosing a replacement

Assuming you won't be using galvanized again, your choice is between aluminum and plastic. Plastic guttering is made of PVC (polyvinyl chloride). It's probably the better choice for a do-it-yourself installation; it is far more widely available than aluminum, and has the edge in terms of cost and durability.

Two different cross-sections are commonly available — half-round and 'square'. The latter is often given a decoratively molded face similar to the more ornate ogee galvanized guttering. This, together with some brands of conventional profile, can be camouflaged by being boxed in with a clip-on fascia panel. Which type you choose is largely a matter of personal taste, but try to choose something that blends into the style of your home.

The size of the gutter

More important than looks is the size of the gutter. Too small, and it will be forever overflowing; too large, and you will have paid more for the installation than is necessary. It's all to do with relating the amount of water the guttering can carry to the amount of water likely to come off the roof during a heavy rainstorm. These calculations are complicated, but you can assume that they were done when the guttering was originally installed. Just measure the existing gutter-

ing at its widest point to find its size, and buy the same again. The most commonly available sizes are 75mm (3in), 100mm (4in), 112mm (4½in), 125mm (5in), and 150mm (6in). If in doubt, consult the manufacturer's literature.

The actual cross-section of the gutter may vary from brand to brand; this can make it difficult to join with existing guttering: for example, the guttering belonging to a neighbor on a semi-detached or terraced house. Most firms offer adaptors to link their product with galvanized guttering, or with a different size from within their range. However, they tend not to offer adaptors to tie in with the equivalent size from another brand, so if possible stick to one brand throughout the installation. If you have to link up with a neighbor's gutter, find out which brand was used, and try to use the same.

There are many different fittings as well as lengths of guttering available on the market. Before you start buying your new guttering get hold of a manufacturer's brochure from the supplier you use and carefully check to ensure you have all the fittings you will need. Make sure you understand how the particular system works before you buy anything.

Taking down old guttering

Galvanized guttering is heavy, and may also be rusted into place, so removing it can be tricky. But there is no need to be gentle with it; it doesn't matter if it breaks. The important thing is to work in safe conditions. If you are wrenching things apart, do it in a controlled way so you don't fall off the ladder, and so that great chunks of gutter don't fall down. If you toss the guttering clear of the house, you might overbalance and fall off the ladder, so aim to lower larger sections gently to the ground with a rope.

Begin with the section linking gutter and downpipe. Cut through the old bolts holding the sections together. Then, if you lift the gutter slightly, you should be able to pull it free from the downpipe. Once it's out of the way, unmake the joints between the sections of gutter (as if you were repairing them), and lift the guttering off its supporting brackets. It may, of course, be screwed directly to the fascia board.

You can now turn your attention to the brackets themselves. These are usually screwed to the fascia board just beneath the eaves of the roof, and can either be unscrewed or levered off with a claw hammer. In older houses the brackets may be screwed to the tops or sides of the roof rafters, to support the weight of the guttering. If there is a fascia board to which you can fit the new gutter, the ends of the brackets can be hacksawed off. Otherwise,

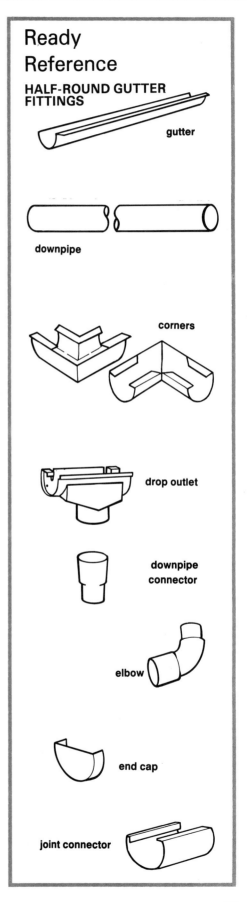

PUTTING UP PLASTIC GUTTERING

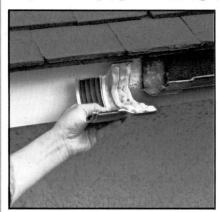

1 If you are joining onto your neighbor's gutter you'll need a special adaptor. Line it with a lump of caulking and bolt it into place.

2 Fix a string at the level of the bottom of the adaptor or end furthest from the downpipe. Hammer a nail into position to hold it in place.

3 Pull the string taut and fix it with a nail at the other end of the gutter run. Make sure it is horizontal by using a spirit level.

4 Fix the brackets at intervals of about 1m (1yd). Drop the first by 6mm (about ¼in) from the string line, the second by 10mm (about ⅜in) and so on.

5 You can now put in the first section of guttering so that it is resting on the brackets, and connect it to the end piece or adaptor.

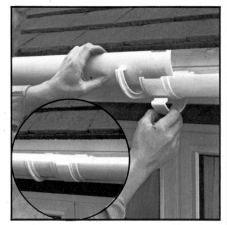

6 Each manufacturer has a different system for making joints. Here the next section rests in the previous one and is then firmly held with a clip.

TIP

7 You will very likely have to cut a section of guttering. Measure it exactly at roof level, then cut it squarely.

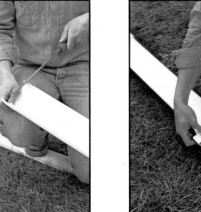

8 In this system, once a section is cut, new notches must be made in the end for the clip. To do this you can use a notch cutter or a wood file.

9 The final corner piece and downpipe fitting is made up on the ground which is the easiest procedure when dealing with small sections.

you will have to lift off some of the roofing to remove them.

When all the old guttering has been removed, inspect the fascia board to make sure it is sound and securely fixed. If it is, fill the old screw holes and paint it before fixing the new guttering. If it isn't, it will have to be replaced. You'll find more information about this in another section.

Fixing new guttering

The obvious first step is to assemble the various bits and pieces you need, and you can use the old guttering system as a model to decide what's required. It's best to measure up the length of the guttering itself, allowing a little extra to be safe.

At the end of the run furthest from the downpipe, fix a gutter support bracket as high up the fascia as possible, and about 150mm (6in) from the end. The fixings here, and elsewhere, are made with 25mm (1in) screws. Choose ones that are galvanized to stop them rusting. Insert a nail into the fascia board level with the bottom bracket.

At the other end of the run, 150mm (6in) from the downpipe, fix another nail, tie a length of string tightly between the two, and use a spirit level to check that this string is level. When it is, lower the second nail by the amount needed to ensure that the guttering runs downhill towards the outlet. This 'fall' varies according to the type of guttering, so check the manufacturer's recommendations. Usually, it is in the region of 5mm (3/16in) for every metre (39in) of gutter run. Once you've found the right line for the gutter, fix another bracket level with the lowest nail.

The next job is to fix the next bracket 1m (39in) from the one at the downpipe end of the run, using the string as a guide to set it at the correct level. Use these two brackets to support a length of gutter with the downpipe outlet attached.

Exactly how you join the gutter to the outlet — or indeed make any other joins in the guttering — will vary from brand to brand. With some, you slip the ends of the components into a special jointing piece called a union, and clip the whole lot together. With others, one of the components will have a union built into its end.

Now work your way along, building up the gutter run as you go and adding additional support brackets as required, again using the string as a guide. In most cases, you will need a bracket every metre, plus one on each side of every join — though some ranges contain combined unions and support brackets. Check the manufacturer's recommendations.

The only problem you may run into is when you have to cut the guttering to length, either to go round a corner, or to finish the run with a stop end. Do the cutting on the ground using a hacksaw, making sure that you cut the end square. Any roughness left by the saw should be cleaned up with a file. If you want to turn a corner, fix the corner piece before cutting the straight piece of gutter to length. You can then use it to work out exactly how long the straight gutter length needs to be. When cutting to finish at a stop end, it is usual to leave about 50mm (2in) of gutter projecting beyond the ends of the fascia.

When you've finished the job and checked to see that all the joints are properly connected, take a bucket of water to the highest point of the gutter and pour it down. If the gutter doesn't drain all the water then go back and check your work.

10 When the whole system is up, you should check that it will work by pouring water in at the point furthest from the downpipe.

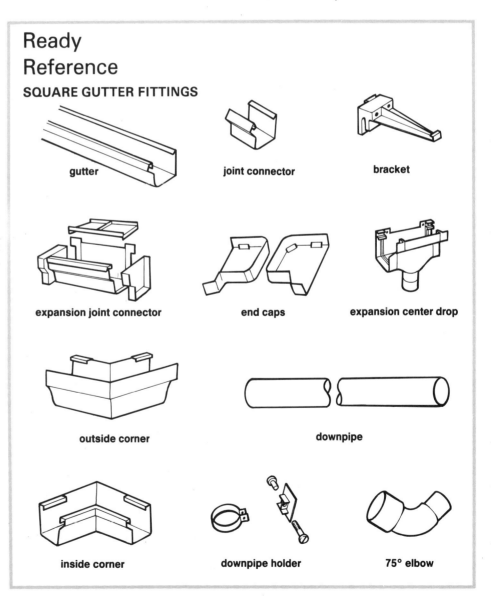

Ready Reference

SQUARE GUTTER FITTINGS

gutter

joint connector

bracket

expansion joint connector

end caps

expansion center drop

outside corner

downpipe

inside corner

downpipe holder

75° elbow

TAP IS LEAKING

Although taps are in frequent use, they rarely need maintenance. But if one starts to leak don't ignore it. Leaking taps are not only annoying and wasteful, but also, if they are hot taps, expensive — you've paid to heat the water going down the drain.

A tap is a device for controlling the flow of water at an outlet point, and is opened and closed by turning a handle. This may be a 'tee' or 'capstan' type (so called because of the shape) fitted onto a stem rising from the body of the tap. Or it may be a 'shrouded head', covering all of the upper part of the tap.

Turning the handle clockwise forces a valve stem down onto a valve seating in the waterway of the tap and stops the flow of water. Because metal against metal doesn't make a very tight seal, a synthetic rubber disc — a washer — is attached to the base of the stem so that it beds firmly onto the seating.

Turning the handle counter-clockwise raises the stem from the seating and allows water to flow. When you open a tap water pressure will also force water around the valve stem and, unless there is some way of preventing it, this would escape from around the stem. To get around this problem some taps have 'O' ring seals fitted to the stem while older taps have greased wool packed tightly in a packing nut around the stem. More modern taps have rubber tube for packing.

Mixers work in exactly the same way as ordinary taps except that they have only one spout that combines the flow of water from the hot and cold supplies. On kitchen mixers particularly this spout can be swivelled so that it can be pushed to one side to give better access to the sink or can supply a double sink.

When a tap starts to leak, there's a strong temptation either to ignore it or to try to stop it by closing it as tightly as you can. Such action is invariably ineffective and could lead to the valve seating being permanently damaged.

Where leaks occur

Basically there are three places a tap can leak: at the spout, in which case the washer and perhaps the seating will need looking at; at the stem when the tap is turned on, which means either the packing or the 'O' ring has failed; or at the swivel point at the spout of a mixer tap, which means that the 'O' ring is at fault. All these repairs are easy to deal with. But first you must know the type of tap and the terminology related to it.

How washers are replaced

Conventional pillar tap This is the basic type of tap design and provides a good example of the procedure to follow when replacing a washer. These taps are commonly used for the hot and cold water supply over the kitchen sink and in this position they are probably the most frequently used taps in the house. It's quite likely that sooner or later the washers will need replacing.

To do this you'll first have to turn off the water supply either at the main entry or at the shut-off valve under the sink which when shut cuts off the supply either to the hot or cold tap without affecting the rest of the system. Turn on the tap fully so it is drained before you start work.

Usually with a pillar tap the stem rises out of a cap or packing nut, which you should be able to unscrew by hand. If this proves too difficult, you can use a wrench, but pad the jaws thoroughly with rag to avoid damaging the finish on plated taps.

Remove the entire stem from the faucet by turning it counter-clockwise. The defective washer is held in place at the bottom with a setscrew. Remove the screw and replace the washer. In an emergency, you can usually reverse the old washer.

Rub some petroleum jelly on the stem and place it back into the faucet body. Turn the water back on at the shut-off valve, turn on the tap and let the water run gently for 15 minutes to remove any air trapped in the pipes.

Tap with shrouded head This is basically a pillar tap where the stem is totally enclosed by a cap that also acts as a handle to turn the tap on and off. Some shrouded heads are

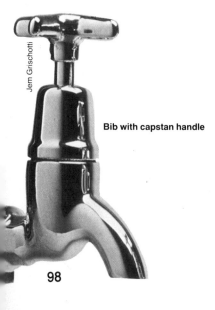

Bib with capstan handle

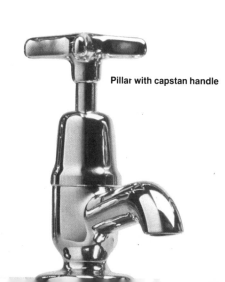

Pillar with capstan handle

Pillar with shrouded head

These three photographs show examples of shrouded mixer taps. You must first remove the cap before you can reach the spindle for repair. Different manufacturers have different methods of fastening the cap so you may have to experiment for removal. Once the cap is removed, repair is identical to the pillar tap.

made of plastic and care is therefore needed when using wrenches. But the mystery of this tap is how to get to the inside — and methods vary with the make of tap.

Some shrouded heads can simply be pulled off, perhaps after opening the tap fully and then giving another half turn. Some are secured by a tiny setscrew in the side. But the commonest method of attaching the head is by a screw beneath the plastic 'hot' or 'cold' indicator. Prise the plastic bit off with a small screwdriver to reveal the retaining screw (normally a cross-headed screw). When the shrouded head has been removed, you'll find that you can unscrew the packing nut to reach the interior of the tap in the same way as with an ordinary pillar tap. Rewashering can then be done in the same way.

Washerless faucets Modern washerless faucets rarely need repair, but when they do, the task is easier to handle than that of faucets with washers. Instead of washers, these faucets use rubber diaphragms or metal to metal contact to stop water flow.

Usually a stem nut rather than a packing nut holds the parts together. Use a wrench to unscrew the stem nut and lift out the assembly.

Use the old assembly as your guide for purchasing a replacement kit.

Bib taps These taps are treated in exactly the same way as a conventional pillar tap.

Bathroom mixer

Kitchen mixer

REPLACING A PILLAR TAP WASHER

1 Pillar taps should be opened fully after turning off the water supply. Now unscrew the cap.

2 Lift up the cap so you can slip an adjustable wrench in to undo the packing nut.

TIP

If there isn't enough space for the wrench, undo the setscrew and then remove the handle.

If the handle won't come out, put a wedge under the cover and try to close the tap and force the cover up.

3 With the handle fully opened, the packing nut can be removed.

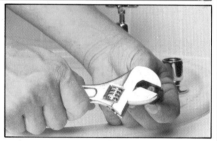

4 Some taps have the washer fixed by a nut; in others it has to be prised off.

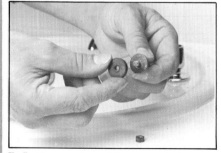

5 Push a washer of the correct size over the end. If held by a nut, clean it with steel wool before replacing it.

6 Push the unit back onto the packing nut and replace in the tap. Turn the handle to half close the tap, then restore the water supply.

SHROUDED TAP

1 With a shrouded head tap, you can either pull it off or prise off the indicator cap with a screwdriver after turning the water supply off and the tap on.

2 Undo the retaining screw (probably a cross-headed type so you'll need the right screwdriver) and then you will be able to pull off the head.

3 Hold the spout to prevent damaging the basin while you unscrew the packing nut using an adjustable wrench.

4 Unscrew the retaining nut, remove the old washer and replace with one of the correct size. Reassemble the tap, then restore the water supply.

Jem Grischotti

Jem Grischotti

WASHERLESS FAUCETS: WATER PIPE AND DRAIN CONNECTION

1 *Assemble spacer and nut to studs then clip under sink with washer. Insert clip and seal (above) into the faucet adaptor.*

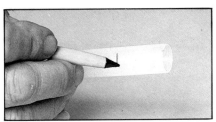

3 *Measure and mark the tubing ⅝'' from the end. This mark will act as a guide when inserting the tube into the coupling nut.*

5 *Remove the nut and gasket from the pop-up body. Put putty under pop-up flange and install in sink. Hand tighten nut making sure the pivot opening faces the faucet.*

2 *Screw coupling nuts onto the faucet adaptors. Hand tighten the coupling nut while griping the faucet adaptor and tube to prevent twisting.*

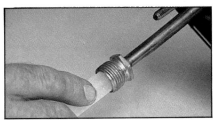

4 *When using ball-nose flexible supply lines, remove inner portion of nut, insert tube through nut and into adaptor.*

6 *Insert pivot rod assembly into pivot opening pressing on the yoke until it locks in place. Insert life rod and adjust pivot rod so that when lift rod is pushed the stopper will open.*

Repairing a poor seating

Sometimes a tap will continue to drip although you've changed the washer. This is usually because the valve seating has become scored and damaged by grit, so the washer can't make a water-tight connection.

You can use a reseating tool to put the problem right. This entails removing the packing nut after the water has been turned off, inserting the tool into the body of the tap and turning it to cut a new seating. It won't be worthwhile buying one of these tools for what is a once-in-a-lifetime job, but you may be able to rent one from a tool rental company.

An alternative method, and certainly one that's a lot easier, is to use a nylon 'washer and seating set'. Again with the water supply off, the packing nut and the washer and stem are removed from the tap end and the nylon liner is placed in position over the seating. The stem and washer are then inserted into the packing nut, which is screwed back onto the tap. The tap handle is then turned to the off position. This action will force the liner into and over the old seating to give a water-tight joint.

You can also use a domed washer to cure a poor seating. It increases the surface area in contact with the waterway and so

Ready Reference

WHAT'S GONE WRONG?

Check out the problem first.
Washers may be worn or disintegrating. Replace with 12mm (½in) or 18mm (¾in) synthetic rubber washers, available from hardware stores. A good tip for a temporary repair is to reverse the old washer.

'O' rings that look worn may also cause leaks. Choose the same size so they fit snugly.

Valve seating is damaged if rough and uneven. You can:
● use a domed, not a flat, washer

● fit a washer and seating set which covers up the damage

● buy or rent a reseating tool to grind the damaged seat smooth

TIPS TO SAVE TIME AND TROUBLE

● If you can't undo the nut holding the washer to the jumper, buy an all-in-one jumper and washer set.

● If a metal cap is stuck pour very hot water over it. It should then unscrew.

● After repairing a tap, leave the water to run gently for 15 minutes to remove any air trapped in the pipes.

LEAKAGE UP THE STEM

1 If the tap has a packing gland around the stem, first try to tighten the packing nut.

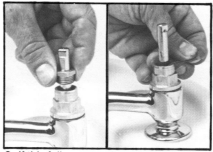

2 If this fails to stop the leak, remove the nut and then pick out the old greased wool stuffing.

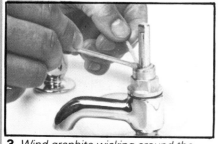

3 Wind graphite wicking around the stem, packing it down tightly.

4 Alternatively you may be able to use a rubber packing washer which just has to be slipped on.

REPLACING 'O' RING SEALS

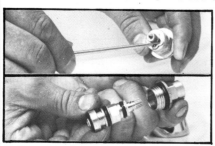

1 To get to the seals on a tap, remove the packing nut and prise off the clip which holds the stem in place.

2 Use a thin-bladed screwdriver to work off the worn 'O' rings and then replace them with new ones.

3 At the swivel point of a spout, first undo any setscrew. Now twist the spout to one side and gently ease it from the mounting.

4 Prise off the worn seals with a screwdriver and then slip new ones into position. Replace the spout back in the mounting, restore water.

effectively cuts off the flow when the tap is turned off even though the top of the valve seating may not be smooth.

Repacking

This is necessary when you turn the tap on and water bubbles up the stem towards the handle. At the same time the tap can be turned on and off far too easily — you might even be able to spin the handle with a flick of the fingers. This fault is a common cause of water hammer — heavy thudding following the closure of a tap or float-valve — that can result in damage to the plumbing system.

Leakage up the stem is most likely to occur in rather old-fashioned — but still very common — taps in which the stem passes through a packing gland filled with greased wool. It's inevitable that water containing detergent will be splashed onto the tap and this may result in the grease being washed out of the gland. The leakage can also be created if you run a garden or washing machine hose from the tap.

Fortunately, to make a repair you don't have to cut off the water supply to the tap, but you must be able to get at the packing nut. This is the first nut through which the stem passes.

Giving the packing nut about half a turn may be enough to stop the leakage up the stem, but eventually all the adjustment available will be taken up and you'll then have to repack the gland. When the packing nut has been unscrewed and removed, the old packing material can be taken out and replaced with graphite wicking. The wicking is wound around the stem and packed down tightly before the packing nut is put back and tightened until the tap handle can be turned fairly easily but without any leaks occurring.

Replacing an 'O' ring

Many modern taps have 'O' ring seals instead of a packing gland or stuffing box. If an 'O' ring fails, the remedy is simply to undo the packing nut, pick out the old 'O' ring and replace it with a new one. Leaks from taps with this fitting are rare. 'O' rings are also found at the swivel point of many mixer taps and if a leak occurs here you have to remove the spout to make the change — but this is usually only held with a setscrew.

Keith Morris

EMERGENCY PIPE REPAIRS

A leaking pipe is no joke. First you have to stop the water – so you need to know where to turn if off – and then to make some kind of emergency repair, even if it's just a holding operation.

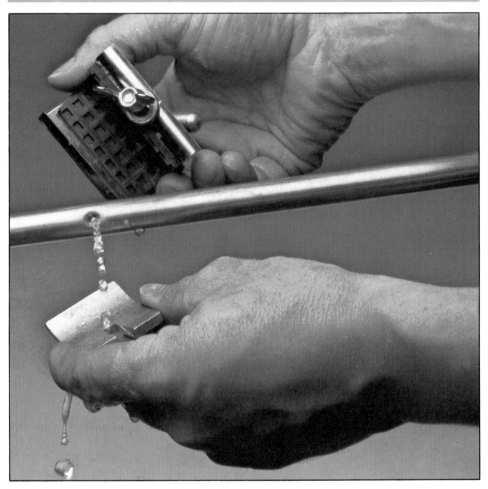

Leaks in domestic plumbing systems have a nasty habit of happening at the most inconvenient of times, often when it isn't possible to carry out a proper permanent repair. What you need is a plumbing emergency first aid kit, and there are now several products available that will at least enable you to make a temporary repair and get the water flowing again.

With any leak, the vital first step is to stop the flow of water. Even a small leak can create a surprisingly large pool of water in no time. Stopping the flow in any pipe is relatively easy provided that you know the locations of the various shut-off valves that isolate parts of your water system, or cut it off completely from the main supply.

Water comes into the house through a pipe known as the rising main, and because water in this pipe (and others leading from it) is under pressure, leaks from it will be particularly serious. It enters the house underground, and from there leads to all the cold taps and a water heating system.

Leaks can result from a number of causes. Pipework may have been forced or strained at some point, resulting in a leak at one of the fittings connecting the lengths of pipe together, or in a fracture at a bend.

Corrosion within pipes may lead to pinholes in pipe lengths, while frost damage can lead to bursts and splits in pipes and to leaks at fittings caused by ice forcing the fitting open. Whatever the cause, cutting off the water supply to the affected pipe is the first vital step.

Ready Reference

TURNING OFF THE SHUT-OFF VALVE

Make sure the family knows where the main shut-off valve is.

● do not force the handle if it has seized up — it could break it off.
● use a hammer or wrench to tap the fitting while pouring penetrating oil down stem.
● if you can't free it call the water authority emergency service — they can turn the water off where your supply pipe leaves the house.
● don't reopen stop valve fully when turning on the supply until a permanent pipe repair is made. This reduces water pressure on a temporary seal.

TIP: MAKESHIFT REPAIRS

If you don't have the right materials at hand, try this:
● bandage insulating tape round the pipe and hole
● cover with a 150mm (6in) piece of garden hosepipe slit along its length and tie with wire at each end, twisting ends of wire together with pliers
● wrap more tape tightly over this

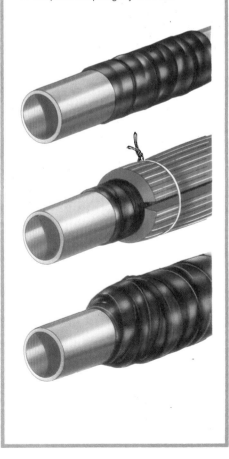

Where to turn off the water

EMERGENCY REPAIRS

● One type of repair kit is based on a two-part **epoxy resin plastic putty** supplied as two strips of differently colored putty in an airtight pack. When the strips are thoroughly kneaded together, the putty is packed firmly round the pipe, where it will harden to form a seal. However, this hardening process takes up to 24 hours and the water supply will have to remain off for this period. (If you don't need to use all the pack in one go, reseal it immediately).

Equal amounts of putty should always be used and mixed together thoroughly until a uniform color results, otherwise it won't harden properly. It's also essential that the pipe or joint is scrupulously rubbed down and cleaned with alcohol or nail polish remover. This will ensure a good bond between the putty and the metal.

● One of the most valuable aids is a multi-size **pipe repair clamp** which has the added advantage of being reusable. It consists of a rubber pad which fits over the hole (for this repair it's not necessary to turn off the water) and a metal clamp which draws the rubber tightly against the pipe when it is screwed in place.

Position the pad and one side of the clamp over the hole, and link the two parts of the clamp together, making sure that the pad is still in place. Tighten the wing nut fully. If the position of the hole makes this difficult, use blocks of wood to hold the pipe away from the wall. This method of repair cannot, of course, be used to mend leaks occurring at fittings.

● Another product uses a two-part **tape** system which builds up waterproof layers over the leak — in the true sense this does form an instant repair. The area round the leak should be dried and cleaned and then the first of the tapes is wrapped tightly round the pipe, covering the leak and 25mm (1in) either side of it. Then 150mm (6in) strips of the second tape, with the backing film removed, are stuck to the pipe and stretched as they are wound round, each turn overlapping the previous one by about half the width of the tape. This covering should extend 25mm (1in) beyond either end of the first layer of tape. The job is completed by wrapping the first tape over all the repair.

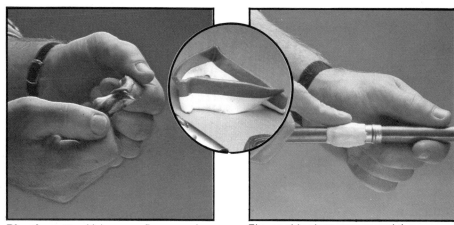

Plastic putty *Using your fingers, mix together equal amounts of the two putty strips. It's ready for use when the color is even all through.*

Thoroughly clean area round the leaking pipe, then pack putty round fitting. It can be sanded smooth when it's completely hard.

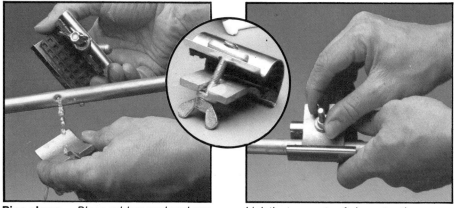

Pipe clamp *Place rubber pad and one side of metal clamp directly over leak in pipe. There's no need to turn off the water with this type of repair.*

Link the two parts of clamp togther, being careful to keep it in position. Screw down wing nut to secure rubber pad against pipe.

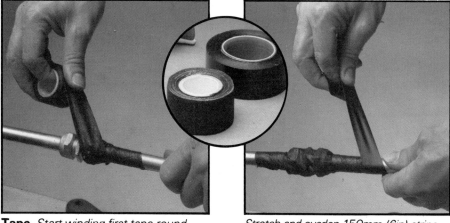

Tape *Start winding first tape round pipe about 25mm (1in) from the leaking fitting. Continue over the joint and for 25mm on other side.*

Stretch and overlap 150mm (6in) strips of second tape round pipe. Continue 25mm (1in) either side of first tape. Finish off with layer of first tape.

CLEARING BLOCKAGES

There are few plumbing emergencies quite as unpleasant as a blocked drain or waste pipe. However, it's usually possible to cure the problem if you know what to do when you've tracked down the blockage and you have the right equipment.

Professional plumbers rarely relish being called out to deal with a blockage. There *are* specialist drain clearance firms, but they can't always be contacted quickly in an emergency — and their charges reflect what can sometimes be the unpleasantness of the job. Drain or waste-pipe clearance is usually well within the capacity of the householder, and there are certainly few more cost-effective do-it-yourself jobs about the house.

Coping with blocked sinks

The outlet of the sink, usually the trap immediately beneath the sink itself, is the commonest site of waste-pipe blockage. Usually the obstruction can be cleared quickly and easily by means of a sink-waste plunger or force cup. This is a very simple plumbing tool obtainable from any hardware or department store. It consists of a rubber or plastic hemisphere, usually mounted on a wooden or plastic handle. Every household should have one.

To use it to clear a kitchen sink waste blockage, first pull out the plug and then lower the plunger into the flooded sink so that the cup is positioned over the waste outlet. Plunge it up and down sharply half a dozen or more times. Since water cannot be compressed, the water in the waste between the cup and the obstruction is converted into a ram to clear the blockage. The overflow outlet is sealed to prevent the force being dissipated up the overflow.

If your first efforts at plunging are unsuccessful, persevere. Each thrust may be moving the obstruction a little further along the waste pipe until it is discharged into the drain gully or the main soil and waste stack.

Should plunging prove unsuccessful you'll have to gain access to the trap. Brass and lead U-shaped traps have a screwed-in plug at the base. With plastic U-shaped and bottle traps the lower part can be unscrewed and removed — see *Ready Reference*. Before attempting this, put the plug in the sink and place a bucket under the trap; it will probably be full of water unless the blockage is immediately below the sink

WHERE BLOCKAGES OCCUR

Blockages can occur in several different places around your home's waste and drain systems. The commonest sites are:

1 *traps under basins, baths and sinks*

2 *toilet traps*

3 *waste pipes running to soil stacks, hoppers or gullies.*

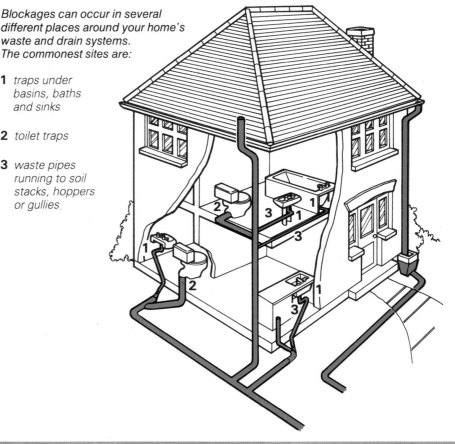

CLEARING BLOCKED TRAPS

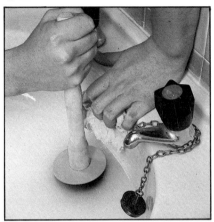

1 *Try using a plunger to clear blocked sinks, basins, baths or toilets. Cover the overflow with a damp cloth, then push the plunger down sharply several times.*

3 *In a confined space like this, you may find it easier to remove the next push-fit elbow before tackling the connection to the waste outlet itself.*

5 *Before reassembling the trap fully, check that the next section of the waste pipe is clear by poking a length of wire down it as far as you can reach.*

2 *If the blockage persists, you will have to open up the trap. Put the plug in the basin and have a bucket handy to catch the trap contents.*

4 *With the trap fully dismantled, wash each component thoroughly to remove the blockage and any scum clinging to the pipe sides. Leave the plug in.*

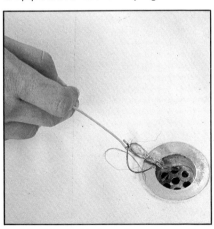

6 *A build-up of hair and scum can often block basin wastes just below the outlet. Fish out as much as possible with a slim wire hook passed through the grating.*

Ready Reference

TYPES OF TRAP

On old plumbing systems you may still come across lead traps, which have a removable rodding eye in the base. On more modern systems plastic traps will have been installed, and it is easy to unscrew part of the trap to clear a blockage.

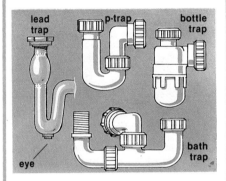

TIP: SUPPORT LEAD TRAPS

Lead traps are very soft, and may bend or split if you use force to open the rodding eye. To avoid this:
● insert a piece of scrap wood into the U-bend of the trap
● undo the rodding eye with a wrench, turning it in the direction shown while bracing the trap with the scrap wood
● reverse the procedure to replace it.

outlet, and the chances are that opening the trap will release it. Having done so, probe into the trap, and into the waste pipe itself. You can buy purpose-made sink waste augers for this purpose, but you'll find that a piece of expanding curtain wire, with a hook on the end, can be equally effective.

Blocked baths and basins
Basin and bath wastes are less likely to be totally blocked than kitchen sink wastes but, when blockages do occur, they can usually be cleared in the same way. (However, be sure to cover the overflow outlet before using the plunger to prevent the force being dissipated up through the overflow opening.) They are, however, very subject to partial blockage. The waste water is often found to run from the bath or basin ever more slowly. This may be due to a build-up of scum, scale and hair on the inside of the waste pipe, and the use of a drain-clearing chemical will usually clear it. These frequently have a caustic soda base, so they should be kept away from children and handled with care, strictly in accordance with the manufacturer's instructions. Before spooning them into the bath or basin waste outlet it is wise to smear petroleum jelly over the rim of the outlet to protect the chromium finish, especially with plastic baths or fittings.

Partial blockage of a wash basin waste may often be caused by hair suspended from the grid of the outlet. This may be all but invisible from above, but probing with a piece of wire (the old standby of a straightened-out wire coathanger is useful) can often produce festoons. If you can't clear the hair by this means, unscrew the nut that connects the threaded waste outlet to the trap and pull the trap to one side. Now use a pair of pliers to pull the hair away from beneath the grid.

CLEARING BLOCKED GULLIES

1 Both surface-water and yard gullies are easily blocked by wind-blown debris such as waste paper and dead leaves. First lift off the gully grating.

2 Try to scoop out as much debris as possible from the gully trap, either by hand or with an improvised scoop such as an old tin can.

3 If the blockage is cleared and the water flows away, scrub out the sides of the gully with a brush and detergent. Clean the gully grating too.

4 Finally, hose the gully out thoroughly with running water. If you are unable to clear the blockage, you may have to rod the drain run from a nearby manhole.

Overflows from gullies
Where waste pipes and downpipes discharge into gullies, the first signs of trouble may be when the gully overflows and the surrounding area is flooded as a result. The gully trap has probably become blocked, either by blown leaves or other debris, or by a build-up of grease and scum on the sides of the trap. Raise the gully grid if one is fitted (and get a new one if it's broken or missing). Then scoop out any debris with a rubber-gloved hand or an improvised scoop, scrub the gully out with caustic soda and flush it through with plenty of clean water before replacing the grid.

Blockages below ground
One sign of a blockage in the underground drains may be a toilet which, when flushed,

fills with water almost to the rim and then very slowly subsides. You'll need a power auger to clear most underground blockages. Most tool rental firms will have power augers available.

Determine where the blockage is and remove the closest clean-out plug. Feed the auger cable into the drainpipe slowly until it reaches resistance. Then feed it more slowly so that it will cut through the blockage. When the cable reaches an impasse, you've probably hit the main sewer.

Remove the cable and flush the drainpipe with a garden hose.

Blocked gutters
Roof rainwater gutters may become obstructed by leaves or other objects. An overflowing gutter isn't an instant catastro-

phe but, if neglected, it will cause dampness to the house walls. An inspection, removal of debris and a hose down of gutters should be a routine part of every householder's preparations for winter.

UNCLOGGING DRAINS

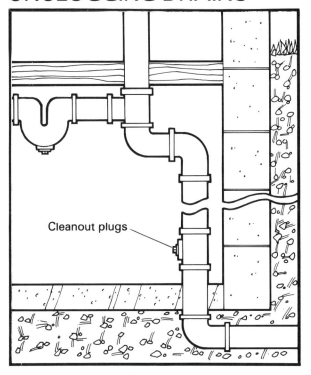

Cleanout plugs

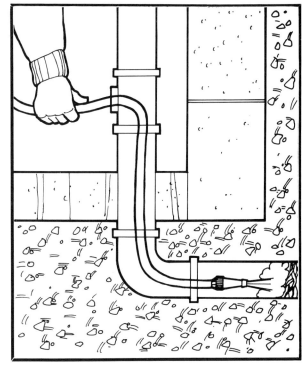

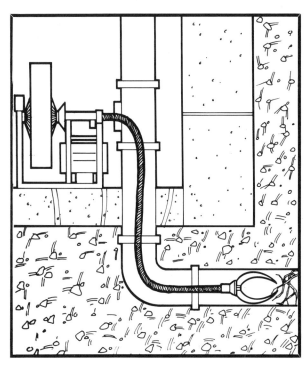

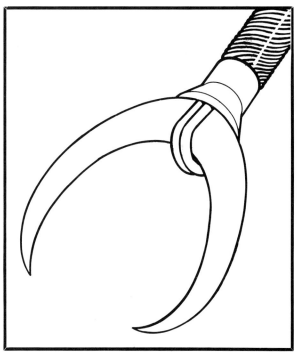

Cleanout plugs allow for easy access to the drain system to clear blockages. A garden hose can be used to flush out soft blockages in the system. An electric auger automatically feeds into the sewer line to clean a blockage. The auger blade is razor sharp and spins on its rod to cut through obstructions.

TOILETS

Don't let a toilet frighten you. Most toilet repairs are within the scope of the homeowner's skills.

A toilet operates through a chain reaction of events. When someone depresses the flush lever, the trip lever pulls the tank ball out of the ball seat, causing the water in the tank to rush out through the ball seat into the bowl. Gravity forces the waste water in the bowl to pass through the toilet trap and into the drain. As the water in the tank drains, the tank ball drops back into position on the ball seat. The float ball, which descends as the water level drops, forces the float valve in the ballcock assembly to open, letting water in through a filler tube to refill the tank and through the overflow tube to refill the bowl. As the water in the tank rises, the float ball ascends, and, at a predetermined point, shuts off the float valve, completing the cycle.

The following is a list of some of the most common toilet problems, along with some suggestions for repair.

Running water, tank won't refill

This means the tank ball isn't positioning itself properly in the ball seat. You may be able to solve this problem by moving the guide arm on the overflow tube to adjust the ball seating. If this doesn't work, then a worn, damaged tank ball could be the problem. To remedy, shut the water off at the stop valve underneath the toilet tank, remove the old ball and replace it with one of the exact dimensions.

The ball seat could also be corroded. To eliminate this problem, shut off the water at the stop valve, drain the tank, let it dry and sand the ball seat until it's smooth. Then turn the water back on.

Another source of the problem could be in the flush lever, trip lever, lift chain or wires that are bent or misaligned. Reshape these metal pieces if possible, or replace with new ones.

Whistling toilet, water keeps running despite a filled tank

The float valve in the ballcock assembly isn't closing fully. Lift the float arm. If this stops the flow, then the water level in the tank isn't high enough to shut off the float valve. But a higher water level could mean the overflow tube will be filled, causing water to drain into the toilet bowl. The water level should be about 25mm (1in) below the top of the over-

flow tube. To solve the problem, bend the float arm to lower the float ball, which will cause the water flow to shut off sooner. If the float ball won't rise high enough, it could be waterlogged and in need of replacement. Unscrew it and install a new one.

If the problem still isn't rectified, the fault could be in the float valve itself, with a damaged washer or valve seat. Remove ballcock assembly and replace necessary parts.

Tank partially flushes

The tank ball may not be rising high enough to allow the water to drain with any force. Shorten the tank-ball lift wires or chain to correct the problem.

Condensation on tank

Condensation occurs when the cold water in the tank cools the tank walls. When the warm air of the room hits the cold tank walls, water drops form on the tank. To correct the problem, line the inside of your tank with foam sheets that can be purchased from a

plumbing supply dealer. Another, more permanent method is to install a tempering valve, which allows a little hot water to mix with the cold water in the tank, raising the water temperature.

Clogged drains

When the water in the toilet bowl starts to rise above its normal level, you can help prevent overflow by removing the tank lid and closing the flush valve by hand.

Use a stiff wire to remove the obstruction. If that fails, use a plunger, which has a special tip to fit the toilet bowl drain outlet. The plunging action creates a force that either pushes the obstruction into the drain or sucks it back into the toilet.

If the plunger fails to work, a toilet auger will negotiate the curves of the toilet trap to help force the obstruction into the drain.

If neither the plunger nor the auger work, go to the nearest clean-out plug and, again using an auger, work it back toward the toilet.

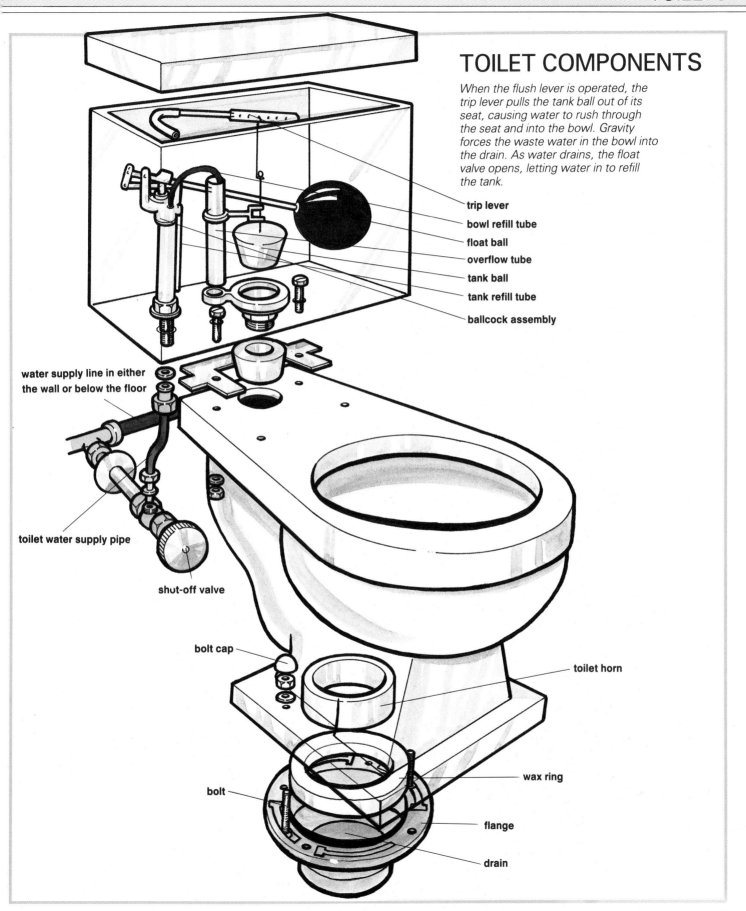

TOILET COMPONENTS

When the flush lever is operated, the trip lever pulls the tank ball out of its seat, causing water to rush through the seat and into the bowl. Gravity forces the waste water in the bowl into the drain. As water drains, the float valve opens, letting water in to refill the tank.

trip lever

bowl refill tube

float ball

overflow tube

tank ball

tank refill tube

ballcock assembly

water supply line in either the wall or below the floor

toilet water supply pipe

shut-off valve

bolt cap

toilet horn

wax ring

bolt

flange

drain

LEAKY BASEMENTS

Protect your home from odors and mildew by taking the necessary steps to keep moisture out of your basement.

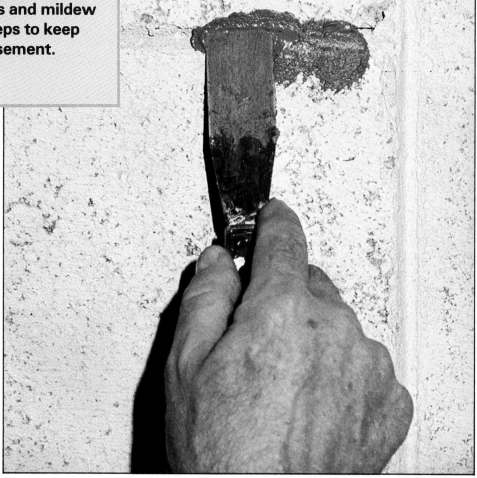

The source of a wet basement is usually on the exterior of the house; therefore the best remedy will be done from the outside. But there are several interior basement repairs that should be attempted first before tackling a major water blockage job from the exterior.

Interior repairs
If your foundation is porous, water could be seeping through the walls and floors and turning into humidity in the basement. High humidity can cause odors and mildew.

Coat your walls and floor with a cement waterproofing material that will expand and harden once it enters the pores of the concrete. To apply the compound, wet your walls or floor, then brush or trowel the cement-based compound over the surface, making sure it's forced into all cracks and crevices. Apply a second coat within 24 hours.

Humidity can also manifest itself in the form of condensation. Warm air is filled with water vapor. As warm air hits a colder surface, water drops or condensation forms. Because basement walls are cold from being next to the cold ground, any warm air inside the basement or warm air coming into the basement through open windows or doors will form condensation on the walls. A heated basement with insulated and finished walls will help solve the problem, but if you prefer to leave your basement unfinished, invest in a dehumidifier to help reduce excess moisture in the air, and cover cold-water pipes with insulation to prevent condensation. Also make sure your clothes drier, which is the major cause of condensation in the house, is vented to the outside.

If there's evidence of water puddling after a rainfall, you could have a crack or crevice in your foundation wall. Even cracks that don't appear wet should be repaired, since they will eventually start leaking.

There are two types of crack — moving and stable. If a crack continues to enlarge, major repairs could be necessary. In this case, it's best to consult a professional.

A stable crack can be repaired with a patching compound. To fix, chisel the crack wider, undercutting the hole so that it's wider at the back. This keeps the patching material from falling out. Brush or vacuum out any dust. Dampen the hole and fill it with a patching compound of 1 part cement to 3 parts sand. A chemical additive should also be mixed in to prevent shrinkage and assist bonding.

If you need to plug a crack while water is seeping through it, use a quick-setting hydraulic mortar. Water is added to the compound, which is then shaped into a plug. After the hole is undercut with a chisel, the plug is inserted and held in place until it hardens.

If water is leaking through the join at the floor and wall, an epoxy resin can be added to make a flexible seal. Chisel out the join, undercutting it on the inside. Vacuum out the dust and fill with the two-part epoxy mix. Use this method only if there has been a period of no rainfall.

Exterior repairs
If the inside wall treatments don't solve your problem, then exterior waterproofing will be necessary. Exterior waterproofing tends to be more effective, because it prevents water from entering the walls in the first place.

A simple exterior remedy is to regrade the soil around the house so that it slopes gently away from the walls, forcing surface water to drain away from the house.

Another method is digging a trench at the foundation. If the cracks are near the surface, dig down below them, patch the wall with asphalt and cover it with a plastic sheet. Backfill the hole with gravel to a depth of about 60cm (2ft), then cover with topsoil. Make sure the grade is sloping away from the house.

A more serious leakage problem lower on the basement wall could be caused by considerable water pressure. The remedy for this would involve digging a trench around the house down to the footings, covering the foundation wall with asphalt and plastic sheeting, and laying new drain tiles to collect the excess water and take it away from the foundation walls. Cover the drain tiles with a thick gravel bed and backfill the trench again, making sure the fill slopes gently away from the house.

EXTERIOR REPAIRS

To waterproof an exterior foundation wall, first dig a trench by the wall. Clean and fill all mortar cracks. When dry, apply a thick coat of sealer. If you need to remove groundwater, dig the trench to the base of the footings and lay new drain tiles with a slope of 12mm (½ in) per 30cm (1ft) leading to a sewer or dry well.

STAIRS

Stringers, treads, risers and balustrade combined make up the parts of a staircase. And each part can develop its own particular repair problem.

Staircases are usually of two basic types — the closed stringer and the open stringer. A stringer is the sloping board running diagonally between floors into which fit the steps. The top edges of an open stringer are cut with sawtooth notches to accommodate the horizontal treads and vertical risers of the steps. In a closed stringer, the top edges are straight and grooves are cut into the stringers to accommodate treads and risers.

Most homes have a combination of closed and open stringers in a staircase. The stringer against the wall is usually a closed one, with the open stringer facing out into a hallway or room.

Repair work is easier on a staircase with an open stringer, since work can be done from above. On a closed-stringer staircase, repairs must be handled from underneath the steps, which may involve removal of plaster or drywall. If there's an additional support running below the steps on a closed-stringer staircase, small repairs become major structural tasks and it might be best to call in the professionals.

An open-sided staircase has a balustrade of newel posts, balusters and handrail.

Most staircase repairs, then, will center around treads, risers and the balustrade. When making repairs, remember that the balustrade is hardwood and pilot holes should be bored for all nails and screws to prevent the wood from splitting. Old glue must be scraped away from joints to allow for proper adhesion of freshly glued joints.

Repairing squeaky treads and risers

Due to the hygroscopic nature (the shrinkage and expansion) of wood and the settling of a house, staircases can develop a number of minor problems that need attention.

The most common stairway ailment is a squeaky tread. This is caused by the tread rubbing against the riser or the stringer.

Your first job is to locate the source of the squeak, and this could be in a number of spots on a step — loose nails, warped treads or risers, loose glue blocks which are underneath the steps to strengthen the tread-and-riser joint, or loose wedges that fit snugly underneath treads and risers in the grooves of a closed stringer.

As mentioned previously, repairs made from above are the easiest, and there are a couple of repairs that can be handled from above the stairs to silence a squeaky tread.

If the squeak comes from the front of a tread at the top of a riser, spiral-shanked floor nails can be driven into the tread-and-riser joint at opposing angles.

If tread movement is substantial when the tread is walked on, you can use glue wedges to repair the spring. Thin wooden wedges coated with a carpenter's glue can be driven into the bottom of the riser, on the underside of the tread where it joins the riser. Use a sharp utility knife to trim the wedges, then cover the repair with a decorative molding strip.

If the squeak is at the end of the tread close to a closed stringer, it could be a result of loosened glue wedges underneath the steps. If you can gain access to the steps underneath the staircase, remove the old wedge with a chisel and remove the dried glue. Cut a new wedge to fit snugly into the gap. Coat the groove and the wedge with glue and drive the wedge into position tightly under the tread. New wedges can also be driven into the tread-and-riser joint for support.

Glue blocks fastened to the tread-and-riser joint can be worked loose by footfalls on the steps. Remove old blocks, cut new ones, coat with glue and screw into position from two sides.

Balustrade repairs

Although a loose baluster can be tightened with glue, screws or wood wedges, a broken baluster presents a danger and needs to be replaced.

Fixing loose balusters with wedges can be handled in the same manner as wedges on treads and risers.

To fasten a loose baluster with a screw, drill a hole at an angle through the baluster and into the handrail, stringer or tread. Drive screw, countersink, and fill the hole with wood filler.

To remove a broken baluster, determine what type of baluster you have. Square-topped balusters fit into a groove in the bottom of the handrail, and the groove between the balusters is filled with a wood block. Round balusters usually end in dowels that fit into holes at both ends of the baluster. Frequently the bullnose molding on the side of a tread will have to be removed in order to replace a baluster.

To remove the baluster, saw it into two pieces, twist them with a wrench to break the glue joint, then pull out the baluster. If the baluster refuses to budge, saw it flush with the tread or handrail, then drill out the ends with a spade bit to create new holes.

PARTS OF A STAIRCASE

A staircase is composed of six parts – stringers, newel posts, balusters, handrail, treads and risers. The stringers support the staircase; the bottom newel post supports the bottom steps; the baluster supports the handrail; the handrail is fastened into the newel posts and baluster; and the treads and risers are the steps. The staircase can have either two closed stringers, or, what is most common, one closed stringer against the wall and one open stringer.

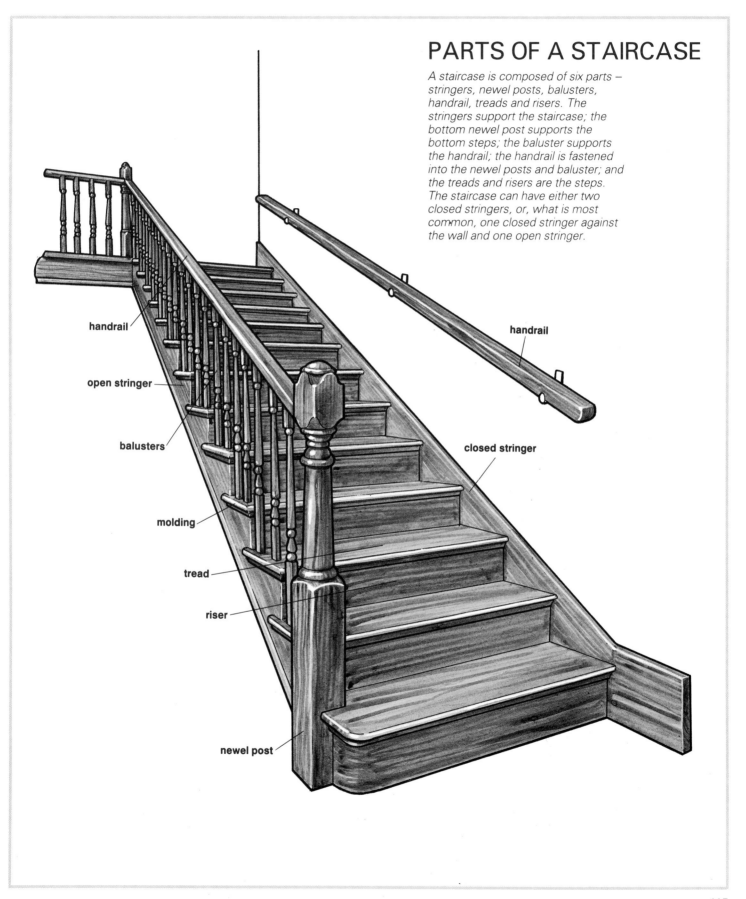

handrail

handrail

open stringer

balusters

closed stringer

molding

tread

riser

newel post

REPAIRING SQUEAKING STAIRS

1 *Drive a series of nails at opposing angles into the tread and through to the riser to silence squeaks that are coming from the front of the tread.*

2 *Coat a wooden wedge with glue and drive it into the bottom or top of the riser to stop squeaks coming from the rear of the tread or from the riser.*

3 *Cut the wedges with a utility knife flush with the base of the riser or tread. Cover the join with a strip of molding to conceal the repair.*

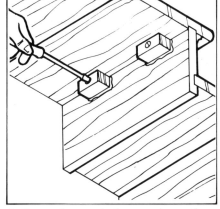

4 *To repair squeaks from underneath the staircase, glue and screw wooden blocks at the join of the tread and the riser.*

5 *Metal angle brackets can also be fastened to the back side of the treads and risers both for stability and to silence squeaking.*

6 *Glue-coated wooden wedges can also be installed from underneath the stairway. Drive them into place with a wood block to ensure a tight fit.*

To install the new baluster, coat joint ends with glue; install bottom first then lift up the handrail to position the top. Nails can be driven into the top and bottom for extra support.

A loose newel can be tightened by drilling and screwing from the floor below or through the newel into the stringer.

Treads, risers and stringers
House-settling can cause the stair stringers to pull away from the steps. This gap can be corrected by driving wedges between the wall and the stringer to force the stringer back against the steps. Only small gaps (less than 12mm/½in) can be corrected this way. Larger gaps forced closed by wedges could crack the stringers. A larger gap usually means stair replacement.

If treads are cracked or badly worn, they need to be replaced.

First, remove the bullnose side molding and balusters. Pry up the tread carefully. If the tread is nailed to the top riser, work the tread until there's enough of a gap to insert a saw to cut the nails, then carefully pull the tread off the bottom riser and out from the closed-stringer grooves.

If a new riser is necessary, cut to fit and mitre the corner that joins to the open stringer. Glue in the wedges on the closed-stringer side first then position the riser, making sure the mitred edges on the open-stringer side fit perfectly. Drive nails into the backside of the riser and through to the vertical stringer groove on the closed stringer. Glue and nail the mitre joint.

Cut a new tread to fit. Mark the mitred corner location for the bullnose molding on the open-stringer side and mark baluster locations. Cut the side and mitre corner to accommodate the molding and cut the baluster holes. Make any cuts necessary to fit the stringer shapes. Cut dado to fit the riser tongue.

Fit and glue a wedge into position on the closed-stringer side. Spread adhesive on the stringers, slide the tread into position, closed-stringer-side first, and tap tread to make a tight fit. Nail tread and bullnose molding into place, countersinking nails and filling with wood putty. If the underside of the stairs is accessible, drive nails through the top riser and into the edge of the new tread.

If both sides of the staircase are closed stringers and the underside of the staircase is accessible, treads and risers can be removed by chiselling out old wedges, sawing the riser tongue from above the stairs and pulling the riser loose. The tread is tapped from the front to push it out of its groove.

New treads and risers are cut to fit. New wedges are fitted and glued, then the riser-and-tread joint is reinforced by screwing or nailing.

REPLACING TREADS AND RISERS

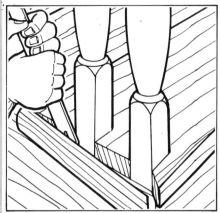

1 To replace treads and risers, you'll first need to remove the balusters. Pry off the side molding on the tread and slide the balusters out from their slots.

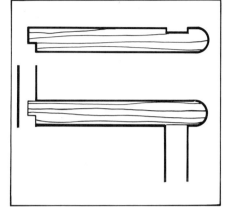

2 Remove any trim from the front of the tread and pry up the tread slightly. Use a saw to cut through any nails, then pry the tread loose.

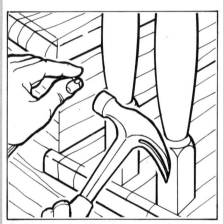

3 Treads can often be reused by turning them over, sanding the underside smooth, then cutting any new grooves into the bottom.

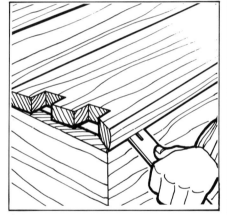

4 When replacing the riser, glue a wedge in place first then position the riser. Hammer nails at an angle through the riser and into the stringer.

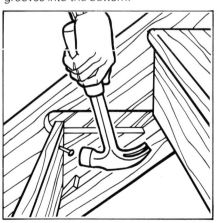

5 Glue and nail the riser mitre joint on the open stringer side of the stairway. Use a nailset to force the nails below the surface then fill with wood filler.

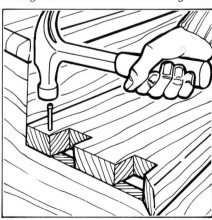

6 Nail the tread into position on top of the riser. One end fits into a groove on the closed stringer side, the other is nailed to the top of the open stringer.

BALUSTERS

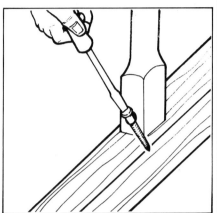

1 Balusters support the handrail and a loose baluster can eventually force the handrail out of alignment. To tighten a baluster, cut a wedge out of hardwood.

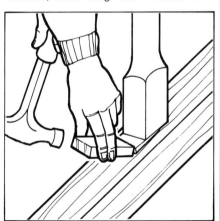

2 Make sure the grain runs lengthwise on the wedge. Coat the wedge with glue and drive it into the gap at the top of the baluster.

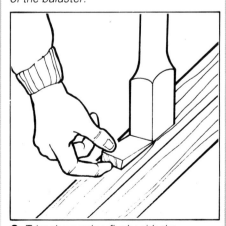

3 Trim the wedge flush with the baluster and let the glue dry before using the handrail. A countersunk screw can be used to refasten baluster.

DOORS
Whether it's changing a lock or shimming a bind, you can easily fix any interior or exterior door problem.

Warping, house-settling, loose or improperly installed hinges can cause a door to bind. And in most cases the remedy is simple.

Binding
To repair a loose hinge, open the door fully and insert a wedge at the bottom of the latch side of the door. This will prevent stress on the one hinge leaf as you remove the faulty hinge. You may be able to solve the problem by installing bigger hinges. If not, enlarge the screw holes to 60mm (¼in) then glue and insert a length of 60mm (¼in) dowel. Sand the dowel flush, then screw the hinge back in place with the original screws.

If the door is binding because of mortises that have been cut too deep, you can shim the hinge to correct the bind. Again, open the door fully and insert a wedge at the bottom of the latch side. If the bind is at the bottom, you must shim the top hinge and vice versa. Remove the hinge leaf from the doorjamb and cut a thin cardboard shim the size of the door mortise. Insert the shim between the doorjamb and the hinge leaf and drive the screws home.

If the door binds at the top or still slightly binds on the latch side after you've shimmed the hinge, plane the edge of the door down at the binding location. You can do this without removing the door. But if the door binds at the bottom, or on the hinge side, door removal is necessary. Use a hammer and pry bar to tap up the head of the hinge pins, remove the hinges and plane the high spots.

Latch and strike adjustment
If your latch and strike plate aren't engaging but the latch is in line with the strike, then place a thin cardboard shim under the latch plate.

If the latch and strike are misaligned, and the range is minor, file the strike plate hole to enlarge it slightly. If the misalignment is greater, remove the strike plate and, using a chisel and mallet, extend the mortise in the proper direction.

Doors that won't close far enough for the latch to engage can be corrected by removing the stop molding, latching the door and drawing a line on the jamb where the stop molding must be repositioned.

Curing warps
Warped doors can be corrected by either supporting the door on blocks and placing heavy weights on the bow for at least a day, or by using a turnbuckle to tighten a wire placed in screw eyes located diagonally across the door.

Replacing a threshold
To remove an old threshold, open the door fully or remove door if necessary. Remove doorstop if necessary and pry up threshold with pry bar or claw hammer. If the threshold extends under the jambs and you can't re-move it intact, saw the threshold into three pieces, remove the middle section and then work out the side sections from under the jambs.

If possible, use the old threshold as a pattern for the new one. Cut the new threshold out of hardwood and make sure it fits snugly against the door trim. Drill holes and counter-sink nails or screws.

Installing new door locks
Door locks can be replaced easily as long as

LOOSE HINGES

1 To repair a door hinge, you must first open the door fully and insert a block of wood at the bottom of the latch side of the door to prevent stress on the hinge.

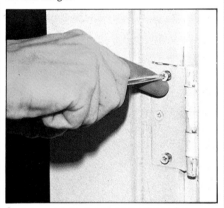

2 A loose hinge can sometimes be repaired by installing a bigger hinge or by enlarging the screw holes, inserting a dowel and screwing the hinge back in.

3 Binding caused by a mortise that is too deep can be corrected by inserting a cardboard shim between the jamb and hinge leaf on the non-binding hinge.

DOOR REPAIRS

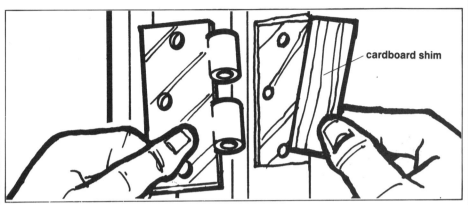

cardboard shim

Sometimes a door will resist closing. A narrow cardboard shim placed between the hinge leaf and door jamb may be all that's necessary to repair the problem.

1 File away small portions of the strike plate to enlarge the opening if the latch is only slightly misaligned with the strike plate.

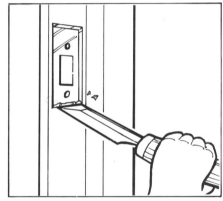

2 If the misalignment is too great to allow for filing of the strike plate opening, or if the door rattles, cut a new mortise and relocate the strike on the jamb.

1 To replace a threshold, saw or chisel the old one out. Use it for a pattern if possible. Cut the new saddle and tap it gently into place.

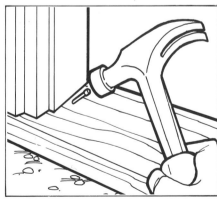

2 Predrill nail holes on each side of the threshold. Drive finishing nails into place, countersinking them with a nailset. Fill holes with wood filler.

you know the type of lock on your door and are sure of your measurements when buying a replacement lockset.

The three major lock types found in most homes are the mortise lock, cylindrical lock and the tubular lock.

Most mortise locks are found on front-entry doors. The lockset usually has a latchbolt and a deadbolt combination in a rectangular box that fits into a recess in the edge of the door. The door must be at least 3.5cm (1⅜in) thick to accommodate these locks.

To install a mortise lock, make the location for the cylinder hole and spindle using a template (usually provided with the lockset). Drill the holes. Mark the location of the lock body on the edge of the door and drill a series of holes the depth of the lock body into the door edge. Use a chisel to remove the excess wood and then insert the lock body to check for fit. Once the body fits, mark the face plate outline on the edge of the door, remove the lock body and then cut the mortise for the face plate to ensure a flush fit. Screw the body into position, attach the handle and knob. The interior knob is usually locked into place with a setscrew.

Mark the strike plate position on the doorjamb. Check to make sure it's accurate and then chisel the mortise and holes for the latchbolt and deadbolt.

Cylindrical locks are inserted through a hole cut in the face of the door and a recess cut in the edge of the door for the latch. The exterior knob has a keyway and the interior knob has a push button to unlock the latch.

To install a cylindrical lock on an old door, remove the old lock and strike plate. Measure the diameter of the cylinder hole and latch hole to ensure that the new lock you buy will be the correct size.

To install a cylindrical lock on a new door, use the template provided with the lockset kit and, with a hole saw, drill the holes in the door face and edge. For the cylinder hole, drill from both door faces into the center to prevent fraying or splitting of the wood. Make sure the hole for the latch is in the center of the door edge and is perpendicular to the cylinder hole.

Insert the latch and with a sharp pencil mark the outline of the face plate on the door. Remove the latch and chisel the mortise, making sure the face plate will sit flush with the surface of the door edge. Screw the latch into position.

Mark the center line of the strike plate on the doorjamb with a vertical and horizontal line to match the center on the latch. Drill a hole at the center point to accept the latch. Line up the strike plate screw holes with the vertical line, making sure the center of the strike plate is in the center of the latch hole you just drilled. Mark the outline of the strike plate on the jamb and cut the mortise with a chisel to ensure a flush fit for the strike plate. Install the strike plate then install the knobs, following the instructions in the lockset kit.

Tubular locks are similar to cylindrical locks, except they're not as sturdy and do not have a keyway, although some can be locked with a push button. They are used on interior passage doors. Installation of the tubular lock is identical to that of the cylindrical lock.

Repairing sliding doors
Closet bypass doors (sliding doors) are usually hardboard panels supported by a top and bottom rack in which wheels glide to facilitate door movement. They can develop problems with misaligned wheels or bent tracks.

Determine the cause of the problem and then remove the door panels. Top-hung doors are removed by lifting the door up and swinging the bottom out to clear the track. If the top track has a space where wheels can be removed, slide the door until the wheels are in position, then lift the door out of the top track.

If the tracks are bent, place a block of wood against the track and hammer the wood lightly, moving the wood along the track as you hammer until the track is straight. Make sure all screws are securely fastened, since a loose screw can cause a bind in the track.

Check wheel alignment. Any misaligned wheel can usually be set with an adjustable screw on the wheel assembly.

To rehang the door, put the top into position first.

FLOORS

Squeaks, sags and splits are part of any homeowner's vocabulary when it comes to keeping floors in top condition.

Most homeowners have experience with squeaky floors. The pattern of noises that follows you as you walk across a floor usually means some loose floor boards. Repairing squeaks in either the finished flooring or subfloor is a fairly simple procedure, but a sagging floor is a major problem that should be dealt with immediately.

Sagging floors

Floor-sagging is a result of weakened joists and posts. This weakness has a number of causes, including improper original construction, house-settling which shrinks or warps the joists, heavy loads on a floor not built to handle them, rotting wood, or house additions that put stress on the existing floor.

If left unrepaired, a sagging floor can cause major structural damage to a house. Sagging floors will show up in windows that won't open no matter how hard you try or what method you use, doors that jam tightly, cracking plaster and sloping floors that have lost their feeling of solidity.

To correct a sag, install jackposts in the basement. These posts are made from two telescoping steel tubes with an adjustable steel-pin locking mechanism.

To use the jack, place a large wooden beam or concrete footing on the concrete floor and position the jack base plate on it. Position another beam under the joists and slide the top plate of the jack into position under the top beam. Turn the jack handle slowly until you feel slight resistance. At this point you *must* stop the jacking and wait 24 hours before any more pressure is applied. Any further lifting of the steel jack could cause serious structural damage to the house — joists and studs could crack and wall plaster could fall. After at least twenty-four hours, turn the jack handle no more than 6mm (¼in). Wait a week before turning another 6mm (¼in). The process should be done slowly over a number of weeks to prevent structural damage. Keep checking the level of the floor to determine when the sag has been corrected.

Squeaky floors

A floor is actually two layers thick. The top layer (the finished flooring) is either wood or a surface covering such as linoleum, and the subfloor is usually plywood sheathing.

JACKPOST

An adjustable jack post offers a permanent solution to a sagging floor. The bottom plate is secured to a concrete footing at least 24'' square and 12'' thick. Check your local building code for steel jack post installation requirements.

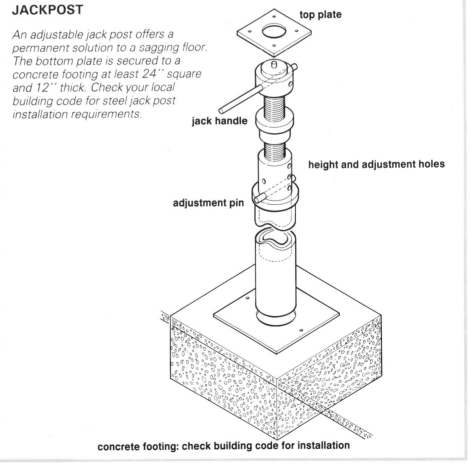

concrete footing: check building code for installation

When a floor squeaks, it usually means loose boards in either the finishing or subflooring.

If the joists under the floor are exposed, the damage can usually be repaired from underneath. Locate the source of the squeak and drive a wedge between the subfloor and the top of the joist to support the loose boards. Or you can nail a 2 × 4 to the side of the joist, with the top edge of the 2 × 4 forced tight against the bottom of the subfloor to take up the slack.

If joist movement is causing the squeak, toenail some diagonal bridging between the joists to stop the movement.

If the squeak is between joists, diagonal bridging may be helpful, or you can install pieces of 2 × 8 at right angles between the joists, forcing the top edge of the 2 × 8 tight against the subfloor.

Loose or warped boards on finished flooring can be repaired by drilling clearance holes into the finished floor and driving flooring nails through the board into the subfloor. When possible, nail into a joist.

Squeaks in floors where there are no exposed joists must be handled from above. Locate the squeak, and drive flooring nails through the floor and into a joist. To find the joist, hammer-tap a block of wood over the floor until you hear a solid tapping sound rather than a hollow one. The solid sound will mean you've found the joist. Countersink the nails on a wood-finished floor and fill with a matching wood putty.

Repairing floorboards

To replace split or worn floorboards, drill holes across the width of the damaged board to provide an opening for grasping the board for removal. Make sure you don't drill into the subfloor. Use a stop block on your drill bit to ensure the holes go through just the finished flooring. Chisel-cut the tongue of the damaged board and then remove the board.

Cut a new piece to fit exactly and chisel off the bottom half of the groove side so the board will fit over the tongue of the adjoining floorboard. Coat the board with glue and put it in position, tongue side first. Hammer into place with a mallet and wood block. Drill clearance holes. Drive and countersink flooring nails, then cover the nail holes with wood filler.

Refinishing a hardwood floor

Remove the shoe molding from the baseboard. Working with the grain, sand the floor with a drum sander until bare wood is exposed. Use a coarse sandpaper for the rough sanding.

Then use a finer grade of sandpaper and

CORRECTING SQUEAKING FLOORS

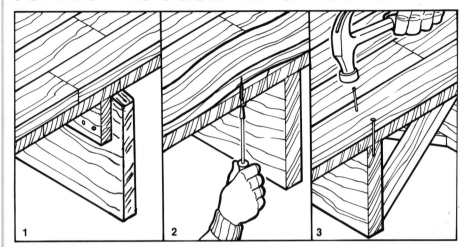

There are several methods of correcting squeaking floors. You can add hardwood strips at the join of the joist and subfloor (1). You can screw from the bottom into the floor (2). You can drive nails dovetail fashion through the finish floor into the joist below, countersinking and filling the nail holes, or you can add additional bridging for rigidity (3).

REPAIRING FLOOR PLANKS

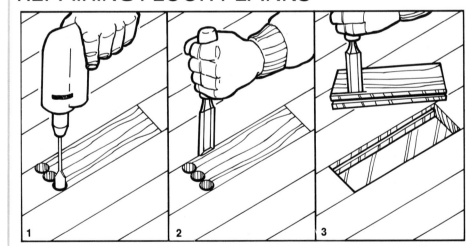

To repair a wood floor plank, first drill holes in the center of the board (1). Chisel out the tongue of the board (2), remove it from the floor and trim opening edges. Cut a new board to fit and chisel off the lower half of its groove (3), so that it will fit over the adjoining tongue. Glue and tap into place. Sink nails at ends.

resand the entire floor to remove scratches. Overlap sanding areas to prevent visible lines.

If you plan to stain the floor another color, apply two coats of a penetrating stain and then finish with a durable, scuff-resistant clear finish. Apply two coats of the finish for full protection.

SIDING

Vinyl and aluminum siding have all but replaced wood as exterior cladding materials. Although vinyl and aluminum require minimum upkeep, wood can create a series of problems you'll need to contend with.

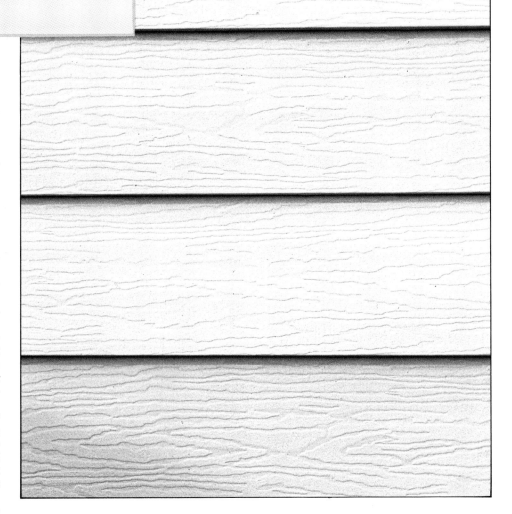

Traditionally, wood and hardboard siding were the materials used in house construction. However, with the advent of aluminum and the newest siding material, vinyl, homeowners attempting re-siding jobs have moved toward the modern materials, which will not corrode, rot or warp. Nor do they need to be painted. In fact, aluminum and vinyl will probably outlast the house! Both require minimum upkeep for long-lasting beauty.

Wood siding

Decay, warps, splits and peeling paint are the problems you can encounter with wood siding. Any damaged wood panel should be replaced as soon as possible, because moisture can seep into the cracks or splits and start to destroy the walls.

Peeling paint is usually caused by moisture that gets into the wood and forces the paint film away from the wood. Repainting over a wet board won't solve the problem; the paint won't adhere to the dampness and will bubble and peel again.

If only a couple of boards are damaged by moisture, they can be replaced. To remove a damaged board, insert wedges in the bottom of the board on top of the damaged piece. Use a hacksaw to cut the nails that join the two pieces, then remove the damaged siding.

Cut a new board to fit, and drive it into place using a hammer and a wood block to prevent damage to the siding. Use galvanized nails to fix the board in place. Countersink the nail heads, fill with a waterproof putty and repaint the board.

Less serious moisture problems can be handled by inserting wedges into the bottom of all the boards to allow moisture to dry out. More serious moisture problems can be helped by the installation of a venting system to release the moisture. Holes are bored into the siding and aluminum or plastic vents are inserted.

Warped wood can sometimes be repaired without removing the siding. Try hammering the board back into place, using ring-shank nails for a tighter grip. Warping can also be treated by sawing a series of cuts slightly more than halfway up the siding panel in the

area of the warp. This allows the wood to spring so it can be nailed back in place with ring-shank nails. Fill all saw cuts with exterior caulking to repel moisture. Smooth the cuts and repaint the siding.

Splits and cracks can also be repaired without removing the siding, by using the above method of ring-shank nails and caulking or by using a waterproof glue. Pry out the split portion so that you can liberally apply glue to the edges of the split. Force the two pieces together and clamp them by using a support from below the siding panel, such as a wood block nailed into the siding. Once the glue has hardened, remove the support and nail the panel back in place. It's preferable to drill pilot holes for the nails to prevent further splitting of the wood. Remember to use galvanized nails for exterior work.

Hardboard siding

Hardboard is ground wood that has been heat-compressed. This siding material requires little maintenance other than painting, but it does sometimes split from moisture penetration.

You can follow the steps under wood siding for replacement of a hardboard siding panel, or, if the damage is in only one small area of a panel, a hole can be cut in the siding and a new piece of hardboard cut to fit. The joint should be caulked to prevent further moisture damage.

Cedar shakes

The smaller size of cedar shingles or shakes makes them easier to repair than panelling. The damaged shake can be forced out by removing the nails, and a new one inserted

123

and nailed in place. A brand-new shake will contrast very prominently with the old shakes. If you can, use a shake from another part of the house that isn't as visible for the replacement, then nail a new shake in that location. The repaired portion of the visible side of the house will then have the same weathered look as the rest of the shakes.

Aluminum siding

As mentioned previously, there's little that can go wrong with this type of siding. It will last for years, and about the only serious problem that can occur is a dent.

Properly applied siding will mean that a dent won't be very noticeable and no repair action need be taken. If the dent is noticeable, remove the panel, force out the dent from the back, then reapply the panel.

Aluminum doesn't need painting. The only maintenance necessary is a washing down once a year.

Vinyl siding

Vinyl is a fairly new siding material, which offers some advantages over aluminum. It won't dent or scratch. This means little need for siding repairs.

Both aluminum and vinyl expand and contract with temperature changes, so the creaking you hear outside your walls is not necessarily a cause for alarm.

As with aluminum, vinyl should also be maintained with an annual washing down.

WOOD SIDING REPAIRS

To replace cedar shakes, cut the nail of the damaged shake with a hack saw blade. Chisel out the shake then apply a new one of the same size and thickness.

Splits in wood siding can be repaired with nails and caulking or a waterproof glue. Pry out the split portion; apply glue; then force the pieces together with nails.

ROOFS

A leaky roof can create some major structural damage if left unchecked. Taking the time to repair a leak will save you some costly structural repairs in the future.

Keeping your shingles in good repair is the first step in preventing roof leaks. Whether your shingles are asphalt, slate or wood, you can repair any damage and help keep your rafters, and the rooms below, dry.

But shingles are only one source of the problem. Flashing around chimneys and vents can also pull away causing water damage in the house.

Should a leak develop in your roof, find and repair the leak first, then tackle any asphalt or flashing problem to prevent further damage.

Locating and repairing leaks

If a wet spot appears on your ceiling, there's a hole in your roof that needs repair. But finding that hole is not always an easy task. The hole may not be directly above the wet spot, and you'll have to determine the water path before you can find the source of the leak.

If you have no access to an attic (so you can find the leak from under the roof), measure the distance from the wet spot on the ceiling to a side of the house. Then, on a dry and windless day, transpose that measurement to the roof. Search in a broad area around your pinpointed measurement to find the leak. Leaks are usually caused by loose, torn or missing shingles, and defective flashing.

If you have access to an attic, grab a flashlight and search out the leak during a rainfall. Start your search directly above the water mark on the ceiling then follow the rafters to find the source, since water tends to leak down the rafters before dropping off to the attic floor.

Drive some nails or a wire through the hole to give you an exterior marker for your outside repair work. Temporarily fill the hole with a caulking compound to help reduce water intake while you wait for a dry day to repair the hole.

Asphalt shingles

Cracked, torn or missing asphalt shingles can cause water damage in the rooms below. But with a little care, shingles can be replaced without the need for major repair work.

A very small crack in the shingles can be filled with asphalt roofing cement, but with larger cracks or tears the shingle should be replaced.

You'll first need to lift the shingle on top of the damaged one to get at the nail. With the top shingles raised slightly, pry up the nails holding the damaged shingle in place. Watch that you don't damage the roofing paper under the nails. Remove the old shingle and put a new one in place, making sure the top of the new shingle fits under the bottom of the shingle on top. With the top shingle raised slightly, nail the new shingle in place using roofing nails. Place some asphalt cement over the head of the nails and let the top shingle fall back into place.

If you need to replace from several courses, the procedure is the same as above, but you must remember to align the lower edge of the new shingles with the lower edge of the existing course. The joints should be staggered to match the existing pattern.

Since asphalt shingles tend to be more pliable when warm, wait for a sunny, warm day to do your repair work. The shingles will then be more flexible, preventing further damage to surrounding shingles.

To replace a ridge shingle, nail down the bottom shingle at the four corners and cover the nail heads with roofing cement. Apply cement to the back of the new ridge shingle and position it, making sure it overlaps the bottom shingle by about 7cm (3in). Nail in place and cover nail heads with cement.

Slate shingles

If a slate shingle is cracked but is otherwise in

good repair, fill the crack with roofing cement, smoothing the cement down with a putty knife.

Slate shingles crack easily, so exercise caution when working on a slate roof.

To replace a slate shingle, use a nail ripper to remove the nails. Hammer the nails from the inside of the house first, if possible, to give you a better grip with the nail ripper and to help prevent cracking of other shingles.

If you need to cut a shingle to fit, score the cut line with a glass cutter, then snap the shingle in two over a straight edge. Hold the shingle in place on the roof and mark the location of the two nail holes. Pre-drill nail holes in the shingle to prevent cracking.

Apply roofing cement to the exposed area of the roof and to the back of the new shingle. Put shingle in place and nail into pre-drilled holes. Cover the nail heads with roofing cement.

Wood shingles

Warping or splitting is the major cause of damage to wood shingles, which means you will need to replace rather than repair them.

Remove the damaged shingle by first splitting the shingle with a chisel and mallet to dislodge it from the nail heads. Since wood isn't flexible, you can't lift the shingle on top to get at the nail heads. Take care not to split any surrounding shingles.

Measure the space for a new shingle and cut the new shingle to fit, reducing the size by about 1cm (3/8in) to allow for expansion of the shingle during wet weather.

Push the new shingle up against the nails left by the old one. Push hard enough to make a mark on the wood. Remove the shingle and cut slots where the existing nails will slide in. Make the slots deep enough so that when you push the shingle into place, the lower edge of the shingle will line up with the lower edge of shingles in the same course. Nail the new shingle in place gently, to prevent splitting. Countersink nail heads and cover with roofing cement.

Flat roofs

A flat roof is comparatively easy to repair, and leaks are usually easy to find; the damaged area in most cases will be directly above the water spot on the ceiling.

Flat roofs are covered with asphalt-coated felt paper. The paper is sometimes covered with gravel to protect the roof from the sun.

To repair a leak, you must first sweep the gravel away from the damaged spot. Don't use a shovel, since it can cause further damage.

When the damaged area is exposed and clean, you can determine the type of repair needed.

To repair a blister, slice through the center of the blister — making sure not to cut through the bottom layer of paper — and expose the two flaps. Allow the blistered area to dry. Once dry, force roofing cement into the blister and nail both sides of the slice, using roofing nails. Cover the repair with a shingle patch and nail around the four sides of the patch. Cover nail heads with roofing cement. There will be no need to reapply the gravel.

A more extensively damaged area is best repaired by cutting away a square patch from the surrounding area. Make sure you cut only the top layer.

Apply roofing cement over the exposed area and try to force some of the cement under the paper around the sides of the cut. Apply a patch of roofing felt to fit the area and nail around the four sides. Cut a patch with a 7cm (3in) overlap to cover the repaired area. Apply roofing cement to the underside of the new patch and nail into place. Cover nail heads with roofing cement.

If your roof develops several leaks, it would be best to cover the entire roof surface with black asphalt roof paint. Make sure the surface is clean and free of gravel. Starting at the highest point of the roof (even flat roofs have a slight pitch for drainage), apply paint with a long-handled brush to sections no bigger than 2sq m (25sq ft) at a time.

Repairing flashing

Flashing is used as a watertight seal wherever shingles cannot be used. You'll find flashing where the chimney meets the roof, around roof vents in valleys, around dormers and where flat roofs meet a wall.

Aluminum, copper, plastic, felt, rubber and galvanized steel are the materials flashing is made from; however, the metal flashing is the more durable and leak resistant.

Flashing is joined to the roof with roofing cement. Over the years the cement can break down, creating holes in the material and possible areas for water leakage.

Inspect your flashings once a year, and if you notice any holes or cracks, refill them

with roofing cement. Larger holes should be filled with roofing felt and then coated with roofing cement.

Chimney flashing is imbedded in mortar, and sometimes this mortar will break down or the flashing will pull away. This calls for immediate repair work, since flashing that has pulled away from the chimney will act as a funnel to collect volumes of rainwater. To repair, clean out the old mortar with a chisel and mallet, reposition the flashing and refill the channel with a new mix of patching mortar. Fill a caulking gun with roofing cement and apply the cement to the join where the metal meets the chimney.

If leaks develop around the vent pipes, apply roofing cement around the flashing area and a few inches up the pipe. If the lead caulking around the neck of the vent pipe becomes too loose, tap it with a chisel or screwdriver until it fits tightly all the way around the pipe.

To replace the flashing around a vent pipe, remove the shingles from around the pipe and, without damaging the roofing felt, chip off the old flashing. Position new flashing and reinstall new shingles. Apply roofing cement over shingle nail heads.

If the chimney flashing needs to be replaced, first chisel out the mortar and roofing cement, holding the cap flashing in place. Pry up the shingles from around the flashing, then, without damaging the roofing paper underneath, remove the flashing. Keep the flashing intact to use as a pattern for cutting the new flashing. Cut the new copper flashing to fit around the chimney and apply the base flashing at the lowest part of the

FLASHING

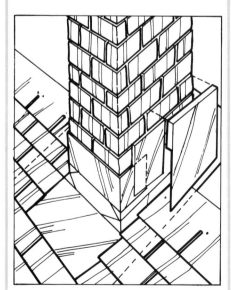

Chimney flashing prevents leaks at the join of the roof and chimney. Flashing is usually made of copper and is bent to conform to the shape of the roof.

LOCATING LEAKS

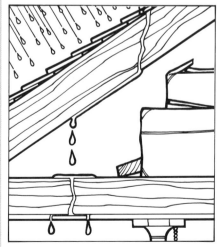

1 Water travels down the rafters from a leak in the roof, so the wet spot on your ceiling may not indicate the exact location of the roof leak.

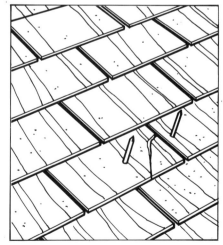

2 Search a wide area of the rafters and once you've found the leak, drive nails through the roof to mark the location on the exterior.

VALLEY FLASHING

Open-valley flashing is usually made of copper and is preferable to closed-valley flashing. Shingles stop before entering the valley leaving an open *space for water runoff. On closed valleys, shingles cover the flashing and there is the potential for water seepage.*

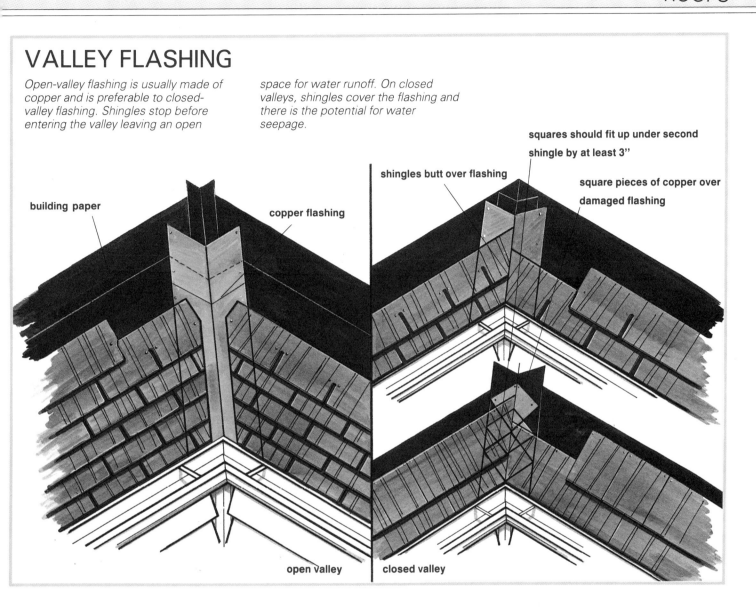

building paper

copper flashing

shingles butt over flashing

squares should fit up under second shingle by at least 3"

square pieces of copper over damaged flashing

open valley

closed valley

chimney first. Use roofing cement to hold the flashing in place. Apply the step flashing up the sides of the chimney, overlapping each piece of metal, then apply the top plate last. Bend the top and sides of the cap flashing so that it will fit into the mortar joints. Position in place and apply new mortar. Caulk around the join with roofing cement. Reapply the shingles and caulk all edges with roofing cement.

Valley flashing, used where two slopes of a roof meet, is used two different ways — open valley, where the shingles stop before entering the valley; and closed valley, where

shingles are butted together right into the valley.

Repairing open-valley flashing is easier, because no shingles need to be removed. Cut a piece of flashing to fit the hole in the valley, overlapping the hole by at least 25mm (1in) on all sides. Apply roofing cement around the hole and press the patch in place. Caulk around the edges of the patch with roofing cement.

To repair a closed valley, first remove all the surrounding shingles. Then cut squares of metal to fit at least 5cm (2in) under the second shingle on each side. Bend the metal

diagonally to fit the valley and place directly over the old flashing and under the shingles. Use roofing cement to hold the metal in place and to fill the area between the shingles and the new flashing. Replace shingles.

To replace roll-roofing flashing, use a putty knife to pry loose the cement that fastens the shingles to the roll roofing. Remove any holding nails. Cut a new piece of flashing the same size as the old, placing it in position under the shingles and nailing in place where the shingle overlaps. Cover nail heads with roofing cement and cement the shingles to the flashing.

WINDOWS

Whether a window is wood, vinyl or aluminum, the material expands and contracts with temperature changes creating problems that can be corrected with a minimum amount of work.

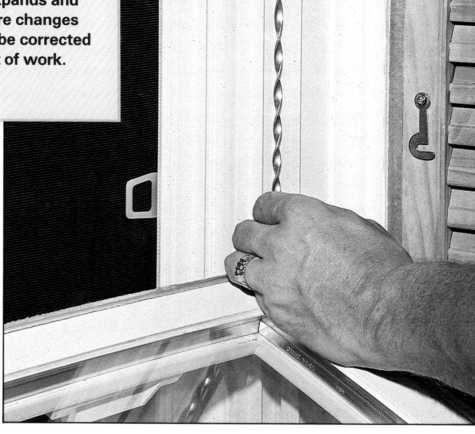

Windows are available in several different types. You'll find wood, aluminum, vinyl and steel windows, in a style range of double hung, casement, sliding, awning and jalousie.

Double-hung windows have an upper and lower sash that operate on a system of weights, springs, chains or cords. The lower sash moves up and the upper sash can sometimes be moved down.

On a casement window, the sash swings out from the frame on hinges attached to one side of the sash. Most are operated with a crank attached to the windowsill.

On sliding windows, the sashes move from side to side on a track or on rollers.

Awning windows are hinged at the top and swing out from the bottom, usually with the aid of a crank attached to the windowsill.

Jalousie windows are glass-louvred windows where each piece of glass pivots on a pin. The glass louvres are opened and closed by a crank handle on the windowsill.

Wood windows, while traditional and in some styles arguably the most beautiful windows, also require the most upkeep. The wood needs to be painted regularly; the sashes can warp in their frames; and the wood is subject to rot.

Aluminum and vinyl windows also expand and contract with temperature changes but are of long-lasting materials that require minimum maintenance.

Steel windows need upkeep because they're prone to rust.

Repairing double-hung windows

Since most double-hung windows are wood, one of the major problems with this type of window is sticking caused by a build-up of paint.

To correct the problem, work a putty knife around the sash and the stop molding to loosen the paint seal. Use a chisel to remove lumps of paint and work a pry bar under the bottom of the window to try to force the window up.

Once the window is open, sand the stop molding and parting strip to remove the paint from the sliding edges, and then lubricate the moldings with some paraffin wax or spray silicone.

If the window is stuck in the open position, place a wood block on the top edge of the sash and hammer the window down gently, working the wood block and hammer over the entire top edge of the sash. Then remove the excess paint from the top part of the window frame, sand and lubricate the moldings. Work the window up and down a few times so you'll have an even, thin coating of lubricant.

Expansion of a wood window due to humidity can cause the window to become immovable. The problem can be corrected by removing the top molding with a chisel and a hammer, making sure you don't damage the molding. Then sand the sash without removing it from the frame. Lightly tack the stop molding in place and test the window. If it still sticks, try tapping the grooves in the window frame with a wood block and a hammer to force the frame slightly outward. If this fails, you'll have to remove the sash and plane the edges of the sash, stop molding and parting strip.

Remove the sash by taking out the stop molding and parting strip. Pull gently on the sash to remove it from the frame, remove the sash cords, then lift out the sash for planing.

Plane and test-fit until you've restored the window to its original shape.

A common malfunction of the double-hung window is a broken sash cord or chain. The cord allows the sash to be opened and closed properly. With a broken cord, the window will do neither.

You'll need to remove the sash and sash cord to make the repair. Remove the screws from the sash-weight pocket cover in the window frame and remove the sash weight. If cord is currently used on your windows, it's best to replace it with a chain. Chain will last longer than cord, reducing your chances of future repair.

Thread one end of the chain through the pulley to the sash weight, then tighten the chain securely to the weight. Put the weight back into its opening. Grab the chain at the pulley and raise the weight until it touches the pulley. Secure the chain so the weight will stay in place, then screw the chain into position in the sash groove, using wood screws through the chain links. Replace the sash-weight pocket cover and replace the sash.

Some windows will not have a sash-weight pocket cover, and you'll need to remove the window frame to get at the sash weight.

Many modern double-hung windows, particularly aluminum and vinyl windows, have spring-lift sash windows. An aluminum tube runs down the sash channel and inside the tube there's a spring around a twisted rod. The spring is kept taut by the rod, enabling the sash to remain open in any position and allowing movement of the window with only slight pressure.

If you're experiencing difficulty with window movement, you may just need to adjust the spring tension. Remove the screw from the tube, making sure you hold the tube and the screw firmly so that the spring won't completely unwind. Adjust the spring a few turns in either direction to compensate for your problem — if the window doesn't rise properly, the spring needs tightening; if it won't close properly, loosen the spring. Again, make sure both the tube and the screw are held firmly. Reattach the tube and test your window.

Repairing casement windows

Repairs to wooden casement windows usually involve tightening loose hinges and cleaning the crank handle. If the window doesn't close properly, it could mean loose hinges. If the holes are too loose to accept the screws, remove the hinge leaf, drill 6mm (1/4in) holes where the screw holes are located and fill the holes with a 6mm (1/4in) dowel. Make sure the fit is tight. You can then reattach the hinge leaf.

Sometimes swollen wood will prevent the windows from closing. Plane the window slightly to fit. Remember that swollen wood will usually shrink in drier weather and if too much wood is removed, there could be a gap between the window and frame after the wood shrinks.

The crank handle needs lubricating from time to time to compensate for dirt build-up in the mechanism. Apply a silicone spray and light oil to the crank works for ease of operation.

If the crank doesn't work, the gears may be broken. Loosen the set screw and remove the handle of the crank, then remove the housing screws. Slide the arm until it leaves the window track. Replace the gears in the housing if they're broken, or clean the debris from around the gears if they're just not operating efficiently. Replace the mechanism.

Repairing sliding windows

Sliding windows move along a track at the top and bottom. Most are made of aluminum and require little in the way of repair.

A slider that sticks can be corrected by lubricating the tracks with some paraffin wax. If the track is bent, re-form it using a wood block and a hammer.

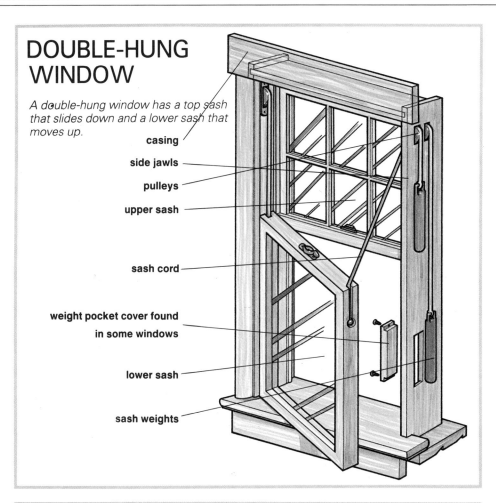

DOUBLE-HUNG WINDOW

A double-hung window has a top sash that slides down and a lower sash that moves up.

casing

side jawls

pulleys

upper sash

sash cord

weight pocket cover found in some windows

lower sash

sash weights

REPAIRING CASEMENT WINDOWS

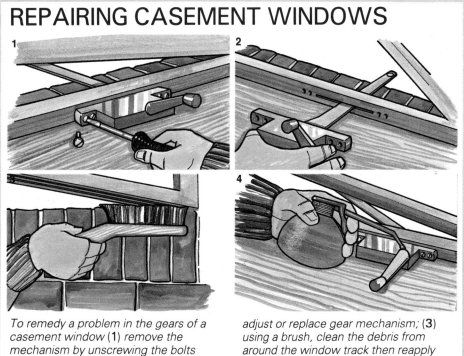

To remedy a problem in the gears of a casement window (**1**) *remove the mechanism by unscrewing the bolts that hold it to the frame;* (**2**) *slide the arm free of the window track and* adjust or replace gear mechanism; (**3**) *using a brush, clean the debris from around the window track then reapply the gear box;* (**4**) *oil the handle and hinges once a year.*

REPLACING AWNING WINDOWS

1 Unscrew the operating handle from the sash and tilt the window flat.

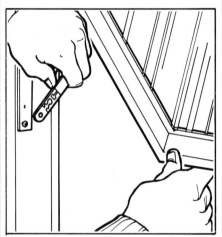

2 Detach the hinges from the side and remove window. Reverse procedure to replace window.

3 The crack handle and the joints of the arms should be oiled regularly.

JALOUSIE SLATS

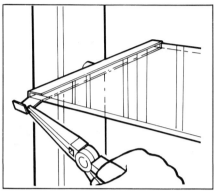

1 Bend the retaining clips back to clean the thickness of the glass.

2 Remove the glass by sliding it out of its metal frame. Insert new glass.

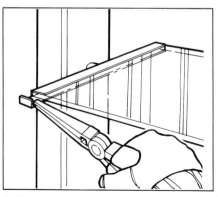

3 To keep the new glass in place, bend the retaining clip back into its original position.

Awning and jalousie windows

Both these windows operate on the same principle — the glass swings out from the bottom on hinges (awning windows) or pivots (jalousies) to provide for ventilation as well as keeping rain out of the house.

Repairs to both these window types usually involve simply regular lubrication of the pivots or crank handles and a tightening of the hinge screws.

CAULKING

Caulking is a quick and easy way to keep the elements outside where they belong.

Caulking is a resilient material used to fill joins between different parts of a house to keep those joins air- and watertight.

Caulking compound is a mixture of pigment and natural or synthetic oils that make the compound elastic and resilient. It adheres to wood, metal, masonry and ceramic, keeping its elasticity so it can expand and contract with surrounding surfaces.

There are five different types of caulking compound — oil based, which will adhere to most surfaces; latex based, which can be cleaned up with water, is fast drying, and can be painted; butyl rubber, which is a long-lasting caulking used mostly for metal to masonry joints; polyvinyl acetate, which adheres to all surfaces; and silicone caulking, which is a long-lasting compound that adheres to any surface except paint.

Although available in a wide range of colors, the most common colors are white, gray and black. The compound can be purchased in bulk quart or gallon form or in disposable cartridge for use in a caulking gun.

For efficient application, caulking is usually applied with a gun which forces the compound out through a nozzle. The nozzle can be cut at various levels to control the width of the caulking bead you lay. If you purchase your compound in bulk, it can be loaded into a full-barrel gun for application. Caulking is placed into the barrel and a cap containing the nozzle is screwed into place. As the trigger of the gun is squeezed, a plunger in the barrel is activated, forcing the compound out through the nozzle.

Buying compound in bulk is efficient only when large areas of one color are to be caulked. Otherwise you need to clean the barrel of one color of caulking before you can refill the tube with another — a time-consuming and messy job. Therefore, most homeowners prefer to buy the compound in disposable cartridges. These cartridges are operated in a half-barrel gun in which the top half of the barrel is missing for easy insertion of the cartridge. Changing colors simply means changing the cartridge.

To operate the gun, squeeze the trigger with a steady, uniform pressure and tilt the barrel at a 45° angle in the direction of the movement. The object is to lay down a neat, continuous convex bead of the compound on both sides of the join to be sealed.

Before you can start, however, any old caulking must be removed, otherwise the new caulking won't adhere. Nor will caulking adhere to a greasy, damp or dirty surface. Clean the surface and rub it with a cloth soaked in solvent to ensure a clean base for adhesion.

Caulking is used to seal around door and window frames, where the chimney meets roof shingles, between steps, porches, patios and the main body of the house, around all roof flashing, at siding corners, to fill fine cracks in stucco, siding or woodwork or beneath windowsills.

Inside the house, caulking is mostly found around the edge of the bathtub where the tub meets the walls. But any small cracks in the bathtub area can be filled with caulking to prevent water seepage. Caulking can also be used as a gasket around taps where the faucet body meets the sink. This will help keep water out from under the taps, preventing possible corrosion of the metal. Caulking is also used to seal air leaks around windows.

Bows in a wall will prevent new baseboard molding from fitting flush to the wall. To remedy, fasten the baseboard and fill gaps with caulking before painting.

If you need to fill large cracks, don't proceed to fill up the hole with caulking. The large amount of caulking needed may have trouble drying. Instead, buy some oakum, a rope-like substance available in hardware and marine-supply stores. Fill the crack with the oakum to within 25mm (1in) of the surface, then apply the caulking.

Caulking can also be bought in dried-rope form, which is unwound from a roll and forced into cracks by hand.

FENCES

Wood fences require little maintenance beyond regular painting and staining. But if you've noticed decay on a part of your fence, repair it now before it weakens the structure.

Wood fences will start to decay after a number of years. The major area for rot attack is the fence post, since it sits in the ground and comes into contact with insects and moist earth.

A properly set post will last several years, but should you notice rot and decay of the wood, the post should be replaced or repaired before it causes further damage to the fence.

To set a post, use a post-hole digger to make the hole. The post should have one-third of its length buried underground, but for better support and to prevent heaving, bury the post below the frost line.

Wood that comes into contact with the ground must be treated to reduce decay. It is advisable not to use creosote or pentachlorophenol to treat the wood yourself. Controversy surrounds the harmful health effects of these two preservatives. There are wood preservatives on the market that contain neither creosote nor penta. You can also use commercially available pressure-treated wood for your posts. This wood is chemically treated in factories following government regulations, and some manufacturers claim their product will last 60 years. Try to buy pressure-treated wood to the length and width you need. Any cuts made in the wood must be chemically treated to prevent decay.

Wear gloves and goggles when applying the chemical and avoid breathing the fumes. It's also advisable to protect yourself when cutting commercially treated wood. Wear a respirator to avoid breathing sawdust.

Place a flat rock or some gravel in the bottom of the hole for drainage. Set the post in the hole and hold it in place with braces. Make sure it's plumb. Mix up some concrete and fill the hole with it. A hole that is slightly wider at the bottom than it is at the top will be stronger support for the post once it's filled with concrete. Make sure the concrete rises above ground level; tap it well to remove air bubbles, then slope it up toward the post at a 45° angle to allow for water runoff.

Once the concrete has hardened, any gaps between the post and the concrete should be patched with asphalt cement to prevent seepage.

If the decay is in only one section of the post, it may not be necessary to replace the entire post. Cut the decayed area out. When the decay is below ground level, drive two long pressure-treated boards into the ground on either side of the post and fasten the boards to the post using galvanized nails or screws. Make sure the bottom of the post is several inches above ground level to help prevent further decay.

When the top of the post is decayed, replace it with a new piece of lumber and fasten it to the bottom piece using a half-lap joint. Although the above repairs are possible, it's best to replace a fence post completely once it's rotted. Dig out the old concrete and the post and follow the instructions for setting a new post.

In most cases, it's possible to replace a fence rail without moving the posts. First, remove the pickets. If your rail is fitted into post sockets, remove all the nails and saw the rail as close as possible to the post. Replace with a new rail fastened with an angle iron against the post. Make sure the ends of the new rail have been treated with a pressure-treated wood sealer. Use galvanized nails or screws to fasten the bracket.

Rotted rails that are fastened with angle irons can be replaced by simply removing the angle bracket, cutting a new rail to fit and replacing the rail and angle iron.

To ensure a tight bond between rail and post, you can caulk around the rail with a weather-resistant caulking to prevent moisture from seeping in.

To replace pickets, remove the decayed board. Use the old board as a cutting pattern for the new piece. Seal the ends of the new picket and attach to the bottom and top rails of the fence using galvanized nails.

SETTING A FENCE POST

Use a post-hole digger to make the hole. Add some gravel to the bottom of the hole then set the post in place. Hold with braces and check for level. Pour concrete into the hole to secure the post. To prevent heaving of posts, holes should be dug below the frost line. Support wobbly posts temporarily with wedges.

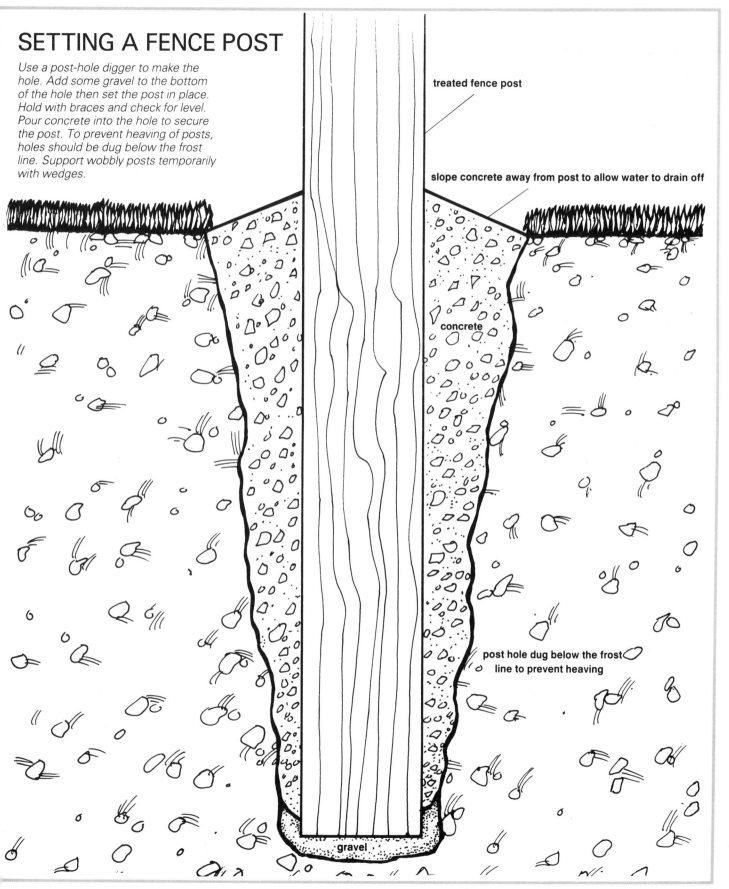

treated fence post

slope concrete away from post to allow water to drain off

concrete

post hole dug below the frost line to prevent heaving

gravel

DRIVEWAYS AND SIDEWALKS

Constant ground shifting can cause cracks in driveways and sidewalks. A regular maintenance program is important to keep them in top shape.

Although asphalt driveways can withstand much of the abuse dealt them by the weather, they do tend to develop cracks and pits over time that need to be repaired to ensure a long life for the driveway.

A basic maintenance program for asphalt driveways involves the annual application of a blacktop sealer to protect the driveway against the sun, rain and snow. The waterproof sealer comes in premixed 19L (5gal) pails. The contents of one will cover from 20 to 40 sq m (200 to 400sq ft) depending on the thickness of application.

To apply, sweep the driveway clean of all debris and scrub oil spots with water and detergent. Don't use an oil solvent to clean off grease or oil, since it tends to soften the asphalt. Rinse the driveway thoroughly.

Pour some of the sealer onto the driveway and spread with a broom or roller. Make sure the driveway is wet for easier application. Use light strokes to help fill shallow pits and cracks but don't apply too much sealer. Wait until the sealer is dry to the touch before applying a second coat to cover any shallow pits or cracks missed in the first application. Try to ensure that the driveway is left untouched by traffic or rain for at least 24 hours.

Larger cracks or pits should be filled before applying the sealer. To fill a hole or crack, apply a premixed asphalt-patching compound to within 25mm (1in) of the driveway surface. Tap it down firmly, then apply more compound to a level of about 12mm (½in) above the driveway surface. Smooth the compound with a 2 x 4 or by running your car over the patch a few times. Deep holes should be half-filled with coarse gravel before applying the compound. Once the patch is dry, you're ready to apply the blacktop sealer.

Asphalt driveways are also subject to large-scale damage that most often results from improper construction.

Large-scale cracking, or alligatoring, can result from several poor construction techniques. In most instances, a professional will need to apply a hot-patch treatment to repair the damage.

Large voids may also need professional work, since they could require a new layer of asphalt on the driveway.

Gravel driveways are subject to heaving, creating a washboard effect. If the heaving covers a large area, you'll need to remove gravel and topsoil layers of the driveway until you're down to the subsurface, which can be gravel, clay, rock or hard earth. Rent a compacter and compact the heaved areas, going over the driveway until the surface is level. Then regrade with topsoil and gravel, crowning the driveway in the center and sloping toward the sides. Then compact the surface again. Make sure the gravel you use has a large number of small fines in it for proper compaction.

Small heaved areas can be treated by simply adding more gravel to the hollow, compacting and repeating the procedure until the surface level is reached.

Sidewalk repairs

Like driveways, concrete sidewalks suffer from constant ground shifting. Cracks can appear in a concrete walkway, and pavers and flagstones can lift with the moving ground.

To repair a shifted slab, pry up one end of the concrete with a crowbar. Slip a round broomstick or pipe under the raised end to help you roll the slab out of the way. Tamp the ground even and fill any low spots with gravel. Add mortar dabs if mortar was used previously. Make sure the ground surface is tamped solidly and evenly, then replace the slab.

Repairing concrete is slightly more difficult than fixing a lifted paver but is certainly within the realm of the do-it-yourselfer.

Concrete is composed of 1 part Portland cement, 2 parts sand and 3 parts fine gravel. However, you can buy premixed concrete

REPAIRING A SIDEWALK

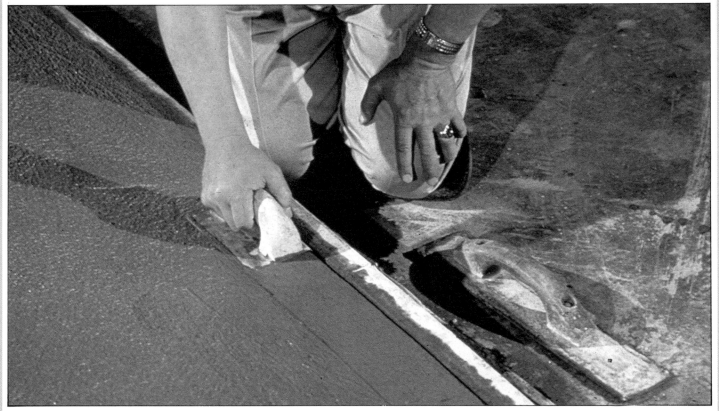

If a large section of the sidewalk develops cracks, it's best to replace that section. Chop out the old concrete; erect a form; pour your concrete mixture; trowel it smooth; slightly roughen the surface with a broom for grip; run an edging tool around the sides then let cure for several days.

that has either a latex, vinyl or epoxy base and dries quickly. These premixed concretes are best used for small concrete repairs, since they force you to work with haste.

If a large section of the sidewalk is cracked, it should be removed and replaced. Small cracks can be handled by patching.

To patch, use a cold chisel and hammer to undercut the crack, making the opening wider at the bottom than at the surface. Concrete will only grip the hole if it is undercut. Clean out all loose particles from the crack.

Wet the area inside and on the surface of the crack. If the area isn't wet, the old concrete will draw the moisture out of the patch before the new concrete has a chance to set. Make sure the surface is damp but not running with water.

Trowel in the new concrete, tamp it firmly, then smooth the surface with a trowel so that it's even with the surrounding area. Let the patch stiffen slightly, then lightly run a broom across the new concrete to provide a better gripping surface. Once the patch is stiff, keep it damp with plastic or wet burlap and let it cure for a week.

REPAIRING A HEAVED SIDEWALK

Pry up one end of heaved concrete slab and insert a pipe. Use the pipe to roll the slab away. Regrade and tamp foundation and replace slab.

CHAPTER 5
Heating and Cooling

HEATING AND COOLING SYSTEMS

A properly maintained heating and cooling system will ensure year-round comfort.

The heating and cooling plant of your house provides for your health and comfort. Whether it's an oil, gas or electric furnace, central or room air conditioning, or a heat pump, the system requires regular maintenance.

Oil furnaces

In oil furnaces, fuel oil is sprayed into a combustion chamber where it is ignited, creating heat. Combustion is accomplished by two different methods in the two basic types of residential oil furnaces — the pressure burner and the vaporizing burner.

The pressure burner is the one found in most homes. Oil, as a fine spray, is pumped into the combustion chambers through a nozzle. This spray mixes with air and is ignited by an electric spark.

Vaporizing burners have a pot which contains oil and a flow regulator. A fire is started with an electric spark and the heat from the fire vaporizes the oil. The pool of oil refills as necessary. Air, to keep the fire burning, is fed into the pot through natural draft or through a small fan. Automatic draft regulators can be placed in the vent pipe to ensure a small steady draft for oil-burning purposes.

Your furnace should be checked regularly for a proper fuel and air mix to help avoid soot and to ensure proper combustion.

Many oil furnaces have a stack control that will automatically shut off the oil pump if the fuel spray does not ignite within a given time. The lack of gas passing the control indicates a lack of combustion, and the control will then shut off the pump motor. This prevents an overflow of oil into the combustion chamber. To restart the furnace, follow the instructions in the owner's manual available from the manufacturer. If, after following the manufacturer's instructions, the furnace fails to operate, call for professional service.

In addition to a stack control shut-off, there are a number of reasons why a furnace will fail to operate. You can check the following steps first before calling a serviceman.

Check the furnace fuse and replace if necessary, or reset a tripped circuit breaker. If the new fuse blows or the circuit breaker

trips again after resetting, call for professional service.

Check the oil tank to make sure it is full.

Check to see that the emergency switch hasn't been turned off. This throw switch is usually located close to the furnace on a gray box.

If you have a setback thermostat, check to see that the timer is working. Also check to see that there's no dirt or corrosion on the thermostat contact points.

Gas furnaces

Gas is supplied under low pressure to the burner head, where it mixes with air. A single flame jet or multiple jets on the burner head then ignite the gas-air combination. The hot gases are passed into the vent pipe and out through the chimney, while the warmed air

137

OIL BURNERS

Oil burners come in two styles – the pressure burner (left) and the vaporizing burner (right).

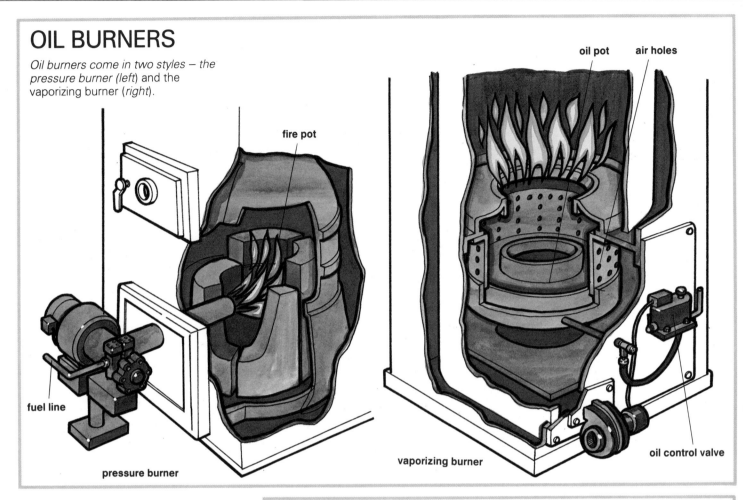

oil pot   air holes

fire pot

fuel line

pressure burner

vaporizing burner

oil control valve

circulating around the outside of the combustion chamber is passed out through the ductwork and into the house.

A pilot light is used to light the burner jets. The flame of the pilot heats a thermocouple, which converts the heat to an electric current. This current keeps a valve open from the main gas-supply line to the burner. If the pilot light goes out, the thermocouple cools off, eliminating the current and forcing the gas-supply-line valve to close. The pilot light can be relighted, but if you've never handled the task before, ask the utility company to send a serviceman to instruct you on how to do it.

A gas furnace needs little maintenance. Inspection by the gas company every two or three years to ensure that the chimney and vents are clean, and that the heat exchanger hasn't developed any cracks, is all that will likely be necessary. However, should an emergency arise, call the gas company for immediate emergency service. If you should smell gas fumes, leave the house immediately and call the gas company from a neighbor's.

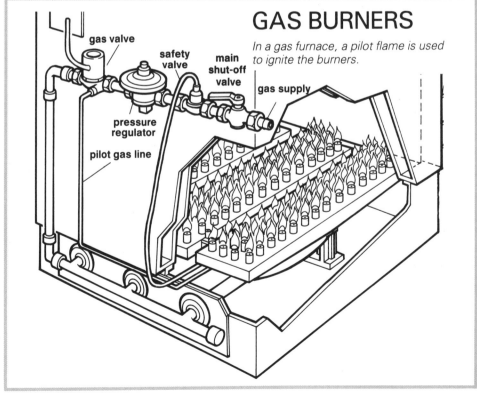

GAS BURNERS

In a gas furnace, a pilot flame is used to ignite the burners.

gas valve

safety valve

main shut-off valve

gas supply

pressure regulator

pilot gas line

ELECTRIC FURNACES

In electric furnaces, an electric current is supplied to heating elements which produce quantities of heat. The heat is then circulated by a blower fan.

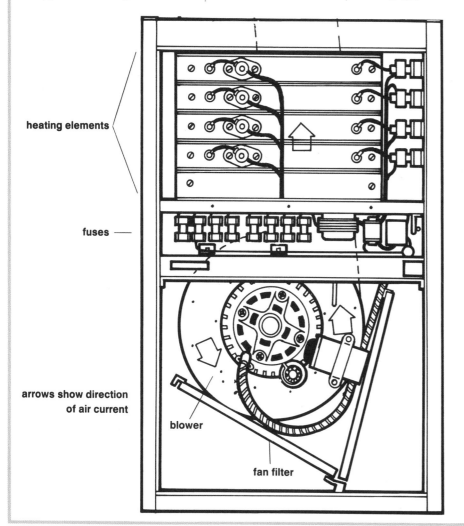

heating elements

fuses

arrows show direction
of air current

blower

fan filter

Electric heating

A well-insulated house can operate on clean electric heat with few maintenance bills and a somewhat constant supply of fuel. However, the cost of heating with electricity tends to be higher than the cost of heating with gas or oil.

Electric heat is simply a current passing through an electricity-resistant conductor. As the current passes through, the conductor heats up, warming the air in the room. There's no combustion necessary and no need for a chimney.

Baseboard heaters are the most popular form of residential electric heating. Heating elements, concealed in thin metal casing, are mounted along the perimeter of a room in place of baseboards. The baseboard heaters are usually wired into individual room thermostats so that you can control the heat in each room.

There are two other types of electric heating without a furnace — the wall heater and radiant ceilings.

The wall heater is a panel usually equipped with a fan to circulate the room air, and is mounted between studs to provide supplementary heating to special areas such as bathrooms or entryways.

A radiant ceiling is a grid of electrical elements imbedded in ceiling panels or plaster. A current passes through the elements, forcing heat down into the rooms below.

The electric furnace has a series of heating elements that take the place of the burner in gas or oil furnaces. A current runs through the elements, which give off heat. The heat is then forced through the house by a blower fan. No chimney is necessary, since electric heat does not give off gases. And since no chimney is necessary and the units are small, they can be installed almost anywhere in the house, including closets.

HEAT PUMP

A heat pump warms a house in winter and cools it in summer. It takes the heat from the outside air in the winter and transfers it inside, reversing the procedure in the warmer months.

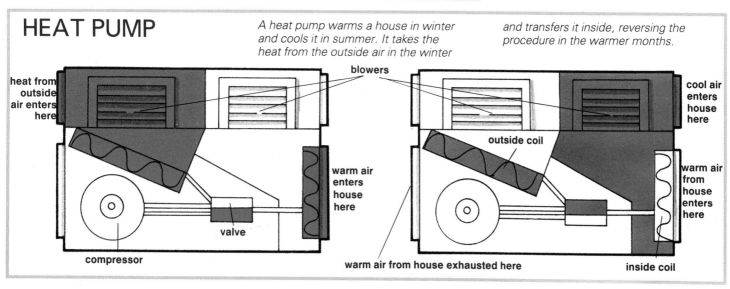

heat from outside air enters here

blowers

cool air enters house here

outside coil

warm air enters house here

warm air from house enters here

valve

compressor

warm air from house exhausted here

inside coil

Heat pumps

A heat pump maintains a constant, comfortable temperature in your home without the need for thermostat adjustment.

The unit will draw heat from the warm air inside the house during the summer and exhaust the heat to the cooler air outside. During the colder months, a heat pump will automatically reverse itself and draw heat from the outdoor air to warm the inside of your house. The operation of a heat pump is most noticeable during the spring and fall months, when the temperature in the morning or evening is quite low, yet the afternoon temperature climbs quite high. By setting your thermostat at the desired temperature, the heat pump will automatically adjust itself to either heat or cool the inside air to maintain a constant temperature reading.

A heat pump has an indoor coil, an outdoor coil and a compressor. To keep your house cool in the warm weather, the indoor coil removes the heat from the indoor air and passes it to the compressor, which exhausts the warm air outdoors. In cold weather, a reversing valve automatically reverses the procedure, so that heat is removed from the outside air and transferred into the house.

When the outdoor temperature reaches freezing, the outdoor coil can develop frost. Water vapor from the air will condense on the coil and freeze. The ice will prevent the coil from picking up enough warmth from the outside air for transfer into the house. A properly functioning heat pump will automatically defrost itself by switching to the cooling mode, transferring warm air from the house to defrost the coil then switching back to the heating mode. While in the cooling mode, the heat pump will switch to a supplementary electric heating system inside the house to keep warm air inside. This supplementary system will work continuously until the coil is defrosted. A regular check of the outside coil is therefore necessary to ensure that the supplementary system is not running continuously but only for the duration of the defrosting action.

The outside coil should show frost when outside temperatures are below freezing. If it remains warm and dry, that could mean the defrosting action is continuous and the heat pump is constantly working on supplementary heat. Call a serviceman for repair.

If, however, ice is constant on the coil, the defrosting action is not taking place. Adjust the thermostat lower to put the heat pump into the cooling mode, which will bring the warm inside air out to defrost the coil. After about 10 minutes, turn the thermostat back up to ensure a minimal loss of heat from the inside. You may need to follow this cycle for about an hour before the coil defrosts. If the coil doesn't defrost within an hour, call a serviceman.

HEAT PUMP SENSING SYSTEMS

The automatic switching of the heat pump is handled by either a sensing tube (1) or a sensing bulb (2).

If the unit defrosts but immediately ices up again, you may need to clean the sensing bulb or tube.

Some heat pumps have a sensing bulb or thermostat at the end of a copper tube clamped to the edge of the outside coil or found inside a sleeve attached to a refrigerant pipe. When the coil temperature reaches freezing, this thermostat switches the unit to defrost. Corrosion or dirt can prevent the thermostat from working properly. Clean the bulb and sleeve of dirt, and sand off any corrosion.

In place of the sensing bulb, other heat pumps have an air-flow sensing tube. As the heat pump fan sucks air through the tube, the defrost switch is kept open. When ice builds up on the coil, blocking the flow of air through the tube, the switch closes, putting the unit into the defrost mode. Dirt build-up can prevent the switch from closing, which means the defrost mode cannot be activated. Keep the tube clean for proper operation.

Air conditioning

There are two basic types of air-conditioning systems for the home — central air conditioning, which cools the entire house and is usually operated through the furnace ductwork; and room units, which cool only the room in which they're located.

If you're planning on installing air conditioning, keep in mind that a room unit for every room of the house will be more expensive to operate than central air conditioning. However, installation costs of central air will be quite high if there's no usable ductwork in your house and a separate ducting system needs to be installed.

The efficiency of any air-conditioning system is measured in BTUs (British Thermal Units) or tonnage. A BTU is the amount of heat removed in an hour. Tonnage is the comparative cooling effect of melting a ton of ice in an hour. There are 12,000 BTUs in 1 ton. Although air conditioners are sometimes rated by horsepower, avoid this as a measurement, because there can be a wide range in BTUs in two units rated at 1 horsepower. And it's the BTU measurement you need to determine the cooling capacity for your air conditioner. Generally, 12,000 BTUs are the equivalent of 46m² (500ft²) in a home.

Room Air Conditioners A room air conditioner is designed to cool only the room in which it is situated. The units are usually fastened to the windowsill, but can also be installed in a sleeve that fits through the wall.

In these units, warm air passes over the cooling coil and loses its heat. With the help of a fan or blower, the conditioned air is circulated in the room. The heat that was removed from the air forces the cold liquid refrigerant in the evaporator to vaporize. The vaporized refrigerant is transported to the compressor, which compresses the vapor and raises its temperature to a higher degree than the outside air. By then the refrigerant is hot and moves to the condenser, where the vapor liquifies and gives up the room heat to the outside air. The hot refrigerant then pas-

INSTALLING AN AIR CONDITIONER

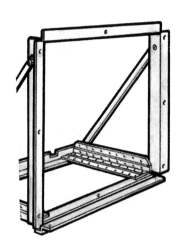

To install a window air conditioner, first assemble the frame.

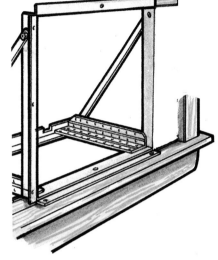

Attach it to the mounting frame in the center of the window.

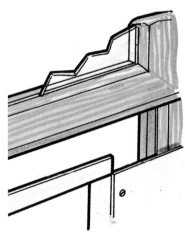

Add weatherstripping to prevent air leaks around the joins.

Slide the air conditioner into place and seal with the supplied rubber gasket.

middle of your opening and insert a pre-assembled wood frame into the opening. Attach the unit housing, caulking around the outside edges to prevent water or air seepage. Apply any finishing woodwork, then insert the air conditioner.

Small units can be handled by the 120-volt house current, but larger units may need a 240-volt outlet.

A time-delay fuse should be used in the circuit that contains your unit, since there is usually a great surge of power when the unit starts up, which could cause an overload on a regular fuse.

Central Air Conditioning Central air-conditioning systems are less expensive to operate, run more quietly and offer better cooling than individual room units. There are two types of systems available.

The single package system has all the components in one package. It can be installed indoors; however, the noise and vibration make outdoor installation preferable. If installed outdoors, a connecting duct needs to be installed through the wall into the unit at one end and the existing ductwork at the other.

The most popular central air system is the split system, where the condenser and compressor are located outdoors to minimize noise and vibration and are connected by copper tubing to the cooling coil located on the furnace, where the furnace blower and ducts are used to circulate the air through the house.

Most air conditioners need a special line to the fuse box to accommodate a voltage higher than regular household voltage; however, regardless of requirements, a separate line should be run between the fuse box and the air conditioner to eliminate overloading of household circuits.

Always check to make sure your installation complies with local building codes.

Electronic Air Cleaners Electronic air cleaners, not to be confused with table-top models that serve a similar but more confined use, are attached to your furnace to eliminate dust, smoke and pollen from the air. They make housework easier by cutting down on the dust, and they also provide cleaner air for allergy sufferers.

When particles enter the cleaner, they receive a positive charge and are attracted to negatively charged collecting plates, where they remain.

The movement of air through the cleaner is constant and air flow is provided by the furnace blower.

The only maintenance necessary for these units is regular cleaning of the collector plates.

ses through a restrictor, which lowers its temperature and liquifies the refrigerant, which then re-enters the evaporator to repeat the cycle.

When buying a room air conditioner, check for thermostats and automatic fan controls so that cooling can be regulated. Also make sure there's a built-in compressor shut-off for protection against overheated motor windings, and make sure there's an effective method of condensation disposal.

If you're installing the unit in a bedroom, you might want to check noise and vibration levels as well.

Many smaller air-conditioning units come with a do-it-yourself installation kit, which you and a helper can follow to ensure proper installation.

Window units are usually fastened to the window by mounting frames with a rubber gasket forced tight around the entire unit to prevent air leakage to the outside.

Units can also be mounted through the wall. Find the studs on the inside wall and, with accurate frame-opening measurements, cut the wallboard away. With a drill and long drill bit, cut through to the outside wall to indicate the four corners of your cut. Remove the outside wall and insulation. Saw off the portion of the stud that falls in the

CENTRAL AIR CONDITIONING

A split system central air conditioning system is the most popular system because the compressor unit is located outdoors for quieter operation. The compressor is connected to the furnace by copper pipes, and the furnace ductwork and blower are used to cool the house.

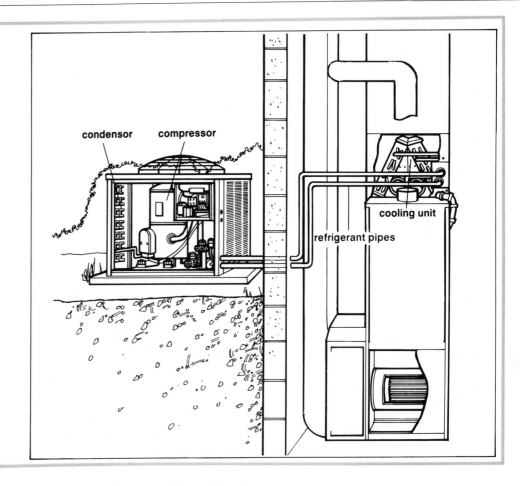

condensor   compressor

cooling unit

refrigerant pipes

FIREPLACES AND WOOD-STOVES

Fireplaces and woodstoves can be an effective secondary heat source for your home if energy-efficient equipment is used.

Although fireplaces were once considered a major source of heat for the home, they are now used mainly for decorative purposes and as supplementary heat sources. Unless your fireplace uses the latest energy-efficient equipment, it can only be considered an inefficient source of heat. It will also use a significant amount of the warm air from the house for combustion, defeating the purpose of using a fireplace as a supplement to your home heating system.

Improving fireplace efficiency

There are several ways of improving the heating efficiency of your fireplace as well as protecting against removal of too much heated air from your house. Since almost two-thirds of the heat from a fireplace is wasted up the chimney (along with almost four times more air than is necessary for combustion), it is wise to take some efficiency steps to save on energy dollars.

While a fireplace screen can be essential to keep live sparks from flying out beyond the hearth, the screen can rob up to 30 percent of the heating efficiency of a fireplace. A way to correct the situation is to use a screen that is higher than the fireplace opening and to place the screen as far away as possible from the fireplace face. This will allow extra heat to escape through the opening created at the top of the screen.

A damper that functions improperly can be a major source of fireplace inefficiency. Inspect your damper regularly to ensure a tight fit when closed. This prevents warm room air escaping up the chimney when the fireplace isn't in operation. The damper needs to be open when lighting a fire, to provide enough draft for combustion.

If your damper needs replacing, you might consider installation of a chimney-top damper. As the name implies, this damper is installed on top of the chimney, keeping rain out, retaining chimney heat and lessening creosote build-up.

Check your chimney regularly for creosote build-up. Excess creosote can be ignited by sparks from the fireplace. To keep the flue clean, a chimney brush can be worked down the flue from the roof and up the chimney

from the firebox. Also make sure you vacuum the smoke shelf directly behind the damper to keep it clean. If your chimney has any bends, which is the case with many of the modern metal chimneys installed with new fireplace units, make sure a clean-out trap is located at the elbow of the bend to facilitate creosote removal.

If creosote build-up is persistent, start building smaller, hotter-burning fires to burn the creosote off the flue. A hotter fire is a roaring fire that needs plenty of air to burn. Keep glass fireplace doors open, if you have them, to ensure enough draft.

To retain more heat in the room in which your fireplace is located, try burning coal. It offers almost double the heat capacity of the usual hardwood fuel. However, make sure it's coal and not charcoal. Charcoal will emit toxic fumes.

Another way to deflect heat into the room is by using a metal heat reflector or fireback. Firebacks can be aluminum or foil, but most homeowners invest in the decorative cast-iron type, which is about 25mm (1in) thick. To install a fireback, place it against the back wall of the firebox, with the bottom edge resting on the hearth. Use masonry anchors and steel screw hooks or lag bolts threaded through lead shields drilled into the masonry to fasten the fireback.

Although glass doors covering the firebox opening will help prevent heat loss from the room, they will not add heat from a burning fire to the room. There's a bit of a catch-22 situation with glass doors. They do prevent heat from escaping, but they also prevent a constant supply of air to the fire. This results in a slower, cooler-burning fire that creates

the potential for faster creosote build-up in the flue. Try not to consistently burn a fire with the glass doors shut. Every third or fourth fire should be a hot fire, with glass doors left open, to help minimize creosote build-up. With the doors open, you'll be providing a supplementary source of heat to the room. If sparks from the fire are a concern, put a fireplace screen across the opening, but remember that a screen reduces heat gain in the room. Most glass door units have built-in roll-back screens for this purpose.

Glass doors are particularly useful when the fire is waning and there's no heat being given off from the firebox. If the doors aren't closed, you'll simply be losing heat from the room up through the open damper.

A word of caution: always keep the damper open until the fire is extinguished. Flames and smoke from even a smouldering log can produce toxic gases. The only escape route is up through the damper.

To maintain your doors, check them regularly for defects, particularly cracked glass. Although the glass is tempered and can withstand high temperatures, a build-up of soot and creosote will reduce the ability of the glass to withstand temperature changes. Clean the glass with a cleaner recommended by the manufacturer. And after a fire, make sure you clean the doors only when the glass has reached room temperature.

Replacing your grate with a tube grate is one way of gaining more heat from the fireplace. These grates are composed of C-shaped tubes with both ends exposed. A fire is built on the bottom portion of the grate; air

143

Ready Reference

FIREPLACE AND CHIMNEY MAINTENANCE

Good maintenance practices are essential to ensure safe, efficient operation of your fireplace.

The biggest hazard in any fireplace is creosote build-up. When wood burns too slowly and too coolly, gases condense in the chimney and form a creosote layer on the flue. Creosote is flammable and can be ignited by sparks from the fireplace. The amount of creosote build-up depends on the type of fuel used, how hot the fires are and the size of the chimney. Wet wood, slow combustion and oversize chimneys add to creosote build-up.

CLEANING YOUR CHIMNEY

You can clean your own chimney with a stiff-bristled chimney brush and extension handles. You'll need to clean the flue down from the roof and up from the firebox. A mirror and a strong light will help ensure that you're removing all the creosote.

Masonry chimneys and fireplaces should also be checked regularly for cracks in the mortar and loose bricks. They'll need to be repaired for efficient fireplace operation.

CHIMNEY LINERS AND CAPS

Many older homes have no chimney liners, which are essential if you plan to use your fireplace frequently. Check the condition of your liner regularly and have a damaged one replaced.

Chimney caps are also important, to prevent moisture from entering the chimney. Water will eventually deteriorate the inside of your chimney. Replace a deteriorated cap.

FIREBOXES

Make sure the interior of your fireplace is in good condition. There should be no cracks in the firebox or in the hearth. Masonry fireboxes should be lined with firebrick.

Scrub your firebox walls with a stiff-bristled brush to eliminate any creosote and soot build-up.

GLASS DOORS

Glass doors will prevent heat loss from a room, but they can also create cooler burning fires which may cause creosote to build up more quickly in the chimney.

is collected in the openings in the bottom tubes and circulates through the tubes. As it circulates, the air picks up heat and is expelled through the top openings in the grate. Some units have blowers to force the heated air into the room. Whichever type you buy, the top tubes of the grate must be flush with the fireplace face and sit no lower than 5cm (2in) below the top of the face. Otherwise the heated air will not enter the room but will be circulated within the firebox instead.

Combination units are available that provide the benefits of a tube grate and blower along with glass doors. These are efficient units, since they allow warm air to circulate from the fire into the room. Even with the glass doors closed, they allow for good combustion, minimizing creosote build-up while preventing heated air from escaping up the chimney.

In both the tube grates and the combination units, you'll need regular maintenance of the interior of the tubes. Any build-up of soot or creosote will prevent an efficient movement of air through the tubes.

Fireplace inserts are a popular means of getting more heat from the fireplace. The insert has a firebox enclosed in another box. Air enters not only the firebox for combustion but also the secondary box, where it circulates around the outside of the firebox, picking up heat and discharging it into the room.

WOODSTOVES

A freestanding woodstove or fireplace stove is an efficient means of adding heat to your home. Airtight woodstoves properly connected can produce almost six times more heat than a masonry fireplace.

Most modern woodstoves are airtight and contain baffles and fans for efficient operation. A baffle divides the firebox into two sections, minimizing heat loss up the flue. A baffle also provides control for secondary combustion. Air enters the woodstove from a low air intake for primary combustion. Unburned gases move toward the rear of the stove and, if a baffle is in place, will not escape up the flue but will move toward the front of the stove underneath the baffle. Where another air intake allows for secondary combustion to burn off the gases, creating more heat and minimizing creosote build-up.

Follow the maintenance procedures under fireplaces to ensure a creosote-free firebox and flue.

FIREPLACE INSERTS

A fireplace insert draws room air through the bottom grate and circulates the air around the firebox and out through a grate in the top of the unit. As the air circulates, it is heated. Combustion air is brought into the fire chamber through a grille located at the bottom of the glass doors. While this type of unit does heat your room, it also provides for a cooler-burning fire, creating the potential for creosote buildup on the flue. Frequently burn fires with the glass doors open. This makes for a hotter fire and helps burn off creosote.

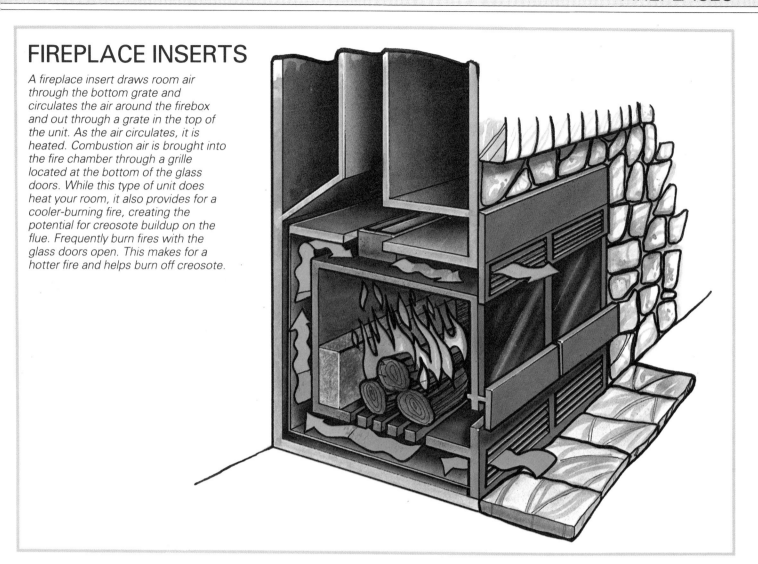

AIRTIGHT WOODSTOVE

A baffle divides the firebox of a woodstove into two sections, minimizing heat loss up the flue and allowing secondary combustion to take place.

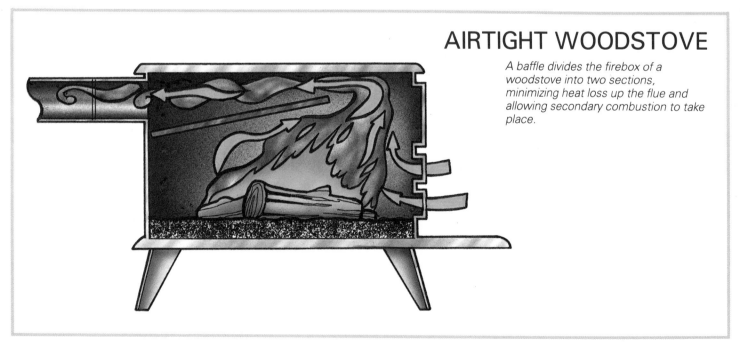

HUMIDIFIERS AND DE-HUMIDIFIERS

Regulate moisture content in household air to prevent condensation damage and to increase comfort.

A s the temperature drops, the ability of the air to hold moisture decreases. Therefore, in winter months the air becomes drier. Coupled with the dry heat produced from forced-air furnaces, the air inside a house can become too dry for comfort. To compensate for the lack of comfort, we need to turn our thermostats up to at least 24°C (75°F).

However, by adding a power humidifier to your furnace, you increase the moisture content of the air, and in so doing can decrease the thermostat setting and still maintain a comfortable level of heat.

Relative humidity, defined as the actual amount of water vapor in the air compared to the actual amount of water vapor the air can hold, should be between 30 and 45 percent. Power humidifiers allow you to set the humidity level for maximum comfort.

There are two different types of power humidifiers used in homes. The most popular is the evaporator type, which forces warm air through a stationary or moving wet pad where it picks up moisture and then goes back into the supply duct and out into the house. This type of humidifier is designed for homes with forced-air heating, but there are other types of evaporator humidifiers that come equipped with a blower fan that can be installed with different heating systems. With this type of humidifier, hot water evaporates and is circulated to a central grille in the house.

The second type of humidifier is the atomizer. It breaks water into fine particles which are then absorbed by the surrounding air. Because this type of humidifier can operate independently of the warm air in the furnace, it can be located almost anywhere in the house where water and electrical connections are convenient.

The evaporator type of humidifier is usually attached directly to the warm-air plenum of the furnace. A copper tube is attached to the nearby cold-water pipe, providing a constant supply of water to the humidifier. As water moves up from the water trough and into the wet pad, where it evaporates into the warm air, the float moves down, opening the valve to allow more water into the trough.

The inside of the unit has a tendency to become coated with mineral deposits from

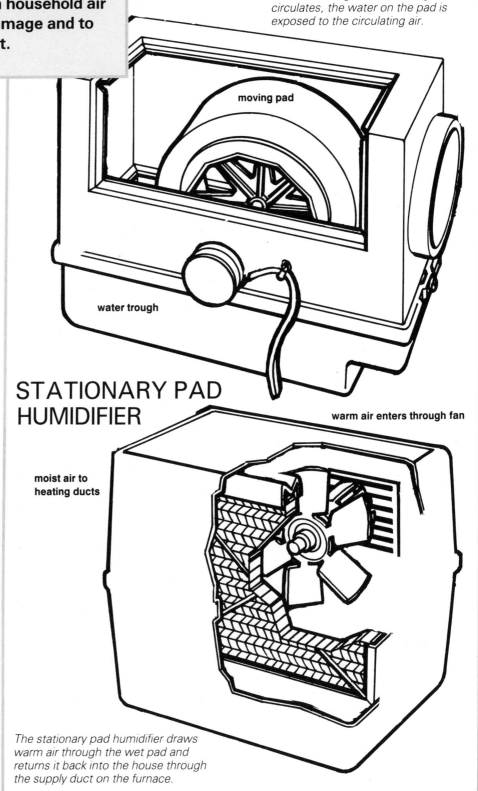

MOVING PAD HUMIDIFIER

In the moving pad humidifier, the pad revolves through a water trough. As it circulates, the water on the pad is exposed to the circulating air.

moving pad

water trough

STATIONARY PAD HUMIDIFIER

warm air enters through fan

moist air to heating ducts

The stationary pad humidifier draws warm air through the wet pad and returns it back into the house through the supply duct on the furnace.

HOW A DEHUMIDIFIER WORKS

In a dehumidifier, a motor and fan draw wet air through the back of the unit and over refrigerated coils. The moisture condenses and drops into a collection bucket. The dry air is then forced out the front of the unit.

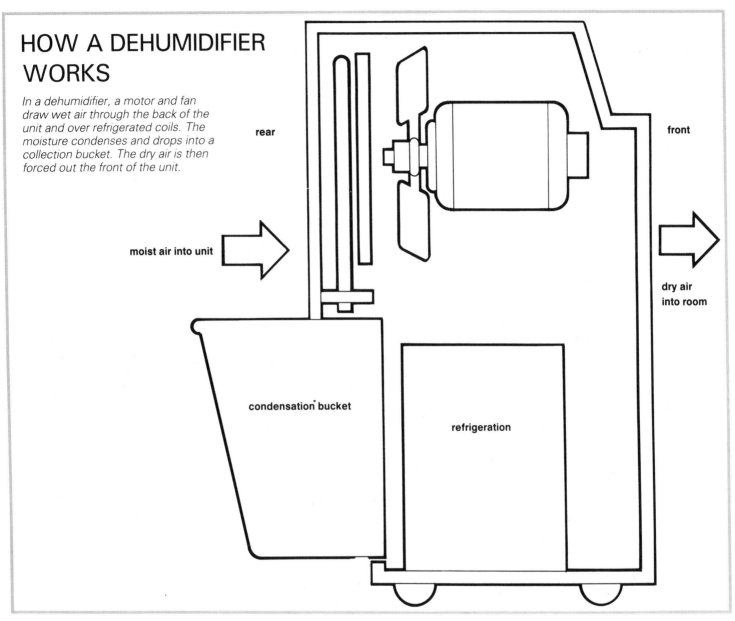

rear

front

moist air into unit

dry air into room

condensation bucket

refrigeration

the water. When you shut the humidifier off for the summer, remove the wet pad and float from the unit and scrub them free of deposits. The wet pad can be soaked in a vinegar and water solution until it comes clean. Scrub the sides of the unit with sandpaper to eliminate the build-up. The humidifier will be in clean condition for winter operation.

Dehumidifiers

While in the winter months some houses suffer from too little humidity, the summer months can bring too much moisture into the air. Even in winter, frequent showers, drying clothes and cooking can contribute excessive amounts of moisture to the air. There are several methods of eliminating excess air moisture, including bathroom ventilation fans to force wet air outside, making sure your clothes drier is vented to the outside, a hood over the stove top with access to an outdoor vent, and dehumidifiers that remove moisture from the air and deposit it into buckets.

A fan in the dehumidifier draws wet air through the back of the unit and over refrigerated coils. The moisture condenses on the coils and drips into a bucket, while the dried air continues through the dehumidifier and out through the front into the room.

A humidistat control on the unit allows you to adjust for the amount of moisture you want removed from the air, and the unit turns off automatically when that level is reached.

Most dehumidifiers have a capacity for removal of 5 to 14L (10 to 30pt) of water, which is the amount of water removed from the air in a 24-hour period at 60 percent relative humidity and an air temperature of 26°C (80°F). A 14L (30pt) capacity unit would be enough to handle the demands for a basement, providing air moves freely through the basement.

When buying a dehumidifier, make sure the capacity can handle your needs. Also look for a unit that has a humidistat, so that you can preset a humidity level for comfort. The unit should also have a catch bucket for the condensation or a hose connection that attaches to the nearest drain for continuous removal of water. With the catch bucket, make sure the unit has an automatic overflow control that will shut off the dehumidifier when the bucket becomes full. Most units have a red signal light to indicate this.

Clean the filter at the back of the unit regularly, and keep dirt and dust from the air-drying coils.

ATTIC VENTILATION

Static and power ventilators provide air movement in the attic to eliminate condensation problems and extreme heat build-up.

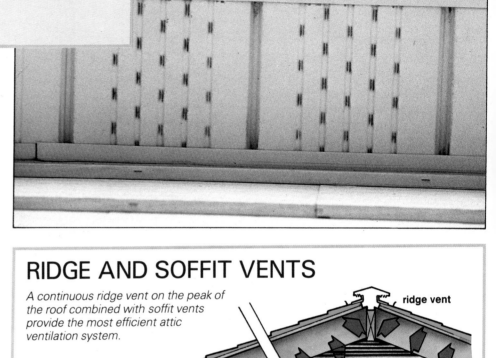

No matter how well insulated your home is, nothing will keep hot air from rising up through it. As the heat rises during the hot months, a well-insulated attic will trap the hot air, which can create a temperature difference of up to 10°C (50°F) between the air in the attic and the outside air. This extreme heat will force its way back down into the house unless your attic has adequate ventilation to moderate the temperature.

Without attic ventilation, the winter months will see condensation forming in the attic, destroying the effectiveness of your insulation and creating an escape route for the warm air in the house.

To ensure that the air in the attic doesn't have a chance to remain static, you should have about 77cm² (1ft²) of ventilation for every 14 to 23m² (150 to 250ft²) of attic space. To accomplish this, there are several varieties of both static and power ventilators that are easy for the do-it-yourselfer to install.

Static ventilators

You'll need a series of different types of vents to provide adequate attic ventilation. Soffit vents are the most familiar type. They're metal grates placed horizontally on the soffits to keep weather out and to allow cool air to enter the attic and flow along the attic floor.

Another type of static ventilator is the gable-end louvre, which is usually triangular and fits under the peak of the roof in the gable ends. Air is drawn in through one ventilator according to the direction of the wind, falls to the floor of the attic and moves across the attic floor and out the ventilator at the other side of the roof.

Both these types of ventilators are good at removing air that sits along the attic floor. However, both do little to ventilate the warmer air that collects at the peak of the roof.

To exhaust this warmer air, roof louvres of wood, aluminum, steel or plastic can be mounted near the peak of the roof. These ventilators are covered and screened to prevent rain and snow as well as birds, animals and insects from entering the attic.

Turbines are another type of ventilator,

RIDGE AND SOFFIT VENTS

A continuous ridge vent on the peak of the roof combined with soffit vents provide the most efficient attic ventilation system.

ridge vent

gable vent

soffit vent

placed close to the roof peak to eliminate warm air. Turbines are metal with multiple fins that rotate in the wind. However, this type tends to remove warm air only from the immediate area of the turbine.

Ridge vents are arguably the best vent to install to remove hot attic air. These aluminum vents are placed over the ridge of the roof the entire length of the peak, providing the warm air with a large avenue of escape.

For effective attic ventilation, the best combination of vents to use is the soffit and ridge vent. The soffit vents take care of the cooler air along the floor of the attic, while the hot air that rises in the attic can be ex-

hausted through the ridge vent.

Roof louvres combined with soffit vents will also provide a similar effect. However, you must remember that one roof louvre won't do an efficient job. You'll probably need multiple louvres to remove all the hot air around the peak of the roof.

Power ventilators

Power ventilators are basically electric fans that exhaust air to the outside. Some units have a thermostat that will automatically turn on and shut off the ventilator when preset temperature levels have been reached.

C--N--ENS-TI--N causes and cures

Condensation in buildings is a bigger problem now than ever before – the result of changes in building methods and our way of life. To tackle it, you need to know what it is and why it happens.

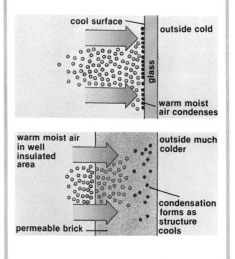

The air around us contains water vapor, and the amount it can carry depends on the temperature — the higher the temperature, the greater the amount of water vapor. If the air becomes cooler, it cannot carry as much vapor, and the excess may be released in the form of water droplets. In the atmosphere this produces clouds and rainfall; in confined spaces like the home it produces condensation.

You can see this happening in a kitchen when you're cooking. A lot of water vapor is created by boiling pans, and this remains suspended in the air in the kitchen as long as the temperature is high. But if the air meets a cold surface — a window, for example — its temperature drops, and the excess water vapor turns back into water, or condenses. Condensation occurs particularly in bathrooms, but can be found throughout your home at some time or another.

Condensation is always a menace, and can lead to corrosion and rot as can any unwanted water. If it forms only a thin film of moisture, this may quickly evaporate when the room heats up, but too often the water seeps into cracks and crevices in the house's structure and starts to cause problems.

The problem of moisture

Dense materials like glass and glazed tiles, are not harmed by moisture and can be easily wiped off. But if it runs off the surface it can carry with it dirt, which can stain nearby materials. Metal surfaces do not absorb moisture, but moisture combined with oxygen in the air will cause iron to rust. If mineral salts are present, or if dissimilar metals are in contact, corrosion may take place.

Some materials, like drywall, lose their strength when wet and may swell and sag. But more damaging is the risk of mold and rot. Mold spores are almost always present in the air, and on the surface of many materials. To flourish, they need moisture, and food which is supplied by general dirt. Condensation provides the moisture. Textured surfaces collect more dirt than smooth surfaces, and are more likely to develop mold growth.

Mold first appears in spots or small patches and spreads to form a furry layer — usually gray-green, black or brown in color. Though unsightly it can easily be cleaned off in the early stages. It may do little harm, but will reappear unless a fungicide is used.

Fungal attack on wood, particularly dry rot, is more serious, causing lasting damage. Once established, dry rot can actually produce the moisture needed for further growth and it can spread extensively through other materials such as brick.

Moisture has another unwanted effect. Many materials, such as sheeps' wool and plastic foam, gain heat insulating qualities through the small pockets of air in them. If this air is replaced by water, then this insulating power is lost. If this happens within a brick wall — so-called 'interstitial' condensation — the wall's resistance to heat flow is decreased and the wall gets colder, producing still more condensation.

How water vapor is created

We can't avoid producing water vapor indoors. For example, during eight hours of sleep, every human body gives off a quarter litre (½ pint) of water. When we are active we make much more.

WHAT CAUSES CONDENSATION

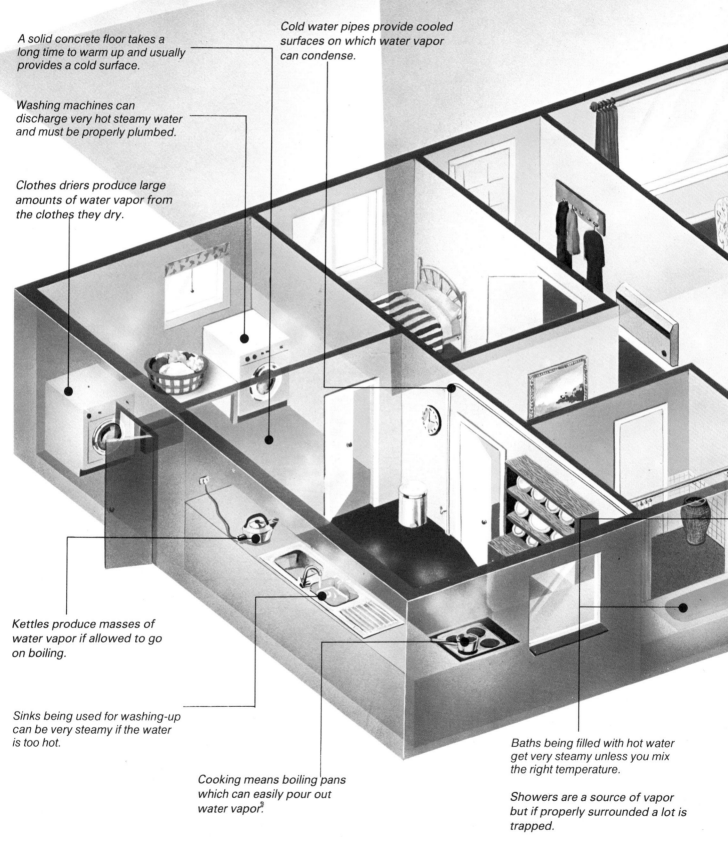

A solid concrete floor takes a long time to warm up and usually provides a cold surface.

Cold water pipes provide cooled surfaces on which water vapor can condense.

Washing machines can discharge very hot steamy water and must be properly plumbed.

Clothes driers produce large amounts of water vapor from the clothes they dry.

Kettles produce masses of water vapor if allowed to go on boiling.

Sinks being used for washing-up can be very steamy if the water is too hot.

Cooking means boiling pans which can easily pour out water vapor.

Baths being filled with hot water get very steamy unless you mix the right temperature.

Showers are a source of vapor but if properly surrounded a lot is trapped.

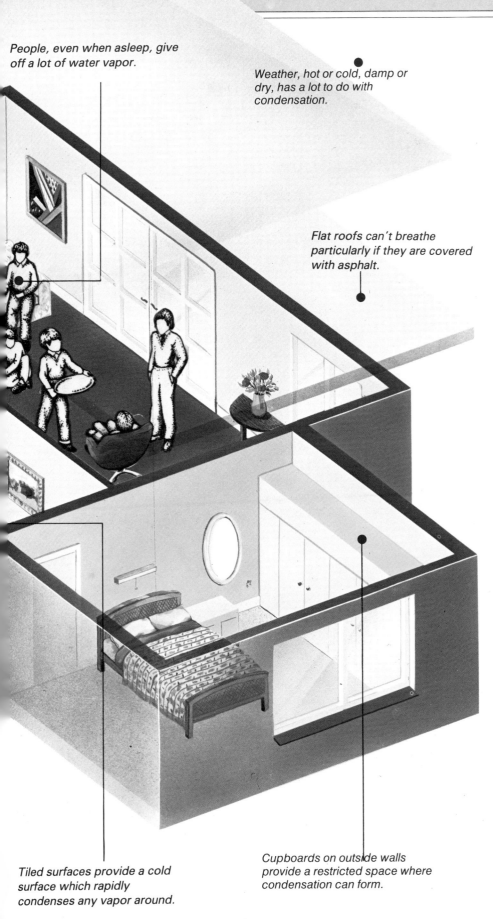

People, even when asleep, give off a lot of water vapor.

Weather, hot or cold, damp or dry, has a lot to do with condensation.

Flat roofs can't breathe particularly if they are covered with asphalt.

Tiled surfaces provide a cold surface which rapidly condenses any vapor around.

Cupboards on outside walls provide a restricted space where condensation can form.

Ready Reference

CAUSES OF DAMPNESS
Condensation is not the only cause of dampness in a dwelling. Before you jump to conclusions, check the other possibilities:
● **rising dampness.** Usually found in older property which has no damp proofer on the outside foundation walls or an ineffective one, but it may also occur in newer property where earth, a terrace, or small extension has bridged the damp proofer
● **rain penetration.** More likely in older houses lacking cavity walls, in parts of the country where there is a lot of driving rain
● **other penetrating dampness.** Can be the result of water getting in through faulty roofs, chimney stacks, ill-fitting door or window frames, or a result of faulty gutters, downpipes or plumbing
● **wet building trades,** like bricklaying, concrete-work and plastering. These use a lot of water which has to be dried out which again requires heat and ventilation.

CONDENSATION CHECKLIST
Once you've eliminated the other causes of dampness, you can justifiably suspect condensation if dampness occurs
● in corners
● over windows
● in unheated rooms
● when double glazing has been installed
● when a fireplace has been blocked up.

SIMPLE CURES
Take condensation seriously: it could seriously damage the fabric of your home. Simple remedies include the following:
● keep doors shut and windows open in steamy rooms
● vent clothes driers direct to the outside
● use a ventilator hood over the stove
● use an extractor fan in the kitchen or bathroom
● fit wind-operated vents if you don't want open windows
● try to keep cupboards and bookcases away from cold outside walls, so condensation cannot form behind them.

INSULATION GUIDELINES
When insulating your home:
● include vapor barriers whenever you are installing wall or loft insulation
● where surface condensation is a major problem, line rooms with polystyrene liner
● when you install attic insulation, see that it is well ventilated, the trap door is draftproofed, and gaps around pipes and cables entering the attic are filled.

KILLING MOLD
Mold growth produced by condensation can be removed with a toxic wash, such as bleach or a fungicide.

HOW TO CURE CONDENSATION

Mechanical ventilators
Powered by an electric motor, these are the sophisticated development of wind-operated vents and obviously much more efficient.

Cavity wall insulation
This reduces heat loss from the house and therefore your heating bills. It also cuts down the incidence of cold outside walls, reducing the likelihood of condensation.

Vented clothes driers
Clothes driers produce masses of water vapor and should always be vented direct to the outside of the house. This can be done via a flexible hose put out a window, but ideally should be through a vent pipe placed in the wall exiting via a protective cowl.

Self-closing doors
Where there are heavy sources of water vapor, as in the kitchen, it is best to contain them rather than let the vapor spread to other rooms where quite often they are likely to condense. A self-closing door is the answer here.

Stove hoods
These are designed to vent hot air and gases coming up from the stove. Those which simply filter the air are really only good for getting rid of kitchen smells, but those which can be vented to the outside air, either directly through the wall or via a fan controlled duct, can cut down condensation risk.

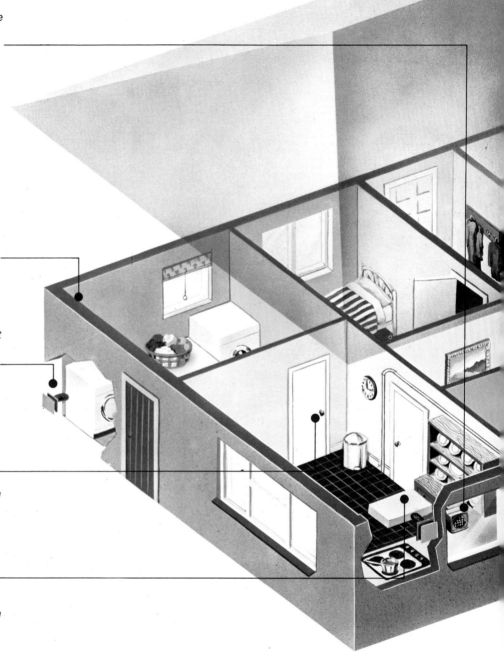

Having a bath or shower can produce two litres (3½ pints) of water vapor. Another offender is dampness. This can penetrate an outside wall or a solid ground floor and later evaporate because of indoor warmth, so adding more water vapor to the air.

Because it is impossible to prevent the creation of water vapor, the main aim then becomes to get rid of it before it can give trouble by forming condensation.

Ventilation is the answer. This can be done by opening windows, installing extractor fans and venting exhaust air from clothes driers to the outside air.

Water vapor moves about. It doesn't only condense on cold surfaces in the room where it is produced; it can penetrate all parts of the home, and is likely to condense in any colder area it reaches. It also rises by convection to cooler bedrooms and the space under the roof.

Warm, moist air gets into the roof space through ceiling cracks, holes used by pipes and electric wiring and gaps around the trap door. It doesn't matter how small the gap — it can still get through as it's a gas. It also

passes through porous plaster or drywall ceilings unless they incorporate a moisture barrier.

Unless there is sufficient ventilation for it to escape to the outside air, it will condense on the roof covering and rafters. The severity of the condensation depends on the roof construction, how well the attic is insulated and ventilated, and how easily moist house air can get into it. However, it can very quickly build up in a poorly ventilated attic, saturating the insulation and making it quite useless. In the end it can soak through the ceiling too.

Attic insulation
Attic insulation is yet another way of retaining heat inside the main part of the house and also contains the risk of condensation, but it must be coupled with the provision of proper attic ventilation, or condensation may become a problem in the attic.

Attic ventilation
This is vital to protect the rafters in your roof from rot attack. The better the attic insulation the greater the temperature contrast between the attic and rooms below, and the greater the risk of condensation.

Wind-operated vents
These small plastic vents set into the window frame usually blow around in the wind, and even a small breeze can make them work. They simply provide ventilation which disposes of unwanted water vapor. While not that effective they are very cheap to install.

Central heating
Usually installed as the source of heat, central heating will also reduce the risk of condensation as the water vapour is not allowed to cool and the temperature differential between different parts of the house is reduced. But effective central heating is rather expensive to run for long periods these days.

Double glazing
This is a highly effective way of retaining heat as 20% is lost through windows which are single glazed. It also ensures that the inner pane of glass is not cold, which is usually the case with single glazing, and thus eliminates a major source of condensation.

Attic insulation certainly makes a house warmer, but means that the roof structure will be colder. This exaggerated difference in temperature enables the water vapor to pass more easily from the house itself to the roof space. Shingles on loosely laid felt will 'breathe' and allow the moisture to disperse, but fully lined roofs tend to trap moist air. Even worse are flat roofs having a lead, bituminous felt or asphalt covering; these cannot breathe at all.

Vapor inside the walls
The better draft-proofed, and more airtight a house, the more likely it is that moist air will force its way into the structure during the winter, possibly leading to condensation.

While 'superficial' condensation is a nuisance and can spoil decoration, it is visible, and serves as a warning to the householder to provide better ventilation. But interstitial condensation can cause serious and lasting damage to a building and, unless it is so severe that dampness shows through on a ceiling or outside wall, it can go unnoticed for

many years. In older drafty houses, risk of 'interstitial' condensation is slight, though superficial condensation will sometimes occur in unheated rooms. Risks increase when fireplaces are blocked up, windows double-glazed, external doors draft-proofed, and attics and external walls better insulated. Builders of new, well-insulated airtight houses should guard against moist air getting into walls and the attic by using vapor barriers, and by ensuring that any air leaking through it is easily vented to the outside.

INSTALLING WEATHER-STRIPPING

Why put up with uncomfortable drafts when you can buy easy-to-install weatherstripping to provide an effective seal against the weather? Here's how to fit some of the more common types.

There's nothing more unpleasant than sitting in a draft. Yet while many of us will complain about feeling shivery, it's surprising how many people are prepared to put up with a cold stream of air blowing round their ankles. However, apart from making your home more comfortable to live in, weatherstripping could also save you a considerable amount of money which will more than pay for the cost of the work. The equation is simple: *drafts = higher heating bills*.

Tracking down the draft
How many times have you heard the expression: 'There's a draft coming from somewhere'? Usually the reason is put down to an interior door that hasn't been closed properly or which has a large gap under it. But in fact, in most instances this isn't to blame. The draft has to come from somewhere, yet in most cases it's coming through ill-fitting window casements, sashes and doors. Fortunately, however, there's a tremendous range of products on the market to deal with virtually every situation and you should choose the type best suited to your needs.

When it comes to installing these devices, carry out the work systematically and don't just block up a few drafts and leave others. You've got to seal the outside of the house and when you've done that it won't matter if you leave an interior door open — it won't on its own cause a draft. However, don't get over-enthusiastic and block up ventilators as it's important to maintain a circulating supply of air in the house — especially where fuel-burning appliances are in use.

Checking frame fit
If a window or door frame has been correctly installed, there shouldn't be a gap between the frame and the wall outside. If there is, say as a result of settlement or a poorly seasoned frame drying out, you may well get a draft through here (as well as penetrating dampness). The answer is to use either flexible crack fillers or caulking, which are most easily applied with a caulking gun. Caulking doesn't set, so it can cater for slight movements in the frame, and by running over the surface with a putty knife dipped in water or turps you can give it a neat, smooth finish.

Using foam strip
Foam strip is probably the most common method of weatherproofing and is easily available in a variety of forms and thicknesses. It's also cheap, but not very long-lasting. However, all you have to do when it wears out is to peel it off and stick on a new strip. Invariably some of the adhesive backing will be left behind when you do this, but it can be removed from the frame by rubbing with a cloth soaked in turps.

Weatherstripping
Being made of metal or plastic, these excluders are more substantial than foam strip. They work on a hinge principle — some are in the form of a flap, others have a V profile — which bridges the gap between the frame and the window or door. The strip can either be fitted to the frame (in the same places you would fit foam strip) or to the window or door itself. If you are installing it round a door then you can't run it down the lock/handle edge: you'll have to use the frame for this part. Generally speaking, fixing to a door is more tricky and you may find it easier to take the door off the hinges first. Weatherstripping can be fitted to the bottom edge, but check that it doesn't drag across a carpet as the door is opened and closed.

Rigid and flexible strip
In contrast to the previous excluders, these strips are fitted to the inner face of the door or window frame on the outside, not in the rebate. They consist of a plastic or aluminum holder with a flexible insert (either a PVC flap or tube) against which the door presses when it's closed. For this reason it's best to position the strip with the door shut so you can see that the flexible strip touches the door along its entire length. You can then open the door to make nailing easier.

Dealing with door bottoms
This is probably going to be where you get most drafts because for a door to operate without sticking there's got to be a small gap between the bottom edge and the sill. But there are a number of devices specially designed to seal this gap when the door is closed. They range in sophistication from a simple flap fitted to the door to two-part sealers which are fitted to the door and sill.

Simple excluders These consist of a brush or PVC strip set in a plastic, aluminum or

WEATHERPROOFING WOODEN FRAMES

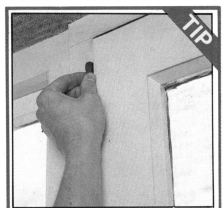

1 If fitting a metal spring strip, there needs to be at least a 2mm (¹⁄₁₆in) gap between the frame and door or window. Check this with a coin.

2 Measure accurately between the door jambs and also down the side, then cut the metal strip to length. Normally it's thin enough to cut with scissors.

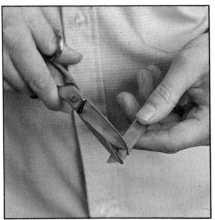

3 So that the spring flaps of the strip complete the seal at the corners, mitre the edges – 45° for the top ends and 20° for the sides is about right.

4 Fix the top strip into position with nails at each end, and then at 100mm (4in) intervals. Next nail the side strips in place down the rebates.

5 Some strip systems have to be nailed to the outside of the door frame. Again you have to mitre the corners of the rubber strip to continue the seal.

6 When the door is closed it presses against the rubber seal and cuts out any drafts. But you may have problems if the door is badly warped.

7 If you're using foam strip on outward opening windows or doors measure the inside of the rebates to see roughly how much strip you're going to use.

8 Press the end of the strip into the corner of the frame, then work along the rebate unrolling the strip as you go. Keep it taut for easier application.

9 If the window frame has warped so that in places it doesn't press against the foam, you can apply a second strip of sealer over the first.

WEATHERPROOFING DOOR BOTTOMS

1 If you're using a sweep, mark the width of the door on the plastic holder, slide back the brush and cut the holder to length with a hacksaw.

2 Push the brush back so that it's flush with the far end, then use the cutting edges of a pair of pliers to cut the strip to the same length as the holder.

3 Position the excluder so that the brush rests on the floor. Fix the outside screws first so you can adjust the bar if the floor is uneven.

4 With this automatic device, make sure that the spring gear and striking bar are on the door opening side. Then cut the bar to length and screw it in place.

5 The spring mechanism means that the bar is raised when the door is opened. Cut the vinyl strip to length and slide it into the groove.

6 Screw the striking plate to the inside of the door jamb. You may have to chisel a bevel on the jamb so the excluder can swing through it when the door is closed.

7 As the door is shut, the striking bar hits the striking plate, forcing the vinyl flap down against the spring and onto the threshold to complete the seal.

8 There are various forms of threshold sealer. With this type, cut the aluminum holder to the width of the door jambs, leaving screw holes at each end.

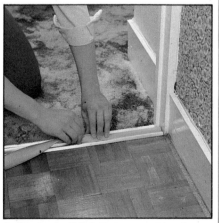

9 When the holder is screwed in place, cut the vinyl strip about 12mm (1/2in) longer than the threshold. Then press the strip into the channel.

wooden bar. They are usually sold in 900mm (36in) lengths but most can be cut down to size. To fit them you just have to nail or screw them to the bottom edge of the opening side of the door (see step-by-step photographs). Where a door has a high sill you'll have to use a type that closes against the sill itself rather than rests on the floor.

Hinged excluders One of the main problems with the simple flat excluders is that they drag across the floor when the door is opened. So to get round this you could install a hinged type instead. These also vary in complexity, but all of them have some form of springing device which lifts a flexible PVC strip clear of the sill when the door is opened. You'll also have to fit a striking plate to the bottom of the door frame which will force the flap down over the gap when the door is closed. A further advantage of these excluders is that they automatically compensate for uneven sills and they can also deal with large gaps (see step-by-step photographs).

Threshold excluders The types used for internal doors are simply screwed to the floor (see step-by-step photographs), but if the gap is too wide you'll have to make some modifications. This may mean mounting the excluder on a strip of wood, fitting a replacement sill or lowering the door on its hinges. If the gap is too narrow for the excluder to be fitted you may have to trim a little off the bottom of the door. Use a plane rather than a saw, and chamfer the door so that it squeezes the flexible part of the excluder as it closes.

Threshold excluders for external doors are more complicated and consist either of a complete replacement sill containing a simple threshold excluder, or a face sealing/combination-type excluder. The replacement sill is no more difficult to fit than a simple threshold excluder, though the ends should be sealed with caulking or putty to stop water getting under them.

In contrast, the second type needs considerable care when it's being installed. Instructions vary, but it is important to ensure that where there are two parts they meet accurately, and that the weather is kept out of the seal, which means screwing a weatherbar along the bottom outside face of the door. Some types even require the door or frame to be shaped to fit the excluder.

Ready Reference

FITTING WEATHERSTRIPPING

Different types of excluder have to be fitted to different parts of a door or window frame, as shown below.

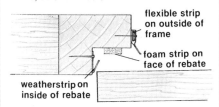

TIP: USE A NAIL PUNCH

To prevent damaging the excluder and frame use a nail punch to drive the fixing nails.

SILICONE SEALANTS

As an alternative to strip excluders use silicone sealant to make a tailor-made gasket. It's ideal for metal frames and badly warped doors and windows.

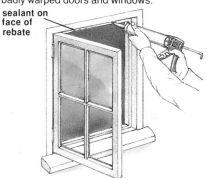

● clean and make good any paintwork
● apply a thin bead of silicone to the face of the frame's rebates and to the side of the rebate on the hinge side
● coat the closing faces of the door or window with special release agent (petroleum jelly, liquid detergent or sticky tape will also do) so they don't stick to the silicone when the door is shut to mold the seal
● leave silicone overnight to cure
● clean up the seal with a sharp knife.

METAL WINDOWS AND FRAMES

These tend to fit better than wooden ones, but if you need to weatherproof them use foam strip or silicone sealant.

LETTERBOXES

Fit a hinged flap over the opening on the inside to seal out drafts. Alternatively fit a brush type excluder.

WEATHERPROOFING SASH WINDOWS

Sash windows are the most difficult type of window to weatherproof. Usually you'll have to use a combination of excluders to make an effective seal.

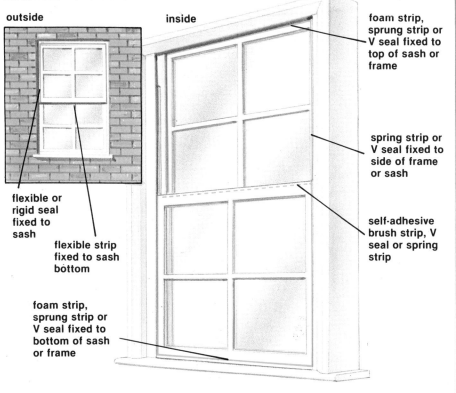

outside

inside

foam strip, sprung strip or V seal fixed to top of sash or frame

spring strip or V seal fixed to side of frame or sash

self-adhesive brush strip, V seal or spring strip

flexible or rigid seal fixed to sash

flexible strip fixed to sash bottom

foam strip, sprung strip or V seal fixed to bottom of sash or frame

FITTING SECONDARY GLAZING

Secondary double glazing — the fitting of fixed, hinged or sliding panes to the inside of existing windows — cuts heat loss and drafts dramatically. If you install it yourself, it need not be prohibitively expensive either.

There are two basic types of double glazing available to the homeowner. Primary double glazing involves the fitting of a sealed glazing unit — two linked panes of glass separated only by a hermetically sealed gap — into an existing or replacement window frame. These sealed units are factory-made, but can be installed by the do-it-yourselfer (see pages 162-165).

Secondary double glazing is the term used to describe the installation of a completely independent second layer of glass (or other glazing material) some distance away from the existing single glazing, either to the inside of the window frame or to the window reveal surrounding it.

The fitting of this form of double glazing is well within the scope of the do-it-yourselfer and offers some advantages over primary double glazing. It is cheaper and quicker to install, since instead of having to order sealed units from a specialist manufacturing company you need only visit your local do-it-yourself shop and collect the necessary kit of component parts.

Sealed units have no weatherproofing abilities when installed in old badly fitting opening windows, whereas secondary double glazing seals the entire frame, acting as both a thermal barrier and weather-proofer.

It is worth noting, however, that primary double glazing is more effective as a thermal barrier and is also less obtrusive, being no more visible than a single pane of glass.

Types of secondary double glazing

An extremely wide variety of secondary double glazing systems exist to cater for virtually all situations (and pockets). Glass is by no means the only material used for glazing. Other products used are clear polyethylene film in varying degrees of strength and clarity, or other transparent rigid plastics.

Methods of framing the glazing also vary enormously, with just double-sided adhesive tape being used for some systems and rigid or flexible PVC or aluminum extrusions for others.

Yet more choice comes with installation methods, where there are fixed, hinged or sliding systems (vertical or horizontal).

Which type to choose

When deciding on a secondary double glazing system, several factors should be considered carefully. Cost naturally plays an important part. If you live in rented accommodation and don't expect to stay for long, or simply want the cheapest form of double glazing for financial reasons, then the chances are that you will find clear polyethylene sheeting will serve your purposes. Attached to the existing window frame with double-sided adhesive tape, the polyethylene will prevent drafts very successfully, but in its most basic form it is not totally clear, is easily damaged, and seldom looks very tidy.

This type of double glazing, although inexpensive and effective, does have one major disadvantage; once fixed, it is there for good — or at least until completely removed and discarded at the end of the winter.

Double glazing of this nature is classed as fixed, but there is another 'fixed' variety which is less permanent and which can be temporarily removed and later replaced successfully. This type generally consists of a sheet of glass or rigid plastic sheet fitted into either a plastic or aluminum frame and then secured to the existing window frame using turnbuttons which hold it firmly in place.

One drawback with fixed systems is that they do not allow for ventilation, and this can be very important. In situations where ventilation is necessary or you simply want easily openable windows, you will have to decide whether to purchase a double glazing system which incorporates sliding panels or hinged ones. And one factor which could help you make this choice is the sort of existing window you have.

Sliding double glazing systems need to have their outer tracks or channels secured to the sides, top and bottom of the window reveal. If your window has no reveal, or this is less than about 40mm (1½in) deep, then you will be unable to fit a sliding system unless you choose a type that is attached to the window frame itself.

Hinged systems are fixed to the existing window's surrounding wooden frame. In some cases, notably on metal windows, catches and stays project into the room past the frame and could prevent a hinged panel closing. The space between old and new panes can, however, be increased to allow for such projections by fitting an additional

FITTING SLIDING TRACK

1 *Measure the height and width of the opening at each side, and write down the smaller measurement in each case if the figures differ.*

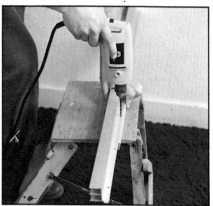

2 *Mark the length required on each of the track sections, cut them with a hacksaw, and file the ends smooth. Then drill holes for the fixing screws.*

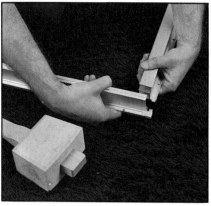

3 *Assemble the track sections on a flat surface. Insert the corner pieces and use a mallet to tap the sections together gently but firmly.*

4 *Lift the assembled frame into place against the window frame, offering up the top track first. Then secure it with just one screw at top and bottom.*

5 *Check that the frame is square by measuring diagonals, and that the top and bottom tracks are level. Add more screws to secure the frame.*

6 *Where screws have to be driven into inaccessible corners, use a short piece of clear plastic tubing to hold the screw on the blade as you drive it.*

wood framework to the face of the existing one, or within the reveal itself.

The width of the frame, whether old or newly-installed, must be sufficient to accommodate the hinge posts and panel surround of the hinged system you have chosen. It is therefore essential, before buying the materials for a hinged system, to check the minimum window frame dimensions recommended by the makers of that system. It is not uncommon for wooden window frames, particularly those around metal windows, to be too narrow for face fixing. Here again the problem can be overcome by fitting a new frame of sufficient width inside the reveal.

An additional inner frame can also be used to increase the gap between panes, as would be necessary if the double glazing were being installed for sound insulation. Where the aim is to reduce noise penetration the ideal gap between panes should be about 200mm (8in). A gap of around 25mm (1in) is the optimum for good thermal insulation when installing secondary double glazing.

Preparing for installation

Once you have chosen the basic variety of double glazing which suits your home and taste, you must study the manufacturer's literature with great care. This will tell you what thickness of glass should be used. It will also detail existing frame size requirements, and indicate the maximum size that any one glazing panel should be. Information will also be provided, particularly with hinged or sliding systems, on how to measure the required sizes for each pane of glass so that this can be ordered in advance.

Some preparatory work may well be needed on the existing window frames. An additional sub-frame may have to be fitted, if,

as described earlier, the present frame is not wide enough or has window fittings projecting past it. Use prepared lumber painted to match the existing frame. Either secure it directly to the old frame with screws, or fix it to the window reveal with screws driven into wallplugs.

Clean and make good any defects on the old frame. Use weatherstripping on badly fitting opening windows to prevent as much air as possible from outside entering the space between the two glazing panes. It is the movement of air in the cavity that transfers warm air from the inner pane to the outer, and cold air from the outside pane to the inside one. Although the secondary double glazing will stop the drafts, it will be no more use than a single pane of glass at preventing heat loss if there is a howling gale blowing between the panes.

Plan your double glazing so that new

MAKING UP SLIDING PANELS

1 *Follow the instructions for measuring and ordering the glass. Then mark each length of edge section to the correct dimension.*

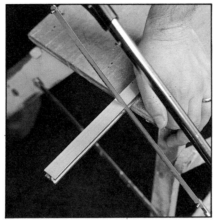

2 *Carefully cut each edge section to length with a hacksaw, making the cut as square as possible and filing away any burr that's left.*

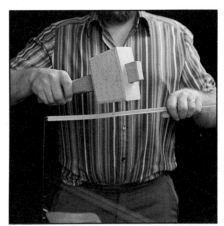

3 *Measure and cut the lengths of glazing gasket using a fine-toothed saw. Then tap them into place along the appropriate edges of the glass with a mallet.*

4 *Tap the top and bottom edge sections into place over the gaskets, add the handle to one of the side sections and then tap the side sections into place.*

5 *With the pane completely framed by the four edge sections and their gaskets, drive in small self-tapping screws to lock the corner blocks in position.*

6 *Move the handle along the groove in the side section to the desired position and then use a screwdriver blade to form a notch in the aluminum.*

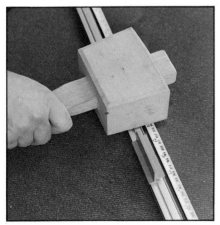

7 *Now use a mallet to tap the handle along the groove and over the burr formed by the screwdriver to lock it in place. Repeat on the other panel.*

8 *Tap the small sliders into the recesses in the two bottom corner blocks of each panel. These help the panels to slide smoothly in the tracks.*

9 *Offer up first the inner and then the outer sliding panels to their respective tracks, and check that they slide from side to side without binding.*

panels match as closely as possible the layout of your existing windows, with vertical divisions kept in line with mullions and opening sections (whether hinged or sliding) aligned with opening windows.

Measure your window opening carefully before ordering any glass. Problems can arise, particularly with sliding systems, if the window opening or frame is not square. If the two diagonal measurements of the opening are not equal, then the opening is definitely out of true, so for all calculations use the shortest width and height measurements.

Fitting the systems

1: Plastic To fit this very basic form of fixed double glazing you will need just a roll of double-sided adhesive tape, a roll of clear plastic, a tape measure and pair of scissors or utility knife.

Stick the tape, without removing the backing paper, to the face of the outer window frame all around the perimeter. Measure the size of the opening and cut a piece of plastic to suit. Remove the backing paper from the top piece of tape and attach the edge of the plastic gently to it. Allow the sheeting to hang down. Check that it fits squarely before removing the backing paper from the other three pieces of tape and securing the plastic to it. Be sure it is stretched taut all the time.

Strong, less creasable plastic, classed as semi-rigid, can be fixed in a different way by cutting it to the exact size first, then attaching the sticky tape to it rather than to the window frame. With the backing paper removed from the top edge only, the sheet is aligned to the head of the window frame, then stuck in place, followed by the other three edges.

2: Non-opening removable panels The most recent version of this form of double glazing uses a PVC extrusion stuck to the window frame, with a second extrusion holding the plastic sheeting in place. The work required involves cutting the PVC extrusion to size and fitting it around the existing frame. Either butt or mitred joints can be made at the corners. The plastic sheeting is then cut to size to fit in the profile. The clip-on extrusion is finally cut to size and snapped into place.

Other variations of this non-opening type of double glazing usually consist of plastic 'U' channelling fitted around pre-cut panes of glass. The glass, now with protected edges, is secured to the window frame with turnbuttons or clips spaced every 300mm (12in) around the perimeter to press the panel firmly against the frame and so exclude drafts. The glass for this type must be cut to size, allowing for the space taken up by the fixing clips on the frame. The panels can be removed and stored elsewhere at the end of the winter season.

Rather stronger non-opening panels can be made using aluminum framing instead of plastic 'U' channel, but these are generally a fixed version of hinged panels.

3: Hinged panels The most common hinged secondary double glazing systems are constructed using glass with an aluminum extrusion frame. The frame incorporates one channel with a plastic glazing gasket for the glass, a weatherproofing insert of either plastic or nylon fibre bristles which press against the window frame, and a second channel into which hinge fittings, turnbuttons and corner joins are fitted. Glass of the specified thickness is cut to size. Some makes can be fitted with more than one thickness of glass, this being determined by the overall panel size. A different size of glazing gasket is used for each thickness.

Once the glass is cut, the glazing gasket can be fitted to it, and the aluminum extrusions cut to length using a hacksaw. Straight cuts are made since the special corner joins eliminate the need for mitred corners.

The panel is then assembled, special care being needed to ensure that the glazing gasket is correctly seated in its channel and that all hinge fittings are properly inserted in the outer edge of the aluminum frame.

Hinge posts are then screwed to the window frame and the panel is lifted into place. Turnbuttons are finally fixed round the other three edges of the hinged panel to ensure that the panel is held tightly against the window frame when closed.

4: Sliding panels Made from either aluminum or PVC extrusions, sliding double glazing units are generally quick and easy to assemble and fit. Normally sold in kit form with everything but the glass provided, the biggest problem is often deciding which part belongs where, so the first step is to identify the different sections. One part of the kit will contain the vertical sections — the frame uprights and glass edging — and the other, the horizontal sections — the top and bottom sliding tracks and more glass edging.

The outer frame is fitted to the window reveal. This will usually involve drilling holes into the reveal sides, top and bottom and plugging the holes to take screws. Great care must be taken to ensure that the top double channel (the deeper one) is fitted directly above and in line with the bottom channel.

With the frame secured, the panes of glass can be fitted with their edge profiles, and the panels are then lifted into position in the sliding channels.

Provided that you have measured the glass correctly according to the instructions given by the double glazing manufacturer, you should find that the panels slide easily and that all nylon fibre weatherstripping built into the system aligns perfectly.

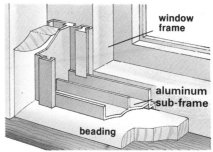

INSTALLING SEALED UNITS

Fitting sealed double glazing units will provide good heat and sound insulation as well as reducing drafts. They are easy to install in either existing or replacement window frames.

It is well known that double glazing offers considerable benefits for the homeowner. It can considerably reduce drafts from around the window area, not only those which enter through badly fitting frames but also down-drafts caused by warm air close to a cold, single pane of glass being quickly cooled and so falling. Eliminating these down-drafts makes for a more comfortable environment and prevents that 'chilly' feeling even though the room is heated. Some forms of double glazing can, to some extent, also reduce the penetration of noise from outside the building, but the major advantage is that the use of two panes instead of one can help reduce heat losses through glazed areas, providing a potential for saving energy and, hence, cutting fuel costs.

By far the most efficient method of achieving such thermal insulation is by the fitting of sealed double glazing units in place of single panes of glass in the window frame. This is known as primary double glazing.

Each sealed unit comprises two sheets of glass separated by a metal, glass or rigid plastic spacer which is fitted around the edges. The air between the two panes is dehydrated so that it contains no moisture, and the entire unit is sealed hermetically so that none can enter. As long as the seal remains unbroken condensation cannot form between the two sheets of glass.

The space between the panes normally varies between 6 and 12mm (¼ and ½in), the wider gap providing the best thermal insulation properties. The glass itself will vary in thickness from 3mm (⅛in) upwards depending on the size of the pane and the position of the window, many different types being available including float, laminated, toughened, standard sheet, tinted and obscured.

All sealed double glazing units are factory made by specialist companies and cannot be assembled at home. However, they can be fitted by the non-professional glazier in much the same way as normal replacement panes of glass (see techniques covered on pages 90-92) either to existing window frames or into new replacement windows.

Local glass merchants are becoming increasingly involved in the supply of sealed double glazing units in a wide range of standard sizes or in made-to-measure form to suit individual requirements, and it is now common practice for complete replacement windows, made from wood, aluminum or vinyl, to be supplied with sealed glazing units fitted as standard.

Fitting to existing frames

There are several factors you should consider in deciding whether or not to replace single panes of glass with sealed double glazing units.

Your existing window frames must be in excellent condition as there is little point in fitting sealed units into frames which may themselves have to be replaced within a few years. If the frames are more than 30 years old they are not likely to be of a standard size and so they would need specially-made sealed units. These would not be reusable in a new standard replacement frame and so this would have to be made specially, too.

Standard size sealed units are, in effect, mass-produced and so are cheaper than specially made ones. They are obtainable virtually 'off the shelf' from many suppliers, particularly for use in wooden-frame windows.

The rebate in the existing frames must be deep enough to accommodate the thickness of the sealed units and still allow them to be puttied in place or fixed with a glazing bead. You are likely to be changing from a single glazing thickness of 3 or 4mm (about ⅛in) to at least 12mm (½in), rising to 18mm (¾in) if you want units with a 12mm gap. For the latter, therefore, you would need a rebate measuring some 30mm (1¼in) from front to back, and not all old frames have this.

It is possible, however, to overcome the problem of too narrow a glazing rebate by using what are known as 'stepped' sealed units. These have one sheet of glass smaller than the other, the larger pane being fitted exactly in the same position as the original single pane with the smaller one on the inside, overlapping the back of the glazing rebate. Such stepped units are readily available to fit standard modern window sizes, or they can be made specially. They can be used in wooden frames but not in steel, which are generally unsuitable for sealed unit double glazing.

The same can be said of any windows incorporating a large number of small panes, such as Georgian styles. The cost of replacing all the individual panes with sealed units

PREPARING THE FRAME

1 *Chop out all the old putty with a glazier's hacking knife or an old chisel. Take care not to damage the wooden window frame.*

2 *The glass will be held in place by small sprigs driven into the glazing rebate. Remove them with pincers or pliers. If straight they can be reused.*

3 *Have a helper tap around the edge of the window inside to free it. Wear gloves, or use a towel, to hold the glass and to avoid cuts.*

4 *With the old glass removed, chop away all remaining traces of putty from the rebate, being careful not to damage it in the process.*

5 *Brush all the dust and debris from the rebate and then prime any areas of exposed wood, allowing the primer to dry thoroughly.*

6 *When the primer has dried, apply a layer of bedding putty to the glazing rebate, working it well into the angle with your thumb.*

would be extremely high, even if the glazing bars were of a suitable size. However, if you wish to keep this appearance, complete sealed units are available that reproduce the Georgian or leaded-light look quite effectively.

If you are quite satisfied that sealed units can be fitted to your existing frames, the first step is to measure the rebate so you can order the correct size. Take great care to get the correct dimensions because, once made, the size of the sealed unit cannot be altered. With standard sizes this is not so much of a problem, but if you are having the units specially made it could prove to be an expensive mistake if you get it wrong. The height and width of the rebate should each be measured in at least two places. If there is a difference between any of the measurements, work with the smaller size. Deduct a further 3mm (⅛in) from both the selected height and width to allow for clearance

around the unit, and this will be the size you should order.

Once you have the new sealed units, remove the putty from the window frame using an old chisel or similar tool and taking care not to damage the wood. Pull out the glazing sprigs with a pair of pincers and carefully lever the glass from the frame. Wear thick gloves or wrap a towel round the edge of the pane to prevent cuts as you lift it clear. If the glass is stuck fast to the old bedding putty, you may find that it can be tapped out from inside by a helper. Only gentle taps should be used to avoid breaking the glass accidentally. If all else fails, break the glass from the inside with a hammer (making sure there is no-one outside who might be injured by the flying fragments) and pull out any remaining glass with a gloved hand or pair of pliers. Clean out the remains of the putty and brush any dust or dirt from

the rebate. Reprime any areas of exposed wood and allow the primer to dry before fitting the new unit.

Line the rebate with a bedding layer of fresh putty, inserting rubber spacing blocks at intervals along the bottom and at each side. These should be cut to a thickness that will centralize and square the double glazing unit in the frame.

Offer up the new unit bottom edge first and gently press it into place with the palms of your hands so that the bedding putty oozes out round the inside edges of the sealed unit. Apply pressure only to the edges of the unit to prevent the glass breaking where it is unsupported in the middle. Check inside that there is about 3mm (⅛in) of putty between the inner face of the glazing unit and the rebate.

Next, very carefully tap in the glazing sprigs, using a cross-pein hammer. Use at least two sprigs per side and slide the head of the hammer across the glass to avoid breaking it. Drive each sprig in squarely so that it does not pinch the glass until only 6mm (¼in) remains visible. If you can't obtain proper glazing sprigs, you can use 19mm (¾in) panel nails with their heads nipped off.

Apply a finishing fillet of putty all round the rebate, pressing it into place with your thumb so that it covers all the edges of the glass. Smooth this off to an angle with a putty knife, making sure it does not project above the level of the rebate otherwise it will be visible from inside the room. Mitre the corners carefully and clean off any excess putty from both inner and outer panes of the unit. Leave the putty to harden for two weeks before applying a coat of primer and finally a finishing coat of paint. The latter should overlap onto the glass by 3mm (⅛in) to ensure a watertight seal.

If stepped double glazing units are to be fitted, a rebate for the stepped portion of the unit can be made by pinning lengths of beading around the inside of the window frame. Extra putty will be needed around this stepped rebate to provide a bed and surround for the inner pane of glass.

New wooden window frames

The increasing use of sealed double glazing units has led to most manufacturers supplying new wooden frames with glazing rebates of sufficient depth to take standard sealed units up to a maximum thickness of about 20mm (⅞in). By choosing your supplier carefully you will be able to order both frames and glazed units at the same time. You won't need to measure for the glass if the frame is one of the many standard sizes available.

If you need to have frames made, you should make it clear to the supplier that you will be fitting sealed double glazing units. He will then make allowance for this when making up the frames.

Normally, the glass is fitted using wooden glazing beads to hold it in place and putty or caulking to provide a seal between the unit and the frame. Acrylic putty is coming into use now and is ideal for double glazing units.

Aluminum and vinyl replacement windows

Although they are still available, it would be difficult to find either aluminum or vinyl replacement windows which are intended for use with single pane glazing. Invariably, such windows are designed to be fitted with sealed units having a 6 or 12mm (¼ or ½in) gap. It is common for companies specializing in these windows to operate a supply-and-fit service. However, most will also work on a

FITTING THE UNIT

1 *Rubber spacing blocks should be set in the putty to centralize the unit in the frame. These can be cut from an ordinary hard pencil eraser.*

2 *Offer up the sealed double glazing unit, positioning the bottom edge first by setting it on the rubber blocks. Then push the unit into place.*

5 *Apply a fillet of putty to cover the sprigs and edge of the glazing unit, trimming it off with a putty knife. Remove excess putty from the glass.*

6 *Carefully mitre the putty at the corners of the glazing rebate with the putty knife. Alternatively, a straight-bladed putty knife could be used.*

supply-only basis. This means that they will provide you with all the component parts ready for you to install yourself.

When doing your own fitting, the only measurements you need to give the supplier are the height and width of the opening into which the window is to be fitted. If the existing outer wood frame is in excellent condition, particularly at the bottom of the jambs and along the sill, you can normally fit the new window in exactly the same place as the old one, with no trouble at all.

If the outer frame is in poor condition and a new one is required, then the window supplier will be able to provide this as well. In this case, the only dimensions he needs are those of the opening in the wall. From these he will be able to calculate all the other sizes. You will, of course, need to specify the style of window, the type of glass, whether or not the glass has to be leaded or fitted with a grille to

simulate a Georgian style window, or be made non-standard in any other way.

The sealed double glazing units fitted in replacement aluminum or vinyl windows are the same as those used in wooden framed windows but the installation method is somewhat different. The glazing unit is always fitted 'dry', rubber or PVC gaskets being used to provide a seal to the frame. No sealants are required at the glazing stage. There are two basic glazing methods in common use. One of them involves making up the frame around the glazing unit. Each frame section, complete with gaskets on either side, is pushed over the sealed unit and then the four corners are screwed together tightly to hold it in place.

The other method is to make up the frame, which has an integral glazing rebate, insert the glazed unit and secure it in place with a 'snap-in' glazing bead. Provided that the

3 Once the unit is in place, use firm hand pressure around the edges to bed it properly in the putty. Don't apply pressure to the center.

4 If the old glazing sprigs are in good condition, re-use them; use new ones otherwise. Slide the hammer across the glass to prevent breakage.

7 Trim the putty which oozes out of the back of the rebate (when the glazing unit is pressed in place) flush with the edge of the frame.

8 Allow the putty to dry for 14 days before applying the first undercoat of paint. The final top coat should lap onto the glass by 3mm ($^1/_8$in).

Ready Reference

TYPES OF SEALED UNIT

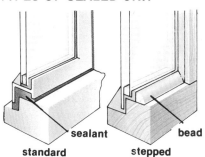

standard   sealant   stepped   bead

There are two types of sealed unit – standard and stepped. The former comprises two similar sized panes of glass held apart by a metal, glass or rigid plastic spacer. It is designed to fit in the glazing rebate in place of a single pane of glass. Where the rebate is too narrow, such as on old wooden windows, a stepped unit may be used.

GLAZING WITH WOOD BEADS

In some cases, glass is secured in the rebate by means of wooden beading pinned round the edge. With this kind of fixing, the glazing unit should be bedded in putty or a sealant before refitting the beading. It may be necessary to use a narrower bead than that fitted originally.

SETTING SPACING BLOCKS

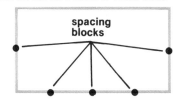

spacing blocks

To keep the glazing unit central and square in the rebate while the putty hardens, rubber spacing blocks should be set at regular intervals along the base of the rebate and at the sides. Set them out as shown. The number along the bottom depends on the width of the unit.

TIP: CLEANING WINDOWS

When fitting a sealed unit to a window on an upper floor, clean off all labels and finger marks from the outside before dismantling your access tower.

---

glazing bead is on the inside (which is becoming standard practice) the sealed unit can be replaced easily if damaged, and the glazing is secure. No potential intruder can prise off the bead and remove the glass from the outside. Gaskets are incorporated in the glazing rebate and glazing bead to ensure a watertight and airtight seal.

Condensation and safety

Obviously, the fitting of sealed double glazing units to old window frames can only be of value if those old frames are in good condition and are not so badly fitting that they let in drafts. This should be checked very carefully beforehand and, if necessary, the frames should be replaced.

Condensation will never appear in the space between the two panes of glass as long as the hermetic seal remains undamaged. Consequently, care should be taken during installation to ensure that the seal is not broken accidentally. Sealed units, may, however, develop condensation on the room side of the inner pane, although this is likely to be far less troublesome than on single glazed windows. The units should never be considered as a complete cure for a condensation problem. Their value lies in their thermal insulation properties and the elimination of down-drafts.

When ordering sealed double glazing units seek the advice of your local glass merchant. He will be able to tell you what thickness of glass should be used and, even more important, the type of glass.

INSULATING TANKS AND PIPEWORK

Worried by the thought of your next heating bill? Concerned by the prospect of your pipes freezing in winter? Proper insulation could well be the answer – and what's more it's cheap and easy to install.

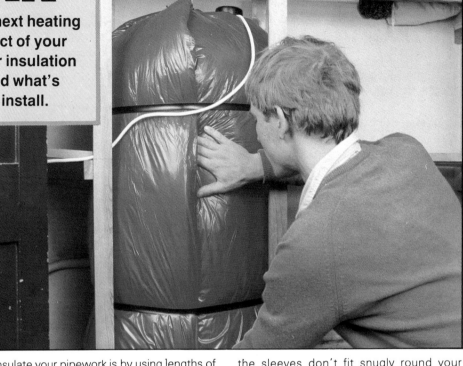

Insulation is important because it reduces heat loss, and when properly applied to your water system it benefits you in a number of ways. Firstly, it saves you money by slowing down the rate at which heat is lost from the pipes and tanks of your hot water system. Secondly, by reducing the heat loss from your cold water system (and even the coldest water contains *some* heat) it tends to keep your cold water warmer in winter, thereby minimizing the risk of frozen pipes. Warmer cold water in winter also means that it takes less energy to heat it up to the desired temperature when it enters your hot water tank. In this respect too insulation saves you money.

So for all the above reasons you should consider properly insulating your pipes and tanks. The cost of the materials you will need is small and the potential savings great.

Before purchasing the insulation material for your pipes and tanks, work out how much you are likely to need. Most tanks will have their capacity and/or their dimensions marked on them somewhere — if yours don't then measure them yourself. You will also need to calculate the combined length of the pipes you intend insulating and establish what their diameter is — though this last measurement is only important if you plan to use split sleeve insulation (see below). As you'll want the insulation on your tanks to overlap that which you fit to any pipes that run into them, it's best to start by insulating your pipework.

Insulating pipes

Two types of pipe insulation are commonly available. The first is made out of a glass fibre or mineral wool material similar to that used for insulating attic floors, but supplied in bandage form (75 to 100mm/3 to 4in wide and 10mm/⅜in thick) generally with a flimsy plastic backing. The second type comes in the form of split sleeves which are made from some sort of foamed material — usually plastic. Both types of pipe insulation have their advantages and disadvantages (see below) and both types are cheap. And since there is no reason why they can't be used side by side on the same pipe system, you'll almost certainly find that the easiest way to

insulate your pipework is by using lengths of both.

The bandage type is fitted by wrapping it around the pipe in a spiral, with each turn overlapping the previous one by at least 10mm (⅜in). It doesn't matter which way round the plastic backing goes. Make sure that the bandage is sufficiently tight to prevent air circulating between the turns, but don't pull it too tight or you will reduce its effectiveness. When starting or finishing each roll, and at regular intervals in between, hold it in place using plastic adhesive tape or string. Tape or tie the bandage, too, on vertical pipe runs and on bends as these are places where the turns are likely to separate. And don't forget to lag any shut-off valves properly — only the handle should be left visible.

Apart from being rather more time consuming to install than split-sleeve insulation the main drawback with the bandage type is that it is difficult to wrap round pipes in awkward places, such as those that run under floorboards. For pipes like these you will generally find that sleeves are more suitable since once fitted they can be pushed into position.

Split-sleeve insulation normally comes in 1m (3ft 3in) or 2m (6ft 6in) lengths. It is available in a variety of sizes to fit piping from 15mm (½in) to 35mm (1½in) in diameter. The thickness of the insulating foam is generally around 12mm (½in). Make sure that you buy the right size sleeve for your pipes — if

the sleeves don't fit snugly round your pipework they won't provide satisfactory insulation. Both flexible and rigid sleeves are available, but as the rigid type isn't much use for pipework that bends frequently, you'd probably be better off using the flexible variety.

Fitting the sleeves is very straightforward. You simply prise apart the slit that runs along the length of the sleeve and slip the insulation over the pipe. It's advisable to tape the sleeve at intervals, and you must do so at joins. At bends, where the sleeves will tend to come apart, you should tape the split lengthways.

Once sleeve insulation has been fitted, it can easily be slid along a length of pipe to protect a part of it that may be hard to get at. However, you should bear in mind that it won't be able to get beyond any pipe clips, very sharp bends or bulky joints it may encounter. You'll find that most flexible sleeves will readily slide round curves and even 90° bends made using soldered fittings, but whenever you run up against problems in the form of bulky compression elbows or tee connectors the sleeves will have to be cut accordingly. However, in some circumstances you might well find that bandage insulation provides the better solution. To fit round a 90° elbow the sleeve should be cut in two and the sleeve ends then cut at an angle of 45° before being slipped over the pipe. You should then tape over the resulting join.

INSULATING PIPEWORK

1 Start by wrapping the bandage twice round the end of the pipe next to the tank. Hold the turns in place securely with string or tape.

2 Wrap the bandage round the pipe in a spiral. Make sure that each turn overlaps the previous one by at least 10mm (³/₈in). Don't pull the bandage too tight.

3 Whenever you finish a roll of bandage and start a new one allow a generous overlap to prevent air circulating between the turns of the join.

4 Finish off the pipe in the same way that you started, with an extra turn of bandage. Lastly, check the pipe to make sure all the insulation is secure.

5 Fitting split-sleeve insulation is simple. You simply prise apart the split and slip the sleeve over the pipe. Use tape to keep the sleeve in place.

6 At bends, where the sleeve tends to come apart, tape the split lengthways. Tape the sleeves, too, whenever you join one to another.

7 At tees, first cut a 'notch' from the main pipe sleeve. Then shape the end of the branch pipe sleeve to fit and slot it into place. Tape the join.

8 Use split sleeve insulation on pipes that would be hard – or impossible – to fit with bandage. Slip the sleeve over the pipe and slide it into position.

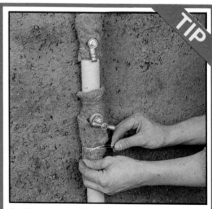

TIP

9 Sleeve and bandage insulation can – and sometimes must – be used together. A shut-off valve, for example, can only be properly lagged with bandage.

INSULATING YOUR ROOF

About a quarter of the heat lost from an uninsulated house goes through the roof, and so some kind of roof insulation should be your first priority for saving money on heating bills.

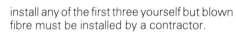

Houses leak heat like a sieve. Up to 75 per cent of the warmth generated within the house finds its way to the outside world through the roof, walls, windows and doors, and this represents an enormous waste of energy and money.

Insulation reduces the rate at which heat passes through the various parts of your house's structure, by trapping 'still' air within the insulating material itself. Still air doesn't conduct heat much and so wrapping your house in suitable insulation serves the same purpose as putting a tea-cosy on a tea pot: the tea stays hot for far longer. The converse is true during the summer: the insulation bars the heat of the sun.

About a quarter of the heat lost from an average house goes through the roof, and this is an easy area to insulate effectively. What you do is to put your insulation in one of three places: on the highest ceiling; on the attic floor; or on the inside of the roof itself. Insulating the attic floor is the simplest and most effective of these: you should insulate the ceiling where there's no attic or the roof slope where the attic space has been converted into living accommodation.

Why you should insulate
The savings you can make by insulating your attic depend on whether there's any insulation there already (it's the first layer that's most effective), how much you put in, and whether you can control or alter your heating system to take advantage of the insulation. The last point is important: if you install attic insulation and leave central heating controls as they are with a thermostat in, say, the living room, the most noticeable effect will be warmer rooms upstairs rather than dramatically decreased fuel bills. If, however, you can lower the temperatures in upstairs rooms, or keep them the same as before, by fitting thermostatic radiator valves or by turning radiators down (or off), your house will lose less heat and your fuel bills will be lower.

Types of insulation
There are four main types of attic insulation you can use: blanket, loose-fill, sheet (see *Ready Reference*) and blown fibre. You can

install any of the first three yourself but blown fibre must be installed by a contractor.

The most extensively used attic insulation material is rolls of glass fibre or mineral fibre blanket, which you lay between the joists of the attic floor. You can choose from either of two thicknesses: 80mm (just over 3 in) and 100mm (4in).

Although you'll benefit in terms of warmer rooms by installing thicker insulation, the more you put in, the less cost effective it becomes. From a practical point of view thicknesses greater than 125mm (5in) will probably take the insulation over the top of the joists, making walking about or storing things in the attic rather difficult.

To save storage and transportation space the material is compressed when rolled up and packaged but it regains its original thickness quite quickly when unwrapped. The most common width of roll is 400mm (16in). Lengths vary from brand to brand, but they're usually about 6 to 8m (20 to 25ft) long. Some glass fibre insulation is available in 600mm (2ft) wide rolls for use in attics with wider-than-usual joist spacings.

The 400mm (16in) width is the most suitable size for most houses and allows a little to turn up where it meets the joists. Joists are usually 400mm (16in) apart but they might be as much as 450mm (18in) or as little as 300mm (1ft). If you have narrow-spaced joists the 600mm (2ft) width is probably the best to use: you can

cut a roll in half with a saw while it's still in its wrapper.

Working out how much insulation you'll need is simply a matter of multiplying the length of the attic floor by the width to calculate how many square yards there are, and then checking the chart in *Ready Reference*.

Remember that the 100mm (4in) thickness of blanket insulation comes in shorter length rolls than the 80mm (3in) thickness. An 8m (26ft) roll, 400mm (16in) wide, covers 3.2 sq m (35 sq ft). For blanket insulation, ignore the joists in your calculation; for loose-fill and sheet insulation, include the joist size, otherwise you could end up with 10 to 15 per cent too much. Loose-fill insulation comes in bags, typically containing 110 litres (4 cu ft). This is enough for 1.1 sq m (12 sq ft) laid 100mm (4in) deep. By far the most effective material is called vermiculite, which is made from a mineral called mica, though you might also find expanded polystyrene granules, loose mineral wool or cellulose fibre being sold as loose-fill insulation.

Thickness for thickness, vermiculite is more than twice the price of glass fibre blanket and it's not as effective. To get the same insulating effect as 80mm (3in) of glass fibre, you'd need 130mm (about 5in) of vermiculite, which might well come over the top of the ceiling joists.

Another disadvantage of loose-fill insulation is that it can blow about in a drafty attic:

WHERE TO INSULATE

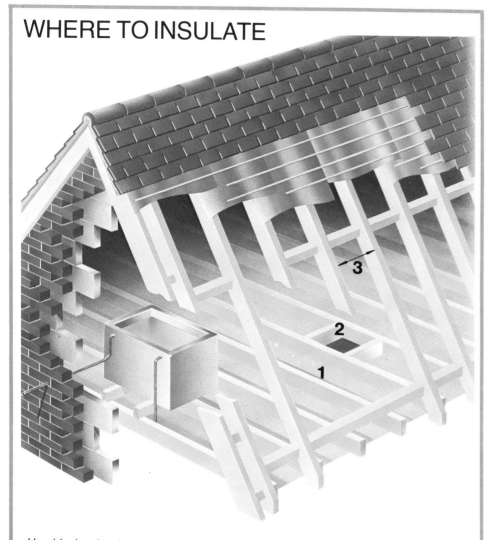

Use blanket insulation between the joists (1) or lay loose-fill or sheet materials; insulate the attic hatch (2) by sticking on a sheet of polystyrene; clad the rafters (3) with drywall or fix blanket insulation between them.

Ready Reference

TYPES OF ROOF INSULATION

There are three types of attic insulation you can lay yourself:

● blanket insulation consists of rolls of glass or mineral fibre matting, 80 or 100mm (3 or 4in) thick by about 6 or 8m (20 or 26ft) long. It's unrolled between the joists

● loose-fill insulation can be a granulated mineral called vermiculite, expanded polystyrene granules, mineral wool fibre or cellulose fibre, available in bags. It's tipped between the joists and spread out to an even thickness – 100mm (4in) for fibre types, 125mm (5in) for granular materials

● sheet insulation is either expanded polystyrene between the joists or rafters, or fibreboard, which is laid across the joists with loose-fill or blanket insulation underneath.

LEVELLING GRANULAR INSULATION

To lay granular materials to the correct depth — 100mm (4in) — make a 'spreader' from an offcut of chipboard, which you draw along the joists. Ensure:

● the body of the spreader just fits between the joists

● the arms rest on the joists

● the depth of the body is 100mm (4in) above the attic floor.

If your joists are only 100mm (4in) deep, lay the material flush with the top of the joists.

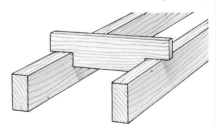

HOW MUCH INSULATION

To work out how many rolls of blanket insulation you'll need:

● multiply the length by the width of the attic to get the number of square yards

---

this is most likely to be the case round the outside edges of the roof, by the eaves, where there are always some gaps. However, it's good for unevenly-spaced joists where other types of insulation might leave gaps.

To lay loose-fill insulation, you simply empty out the bags between the joists and spread it to an even thickness.

Sheet insulation isn't used much for attic insulation, though it's sometimes used for insulating between rafters, over solid walls and on flat roofs. The best type of rigid sheet for attic insulation is expanded polystyrene. It comes in various thicknesses in sheets from 1200 × 2400 mm (4 × 8ft). You'll have to cut it up to get it through the attic hatch, and then cut each strip to the precise width required to match the joist spacing.

Other sheet materials such as fibreboard or chipboard can be laid across the joists, with loose-fill or blanket insulation sandwiched underneath. You can walk on chipboard, so it's also suitable for use as a floor, but fibreboard won't support your weight.

Blown fibre insulation costs little more than installing glass fibre blanket but it must be installed by a contractor. The three common materials are mineral fibre, pelleted glass fibre and cellulose fibre. It's easy and quick to put in, and will cover all the nooks and crannies that are difficult to reach by other methods.

Preparation

Attics are usually dirty places, so it's advisable to wear some old clothes, preferably ones you can throw away afterwards.

Blanket insulation, especially glass fibre, can cause irritation to the skin, so you must wear rubber gloves when handling it. Remove your wrist-watch and roll up your sleeves. It's

LAYING BLANKET INSULATION

1 *Clean up any dust and dirt from the attic floor.*

2 *Starting from the eaves, unroll the insulation between the joists. Leave a small gap at the eaves to allow air to circulate in the attic space.*

3 *If the headroom at the eaves is limited, unroll the blanket and push the end gently into the eaves with a broom. Take care not to tear the insulation material.*

6 *Once you've unrolled the blanket, return to the other end and press it down. Where you're joining one roll to another, butt the ends together.*

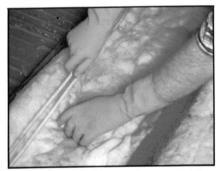

7 *The electric cables serving your lighting system are probably lying loose on the loft floor. Never cover them with insulation: lay them on top instead.*

8 *An even better solution is to attach loose cables to the side of a joist, if there's enough slack. Use cable clips to hold them in place.*

also sensible to wear a simple mask to cover your nose and mouth as the insulation material is not only unpleasant but dangerous to inhale. Loose-fill is a dusty material and you'd be wise to wear a pair of protective goggles — as well as a mask — when laying this. You can buy a mask, with replacement lint filters, and the goggles, all of which are available from most hardware stores.

You'll need a good light to work by; a fixed attic light is best, but if there isn't one, you could rig up an inspection lamp or even a table lamp. Don't, however, use a torch: you'll have enough to contend with without having to carry and aim a light. Don't use a naked flame because the risk of fire is high in the enclosed space of the attic.

Be careful where you tread. The space between the joists — the ceiling of the floor below — is only drywall or, in older houses, lath and plaster, and neither will support your weight. Rather than balancing on the joists — especially when you're carrying rolls or bags of insulation — it's better to have a short plank or piece of chipboard to stand on, but make sure that both ends are resting on a joist without overlapping, or it could tip up

under your weight.

Before you start to lay the insulation you should remove any boxes or other items you have stored in the attic to give you plenty of room to maneuver: if there's too much to take down from the attic, you can shift it up to one end of the attic, lay the insulation in the free area, then move the boxes back again and lay the other half.

Clean up the spaces between the joists using a vacuum cleaner with a nozzle attachment to enable you to reach awkward corners. If you don't have one you can use a soft-bristled broom or a hand-brush and a dust-pan, but you'll stir up a lot of dust in the process.

Laying the insulation

Laying the blanket type of insulation is simplicity itself: all you do is to start at the eaves and unroll the blanket between the joists. On widely spaced joists it'll just lie flat on the attic floor but if the joist spacing is narrow, or irregular, you can tuck it down and allow it to curve up the sides of the joists. Cut or tear

LAYING LOOSE-FILL

Left: Stop the loose-fill insulation from falling into the wall cavity at the eaves by placing a few bricks or a chipboard panel between the joists.

Center: Empty out the bags of loose-fill between the joists; stand on the footboard across the joists.

Right: Use a wooden spreader to even out the insulation to the correct level.

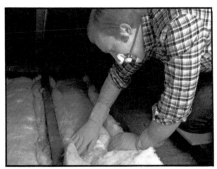

4 The blanket can either lie flat between the joists or, if the joist spacing is narrow or irregular, you can allow it to curve a little way up the sides.

5 Continue to unroll the blanket between the joists. As the attic floor won't support your weight, work from a plank or board placed across the joists.

9 When you've secured the cables to the side of a joist you can lay your blanket in the usual way; if it still covers the cable, you should cut it away.

10 Where there are cross beams, lay the blanket over the top, cut it with a sharp knife and push the ends under the obstruction. Butt the ends together.

Ready Reference

LAGGING THE PIPES

You can lag pipes in the loft space with:
- mineral fibre rolls, wrapped on diagonally like bandages and secured with wire, adhesive tape or string or

- strips of blanket insulation wrapped on and tied in place or
- proprietary foam tubes slit down their length so they can be slipped on the pipe.

You needn't lag the pipes if they're contained within loose-fill insulation or they'll be covered with blanket insulation.

INSULATION

small pieces of blanket from the roll to fit very small nooks and crannies.

Butt up new rolls and allow for extra material at beams and pipes that are set at right angles to the joists. Cut the insulation and tuck it under the obstruction, then butt up the next piece to it.

Cut a square of blanket to cover the top of the attic hatch cover and tack it in place, leaving an overlap to stop drafts getting into the attic space.

If you're laying one of the loose-fill materials you'll have to stop it from falling into the wall cavity at the eaves. Place a few bricks on edge, or a panel of chipboard, between the joists near the eaves, to contain the granules.

Empty out the bags between the joists, starting at the eaves, and use a specially shaped spreader (see *Ready Reference*) to spread it to the correct thickness.

Insulating pipework

If the pipes lie within your loose-fill or under your blanket insulation there's no need to lag them separately, but if they're positioned above you'll need to wrap them with pieces of blanket insulation, ready-made mineral fibre rolls or pre-formed pipe insulation.

To prevent electric cables overheating you shouldn't cover them with insulation. Attach them to the side of a joist or, if you're using blanket material, lay them on top. If your wiring is the old rubber-insulated sort you'd be wise to replace it.

Another point to watch now that the attic will be much colder is the risk of condensation in the attic space. This can be a serious problem, which can rot the roof framing and soak the insulation, making it useless. To avoid this, ensure that there's sufficient ventilation in the attic by leaving gaps at the eaves 10mm (⅜in) all the way round. Don't fill the gaps with insulation. Also, make sure that the gaps around pipes and the attic hatch are well sealed to keep moisture out.

INSULATION ALTERNATIVES

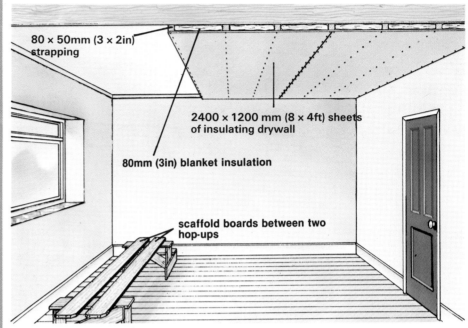

80 × 50mm (3 × 2in) strapping

2400 × 1200 mm (8 × 4ft) sheets of insulating drywall

80mm (3in) blanket insulation

scaffold boards between two hop-ups

If your house has a flat roof you won't have an attic so you'll have to insulate the underside of the ceiling instead (above). To do this, you can nail up sheets of insulating drywall directly to the joists, which have an insulating layer and a vapor barrier that prevents moisture penetrating the surface. Or you can nail strapping to the ceiling joists and sandwich blanket insulation between the false and the real ceiling.

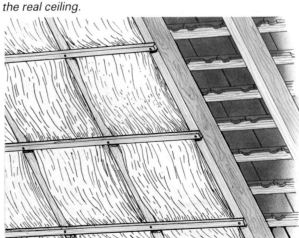

You need to insulate the rafters only if you're converting your attic into a habitable room. You can use most of the materials that you use on the attic floor but the easiest are the sheet materials, which you can secure across the rafters (above) and the blanket materials, which can be pushed between the rafters and held in place with strapping (left). You can also buy insulation blanket with a paper cover.

CHAPTER 6
Fitting and Fastening

ADHESIVES

To get the best results you have to pick the right adhesive for the materials you want to join, and then use it in the correct way. But the range available can make your choice extremely confusing.

The idea of an adhesive is easy to grasp: it sticks things together. In practice, however, there's a lot you need to know about the different types of adhesive on the market: how each works, what it will (and will not) stick together, how long it takes to set, whether the bond is heat-proof or waterproof, and so on. Equipped with this information, you can then begin to make the correct choice of adhesive type for the job you want to do.

Here you will find a brief description of the major types of adhesive, and a table that tells you which type to use to stick various materials together. Remember that adhesives should always be used exactly as directed by the manufacturer for the best results. They should also be treated with respect as they can damage the skin; furthermore, their fumes may be dangerous to inhale and highly inflammable.

1 Animal and fish glues
Also known as 'scotch' glues, these are the traditional woodworking adhesives, and come in either liquid form, or as solid chunks or sheets that you have to melt down. They are capable of producing a very strong bond, but have no gap-filling ability, so that woodworking joints must fit very tightly. They dry rather slowly, and are seriously weakened when exposed to dampness, however slight. They have now been almost completely replaced by modern synthetic adhesives.

2 PVA adhesives
PVA (polyvinyl acetate) adhesive is a white liquid which dries clear in under an hour, producing a strong bond within 24 hours. It is now the most important woodworking adhesive indoors,

but can be used on most dry, porous surfaces. It is widely employed within the building trade as a bonding agent for concrete, and a masonry sealant. However, PVA adhesives do have limitations. They are not good at filling gaps, so woodworking joints must have a good fit, and must be clamped until dry. The bond doesn't stand up well to stress, and is weakened by exposure to moisture. PVA adhesives also have a tendency to stain some hardwoods.

3 Aliphatic resin adhesive
This woodworking adhesive comes as a powder that you mix with water, and dries to a pale yellow color. It stands up to low temperatures and dampness better than PVA, and gives a stronger bond. However, it is weakened by water — though its strength returns as it dries out again. It can also take up to 6 hours to set so joints must be clamped. It stains many hardwoods.

4 Resorcinol Formaldehyde adhesive
An excellent woodworking adhesive, giving a strong, rigid, extremely water-resistant bond. The snag is that it comes in two parts which must be mixed together, so some wastage is inevitable. It stains most hardwoods rather badly.

5 Urea-Formaldehyde adhesive
Another two-part woodworking adhesive, urea-formaldehyde – often referred to simply as 'urea' – is the usual choice for exterior

woodwork. As well as giving a very strong bond, and having the ability to bridge gaps, it stands up very well to just about everything the weather can throw at it. These qualities also make it useful in many indoor situations. Unfortunately, it dries rather slowly and joints must be clamped for up to 6 hours. When used on hardwoods it may stain.

6 Contact adhesives
Normally based on synthetic rubber, these get their name from the way in which they are used. You apply a thin coat to both the surfaces to be joined, allow it to become touch dry, and then achieve an instantaneous bond by bringing the surfaces into contact with each other. The resulting bond will resist being pulled apart, but in time some sideways slippage may occur. For this reason, contact adhesives are not suitable for general woodwork and repairs.

Their main use is for sticking down sheet materials such as plastic laminate and cork tiles. Obviously, the fact that the adhesive bonds on contact can cause problems where accurate positioning is required, as you cannot make minor adjustments once the surfaces have been brought together. But some contact adhesives are available which have a delayed action, and so overcome this problem to a certain extent. The petroleum-based solvent used in most brands gives off vapor which is dangerous and unpleasant to inhale, and also highly inflammable. You must be sure to work in a well-ventilated area, and, if this is not possible, use a water-based contact adhesive instead.

7 Latex adhesives
In many ways these are similar to water-based contact adhesives, except that they use natural rubber (latex), and can either be

used as a contact adhesive, or as an ordinary adhesive where you bring the surfaces together while the adhesive is wet. They are a little too expensive to be used on large areas and so are generally used for such tasks as joining fabrics, sticking down carpet, and so on – situations in which the flexible, washable (but not dry-cleanable) bond they produce is a major advantage.

8 PVC adhesives
These stick flexible PVC. The strong, flexible bond they provide makes them the ideal choice for repairing rainwear, shower curtains, beach balls, and things of that sort.

9 Cyanoacrylate adhesives
These are the adhesives ('super glues') once claimed to stick anything to everything in seconds. A cyanoacrylate adhesive will quickly bond a wide variety of materials, but it has limitations. It's expensive, and although you need very little of it, this makes it impractical to use for anything more than small repairs. Surfaces must be scrupulously clean, and a perfect fit, as it has no gap-filling ability whatsoever. Another point to remember is that when used in industry, cyanoacrylate is specially formulated to stick two specific materials together with a very stong bond. Choose two different materials and you have to use a different formula. What the handyman can buy is a compromise formula, and there are therefore some materials that it doesn't stick very well. Glass is perhaps the best example. Ordinary cyanoacrylate is degraded by the ultra-violet radiation in sunlight and glass leaves it exposed and vulnerable. As a result, a special formulation for glass has been brought out to overcome this problem.

Another problem is that cyanoacrylate reacts in a rather odd way with water. The presence of moisture actually speeds up the setting process, but, once set, exposure to water breaks down the bond. Finally, an unfortunate side-effect is that cyanoacrylate adhesive has the alarming ability to stick people to themselves or to their surroundings, so it needs to be used with great care. It is not, however, as dangerous as sometimes suggested: a lot of patient work with hot soapy water often does the trick.

In summary, a cyanoacrylate adhesive isn't as 'super' as it might appear, but it is worth keeping a tube handy for repairs where other adhesives have failed.

10 Epoxy resin adhesives
These are less convenient than cyanoacrylates as they come in two parts, a resin and a hardener, which must be carefully mixed. But epoxy resin adhesives come closer to the 'stick-anything-to-everything' ideal. The strong, heat-resistant, oil-resistant, water-resistant bond that they provide makes them a good choice for small-scale repair work involving metal, china, and some plastics, as well as a variety of other materials. The surfaces must be clean, but since the resin will bridge small gaps without losing strength, a perfect fit is not essential. In fact, for repair work, epoxies have only two major snags. One is that they dry to a pale brown color, which tends to highlight the join, though it is possible to color the adhesive with dry pigment. The second is that they need a setting time of up to 48 hours. This can be overcome by using a fast-setting formulation, which generally

requires at least 24 hours to achieve full strength. Of course, epoxies can be used for large-scale jobs too. The reason why they tend not to be is that they are simply too expensive to use in

11 Acrylic adhesives
This is a two-part adhesive with a difference. It will join the same sorts of material as an epoxy, achieving a bond of only slightly less strength in as little as 5 minutes. You don't have to pre-mix the adhesive and catalyst before you apply them. Instead, you can apply the catalyst to one surface, the adhesive to the other. And most important of all, the surfaces need not be clean. Even oily surfaces can be joined successfully.

12 Plastic solvent adhesives
Although between them, epoxies, acrylics, PVC adhesives, and cyanoacrylates allow you to stick many plastics to themselves, some require a special solvent adhesive. This works by chemically 'melting' a layer of plastic on each of the surfaces to be joined, so that they merge together and produce a 'welded' joint rather like the join in a plastic model kit assembled with polystyrene cement. They work quickly, and give strong results. However, you must be sure to match the solvent to the

Adhesives based on cellulose aren't very strong, but they are fairly waterproof and heatproof, transparent when they dry and they do set quickly. They are most useful as an alternative to epoxy resin adhesives, or to cyanoacrylates, when repairing china and glass.

14 Vegetable gums and pastes
Based on either starch or dextrine, two plant extracts, these are useful only for sticking paper and card, and even here, these days, they tend to be restricted to the 'suitable for children' market.

15 Specialist adhesives
In addition to the general-purpose adhesives we have mentioned so far, you'll find a number of specialized adhesives, such as tile and wallpaper adhesives.

Choosing the right Adhesive...

KEY TO ADHESIVE TYPES

H Clear household	**7** Latex	**14** Vegetable gum
1 Animal and fish	**8** PVC	**Specialist adhesives**
2 PVA	**9** Cyanoacrylate	**15** Wallpaper
3 Aliphatic resin	**10** Epoxy	**16** Flooring
4 Resorcinol formaldehyde	**11** Acrylic	**17** Ceramic tile
5 Urea formaldehyde	**12** Plastic solvent	**18** Expanded polystyrene
6 Contact	**13** Cellulose	

To stick ▽ to this ▷	Wood	Wallpaper	Rubber	Plastic (soft)	Plastic (hard)	Plastic laminate	Plastic flooring	Drywall	Paper & cards	Metal	Man-made boards	Leather	China & glass	Fabrics	Expanded polystyrene	Cork tiles	Ceramic tiles	Carpet
Ceramic tiles	9 10 11	—	—	—	6 9 10 11	6	16	—	—	9 10 11	—	—	—	—	—	6	17 10	6 7
Cork tiles	6 2	15	—	—	—	6	16	—	H 2 7	—	2	—	—	7	—	6	—	7
Expanded polystyrene	18	15	—	—	6	—	—	—	—	—	2	—	—	7	18	18	—	—
China & glass	10 11	—	6 9	—	9 10 11	—	—	H	—	H 9 10 11	—	H 9 10 11	H 9 10 11 13	6 7 H	—	H	—	—
Man-made boards	1 2 3 4 5	15	9 10 11	—	9 10 11	6	16	8	H 2 7 15	6 10 11	1 2 3 4 5	6	9 10 11	6 7	18	6 16	17	6 7
Metal	9 10 11	15	9 10 11	—	9 10 11	6	—	H	—	9 10 11	10	6	9 10 11	6	—	6 9 10 11	9 10 11	6
Paper & cards	2	15	—	H	—	—	—	H 1 2 7 14 15	—	—	H	H	7	—	—	—	—	—
Drywall	2	15	—	—	—	6	16	5	2 15	—	6	6	—	2 15	18	6	17	6
Plastic flooring	—	—	—	—	—	—	16	—	—	—	—	—	—	—	—	16	17	6
Plastic (hard)	—	—	9 10 11	9 10 11 12	9 10 11 12	—	—	H	—	9 10 11	—	—	—	—	—	—	—	—
Plastic (soft)	—	—	9 10 11	8 9 10 11 12	9 10 11 12	—	—	—	—	—	—	—	—	—	—	—	—	—
Masonry	5 10	15	6	—	9 10 11	—	16	6	H 7 15	9 10 11	6 2	—	—	6 7	18	16	10 11 17	6 7
Wood	1 2 3 4 5	15	6 9 10 11	9 10 11	9 10 11	6	16	2	1 2 7 14 15	9 10 11	1 2 3 4 5	6	9 10 11	6 7	18	6 16	10 11 17	6 7

NAILS, SCREWS AND HINGES

Secure fastening involves the use of the right nail, screw or hinge. There's a proper fastener to use for any fastening job.

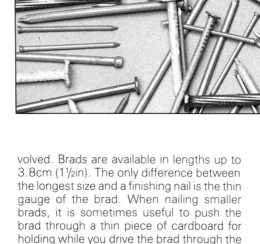

There are a number of nails, hinges and screws on the market. Many have a specific use. This chapter is a guide to help you find the proper fastener for your job.

Nails

Nails, the original wood fasteners, have developed a remarkable number of specialized uses over the years. There's a nail type for almost any nailing task.

One nail won't necessarily handle the job of another, so you need to be aware of the different varieties and their uses, along with a few nailing techniques, to be able to make a secure and durable fastening.

The common nail is the one we're most familiar with. It's a heavy-duty nail used for rough framing and general construction work. This nail has a large flat head that won't pull through the work once stresses are set up on fastened work. The diamond-shaped point makes starting easier, and grooves under the head of the nail offer a bit more holding power.

The box nail is similar to the common nail but is a thinner gauge, making it useful for light work or for use where the heavier common nail might split the wood. These nails also have a grooved shank near the head for better holding strength.

The heads of these two nails are large and very visible once driven home. If you need nailing strength in areas such as trim or cabinetwork but don't want to see the nail head, a finishing nail is used. These nails have a diamond-shaped point at the end and a grooved shank under the head similar to the common and box nails, but the actual head of the nail is smaller than that of the common nail and can be sunk into the wood with a nailset and covered with a wood filler.

Although finishing nails can be used on trim, casing nails are available for these moldings as well. The casing nail is similar to the finishing nail but has a heavier shank for better holding power, and is usually driven flush to the surface and painted over.

In some cases when you're applying molding, the thin trim won't need the strength of a finishing nail. A common brad can be used for light-duty holding where no stress is in-

volved. Brads are available in lengths up to 3.8cm (1½in). The only difference between the longest size and a finishing nail is the thin gauge of the brad. When nailing smaller brads, it is sometimes useful to push the brad through a thin piece of cardboard for holding while you drive the brad through the wood. This keeps your fingers out of the way of the hammer and provides for easier, straighter driving.

The roofing nail belongs to this same family of nails where the shanks have grooves under the nail head. This type has a large flat head to resist pull-through and is used to hold composition boards, shingles and roll roofing. The nail is usually galvanized to prevent rusting. They come in lengths up to 5cm (2in) and usually have a heavy shank. The heavier shank limits their use to roofing, since nailing into thin lumber with a roofing nail will cause the wood to split.

The above nails all feature round, smooth shanks. By notching or threading a shank, the holding power of the nail is greatly increased. An example is the drywall nail. The rings on the shank offer greater protection against popped nails or loosened drywall, a common complaint in homes with gypsum-board walls.

Framing, roofing, siding and flooring nails are all available with ringed or threaded shanks. Although threaded nails are more expensive than conventional nails, you tend to get more nails to the pound.

Threaded nails are available with spiral threaded or ringed shanks, or a combination of both. The most common is the shank with spiral threads. The thread is run at a deep

angle down the shank, rather than a tightly wound thread as you would find on a screw. As the nail is driven by the hammer, the nail forms a spiral groove in the wood, capturing the wood fibres and retaining them along the shank. This prevents nail pull-out caused by stress on the wood. This type of nail is most commonly used for flooring nails to provide a 'squeakless' floor.

The second type is the ringed nail. This type doesn't twist into the wood as it's driven but rather goes straight in. The wood fibres then grip into the grooves created by the rings. These nails are also good for sub-floor installations.

The third type combines the spiral and the ring to form a nail that's similar in appearance to a wood screw. These nails have a tight thread, and twist while being driven.

All these nails are difficult to remove once hammering has started, so don't use them for temporary tacking.

There is a nail on the market specially made for temporary tacking, when you need a tight fit between the pieces of wood being joined. This nail, called a duplex head, has two heads, one at the top of the nail and one slightly lower. The nail is driven until the lower head fits flush to the wood, creating a tight join. The upper head is left protruding for later nail removal.

Nail sizes are designated in inches and sometimes through the use of the term 'penny'. The penny size is denoted by the letter D and was originally used as the price per hundred nails. The term now is used to signify length. The longer the nail, the higher the penny rating.

NAILS

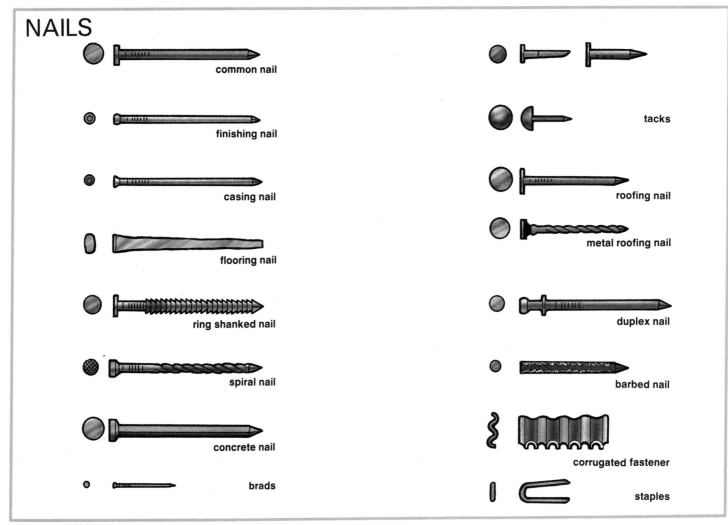

Screws

Screws provide heavy-duty fastening, are stronger than nails and have the added advantage of being removable. If the proper techniques are followed, wood screws are easy to assemble and will form a tight, permanent join.

Although there are several different types of screws used for specific purposes, the most common wood screw types are the flat head, oval head and round head.

The flat-head screw is used where the screw head needs to sit flush with the surface or countersunk slightly below the surface.

Oval-head screws have a tapered body on the bottom of the head, which is sunk into the wood leaving the rounded top of the screw above the surface. These serve a decorative purpose when you want screw heads to be visible and are also slightly easier to remove than flat-head screws.

Round-head screws have a flat head base rather than the tapered, countersunk base of the flat and oval screws. This flat base permits the use of washers when necessary,

SCREWS

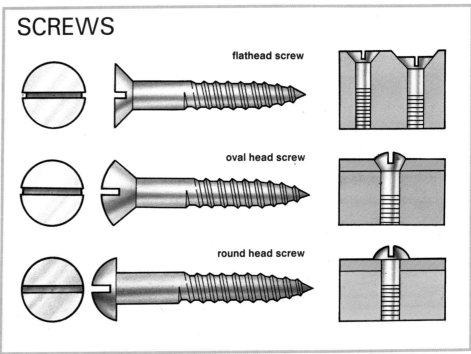

PENNY GAUGE

A penny gauge is a way of determining a nail's size. The rating originally denoted the price per hundred. It is now sometimes used to determine the length of a nail. A 6d nail for example is a 2in nail. Common nail sizes range from 2d to 60d. As length increases, so does the diameter.

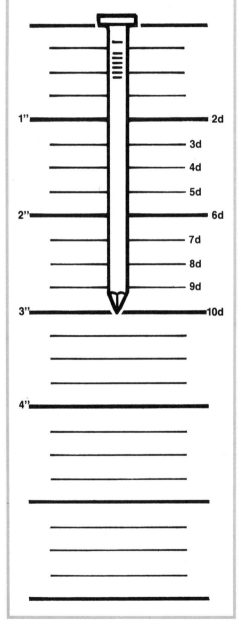

and also allows the use of the screw with thin stock where there isn't enough room for countersinking.

Most screw types are available with a slotted head, which is the most common type; the cross-slotted or Phillips head, which accepts only the Phillips screwdriver and is de-

signed to minimize the chance of the screwdriver slipping; and, in Canada, the Robertson head, which has a square recess to accept the square head of the Robertson screwdriver. This last type of screw greatly reduces the chance of screwdriver slippage.

Screws are available in a variety of lengths and diameters. Buy the size and type best suited to the job at hand. A general rule is to buy a screw three times the length of your thinnest stock so that two-thirds of the screw (the size of the threaded area on the shank) is buried in the base material.

The length of the screw is measured in inches while the diameter is indicated in gauges with 0 (1/16in) gauge being the smallest and about 24 (3/8in) gauge being the largest. The most useful screw diameters for the homeowner range from 3 gauge to 14 gauge. Screws are available in lengths of 4in, but for fastening anything thicker use a lag bolt, which is fastened with a wrench.

Splitting and binding are common problems if screws are used improperly. Screws need a pilot hole drilled in the wood first to enable the thread of the screw to grip the base wood.

Normally, a clearance hole is drilled completely through the top piece of wood. This hole is equal to the diameter of the threaded portion of the shank and should be wide enough to allow the shank to pass through unimpeded. A pilot hole is then driven into the base wood roughly equal to half the length of the thread on the screw and slightly smaller than the diameter of the thread.

To drill the holes, measure and mark your drill point with an X on the top piece of wood. Drill the hole completely through the wood at the center of the X. If the screw is to be countersunk, drill the wider hole on the surface of the board at this point. Check for depth by dropping the screw in place. Drill deeper if necessary. Line up the top piece of wood with the bottom piece exactly where the screws are to be located. Mark the screw location with an awl. Drill the pilot hole in the base wood, line up the two pieces of wood and fasten with the wood screw.

Although soft woods may only need a pilot hole driven into the top piece of wood, it's still good practice to drill a clearance hole for a tighter grip. There's no need to ensure that the screw is threaded through the top piece of wood, since an effective joint is one where the thread is buried in the base wood.

Hinges

Hinges are used to fasten doors and lids while still allowing movement. To accomplish this, there are a variety of hinges that will handle a variety of purposes, from flush-mounted doors to overlay doors and recessed doors.

Hinges made for cabinet doors are usually reversible and can be used to hang a door

Ready Reference

NAIL SIZES

When using nails, regardless of the type, keep in mind that the larger the nail, the greater the holding power. But larger nails also tend to split wood. Therefore, use the largest nail possible for the job but one that isn't large enough to split the wood. A good rule of thumb is to use a nail three times as long as the thinnest piece of wood being joined. This will allow two-thirds of the nail to penetrate the thickest board.

TIP: HOW TO AVOID SPLITTING WOOD

Splitting of very dry wood, or hardwood, can be avoided by drilling a pilot hole in the wood first. Splitting can also sometimes be checked by blunting the tip of the nail before hammering.

DRIVING NAILS

Use a hammer that feels comfortable when swinging. Hammer nails flush to the surface when doing rough carpentry, but when nailing into finished carpentry always stop driving above the surface and use a nailset to drive the nail flush or below the surface. For better holding power, drive the nails at a slight angle to the wood surface and at angles to each other.

SAFETY TIP

Always wear goggles when nailing overhead and when using hardened nails. Hardened nails tend to break rather than bend when hit off-center by the hammer.

DRIVING SCREWS

When driving a screw make sure the blade of the screwdriver fits the screw recess exactly. If it doesn't, you'll damage the screw and possibly cause injury to yourself. For ease of installation, rub screw threads with soap first.

USING SHORT SCREWS IN THICK WOOD

If you're joining two pieces of thick wood, you can still use a short screw provided you counterbore one of the wood pieces so that the entire thread of the screw will still be buried in the second piece of wood.

TIP: DRIVING SCREWS ON AN ANGLE

When driving screws on an angle, chisel out a pocket in the surface of the wood to allow the screws to sit flat against the wood.

either on the left or right side of the cabinet. Many of the hinges for passage doors are not reversible, however, and you'll need to determine the 'hand' of the door before purchasing your hinges. If, when standing on the outside of a passage door, the door swings away from you and to the left, it takes a left-hand hinge. A swing to the right would indicate right-hand hinges. However, if the door opens toward you and to the left, it's considered a reverse door and would take right-hand hinges, or left-hand hinges should the door swing toward you and to the right.

The basic butt hinge is the one most of us are familiar with. This type of hinge is reversible, therefore it can be used with both right- and left-hand doors. The pin is fastened permanently to the hinge, making it impossible to take the hinge apart and making the hinge reversible, since the pin won't fall out when turned upside down. If you want to remove a door fastened with butt hinges, you'll need to unscrew the hinge from the door or jamb.

A loose-pin hinge is not reversible and the 'hand' of the door has to be considered before fastening the hinge. In this type of hinge, one hinge leaf has two knuckles, the other three, which join together and are fastened by a loose pin inserted down the barrel of the knuckles. If you want to remove a door fastened with a loose-pin hinge, simply remove the pins and pull out the door.

As an alternative to the loose-pin hinge, the loose-joint hinge offers the same features, except that during removal the door is raised so that one hinge leaf clears the permanent pin fastened in the barrel of the other hinge leaf.

The rising butt hinge is another hinge that cannot be taken apart. It offers a unique feature for doors that swing out over carpet. As the door is opened, the barrel of the hinge rises slightly, raising the door to allow free movement over the carpet.

Ball-bearing hinges are similar to butt hinges in that they can't be taken apart, but the knuckles of these hinges contain permanently lubricated ball bearings, which makes this type of hinge ideal for use on heavy doors.

The above hinges are the basic types for door installation. They are used mainly for passage doors, although in smaller sizes they do have some applications for cabinet doors. However, cabinet doors offer the options of being mounted as overlay doors, flush doors or recessed doors with concealed hinges, partially concealed hinges or

FASTENING SCREWS

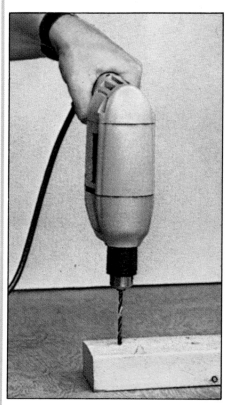

1 *When screwing into wood, a clearance hole is first drilled through the top piece of wood. The hole should have the same diameter as the screw thread.*

2 *A pilot hole is driven into the base wood; the screw is dropped through the clearance hole in the top piece and screwed only into the base wood for an effective joint.*

full-view decorative hinges.

Knuckle hinges and flush-door hinges offer concealment of the hinge except for the knuckle or barrel.

There are several kinds of decorative hinges that can be used when the hinge is part of the design of the cabinet. Many of these are of the butt hinge type, but there are some available that offer partial concealment. One hinge leaf is attached behind the door, while a small decorative hinge leaf is attached to the stile of the cabinet frame.

With the trend toward European cabinets

in kitchens comes the trend toward concealed hinges. No face frame is necessary for the European cabinet, since the hinge is recessed both into the cabinet door and into the interior side of the cabinet. Other types of European hinges offer various opening positions for the door.

Although lids can be fastened with regular butt hinges, a long heavy lid is usually hinged by the piano, or continuous, hinge. This hinge comes in lengths up to 213cm (84in) and is screwed into place through a series of screw holes placed at 5cm (2in) intervals.

DOOR HINGES

Loose pin door hinges are specified as left or right hand door hinges. The hand of the hinge determines the direction of opening for the door.

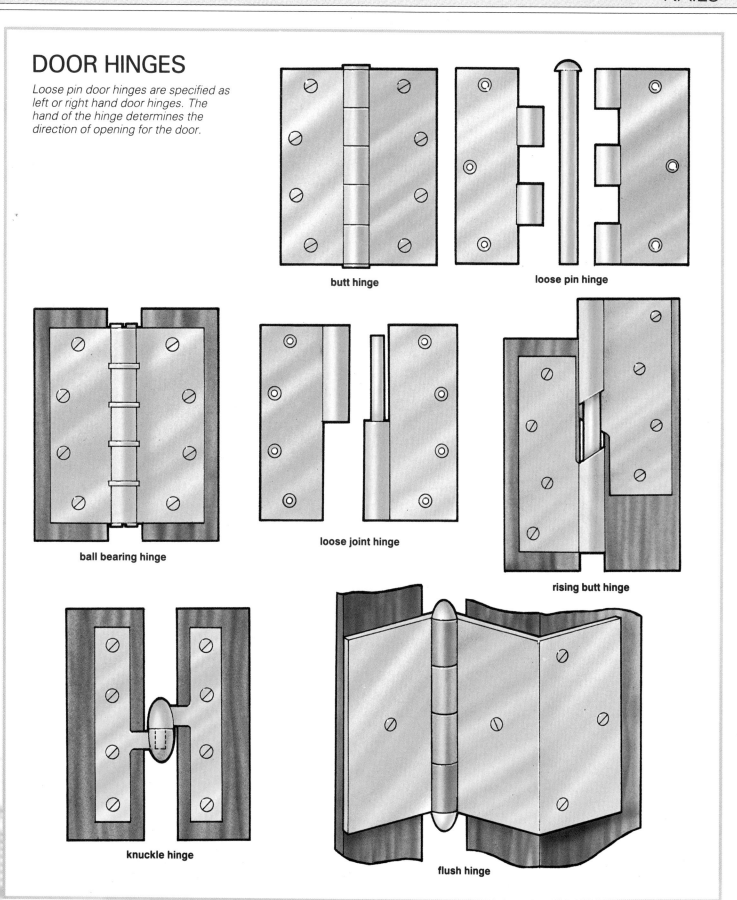

butt hinge

loose pin hinge

ball bearing hinge

loose joint hinge

rising butt hinge

knuckle hinge

flush hinge

DOOR HINGES

The 'hand' of the door must be determined before buying hinges.

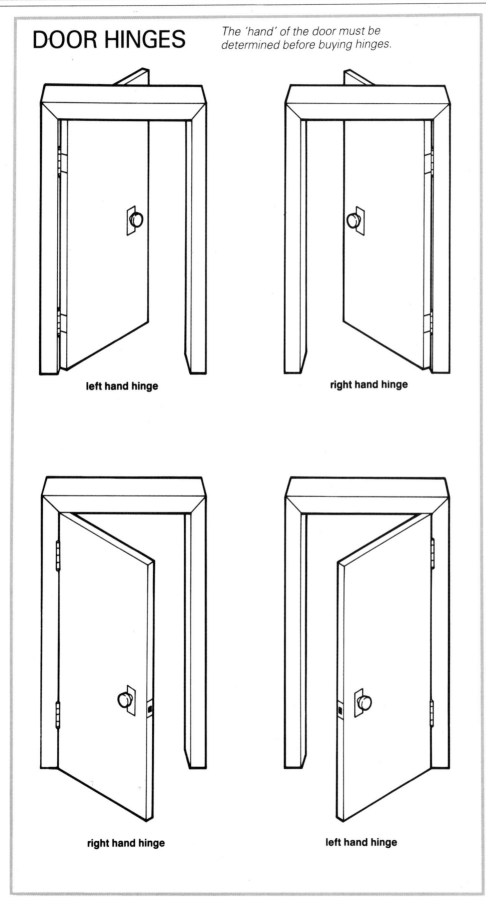

left hand hinge

right hand hinge

right hand hinge

left hand hinge

SIMPLE JOINTS

It's often thought that only elaborate joints give good results in woodwork. It isn't true. There are simple ways to join wood, and one of the simplest is the butt joint. It's easy to make, can be used on natural lumber or man-made boards, and it's neat. What's more, given the right adhesive and the right reinforcement, a butt joint can also be strong enough for most purposes.

The great thing about butt joints is their simplicity. You can use them on any kind of solid wood or man-made board, provided it isn't too thin — not under 6mm (¼in). The only problem you will run into is where you are joining chipboard. A special technique is needed here to get the screws to grip, as is explained later.

Although it is possible to simply glue two pieces of wood together, unless you add some kind of reinforcement the result won't be very strong. So in most cases, the joint should be strengthened with either screws or nails. The question is which? As a rule of thumb, screws will give you a stronger joint than nails. The exception is where you are screwing into the endgrain of solid wood. Here, the screwthread chews up the wood to such an extent that it has almost no fixing value at all. Nails in this case are a much better bet.

Choosing the right adhesive

Even if you are screwing or nailing the joint together, it ought to be glued as well. A PVA woodworking adhesive will do the trick in most jobs, providing a strong and easily achieved fixing. This type of adhesive will not, however, stand up well to either extreme heat or to moisture; the sort of conditions you'll meet outdoors, or in a kitchen, for example. A urea formaldehyde is the glue to use in this sort of situation. It isn't as convenient — it comes as a powder that you have to mix with water — but your joints will hold.

Choosing the right joint

There are no hard and fast rules about choosing the best joint for a particular job. It's really just a case of finding a joint that is neat enough for what you're making, and strong enough not to fall apart the first time it is used. And as far as strength is concerned, the various kinds of butt joint work equally well.

Marking lumber

Butt joints are the simplest of all joints — there's no complicated chiselling or marking out to worry about — but if the joint is to be both strong and neat you do need to be able to saw wood to length leaving the end perfectly square.

The first important thing here is the accuracy of your marking out. Examine the piece of wood you want to cut and choose a side and an edge that are particularly flat and smooth. They're called the face edge and face side.

Next, measure up and press the point of a sharp knife into the face side where you intend to make the cut. Slide a try-square up to the knife, making sure that its stock — the handle — is pressed firmly against the face edge. Then use the knife to score a line across the surface of the timber. Carry this line round all four sides of the wood, always making sure that the try-square's stock is held against either the face edge or the face side. If you wish, you can run over the knife line with a pencil to make it easier to see — it's best to sharpen the lead into a chisel shape.

Why not use a pencil for marking out in the first place? There are two reasons. The first is that a knife gives a thinner and therefore more accurate line than even the sharpest pencil. The second is that the knife will cut through the surface layer of the wood, helping the saw to leave a clean, sharp edge.

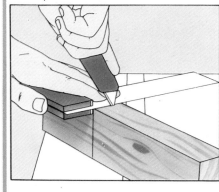

Sawing square

One of the most useful — and easiest to make — aids to sawing is a bench hook. It'll help you to grip the wood you want to cut, and to protect the surface on which you are working. You can make one up quite easily, by gluing and screwing together pieces of scrap wood (see *Ready Reference*).

You also need the ability to control the saw, and there are three tips that will help you here. Always point your index finger along the saw blade to stop it flapping from side to side as you work. And always stand in such a way that you are comfortable, well balanced, and can get your head directly above the saw so you can see what you are cutting. You should also turn slightly sideways on. This stops your elbow brushing against your body as you draw the saw back — a fault that is often the reason for sawing wavy lines.

Starting the cut

Position the piece of wood to be cut on the bench hook and hold it firmly against the block furthest from you. Start the cut by drawing the saw backwards two or three times over the far edge to create a notch, steadying the blade by 'cocking' the thumb of your left hand. Make sure that you position the saw so that the whole of this notch is on the waste side of the line. You can now begin to saw properly using your arm with a sort of piston action, but keep your left (or right as the case may be) hand away from the saw.

As the cut deepens gradually reduce the angle of the saw until it is horizontal. At this point you can continue sawing through until you start cutting into the bench hook. Alternatively, you may find it easier to angle the saw towards you and make a sloping cut down the edge nearest to you. With that done, you can saw through the remaining waste holding the saw horizontally, using the two angled cuts to keep the saw on course.

Whichever method you choose, don't try to force the saw through the wood – if that seems necessary, then the saw is probably blunt. Save your muscle power for the forward stroke – but concentrate mainly on sawing accurately to your marked line.

Cleaning up cut ends

Once you have cut the wood to length, clean up the end with sandpaper. A good tip is to lay the abrasive flat on a table and work the end of the wood over it with a series of circular strokes, making sure that you keep the wood vertical so you don't sand the end out of square. If the piece of wood is too unmanageable, wrap the sandpaper around a square piece of scrap wood instead and sand the end of the wood by moving the block to and fro — it'll help in keeping the end square.

DOVETAIL NAILING

This is a simple way of strengthening any butt joint. All you do is grip the upright piece in a vice or the jaws of a portable work-bench, and glue the horizontal piece on top if it – supporting it with scrap wood to hold the joint square – and then drive in the nails dovetail fashion. If you were to drive the nails in square, there would be more risk that the joint would pull apart. Putting them in at an angle really does add strength.

The only difficulty is that the wood may split. To prevent this, use oval brads rather than round nails, making sure that their thickest part points along the grain. If that doesn't do the trick, try blunting the point of each nail by driving it into the side of an old hammer. This creates a burr of metal on the point which will cut through the wood fibres rather than parting them.

Once the nails are driven home, punch their heads below the surface using a nailset, or a large blunt nail. Fill the resulting dents with plastic wood and sand smooth.

1 *Drive nails at angle: first leans to left; next to right, and so on.*

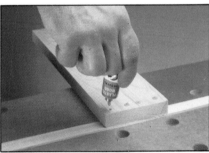

3 *Fill resulting dents with plastic wood to cover up nail heads.*

THE OVERLAP

This is the simplest of all and is one you can use on relatively thin wood. The example shown is for a T-joint, but the method is the same if you want to make an X-joint.

Bring the two pieces of wood together as they will be when joined, and use a pencil to mark the position of the topmost piece on the one underneath. To reinforce the joint, countersunk screws are best, so mark their positions on the top piece of wood, and drill clearance holes the same diameter as the screw's shank – the unthreaded part – right the way through. The screws should be arranged like the spots on a dice (two screws are shown here, but on a larger joint where more strength is needed five would be better) to help stop the joint twisting out of square. Enlarge the mouths of these holes with a countersink bit to accommodate the screw heads, and clean up any splinters where the drill breaks through the underside of the wood.

Bring the two pieces of wood together again using a piece of scrap wood to keep the top piece level. Then make pilot holes in the lower piece using either a bradawl or a small drill, boring through the clearance holes to make sure they are correctly positioned. Make sure the pilot holes are drilled absolutely vertically, or the screws could pull the joint out of shape. Finally, apply a thin coating of adhesive to both the surfaces to be joined (follow the adhesive manufacturer's instructions), position the pieces of wood accurately and, without moving them again, drive home the screws.

3 *Reassemble joint and bore pilot holes in bottom piece with bradawl.*

2 With nailset or large blunt nail, hammer nail heads below surface.

4 When filler is dry, sand flush with surface of surrounding wood.

CORRUGATED WOOD CONNECTORS

Another simple way of holding a butt joint together is to use ordinary metal connectors. Simply glue the two pieces of wood together, and hammer the connectors in across the joint. Note that they are driven in dovetail fashion — the fixing is stronger that way.

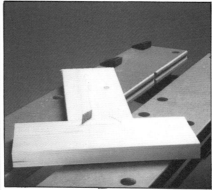

For strength, hammer in connectors diagonally rather than straight.

Ready Reference

MAKING YOUR OWN BENCH HOOK

This a very useful sawing aid to help grip the wood when cutting. Hook one end over the edge of the workbench and hold the wood against the other end. Make it up from off-cuts and replace when it becomes worn.

You need:
● a piece of 12mm (1/2in) plywood measuring about 250 x 225mm (10 x 9in)
● two pieces of 50 x 25mm (2 x 1in) planed softwood, each about 175mm (7in) long. Glue and screw them together as shown in the sketch. Use the bench hook the other way up if you're left-handed.

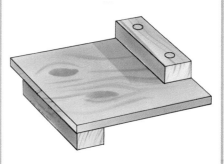

TIP: SAWING STRAIGHT

● hold wood firmly against bench hook and start cut on waste side of cutting line with two or three backward cuts
● decrease angle of the saw blade as cut progresses
● complete cut with saw horizontal, cutting into your bench hook slightly

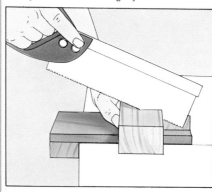

TIP: TO SMOOTH CUT END

● rub with a circular motion on sandpaper held flat on the workbench, so you don't round off the corners
● on large pieces of wood, wrap sandpaper around a block of wood and rub this across the cut end

1 Bring pieces squarely together. Mark position of each on the other.

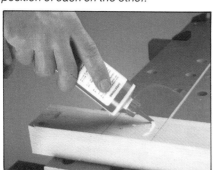

4 Apply woodworking adhesive to both pieces and press them together

2 Drill and countersink (inset) clearance holes for screws in uppermost piece.

5 Carefully drive in screws. If they're tight, remove and lubricate with soap.

FASTENING INTO CHIPBOARD

Because neither nails nor screws hold well in chipboard, how do you hold a butt joint together? The answer is that you do use screws, but to help them grip, you drive them into a chipboard plug. Chipboard plugs are a bit like ordinary wall plugs. In fact, you can use ordinary plugs, but you have to be careful to position the plug so that any expanding jaws open across the board's width and not across the thickness where they could cause the board to break up.

The initial stages of the job are exactly the same as for the overlap joint – marking out, drilling the clearance holes, and so on. The difference is that instead of boring pilot holes in the second piece of wood, you drill holes large enough to take the chipboard plugs. Pop the plugs into the holes, glue the joint together and drive home the screws.

Incidentally, if you can't use any sort of plug at all – for example, when screwing into the face of the chipboard – the only way to get the screw to hold properly is to dip it in a little woodworking adhesive before you drive it home.

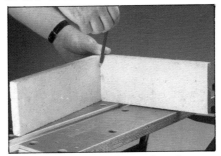
1 Bring pieces together and mark position of overlap with a pencil.

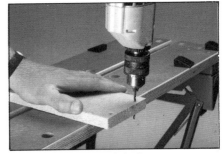
2 Drill and countersink clearance holes in overlapping piece.

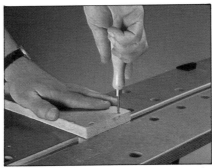
3 Mark screw positions through holes onto end of second piece.

4 Drill chipboard to take plugs, then glue and screw joint together.

REINFORCING BLOCKS

The joints described so far are fairly robust, but if a lot of strength is needed it's worth reinforcing the joint with some sort of block. The simplest is a square piece of timber.

First drill and countersink clearance holes through the block and glue and screw it to one of the pieces you want to join so that it's flush with the end. To complete the joint, glue the second piece in position, and drive screws through into that. You can arrange for the block to end up inside the angle or outside it. Choose whichever looks best and is easiest to achieve.

With the block inside the angle, you'll have a neat joint and the screw heads won't be openly on display. However, in most cases it means screwing through a thick piece of wood (the block) into a thin piece (one of the bits you want to join), so it's not as strong as it might be. If greater strength is needed work the other way round, driving the screws through the pieces to be joined, into the block. You can neaten the result to a certain extent by using a triangular rather than a square block.

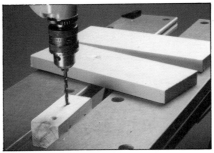
1 Drill and countersink clearance holes through reinforcing block.

2 Glue and screw block in place level with end of one piece of wood.

3 Glue second piece in place and drive screws into it through block.

4 In some cases this joint looks better with block outside angle.

JOINTING BLOCKS

Made from plastic, these are just sophisticated versions of the wooden blocks you can make yourself, and they're used in similar situations. Their only real advantage is that they tend to give a neater result when you're working with veneered or melamine covered chipboard, but only because they come in the right colors. There are basically two kinds to choose from.

The simplest is just a hollow triangular 'block' that comes with a snap-on cover to hide the screws. More complicated versions come in two parts. You screw one half of the block to each piece of wood, and then screw the two halves together using the machine screw provided. It's essential here that both halves of the block are positioned accurately, and since the blocks vary from brand to brand in the details of their design, you should follow the manufacturer's instructions on this point.

1 Screw half of block to one piece of wood and mark position on other.

2 Next, screw second half of block in place on second piece of wood.

3 Finally, connect both halves of block using built-in machine screw.

4 Treat blocks that come in one piece as wooden reinforcing blocks.

ANGLE IRONS

If still greater strength is needed, use either an angle iron or a corner repair bracket to reinforce the joint. These are really just pieces of metal pre-drilled to take screws and shaped to do the same job as a reinforcing block (the angle irons) or to be screwed to the face of the two pieces of timber across the joint (the flat T-shaped and L-shaped corner repair brackets).

In either case, bring together the pieces of wood to be joined, position the bracket, and mark the screw holes. Drill clearance and pilot holes for all the screws, then screw the bracket to one of the pieces before glueing the joint together and screwing the bracket to the second piece. They don't look very attractive, so use where appearance isn't important, ie, at the back of a joint, or where the joint is going to be concealed in some other way.

1 Corner joints strengthened with plywood and an angle repair iron.

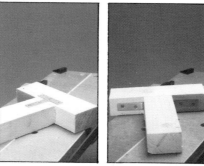

2 T-joints can be simply made with angle irons or repair brackets.

TOENAILING

There'll be some situations where you cannot get at the end of the wood to use dovetail nailing. Here you must use toenailing instead. This means gluing the two pieces securely together and then driving a nail into the upright piece of wood at an angle so it also penetrates the horizontal piece. Put a couple of nails into each side of the upright so that they cross. To stop the upright moving, clamp a block of wood behind it or wedge it against something solid.

Stop movement while driving nails with scrap wood block and C-clamp.

WALL FASTENERS

There's a huge variety of wall fasteners available. Some are designed for solid walls, some for hollow walls. Choosing the right one will ensure that whatever you're fastening stays there.

Two things will decide which type of wall fastener you need: the first is the strength of hold you require — book shelves, for instance, are going to need a much stronger hold than a picture frame — and the second is the kind of wall you're fastening to.

Whether you're fastening to solid walls (either plaster covered brick, stone, concrete, or some other kind of building block) or in hollow ones (plasterboard, lath and plaster, or wood panels fixed to a timber framework), screws are normally used. However, on their own, screws don't grip in masonry, so you have to use some sort of plug.

Hints

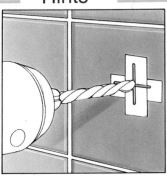

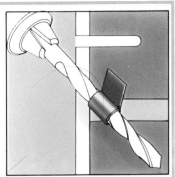

When drilling in hard shiny surfaces — ceramic tiles, for example —you often find that the drill bit wanders out of position as soon as you turn on the drill. To avoid this, cover where you want the hole with sticky tape.

Sticky tape is also handy for making sure you don't drill too deeply. Just wrap it round the drill bit the length of the plug in from the tip, to form a little flag. When the flag touches the wall, you know you've drilled far enough.

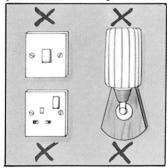

It's not just hard surfaces that can make the drill wander off course. It can happen on plaster, too. Here the answer is to make a shallow dent by turning the bit by hand. The dent should then keep the tip of the drill just where you want it.

Take care when drilling into walls not to go through electric cable. The main danger areas to avoid are above and below light switches or receptacles, and anywhere near wall lights. Also avoid areas near pipes.

The screw used is important for a strong grip. Choose one that will penetrate at least 25mm (1in); more if it is to carry a lot of weight. The screw gauge also matters. The higher the gauge number, the thicker the screw, and the stronger the grip. A No 6 is for light fastening only. A No 8 will do for most other jobs, but for a very sound grip indeed, use a No 10 or No 12.

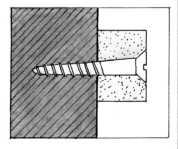

Fastening to solid walls

Drill a hole, insert a wall plug, and then drive the screw into that. As the screw penetrates, the plug expands and presses against the sides of the hole. So long as you don't overtighten it (in which case the screw thread will destroy the plug) the screw will then be very firmly embedded indeed.

You must, though, ensure that the plug expands in solid masonry, rather than in the plaster coating, or in any mortar joins.

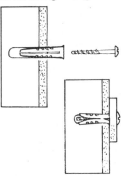

Fibre plugs These are made from compressed fibre with a built-in pilot hole for the screw. They come in various sizes and lengths, and to get a good grip both the hole and plug size must tally exactly with the size of screw. Refer to the manufacturer's recommendations here.

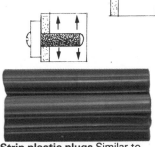

Strip plastic plugs Similar to fibre plugs, these are sold in 300mm (12in) lengths so you can cut off just the amount you need. Again, you must match the size of plug and the hole to take it, with the size of screw, and to help you the plug sizes are color coded. White is for screw gauges 4 and 6 and needs a hole drilled with a No 8 masonry bit; red is for gauges 6 and 8 and needs a No 10 bit; green is for gauges 8, 10 and 12, and needs a No 12 bit; and blue is for gauges 10, 12, and 14, and needs a No 16 bit.

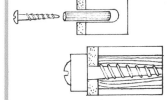

Standard wall plugs Also made from plastic, these give a stronger grip than strip plugs. Designs vary, but all have slits or opening jaws to increase the degree to which the plug can expand, as well as fins and barbs to increase grip. The other advantage of this sort of plug is that, with most brands, one size of plug can take several sizes of screw, without reducing the fastening strength.

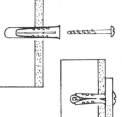

A special version of the standard plug for fastening structural lumber like door frames. It has a built-in brass screw.

Breeze block plugs One thing ordinary plugs are not good at is gripping in soft or crumbling masonry, notably breeze block and aerated concrete block. Here a special plug is required. It consists of a central core surrounded by tough, flexible fins arranged in a sort of spiral. To use it, drill a hole a little larger than the central core, and hammer the plug in. The fins compress, then force themselves against the sides of the hole to hold the plug even if the masonry does give way.

Rawlbolts The thing to use if you need a really heavy-duty grip — for example, fastening a lean-to roof to the side of a house. Rawlbolts work in much the same way as a standard plug, but are made from metal, and come ready-fitted with a bolt. Various sizes are available, and you can choose between a number of types of head, including a threaded stud to take a nut, a hook, an eye, and a normal hexagonal bolt head.

Wooden pegging The solution to the problem of fixing into mortar joints — take a piece of wood, preferably hardwood, roughly 19mm (³/₄in) in diameter, taper one end, and then drive it into a 12mm (¹/₂in) hole with a mallet. You can then screw into it in the same way as any other piece of wood.

Masonry nails Masonry nails are used like any other nail. They are just specially hardened, and designed to penetrate and hold in masonry. They come in sizes to suit most jobs — choose a length that will penetrate the wall by about 19mm (³/₄in) — and, in spite of their tendency to shatter if you don't hit them squarely, they do offer a fast way to get a grip. However, the result is not neat, so reserve them for rough constructional jobs, where looks are not important.

Plugging compound For a relatively light fixing in crumbling walls, use a plugging compound; a fibrous material that you mix with water and pack into the hole using the tool provided. Once the hole is full, make a starting hole with the pointed end of the tool, and carefully drive in the screw. As the compound dries, it "cements" the screw in place.

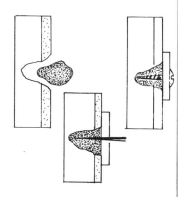

Fastening to hollow walls

Here, getting the screw to grip is even more of a problem than with a solid wall. After all, the screw has nothing to bite on but air. There are a number of ingenious solutions, but virtually all have a snag; remove the screw, and the fixing device is lost inside the cavity.

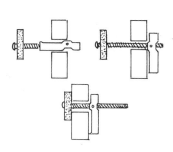

Petal anchors Made from plastic, these are twisted onto the end of the screw and pushed through the hole into the cavity beyond. As the screw is tightened, the anchor's petals open out against the back of the plasterboard, or whatever, thus preventing both anchor and screw from pulling out.

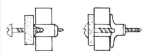

Expanding plugs Designs vary, but all work in the same sort of way. You push them into the hole, insert a screw – some have a built-in machine screw – and tighten up. The plug bulges out inside the cavity until it is too large to come back through the hole.

Gravity toggles The toggle is essentially a small metal hinged device fitted to the end of a machine screw (supplied). When pushed through the hole, it flops down inside the cavity, bridges the hole, and so allows the screw to be tightened. This bridging action is ideal for lath and plaster walls.

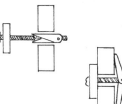

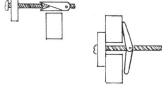

Spring toggles These use the same principle as gravity toggles. The difference is that two sprung metal wings are used to do the bridging job.

Screwing into the framework

The only way to get a really strong grip in hollow walls is to screw directly into the wall's internal wooden framework. This consists of upright 'studs' spaced about 400mm (16in) apart, and horizontal bars put in mainly where there is a horizontal join between drywall sheets. The former offer the strongest support for a fastening.

To locate them, tap the wall until it sounds reasonably solid, then drill a series of tiny test holes until you strike wood. If the studs aren't where you need them, span two with a stout piece of wood screwed in place on the surface, and fasten into that.

SHELVING THE BASICS

There are lots of ways of putting up shelves. Some systems are fixed, others adjustable — the choice is yours. Here's how both types work, and how to get the best from each.

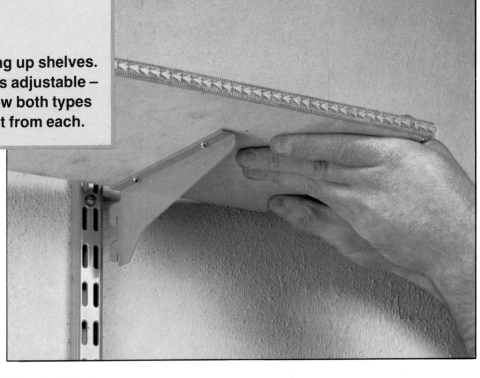

Deciding how much shelving you'll need is always tricky — because, the more shelves you have, the more you'll find to go on them! So it's always wise to add an extra 10 per cent to the specification when you start planning.

Think carefully about what you want to store and display, and try to categorize it by size and weight. The size part is fairly easy. Concentrate first on the depth (from front to back) and length; a collection of paperback books, for instance, might need 3.5m (10ft) of 150mm (6in) deep shelves. Having the shelves a bit deeper than you really need is always worthwhile, and if you add 10 per cent the length should look after itself.

Next, the heights in each grouping will tell you roughly how far apart the shelves must be. Most paperbacks are 175mm (7in) high — allow an extra 25mm (1in) for easy access and removal.

Finally, weight. The trouble here is that, even if you weigh what you'll be storing, you can't translate the result into shelf, bracket and fixing materials or sizes. Instead, think in terms of light, moderately heavy and very heavy. Items such as the TV and stereo, while not especially weighty, are best treated as very heavy, because it would be nothing short of disastrous if a shelf did give way under them!

Shelf design

Where you put the shelves affects the amount of storage you can gain, how you build them, and the overall look of the room itself. This last may not be important in a workshop, for instance, but in a living room, where the shelves may well be the focal point, a bad decision can be serious.

The obvious spot for shelving is against a continuous wall. This offers most scope to arrange the shelves in an interesting and attractive way. An alcove is another possibility. Shelving here is neat, and easily erected; it is a very good way of using an otherwise awkward bit of space. A corner has similar advantages if you make triangular shelves to fit — though they're really only suitable for displaying plants or favorite ornaments rather than books.

Planning it out

If appearance matters and you're putting up a lot of shelves, a good way to plan is by making a scale drawing of the whole scheme to see how it looks. Then check for detail. If your TV has an indoor aerial, make sure you have room to adjust it. With stereo systems, ensure the shelf is deep enough to take all the wiring spaghetti at the back. And do think about the heights of the shelves from the floor (see *Ready Reference*).

Finally, make sure you provide adequate support for the shelves and the weight they'll be carrying. There is no very precise method of gauging this, but you won't go wrong if you remember that for most household storage a shelf needs support at least every 750mm (30in) along its length. This will usually be enough even with chipboard, which is the weakest of shelving materials. But bowing may still be a problem, so for items in the 'very heavy' category it's advisable to increase the number of supports by reducing the space between them.

Which material?

Chipboard is usually the most economical material, and if properly supported is strong enough for most shelving. It can be fairly attractive, too, since you can choose a type with a decorative wood veneer or plastic finish. These come in a variety of widths — most of them designed with shelving in mind.

Natural wood, though more costly and sometimes prone to warping, is an obvious alternative. You may have difficulty obtaining some wood in boards over 225mm (9in) wide, but narrower widths are readily available. For wider shelves, another way is to make up the shelf width from narrower pieces. An easy method is to leave gaps between the lengths and brace them with others which run from front to back on the underside, forming a slatted shelf.

Particleboard and plywood are also worth considering.

Both are a lot stronger than chipboard and have a more attractive surface which can be painted or varnished without trouble. However, in the thicknesses you need — at least 12mm (½in) — plywood is relatively expensive; particleboard is cheaper, and chipboard cheaper still. All these man-made boards need to have their edges disguised to give a clean finish. An easy yet effective way to do this is just to glue and pin on strips of molding or 'beading'. Also remember that the cheapest way to buy any of these boards is in large sheets (approximately 2.4m × 1.2m/8ft × 4ft), so it's most economical to plan your shelves in lengths and widths that can be cut from a standard size sheet.

Shelves needn't be solid, though. If you want them extra-thick, for appearance or strength, you can make them up from a wood frame covered with a thin sheet material. Hardboard is cheap, but thin plywood gives a more attractive edge; alternatively use a wooden edging strip.

BRACKET SHELVING

1 *If your shelves are of man-made board, a good way to give them neat edges is to pin on decorative 'beading', mitred at the corners.*

2 *Begin by screwing the shorter arm of the bracket to the shelf. Position it squarely and in such a way that the shelf will lie snugly against the wall.*

3 *Using a spirit level as a guide, mark a pencil line along the wall at the height where you want the top of the shelf to be positioned.*

4 *Hold the shelf, complete with brackets, against this line, and mark with a pencil through the screw holes in the brackets, so you know where to drill.*

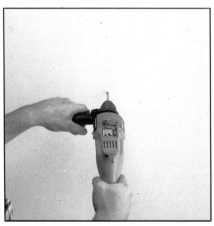

5 *Drill holes in the wall with a power drill, using a masonry bit if necessary, and being sure to keep the drill straight. Then insert plastic plugs.*

6 *Hold the shelf in position, insert one screw in each bracket and tighten it halfway; then insert the others and tighten the whole lot up.*

Ready Reference

PLANNING SHELVES

When you design storage, plan ahead and think about *how* you're going to use it.

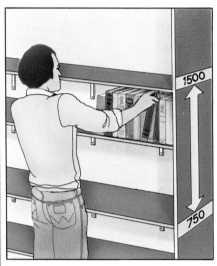

Height. Keep everyday items well within reach. That means between 750 and 1500mm (30 and 60in) off the ground.
Depth. Shelves that are deepest (from front to back) should be lower, so you can see and reach to the back.
Spacing. An inch or two over the actual height of the objects means you can get your hand in more easily.

HOW TO SPACE BRACKETS

Space brackets according to the shelf thickness. Heavy loads (left) need closer brackets than light loads (right).

12mm (½in) chipboard

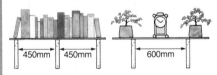

12mm (½in) plywood
19mm (¾in) chipboard

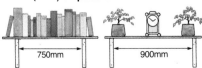

19mm (¾in) plywood

ADJUSTABLE SHELVING

1 Metal uprights come in a range of sizes, but occasionally they may need shortening. If so, you can easily cut them down with a hacksaw.

2 After using your level to mark the height for the tops of the uprights, measure along it and mark out the spacings between them.

3 Hold each of the uprights with its top at the right height, and mark through it onto the wall for the position of the uppermost screw hole only.

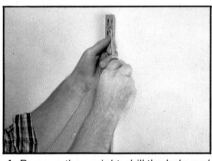

4 Remove the upright, drill the hole and plug it if necessary. Then replace the upright, and fit the screw – but don't tighten it completely.

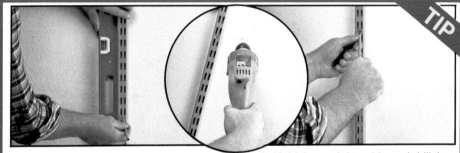

TIP

5 With the upright loose, hold a level against it and adjust it till it's vertical. Then mark through it for the other screw positions.

6 Hold the upright aside and drill the other holes. Plug them, insert the screws and tighten them all up – not forgetting the topmost one.

7 Now you can screw the bracket to the shelf, aligning it correctly and taking particular care over how it lines up at the back edge.

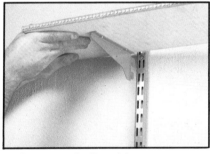

8 One type of adjustable system uses brackets with lugs at the back. It's easiest to let these lugs project behind the shelf when screwing on brackets.

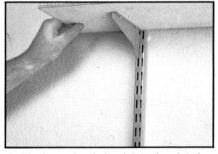

9 The lugs simply hook into the slots in the uprights. Changing the shelf height is just a matter of unhooking them and moving them up or down.

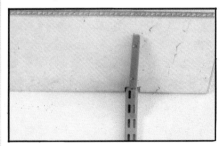

10 If you want the back edge of the shelf right against the wall, notch it with a tenon saw and chisel to fit round the upright. Inset the bracket on the shelf.

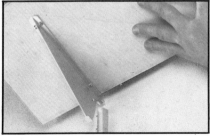

11 The channel system is different. First of all, you engage the bracket's upper lug in the channel and slide it down, keeping the lower one clear.

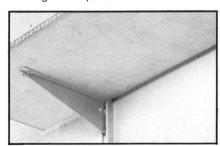

12 When you reach the position you want, level the shelf and the bracket, so as to slide its lower lug into one of the pairs of slots down the upright.

Fastening shelves

The simplest method of fastening shelves is directly to the wall, using brackets. L-shaped metal brackets of various sizes and designs are available everywhere — some plain and functional, some with attractive lacquered or enamelled finishes. It's just a question of choosing ones about 25mm (1in) less than the shelf depth, spacing them the right distance apart and screwing them to both shelf and wall.

If you're filling up your shelves with books, the support brackets won't be seen. But if you're using the shelves for ornaments, the brackets will be visible, so choose a style that blends. Alternatively, you can make up your own brackets from two pieces of wood butt-jointed into an L shape and braced with a diagonal strut or triangular block.

The fastening technique is the same either way. First you draw a line on the wall where the shelf is to go, using a spirit level. Next, attach the brackets to the shelf and put the whole assembly up against the line. Mark on to the wall through the pre-drilled screw holes in the brackets; then take the shelf away and drill holes in the wall, filling each with a plastic plug. Lastly, drive in one screw through each bracket; then insert the rest and tighten them all up.

Because the accuracy of this method relies largely on your ability to hold the shelf level against your line, you may find it easier to work the other way round. By fixing the brackets to the wall along the guide line, you can then drop the shelf into place and screw up into it through the brackets. This works, but you must position the brackets with great care, and avoid squeezing them out of position as you screw them into the wall. That isn't always easy. For one thing, many brackets don't have arms which meet at a neat right angle. They curve slightly, which makes it hard to align the top of the shelf-bearing arm with the line on the wall.

Providing a firm support

Remember that the strength of all brackets depends partly on the length of their arms (particularly the one fastened to the wall) and partly on the strength of your fastening into the wall. The longer the wall arm in proportion to the shelf arm, the better; but it's also important to use adequate screws — 38mm (1½in) No 8s or 10s should do — and to plug the wall properly. In a hollow partition wall you really must make sure you secure the brackets to the wall's wooden framework and not just to the cladding. Even if you use drywall plugs or similar devices (see pages 188-189), a lot of weight on the shelf will cause the brackets to come away from the cladding and possibly damage the wall.

Of course, there is a limit to how much weight the brackets themselves will take.

Under very wide shelves they may bend. With shelves that have heavy items regularly taken off and dumped back on, and shelves used as desk-tops, worktops and the like, the movement can eventually work the fasteners loose. In such cases it's best to opt for what's called a cantilevered shelf bracket. Part of this is set into the masonry to give a very strong grip indeed. Details of its installation vary from brand to brand, but you should get instructions when you buy.

Alcove shelving

All brackets are expensive. However, for alcove shelving there's a much cheaper alternative, and that is to use battens screwed to the wall. All you do is fix a 25 x 50mm (1 x 2in) piece of softwood along the back of the alcove, using screws driven into plastic plugs at roughly 450mm (18in) centers. Then screw similar ones to the side walls, making sure that they line up with the first. In both cases, getting the battens absolutely level is vital. In fact, it's best to start by drawing guidelines using a spirit level as a straight edge.

A front 'rail' is advisable where the shelf spans a wide alcove and has to carry a lot of weight. But there's a limit to what you can do. With a 50 x 25mm (2 x 1in) front rail and battens, all on edge, 1.5m (5ft) is the safe maximum width.

A front rail has another advantage because, as well as giving man-made boards a respectably thick and natural look, it also hides the ends of the side battens. So does stopping them short of the shelf's front edge and cutting the ends at an angle.

The shelf can be screwed or even just nailed to the battens to complete the job.

Movable shelves

Unfortunately, both brackets and battens have one big drawback: once they're fixed, they're permanent. So you might consider an adjustable shelving system which gives you the chance to move shelves up and down. Such systems consist of uprights, screwed to the wall, and brackets which slot into them at almost any point down the length.

There are two main types. In one, brackets locate in vertical slots in the uprights. The other has a continuous channel down each upright. You can slide brackets along it and lock them at any point along the way, where they stay put largely because of the weight of the shelf. With both types, brackets come in standard sizes suitable for shelf widths, and there's a choice of upright lengths to fulfil most needs.

Many shelving systems of this sort include a number of accessories to make them more versatile. These include book ends, shelf clips and even light fittings.

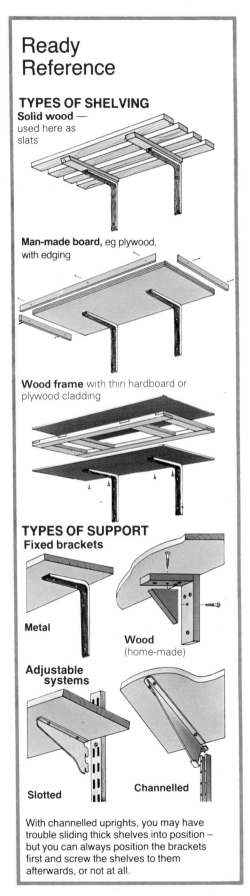

Ready Reference

TYPES OF SHELVING
Solid wood — used here as slats

Man-made board, eg plywood, with edging

Wood frame with thin hardboard or plywood cladding

TYPES OF SUPPORT
Fixed brackets

Metal

Wood (home-made)

Adjustable systems

Slotted

Channelled

With channelled uprights, you may have trouble sliding thick shelves into position – but you can always position the brackets first and screw the shelves to them afterwards, or not at all.

BUILDING SHELVING UNITS

Self-supporting shelves, unlike the wall-mounted type, can be moved wherever and whenever you like – without leaving screw holes to be plugged. Here's how to make them rigid and roomy.

A part from their most obvious advantages over built-in units, freestanding units don't have to be tailored to fit any irregularities of walls and alcoves. But, because they aren't fixed in position, you have to devote a bit more time and thought to making them rigid.

This is often a matter of making a straightforward box, although frame construction is another possibility. Either way, it is important to remember that the shelves themselves won't add much stability, particularly if they're adjustable. You need additional stiffening to compensate the tendency for the whole unit to fold up sideways into a diamond shape.

The basic box
Always keep your materials in mind. The options are, of course, solid wood or manmade boards. Plywood is probably the best all-rounder, but it's quite expensive. Chipboard is cheap, and chipboard screws make a strong butt joint. In solid wood and particleboard, you're restricted by the fact that you shouldn't screw or nail into end grain.

Dowels or plastic jointing blocks are good for assembling most of the structure, but dowels are less than ideal for corners, because a dowel joint isn't all that rigid. A wood strip, glued and screwed into both surfaces, can add some necessary reinforcement; but shelf units often rise above eye level, so be careful that it's not unsightly.

A barefaced housing joint is one remaining possibility – that is, apart from those afforded by power tools. A circular saw or router makes it a lot easier, for example, to cut rebate joints or mitres.

An additional point is that plastic facings such as melamine laminate won't accept glue, so that some form of screw fastening is virtually your only way of fixing other components to them.

Stiffening the unit
The simplest way of making a unit rigid is to pin a back panel to the rear edges of the box and perhaps even to the back edges of the shelves as well.

However, there may be occasions (for example, if the unit is to stand in the middle of a room) when you want a more open, airy look than is possible with this unmodified form of construction. In such cases the answer is to add bracing to the actual box components themselves. Even if you are incorporating a back, the extra stability such bracing provides won't come amiss – especially on large units.

The principle works as follows. Flat boards bend under stress. You can counter this by fixing lengths of reinforcing lumber along them, preferably on edge. Each reinforced board helps to keep the structure stable.

You can even stiffen the open (front) face of the cabinet, by running bracing members across it, provided these are firmly jointed to the cabinet sides — say with dowels, plastic jointing blocks or steel angle repair brackets. A recessed kick does this job and the type of kick that's made up separately stabilizes the cabinet by stiffening its bottom.

Frequently the neatest way of stiffening the front is to place such reinforcement along the shelves – either underneath them (inset if you like) or fixed to their front edges.

Rectangular-sectioned wood such as 25 × 50mm (1 × 2in), or a metal L-section, is ideal here. The procedure has the added advantage of strengthening the shelves, and you can treat intermediate shelves in the same way — not just the top and bottom panels.

Supporting the shelves
You can fix shelves into the unit by any of the methods appropriate for box construction using hand tools. The strongest and most professional of these is to house the shelves into the uprights

A stopped housing makes the neater joint here, since it means the front edge of each upright is unbroken by the ends of the shelves, but a through housing is quite adequate. The other invisible fastening for fixed shelves is dowels. Screws will leave plastic caps showing on the outsides of the side panels.

The choice between these methods depends largely on your materials. A plastic-faced upright panel means the dowel joints can't be glued, so you rely even more than usual on the main box for strength. Wood

A STURDY SHELF UNIT

This unit's top and sides are made of plastic-faced chipboard; the softwood shelves are planed down in the width to match.

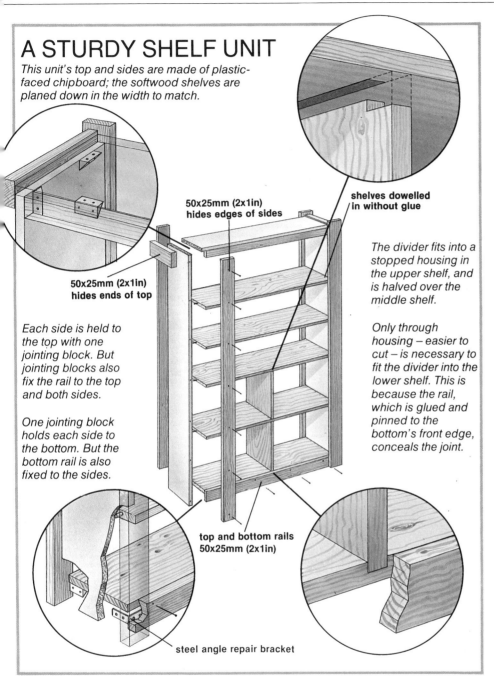

50x25mm (2x1in) hides edges of sides

50x25mm (2x1in) hides ends of top

Each side is held to the top with one jointing block. But jointing blocks also fix the rail to the top and both sides.

One jointing block holds each side to the bottom. But the bottom rail is also fixed to the sides.

shelves dowelled in without glue

The divider fits into a stopped housing in the upper shelf, and is halved over the middle shelf.

Only through housing – easier to cut – is necessary to fit the divider into the lower shelf. This is because the rail, which is glued and pinned to the bottom's front edge, conceals the joint.

top and bottom rails 50x25mm (2x1in)

steel angle repair bracket

Ready Reference

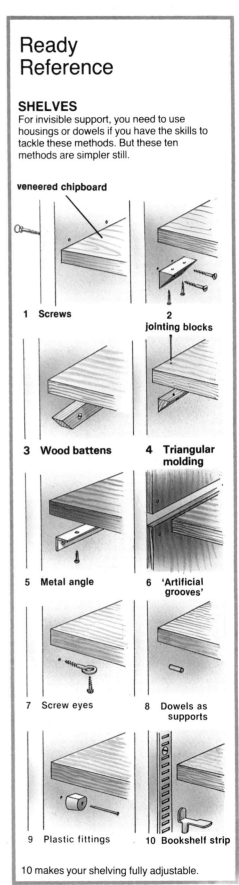

SHELVES

For invisible support, you need to use housings or dowels if you have the skills to tackle these methods. But these ten methods are simpler still.

veneered chipboard

1 Screws

2 jointing blocks

3 Wood battens

4 Triangular molding

5 Metal angle

6 'Artificial grooves'

7 Screw eyes

8 Dowels as supports

9 Plastic fittings

10 Bookshelf strip

10 makes your shelving fully adjustable.

---

shelves can't be screwed in directly because you'd be going into the end grain.

Plastic jointing blocks are an obvious and fairly unobtrusive possibility. Wood battens, glued and pinned, or screwed and if possible glued, to shelves and uprights are tough; they can also be quite neat if you chamfer their front ends, cut them off at an angle, or hide them with a front rail. A triangular-sectioned wooden 'stair rod' molding, or an L-sectioned strip of steel or aluminum, is neater still.

You can create artificial housings by using pieces of wood or board, the same width as the uprights, pinned and glued to their inside

faces, and leaving just enough space for the shelves to fit between them. This means you can make the uprights themselves a bit thinner.

A rather different approach is to let the shelf ends rest on small supports sticking out of the uprights. These might be screw eyes (with screws driven up through them into the undersides of the shelves to fix them in place if necessary); they could be 6mm (1/4in) diameter dowels. You can also get several sorts of plastic studs which screw in, nail in or push into drilled holes. Some are specially designed for glass shelves. And sometimes the hole is filled by a bush which

ASSEMBLING THE CARCASE

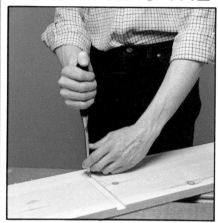

1 After cutting all the shelves to the same length, mark and cut housings for the divider halfway along the shelves above and below it.

2 Use one of the housings as a guide to mark the position of the halving to be cut in the shelf which the divider crosses.

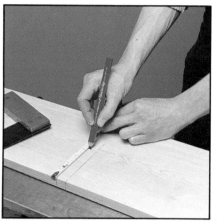

3 Measure halfway across the shelf for the depth of the halving. Then cut the divider to length, and measure and mark it out likewise.

4 Cut the matching halvings in the divider and the shelf it crosses; use a tenon saw across the grain and then a chisel to chop out the waste.

5 Align both uprights exactly and mark on them the height of each shelf (at a point which is halfway across the shelf's thickness).

6 Use a combination square at the same setting to mark the exact dowel positions on both the uprights and on all the shelf ends.

7 Drill all the dowel holes, glue the dowels into the shelf ends, and fit all but the top and bottom shelves to the uprights when the adhesive sets.

8 Screw the top and bottom shelves into position with plastic jointing blocks, or any other appropriate jointing technique.

9 Insert the divider into the unit from the back, using scrap wood to prevent damage to its rear edge as you tap it into position.

ADDING REINFORCEMENT

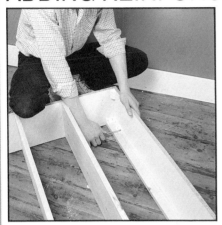

1 *Fix a stiffening rail across the top, screwing it to the uprights and the underside of the top shelf with jointing blocks.*

2 *Glue and pin the kick to the front edge of the bottom shelf (which is cut narrower than the other shelves to allow for this).*

3 *Use steel angle repair brackets to hold the kick firmly to the uprights and thus help to keep the whole unit rigid as well.*

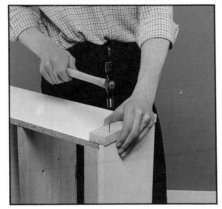

4 *Glue and pin lengths of wood, as long as the uprights are wide, to the ends of the top shelf in order to conceal them.*

5 *Glue and pin further lippings to both long edges of each upright to enhance the unit's appearance and give it extra rigidity.*

6 *Lastly, fill all nail holes with wood filler of the appropriate shade, and varnish the wood parts to improve their looks and durability.*

will accept a number of different types of stud.

Lastly, there's a very neat way to make the shelves in a freestanding unit fully adjustable. This is to use 'bookshelf strip' – metal strips with continuous rows of slots, into which you clip small metal lugs; the shelves rest on these. The strips (of which you'll need two each side) can be simply screwed to the insides of the uprights, or fitted into vertical grooves if you've got the power tools to cut them.

A home-made version of this system uses removable dowels in regular vertical rows of drilled holes.

Installing dividers

For the distances you can safely span with various thicknesses of various materials, see page 191. Really wide shelves may need extra support in the middle. Vertical dividers will provide this, and can also add to looks and usefulness. They're usually housed or dowelled in at top and bottom, and halved over intermediate shelves.

Alternatively, a square- or rectangular-sectioned wooden upright, fixed to the front edges of the shelves, will help matters. It can be glued and pinned to the shelves, dowelled in or notched over them.

Frame shelving

If you only think in terms of box construction, you limit the scope of your projects. A shelf unit's sides can just as well be open frames as single slabs. This gives a lighter look, and also avoids the problems of using man-made boards. But you do need to pay even more attention to making the structure rigid. You'll certainly need extra strengthening pieces running from side to side.

Shelves can be supported in most of the ways already mentioned – with the additional possibility of placing them on the cross pieces in the frames themselves. These cross pieces can even be pieces of broomstick – in other words, each upright is in effect a ladder, with the shelves resting on the rungs.

Box modules

In fact, as far as freestanding shelves are concerned, the possibilities are limitless. One more example may help to demonstrate this. There's no reason why you shouldn't make your 'shelving' up as a stack of completely separate open-fronted boxes. They needn't even be the same depth from front to back. Such a system lets you rearrange its shape completely at will. Its main disadvantage is that most of the panels are duplicated, so the cost of materials goes up. But moving house is easy: each box doesn't even need packing!

As long as you make the structure rigid, the choice of design is yours.

FITTING CURTAIN TRACKS

The precise method you use to fit curtain track will depend on the type you are installing. For a successful result, follow the manufacturer's instructions carefully, but here's a general idea of what's involved.

There is a wide variety of curtain tracks available, ranging from simple plastic or metal track which provides a neat inconspicuous method of hanging curtains to decorative metal rods or wooden poles which are designed to be a feature of the window treatment.

Curtain track has a series of small-wheeled runners, from which the curtains hang by means of hooks slotted into their heading tape. Rods and poles usually have rings which slide along them to carry the curtains, but some, too, have runners concealed in the bottom of the rod or pole. In addition, small curtains may be hung on wire threaded through the hem at the top and stretched between two hooks. Nets, in particular, are often supported in this way. Check with your supplier on types of track available.

Track is fixed by a series of small brackets through which you drive screws. Usually, there is a hole in both the back and the top of the bracket, so that they are suitable for back or top fixing. Poles or rods usually have only two, much larger and stronger, brackets which are fixed near each end. They are suitable only for back fixing. Pole and rod brackets are much more decorative than those of track and are meant to be seen as part of the design. Long poles or rods (usually those over 1200mm/48in) may require an intermediate bracket; check with the manufacturer's instructions about this.

Curtain wire must be fixed inside the window opening or reveal. Poles and rods should be fixed above and outside the reveal, as they are not seen to advantage otherwise. Track can be fitted inside or out, depending on the look you want.

Fastening inside the reveal

There are two advantages to hanging curtains inside the reveal. One is that because the curtains are shorter you need less fabric; it could be much less. The other is that it is normally much easier to fasten inside the reveal. Most windows have frames of wood (even steel and aluminum frames are usually set in a wood surround) and the track or wire can be fixed to this. All you need to do is make a pilot hole for the screw or hook and

then drive it home; this will be even easier if you drill the holes with an electric or hand drill first.

There's also the fact that radiators are often sited beneath a window; you will restrict the emission of heat if you cover them up with curtains hung outside the reveal.

There are some problem areas when hanging curtains inside the reveal. Normally these involve steel windows which are fixed direct to the brickwork of a window opening, so there is no wood surround. Frames like this may incorporate a device for supporting curtain fittings; there may, for example, be integral hooks from which wire can be stretched. But otherwise, there are two courses open to you. With one, you can drill holes in the steel and fix to the frame with nuts and bolts, incorporating rubber or plastic washers to ensure weathertightness. This is a laborious job and you may instead decide to adopt the alternative method of fastening to the top of the reveal. This involves cutting into the lintel, which may be a straightforward or complicated business, depending on the material from which the lintel is constructed. If you are in any doubt, you should seek professional advice.

Fastening outside the reveal

You may decide that you do not like the idea of short-length curtains fitted inside the reveal; and that you would prefer the elegant

look which floor-length curtains can give. If you opt for full-length curtains outside the window opening, the installation normally becomes a little more complicated because you will be involved in fastening into a wall.

If you want the track, rod or pole to be situated immediately above the reveal, you will have to take the lintel which supports the brickwork above into account. In some cases, especially in Victorian houses or even older ones, the lintel may be a wooden one. Fastening into this is just as simple as making them into a wood frame. However, many old houses have lintels of solid stone and in more modern houses the lintel will probably be of reinforced concrete (and in high-rise apartments the walls may be of this material).

The age of your house will give you some idea as to what type of material is used for the lintels, but how can you be sure? In some cases you can see the lintel from outside the house and you will be able to tell just by looking. But if the lintel is concealed you will have to determine the type of material used by other means. You should make a test boring with a drill and bit. You will soon know whether it is stone or concrete on the one hand or wood on the other. (Don't worry about this test hole being unsightly; you can cover it up later on.)

Boring into stone and concrete is a different matter from drilling into ordinary masonry. You will get along better with an elec-

FITTING TRACK INSIDE A REVEAL

1 *Carefully measure the width from one side of the reveal to the other. Make your measurement at the position you intend to fasten the track.*

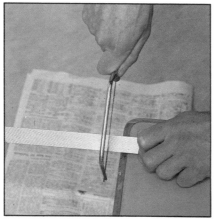

2 *Most tracks can be easily cut to size. Mark off the required length on the track and then cut through it; a fine-toothed hacksaw is suitable for this.*

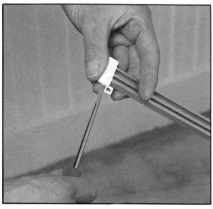

3 *Fit one endcap at the end of the track and slide on the runners. Then fit the second endcap at the other end (don't overtighten these caps).*

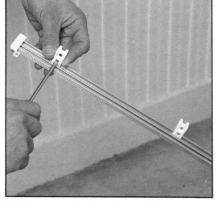

4 *Screw on the brackets. Follow the manufacturer's instructions regarding the position for the end brackets and also the spacing of the rest.*

5 *Hold the track up (here to the top of the reveal), keeping it straight and level, and use a bradawl to make pilot holes for the screws.*

6 *Use an electric drill to bore deeper holes at the positions marked and then replace the track and screw it firmly into place.*

Ready Reference

FASTENING TRACK

Track requires a lot of support brackets. The exact number varies according to the height of the curtains and the weight of the fabric; they can be spaced at intervals as close as 300mm (1ft) and seldom wider than 450mm (18in). Check with the instructions.

TIP: FIT A BOARD

Where the plaster on walls or ceiling is not particularly sound or where you want to avoid a lot of drilling into a resistant surface like reinforced concrete, you can fix the track brackets to a board, which will require fewer fasteners than the track itself. For this:
● fasten the wood with masonry nails which you drive into the wall with a hammer, avoiding drilling and plugging (some masonry nails will go into concrete)
● hide the board if you wish, cover it with the paint you've used on the walls or cover it with wallpaper so it will hardly be noticeable, or
● hack out a trench for the wood in the masonry, using cold chisel and a mallet, and fasten the wood directly to the masonry beneath (you could use an epoxy resin adhesive for this); then cover it up using plaster or filler.

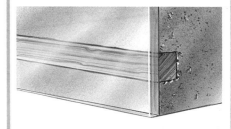

● on a ceiling you can screw the wood to the joists (don't cut out a trench for the wood or you may cause damage).

TIP: NUMBER OF RUNNERS

Don't use more runners than there are hooks in the curtains or the excess ones will cause the curtains to jam.

TIP: SECURE END BRACKET

For cord-operated track where the cord hangs at one side, the bracket which bears the weight of frequent pulling should be extra secure.

FITTING A ROD ABOVE THE REVEAL

1 *With an extendable rod like this one place it up against the wall above the reveal to work out where it will look best and how far to extend it.*

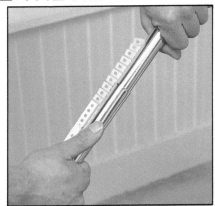

2 *To extend the rod to the required length you simply pull it outwards. Place it back up against the wall to check that it's the right length.*

3 *Longer rods require a central support bracket. Use a pencil to mark off points for this through the screw holes at top and bottom.*

4 *Measure on the rod to work out where the brackets will come and then transfer this measurement to the wall at both ends.*

5 *It's important that you get the rod truly horizontal, so check with a spirit level, and if necessary, adjust the pencil marks you've made.*

6 *Use an electric drill to bore holes at the positions you've marked. You can then fit wall plugs into the holes ready to take the screws.*

7 *Screw the brackets firmly to the wall using a screwdriver. Screws in a finish to match the brackets will normally be supplied with the rod.*

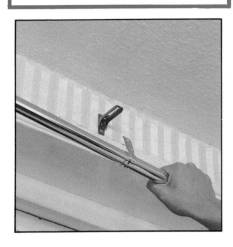

8 *Where you are using a center support as well as the end brackets, fasten one half of the support to the wall; then fasten the matching part on the rail to it.*

9 *At the ends, loosen the rosette screw, leave one runner between the bracket and the rod end and slot the rod in place. Then re-tighten the rosette screw.*

THE FINAL STAGES

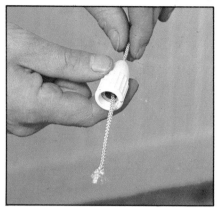

1 *Work out how long you wish the draw cords to be. Cut them if required, then thread them through the acorns supplied and tie knots to secure the ends.*

2 *You can then go ahead and hang the hooks attached to the curtains on the runners, including the master runners in the middle of the rod.*

tric, rather than a hand drill and best of all would be a hammer drill. A two- or multi-speed drill that allows you to work very slowly will make the job easily manageable.

If you don't have a slow-speed hammer drill, then you can adopt the following procedure when dealing with concrete which consists of sand, cement and aggregate with, in the case of reinforced concrete, iron bars in the middle. A bit in a rotary electric drill will cut easily into sand and cement; difficulties will arise when it meets a stone for it will then bore no further. So you should bore in the normal way with your drill and when it seems to stop making progress (a sign that it has come up against a stone) remove it and insert in the hole a percussion bit or jumping bit. To remove the obstruction, strike this a sharp blow with a club hammer and it should cut through or dislodge the flint. Then carry on drilling in the normal way. Any reinforcing bars should be too far from the surface for you to come up against them.

An alternative solution is to aim to avoid the lintel altogether. For this you fasten the rod, pole or track slightly higher up. You will then be dealing with bricks, or in the case of a modern house, building blocks, which are very easy to cut into. In fact the problem with building blocks is that they are soft and it is not always easy to get a sufficiently firm grip in them. However, you should be fine with curtains; the grip has to withstand a certain amount of force when the curtains are drawn, but they need nothing like the support of, say, wall-mounted kitchen cabinets.

One question which will concern you here will be the height of the lintel. Once again, you may well be able to see it from outside and you can then measure it. When it is concealed, working out its height is a more

difficult matter, but in general, 150mm (6in) is normally the minimum thickness for a lintel and 300mm (1ft) the maximum. So if you fasten your track, pole or rod more than 300mm (1ft) above the top of the reveal, it should be clear of the lintel. There are, of course, exceptions to this rule but it is generally the case. Again, you could make a test boring first to make absolutely certain.

If you are using curtain track you could decide to fit it even higher than this, right at ceiling level in fact. Floor-to-ceiling curtains look very striking in any room. You could go further and install curtains to cover an entire wall, even though the window may be comparatively small. It's an expensive treatment but can be a really attractive one, giving the illusion that you have enormous picture windows. It will also make the room much warmer and cosier in winter since the curtains will provide extra insulation.

If you do position the track at the top of the wall and there is no cornice, you can avoid drilling into the wall. Instead, you can top-fix the track to the ceiling by driving screws through the plaster and into the joists above. First, you will have to locate the joists. Sometimes you can actually see them bulging through the plaster. Or in an upstairs room you can look for them in the attic; in a downstairs room, look in the room above. The fixing nails of the floorboards (assuming they are not hidden beneath a floorcovering) will show you their position. Or again, you can test out their position by tapping the ceiling with your knuckles. There will be a distinct difference between the hollow sound when you strike the ceiling between the joists and the solid feel as you hit the part immediately below one. If all else fails you will, once again, have to make a series of test borings.

Ready Reference

FASTENING RODS AND POLES

Rods and poles require far fewer screws than track so there's not the same need to avoid drilling and plugging a wall. Even so, it's worth avoiding fastening into concrete where you can; fasten the rod brackets above or to the side of a concrete lintel. Also, you can, if you wish, make a small backing pad of wood and fasten it to the wall with masonry nails; screw the brackets to this.

FASTENING RODS IN BRACKETS

A typical method of fastening a rod in the end brackets is as follows: loosen the rosette screw (**A**), locate hole (**B**) onto tongue (**C**) in the brackets. One slide (**D**) should always be between the bracket and the end of the rails. Tighten the rosette screw (**A**).

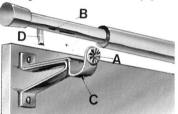

INSTALLING CENTER SUPPORTS

Extra supports for a long rod should be centered between the end brackets. These supports often come in two parts which fit together.

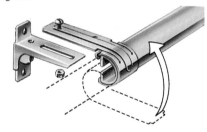

TIP: CENTER MASTER RUNNERS

To center the master runners, pull the cord to open master runner **A** to the right as far as it will go. Lift the cord off the lug on master runner **B**. Hold cords taut, pull master runner **B** to the left as far as possible. Fasten the cord under the locking tongue of master runner **B**.

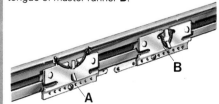

FITTING LOCKS ON WINDOWS

Burglary is a growth industry these days, and windows are particularly vulnerable to attack. But fitting security bolts and latches takes only a few minutes and is a relatively inexpensive job.

Just because you have locks on the outside doors and you are careful to shut all the windows before you go out doesn't mean that your house is safe against a burglar. Such action may deter the thief acting on the spur of the moment, but it won't prevent the committed house-breaker from trying to get in, particularly if he thinks the pickings are worth the risk.

Fortunately, there is a wide range of security bolts and locks available from suppliers to prevent easy access. And the fact that some of these devices are visible from the outside may instantly put off a would-be burglar. You can buy bolts for specific situations — say, for a sliding metal frame, a wooden casement window or a sliding sash window. Some can be used in more than one position, but it's important to follow the manufacturer's instructions closely on where to fit them. There are multi-purpose locks which can be fitted in several ways, but these tend to be more expensive.

Of all the window types, louvre windows still present the greatest security risk. Even if they are closed, it is still relatively simple for a burglar to remove some of the glass slats to gain access to your home. One solution is to glue the glass panes into their holders on either side of the frame, but there is the disadvantage that if you accidentally break a slat it becomes difficult to fit another.

The surest method of all is to fit a grille on the inside of the window. This may seem like drastic action. However, if the window is concealed from general view, this may be the only means of keeping a determined thief out unless a burglar alarm is installed.

Fitting a grille could make your home look like a prison. Fortunately, ornamental designs are available to lessen the impact. Normally you have to order the grille to the size of your window. It is installed by being mortared into the surrounding brickwork — inevitably this will cause some damage to the decoration. Some grilles are hinged and incorporate a lock to secure them in position. This enables the grille to be moved aside so that the glass can be cleaned, and, more importantly, in the event of a fire, you are still able to use the window as an escape route.

PROTECTING YOUR HOME

Railings (1), and a locked side gate, will hamper access to the back of the house. Lock a garage side door (2) with a rim lock or padlock. Fit grilles behind louvre windows (3) and special locks on sash windows (4).

There are special casement locks for wooden or metal windows (5). The outer doors or a porch (6) should be secured with rack or barrel bolts as well as a rim or mortise lock. At the back of the house fit a sliding door lock to patio doors (7). Likewise, aluminum sliding windows (8) should be locked with a similar device. Hinge bolts, rack bolts or barrel bolts will give added security to a back door (9). Secure any garage window (10).

FITTING A PUSH-LOCK

1 *Mark the position of the lock on the fixed and opening sections of the frame. Use the plastic wedge to ensure the lock sits square to the casement.*

2 *Separate the lock from the backplate and screw the backplate to the casement. This is deep enough to receive the bolt so you don't need to drill a hole.*

3 *Push the lock over the backplate and position the wedge, then screw the lock against the side of the frame. Cover the screw holes with plastic plugs.*

4 *A special key is needed to unfasten the lock. Keep it accessible, but out of reach of the window so the frame can be opened quickly in an emergency.*

The simplest security devices, particularly from the point of view of fitting, are those which give added support to the latch and stay already attached to the window. Stay bolts, for example, are available in various designs; some just clamp on, others have to be screwed in place (see *Ready Reference*), replacing the existing stay catch entirely. And if you don't want to go to the trouble of replacing the latch with a lockable version you can always fit a cockspur lock underneath the catch instead (see *Ready Reference*).

Fitting the devices
The step-by-step photographs show how different windows can be secured using various security devices. However, there is little point in fitting a bolt if the frames are rotten or unsound, as the bolt can easily be prised off by any burglar using force.

Most devices can simply be screwed into position on the surface of the opening or fixed frame. But some bolts, for example the rack bolt, have to be concealed within the frame itself, like a mortise lock. For added security it's often advisable to fit two bolts, one at the top, the other at the bottom.

When fitting any of these devices it's important that they can't be removed even if the glass is broken or a hand slipped through a fanlight inadvertently left open. So use clutch-head screws which are almost impossible to remove once they have been driven into place. On metal frames you'll first have to drill pilot holes before you can drive in the screws, but do make sure you avoid the glass. On old galvanized frames, prime any holes with a rust inhibitor before driving in the screws, otherwise your fitting can be forced out by a burglar.

TIP: KEEP KEYS HANDY
Security devices are for keeping burglars out and not you in. In the event of a fire you should be able to unlock them easily and quickly. So keep keys near the window, but out of reach of a burglar's arm stretching through a broken pane.

WINDOW STAY LOCKS
Window stays allow a window to be fastened in the open position. Some stay locks prevent the stay being lifted off the catch and the window being fully opened for access. However, they do not prevent the stay from being cut through. Their main advantage is in preventing young children from climbing out of the window.

Types of stay

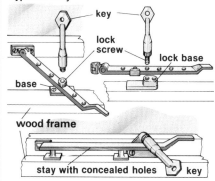

COCKSPUR LOCKS
When set in the closed position, cockspur locks prevent the latch from being opened. There are three main types:
- vertical sliding (A)
- sliding wedge (B)
- pivoting (best on aluminum frames — C).

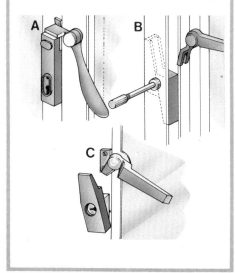

METAL FRAMES

1 Mark and drill holes on the opening frame. Use a depth gauge on the drill bit to prevent overdrilling. Then screw the lock in place.

2 Set the locking staple on the fixed frame and close the lock to keep it in place. You can then mark the holes with a pencil.

3 Unfasten the bolt and push the locking bar to one side. Drill the holes and screw the staple into place, covering the self-tapping screws with plastic plugs.

SECURING SASH WINDOWS

1 There are various types of acorn stop. For the simplest, drill a hole no more than 75mm (3in) above the bottom rail of the outer sash and fit the backplate.

5 Mark the position of the backplate on the outer sash and use a chisel to cut a recess so the plate will sit flush with the surface of the rail.

9 A special 3-stage sash lock is also available. To fit it, hold the striking plate against the outer frame and mark where the recesses have to be cut.

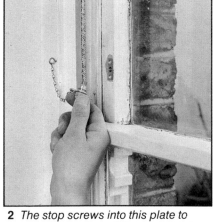

2 The stop screws into this plate to prevent the sashes sliding past each other: fit two for added security. Some stops can be locked in place.

6 Next, screw the backplate into position. With some dual screws there may be a small threaded barrel which you screw in instead of the backplate.

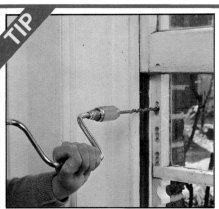

10 It's easier and more accurate to use a brace and bit, rather than an electric drill, to cut the recesses so that the striking plate sits flush.

3 When fitting dual screws, check that the rails of the sashes are thick enough to take the barrels. Site the locks about 100mm (4in) in from the side edges.

4 Drill a 10mm (³/₈in) diameter hole through the inner sash and for 15mm (⁵/₈in) into the outer one. Mark the bit with tape as a guide.

7 Close the frame, then screw the large threaded barrel of the bolt into the inner sash. Make sure you stop when it is flush with the rail surface.

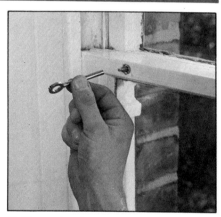

8 To secure the lock you have to screw a bolt through the large barrel on the inner sash and into the locking plate on the outer sash using a key.

11 Use a sharp chisel to square up the edges and clear out the waste in each recess. Then screw the striking plate into position.

12 Screw the locking unit to the top edge of the inner sash with clutch head screws. The locking bar is wound into the striking plate with a special key.

Ready Reference

SLIDING WINDOW LOCKS

The clamp-on type has jaws which are opened and closed with a special key. The lock is placed over the track and against the frame of the closed window and is then locked in position.

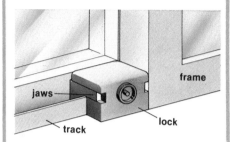

TIP: FIT A DEPTH STOP

When drilling holes in metal (and particularly aluminum) frames, fit the twist drill with a depth stop so there is no risk of drilling into the glass of the window and cracking it, or of breaking the weatherstrip or sealing strip.

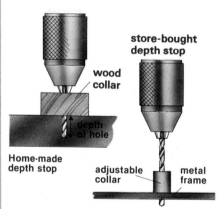

TIP: NARROW STILES

Rack bolts are often too bulky to fit into frames with narrow stiles, but special surface-mounted locks are available. When closed they draw the sash tightly into the frame so the sash can't be levered out. They also help to cut down drafts.

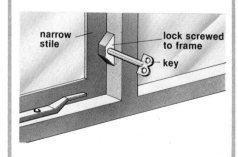

FITTING A RACK BOLT

1 Mark and drill the hole in the frame to accommodate the bolt – vertically, if the frame sides are narrow. Repeat the operation for the keyhole.

2 Next screw the bolt into place. You may have to recess it slightly so that the bottom plate doesn't foul the moving frame when it's being closed.

3 Screw the keyhole plate into position. Coat the bolt with chalk, shut the window and then try to close the lock so the bolt marks the frame.

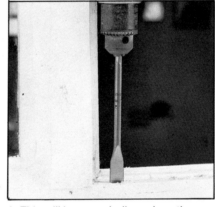

4 This will leave a chalk mark on the fixed frame. You can now drill a hole to receive the bolt. When doing this it's important to keep the drill upright.

5 Screw the backplate over the hole to prevent wear. Again you may first have to recess it so that it doesn't obstruct the frame when it's being closed.

6 For extra security fit two bolts – one at the top, the other at the bottom of the opening edge of the frame. Don't forget to remove the key after locking the bolt.

LOCKING LATCHES

1 Remove the old latch and catch and fill the fixing holes. Sand the newly exposed woodwork, then prime and paint it the same color as the frame.

2 With the window closed, screw the new catch to one window frame midway between top and bottom. Then position the catch in relation to this.

3 When the latch is in the closed position you can insert a special key and wind the locking bar into the backplate to secure the casement.

FITTING LOCKS ON DOORS

There's little point in going to the time, trouble and expense of fitting security devices to windows if you don't carry out a similar operation on doors as well.

A door sitting solidly in its frame may appear an impressive barrier to a would-be burglar, but if it's only fitted with a traditional mortise or rimlock then it's far more vulnerable than you may think. Modern locks, admittedly, are hard to pick; however, a burglar isn't going to waste time trying to do this. He wants quick access, and brute force rather than stealth is often his best means of getting in. Consequently, he may try to force open an outside door either by kicking it or by using a crowbar to lever it free. If the door isn't properly protected, it will only take a few seconds before he's inside.

Attacking the weak points
Your main entry/exit door is the most difficult to make secure. The best protection is offered by a mortise deadlock fitted into the edge of a substantial door. A rimlock is less resistant to forcing, because it is merely screwed to the face of the door.

Check that all fittings — including the hinges — are secure, and that the wood-work is in good condition. Also make sure that the lock cannot be reached by a hand pushed through the letterbox.

For added protection of this door when you're in the house, the simplest device to fit is a door chain. There are various types, but all depend on a secure fitting if they are to be effective. The plate, into which the chain is hooked, is screwed to the opening edge of the door, and the chain staple is screwed to the fixed frame — see step-by-step photographs overleaf. With aluminum doors, it helps to improve the strength of the fitting if a block of wood can be slipped into the door frame section, perhaps through the letter-plate opening or lock cut-out. This will give the self-tapping securing screws more to grip on. Also, fix the chain staple to the wooden part of the door frame and not to the aluminum sub-frame.

Security for other doors
The best protection for other doors is given by substantial bolts. These can be surface-mounted, but make sure that the screws are secure and that they cannot be reached if glass in the door is broken.

Better protection is offered by rack bolts mortised into the door edge at the top and bottom. But it's best not to use these on thin doors as they can weaken the stile. And don't set them into the mortise and tenon joints at the corner of the door as this will also weaken the door structure. As an alternative, you can fit flush or barrel bolts.

Protecting the hinges
The other area frequently forgotten is the hinge side of the door, which is most vulnerable to being kicked in if the door opens outwards. Hinge bolts, however, help prevent this and can be fitted to front doors as well as other external doors. The stud type (see step-by-step photographs) are best set 25mm (1in) inside the top and bottom hinges, but on heavier doors it's best to use the tongue type. The male part is fixed to the edge of the door and a recessed plate is set in the frame.

Patio doors
At one time sliding patio doors had a poor security record, notably because burglars had the audacity to lift the sliding sash clear of the track. This isn't possible with modern designs, which also incorporate a locking device. However, there are purpose-made patio door locks available to give added security (see *Ready Reference*).

Ready Reference

SECURING FRENCH DOORS
Because the doors lock against each other they are awkward to secure. Fit hinge bolts on the outside edges, and rack or barrel bolts which should lock into the top frame and the floor.

PATIO DOOR LOCK
This is screwed to the bottom edge of the inside frame and a bar is pushed into a predrilled hole in the outer one.

PREVENTING FORCED ENTRY

One of the most unpleasant situations anyone can experience is to answer a knock at the door to be faced with someone barging his way in uninvited.

Once the door has been opened, a rim or mortise lock is totally ineffective at keeping an intruder out. But to prevent this happening you can fit one of a variety of door chains so you can identify who is at the door without having to open it more than just ajar.

Most chains can be hooked in position when you are in the house, but there is a type that you can lock in place from the outside to give added protection to the door locks.

Don't forget that you can also fit a door viewer to a solid wood door and this will enable you to see who is on the other side without them seeing you.

1 *Set the door chain centrally on the opening edge of the door. First mark the holes of the plate that has to be attached to the door itself.*

2 *Use a bradawl to mark small starting holes in the door and then screw the plate in position. If the wood is soft, resite the plate.*

3 *Partly drive in the bottom screw of the staple that holds the chain in place on the frame. Slip the chain over the staple and fasten both screws.*

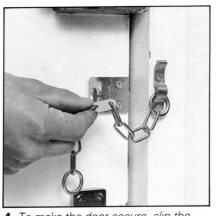

4 *To make the door secure, slip the tab on the linkage through the slotted ring on the plate and draw the chain back to lock against the plate.*

5 *A door viewer should be fitted centrally at eye level to a solid wood door. It allows you to see who is on the other side without them seeing you.*

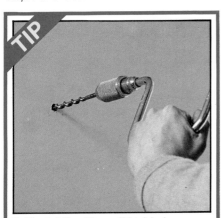

6 *Next drill a 12mm (1/2in) hole through the door. If using an electric drill hold a wood block at the back of the hole to prevent splitting.*

7 *Push the barrel through the hole from the outside of the door so the flange surrounding the lens of the viewer presses tightly against the door.*

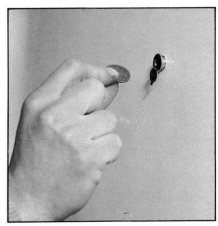

8 *On the inside, screw the eyepiece, which sometimes has a swivel cap over the end, to the barrel using a coin. This will hold the viewer firmly in place.*

SECURING DOOR EDGES

1 Rack bolts for doors have a longer barrel than their window counterparts. First mark the position of the barrel and the keyhole on the edge of the door.

2 Drill the barrel hole and keyhole, then cut a recess so that the plate of the bolt sits flush with the door edge. Check that the barrel hole is deep enough.

3 Screw the bolt and keyhole plate into place. Chalk the end of the bolt, close the door, then use the special key to try to lock the bolt.

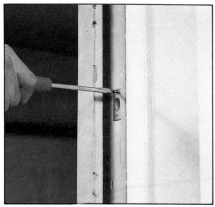

4 Where the bolt makes a chalk mark on the frame, drill a suitably-sized receiver hole. This should be protected by a metal plate recessed into the frame.

5 To fit a stud-type hinge bolt, drill a 10mm (3/8in) diameter hole about 38mm (1 1/2in) into the closing edge of the door. Tape the bit to act as a depth stop.

6 Drive the ribbed part of the bolt into the hole with a hammer. Then partially close the door so that the bolt makes a mark on the door frame.

7 Measure how far the stud protrudes from the door edge and then drill a 12mm (1/2in) diameter hole in the door frame to slightly more than this depth.

8 This hole in the frame is covered with a mating plate; you will probably have to recess this to ensure that the door can close properly without sticking.

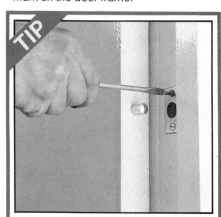

9 Screw the mating plate into the recess, making sure you drive the screws squarely into the countersunk holes so they don't foul the door.

CHAPTER 7
Plumbing

HOME PLUMBING SYSTEM

An understanding of how your plumbing system works makes for easier repairs.

A home plumbing system is made up of three different parts: the water supply lines, the drain-waste-vent (DWV) pipes, and the fixtures.

Water enters your home through a main from a municipal system or a well, and travels to the hot-water heater where the supply line splits into two. One line enters the heater, where it is warmed and returned to a hot-water supply line. The other line is the cold-water supply. The hot-water and cold-water supply lines then run parallel to each other from the hot-water heater to the fixtures in the home.

The fixtures are the water control outlets in your house — the bathtub, sinks, toilet, dishwasher or clothes washer. Faucets or electrical controls regulate the amount of water that enters the fixture, while the drain-waste-vent connection on each fixture allows drainage of used water.

The DWV pipes are attached to the bottom of each fixture, allowing water to drain from the fixture into a soil stack, where the waste water is transported to the main house drain and out into the sewer system.

Water enters your house from the municipal water system, a lake or a well, through a 20 or 25mm (3/4 or 1in) diameter pipe. As it enters the home, it passes through a main shut-off valve. If any plumbing repair work is necessary, this is the valve to close to ensure that no water enters the system while you're working on it. For localized repair work, shut-off valves are often located near each of the fixtures as well, so that you can shut off the water to a specific fixture without affecting the rest of the water system in the house. Your water meter is usually located next to the main shut-off valve, but may also be found on the exterior of your house or buried in the lawn.

As the water enters the house, it travels through a 2cm (3/4in) pipe directly to the hot-water heater, usually located somewhere in the basement. Before entering the heater, the 2cm (3/4in) pipe is stepped down into two 13mm (1/2in) pipes; one entering the heater, the other becoming the cold-water supply line for the house.

Cold water enters one side of the heater and exits as hot water, usually through a pipe at the top of the heater. This pipe becomes the hot-water supply line. These two pipes then travel throughout the house, parallel to each other and about 15cm (6in) apart, on a direct route to each bathroom, kitchen, laundry room or outdoor faucet. As the pipes travel through the walls they're known as risers.

A 10 to 12mm (3/8 to 1/4in) diameter pipe, one for the hot water and one for the cold water, leads from the risers to the fixture, with the hot-water pipe on the left and the cold-water pipe on the right.

Every water pipe has a piece of capped pipe attached to it at the spot where it enters the fixture. This capped pipe is called an air chamber. It diminishes hammering in the pipes when the faucet is closed. Since water pressure in your system is at a constant level of about 27kg (60lb), these air chambers absorb the shock created by opening and closing the faucet. The simple act of opening and closing a faucet can build up a pressure of several hundred pounds, and that pressure needs to be absorbed somewhere other than in the water supply pipes. Without these air chambers, enough pressure can build up to burst the pipes.

Water pipes are made of steel, copper or plastic, and rarely require any repairs. Metal pipes, however, can become corroded or scaled and need replacing.

Fixtures are durable pieces of equipment that control the flow of water from the water supply pipes to the DWV system. Any repair work necessary on the fixtures would likely be centered around the faucets and clogged drains.

The drain-waste-vent system starts at the drain of your fixture. Waste water is carried from the drain through a tailpipe 3.8cm (1½ in) in diameter to a trap usually directly under the fixture. This trap fills with water when the drainpipe is not in use, to prevent sewer gases from leaking back up into the fixture. After the waste leaves the trap, it travels through a larger pipe to the soil stack. The soil stack is about 10cm (4in) in diameter and runs vertically from the drain in the basement to above the roof line. All drainpipes connect to the soil stack, which in turn expels waste out of the house and into the sewer system.

The top of the soil stack protrudes above the roof to allow enough air pressure build-up in the pipe to give free movement of water through the drain system. This pressure also keeps the waste water from backing up into the fixtures. To keep water moving freely through the entire system, every fixture within a distance of 4.5m (15ft) from the soil stack is vented by a 5cm (2in) diameter pipe to the stack. Fixtures exceeding these distances are separately vented through the roof.

Should a blockage problem be created in the DWV system, there are a series of clean-out plugs in the soil stack and house drain that can be opened to enable you to use an auger to clear the blockage.

DWV SYSTEM

The drain-waste-vent (DWV) system is separate from the water supply system. It removes drain water and waste from fixtures.

WATER SUPPLY SYSTEM

Water enters your home through a main supply pipe. It travels through a pipe to the hot water heater where it divides into a hot and a cold water supply system.

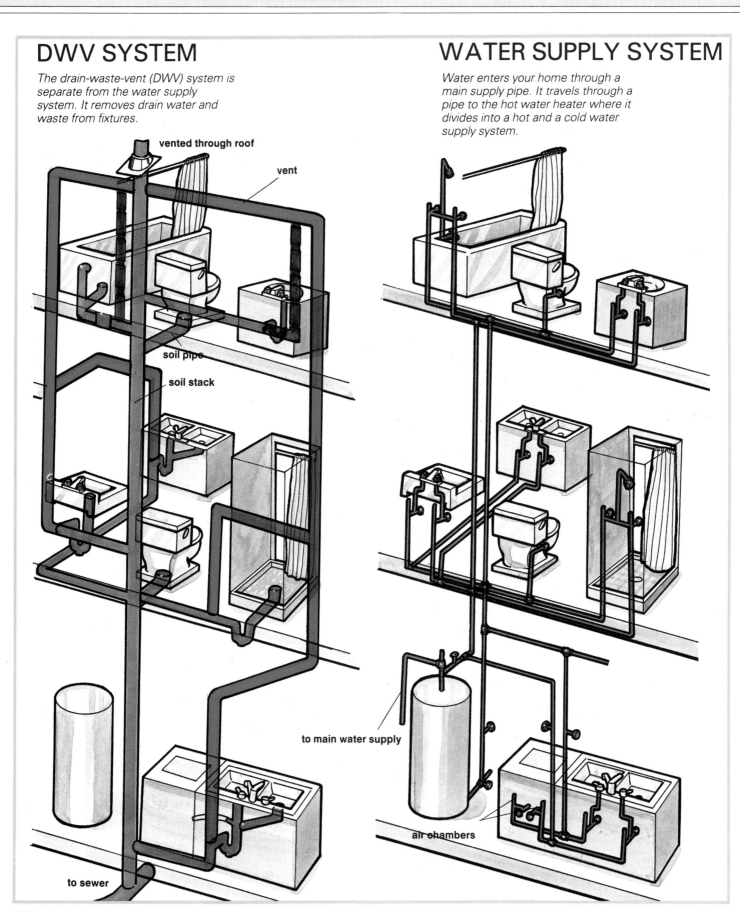

vented through roof

vent

soil pipe

soil stack

to main water supply

air chambers

to sewer

REPLACING TAPS

Changing the old taps on your basin is a bright and practical way of making your bathroom more attractive. It may also be a good idea if they are old and inefficient.

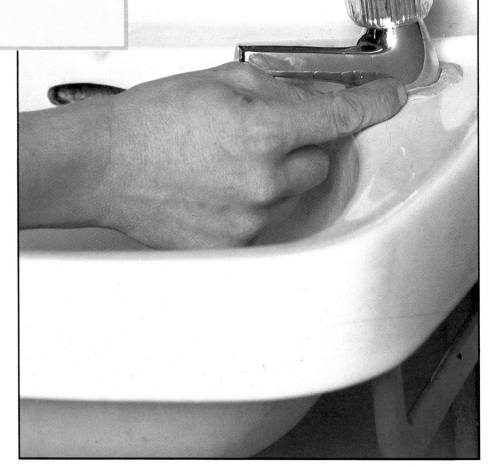

There may be a number of reasons why you wish to replace the taps supplying your sink, basin or bath. They may continually drip or leak, where new taps would give efficient, trouble-free service. Perhaps you want the advantages that mixers have over individual taps or perhaps it is simply that the chromium plating has worn off leaving the taps looking incurably shabby.

It is more likely, however, that appearance, rather than malfunction, will be your reason for changing. There are fashions in plumbing fittings as in clothing and furniture. Taps of the 1950s or 60s are instantly recognizable as out-of-date in a bathroom or kitchen of the 1980s. Fortunately, fashions in sinks, basins and baths have changed rather less dramatically over the past three decades. There is probably no more cost-effective way of improving bathroom and kitchen appearance than by the provision of sparkling new taps or mixers.

Choosing taps

When you come to select your new taps you may feel that you are faced with a bewildering choice. Appearance, the material of which the tap is made, whether to choose individual taps or mixers and — for the bath — whether to provide for an over-bath shower by fitting a bath/shower mixer: all these things need to be considered.

Most taps are made of chromium-plated brass, though there are also ranges of enamelled and even brass-plated taps and mixers. Although taps and mixers are still manufactured with conventional crutch or capstan handles, most people nowadays prefer to choose taps with 'shrouded' heads made of acrylic or other plastic.

There is also a very competitively priced range of all-plastic taps. These usually give satisfactory enough service in the home, but they cannot be regarded as being as sturdy as conventional metal taps, and they can be damaged by very hot water.

So far as design is concerned the big dif-ference is between 'bib taps' and 'pillar taps'. Bib taps have a horizontal inlet and are usually wall-mounted while pillar taps have a vertical inlet and are mounted on the bath, basin or sink they serve.

Taking out old basin taps

When replacing old taps with new ones the most difficult part of the job is likely to be — as with so many plumbing operations — removing the old fittings. Let's first consider wash basin taps.

You must, of course, cut off the water supply to the basin. Then run the bathroom taps until water ceases to flow.

If you look under the basin you will find that the shanks of the taps are connected to the water supply pipes with small, fairly accessi-ble nuts, and that a larger — often inaccessible — locknut secures the tap to the basin. The nuts of the swivel tap connectors joining the pipes to the taps are usually easily undone with a wrench of the appropriate size. The locknuts can be extremely difficult — even for professional plumbers!

There are special wrenches that may help but they won't perform miracles and ceramic basins can be very easily damaged by heavy handedness. One way is to disconnect the swivel tap connectors and to disconnect the tap from the waste outlet. These are secured by nuts and are easily undone. Then lift the basin off its brackets or hanger and place it upside down on the floor. Apply some penetrating oil to the tap shanks and, after allowing a few minutes for it to soak in, tackle the nuts with your wrench or basin wrench.

Ready Reference

EQUIPMENT CHECKLIST

For replacing existing taps, you will need the following tools and equipment:
● new taps of the right type and size
● an adjustable wrench
● a basin wrench ('crowsfoot')
● penetrating oil
● plumber's putty

You may also need tap shank adaptors (if the new taps have shorter shanks than the old ones) and new tap connectors (if your new taps have metric shanks instead of imperial ones).

WHAT ABOUT WASHERS?

With ceramic basins, use a plastic washer above and below the basin surface (A) so you don't crack the basin as you tighten the locknut. You can use plumber's putty or a gasket instead of the upper washer.

A

washer
—locknut

TIPS TO SAVE TROUBLE

● to undo stubborn locknuts, add extra leverage to the wrench by hooking another wrench handle into its other end
● grip the tap body with a second wrench to stop it turning; otherwise the tap could crack the basin
● if this fails, squirt penetrating oil around the locknuts. Leave for a while and try again

REMOVING OLD TAPS

1 You can change taps by removing the basin completely. Loosen the two tap connectors carefully with an adjustable wrench.

2 Disconnect the waste trap connector using an adjustable wrench. Take care not to damage the trap, particularly if it is lead or copper.

3 Undo any screws holding the basin to its brackets on the wall, and lift it clear of the brackets before lowering it carefully to the floor.

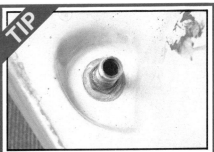

4 Check the condition of the locknuts, which may be badly corroded. It's a good idea to apply penetrating oil and leave this to work for a while.

5 Use a wrench (with extra leverage if necessary) to undo the locknut. If more force is needed, grip the tap itself with a wrench to stop it turning.

6 Remove the locknut and any washers beneath it and the basin. Old washers like these should always be replaced with new washers.

You'll find they are much more accessible. Hold the tap while you do this to stop it swivelling and damaging the basin.

Fitting the new taps

When fitting the new taps or mixer, unscrew the locknuts, press some plumber's putty around the shank directly below the tap body or fit a plastic washer onto the top shank. Push the shanks through the holes in the basin. Slip flat plastic washers over the shanks where they protrude from beneath

the basin, screw on the locknuts and tighten them up. Make sure that the taps or mixer are secure, but don't overtighten them.

All that remains to be done is to connect the swivel tap connectors to the shanks of the new taps or mixer. You will see that a tap connector consists of a lining — with a flange — that is inserted into the tap shank and is then secured by the coupling nut. This nut is provided with a washer to ensure a watertight connection. When renewing taps you may well need to renew this small washer.

FITTING NEW TAPS

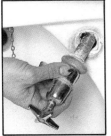

1 Remove the tap and clean up the basin surround, chipping away scale and any old putty remaining from when the tap was originally installed.

2 Now take one of the new taps and fit a washer or plumber's putty around the top of the shank before pushing it into the hole in the basin.

3 Twist the tap so that it's at the correct angle to the basin and is firmly bedded on the putty. Then push a washer onto the shank.

4 With the washer firmly in place, take the new locknut and screw it up the shank of the tap by hand.

5 Tighten up the locknut until the tap assembly is completely firm, using the basin wrench. Repeat the process for the other tap.

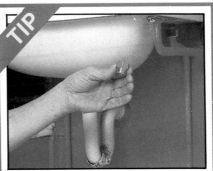

TIP

6 Reconnect all the pipework. Use tap shank adaptors if the new taps have shorter shanks than the old ones.

7 When all is secure, remove any surplus putty from around the base of the taps, wiping it over with a finger to leave a smooth, neat finish.

8 Turn the water back on. Check that the flow from the taps is regular and that the waste trap is not leaking. If it is, tighten up its connectors slightly.

It is possible that when you come to connect the water supply pipes to the taps you will get an unpleasant surprise. The shanks of modern taps are slightly shorter than those of older ones and the risers may not reach. If the water supply pipes are of lead or of copper, it is quite likely that they will have enough 'give' to enable you to make the connection but, if not, there are extension pieces specially made to bridge the gap.

Bib taps

If you're replacing existing bib taps with those of a more modern design, it's a relatively simple matter of disconnecting and unscrewing the old ones and fitting the new taps in their place. However, it's quite possible that you'll want to remove the bib taps altogether and fit a new sink with some pillar taps. This will involve a little more plumbing work. To start with, turn off the water supply and remove the taps and old sink. If the pipework comes up from the floor, you'll need to uncover the run in the wall to below where the new sink will go. You should then be able to ease the pipes away from the wall and cut off the exposed sections. This will allow you to join short lengths of new pipe, bent slightly if necessary, to link the pipe ends and the tap shanks. Alternatively, if the pipes come down the wall, you'll have to extend the run to below the level of the new sink and use elbow fittings to link the pipe to the tap shanks. In either case it's a good idea to fit the taps to the new sink first and to make up the pipework runs slightly overlong, so that when the new sink is offered up to the wall you can measure up accurately and avoid the risk of cutting off too much pipe. Rather than having to make difficult bends, you can use lengths of corrugated copper pipe. One end of the pipe is plain so that it can be fitted to the supply pipes with either a soldered capillary or compression fitting; the other end has a swivel tap connector.

JOINTS FOR COPPER PIPE

Joining copper pipe is one of the basic plumbing skills. Compression and capillary joints are easy to make and once you've mastered the techniques, you'll be prepared for a whole range of plumbing projects.

Connecting pipes effectively is the basis of all good plumbing as most leaks result from poorly constructed joints. For virtually all domestic plumbing purposes you will only have to use compression or capillary joints. Compression joints are easy to use but expensive, while capillary joints are cheap but need some care in fitting.

If you are making a join into an existing pipe system remember to make sure the water supply has been turned off at the relevant shut-off valve either on that section or at the main house entry, and the pipe has been completely drained.

Preparing the pipes
Before joining pipes together, check that the ends are circular and have not been distorted. If they have been dented, cut back to an undamaged section of the pipe using a hacksaw with a sharp blade or a wheel tube cutter (see pages 221-223).

The ends should also be square. Use a file to make any correction and remove ragged burrs of metal. If you're using a capillary joint clean up the sides of the pipe with abrasive paper or steel wool.

Compression joints (friction joints)
A compression joint, as its name implies, is made by compressing two brass or copper rings round the ends of the pipes to be joined, so forming a watertight seal.

Although not the cheapest means of joining a pipe, a compression joint is the easiest to use and requires only the minimum of tools. It comprises a central body with a compression nut at each end which, when rotated, squeezes the compression ring tightly between the pipe end and the casing. This is the most commonly used type of compression joint suitable for most internal domestic plumbing purposes.

How a compression joint works
The compression ring is the key part of a compression joint. When the compression nut is rotated clockwise the compression ring is forced between the casing and the pipe and is considerably deformed in the process.

A watertight seal is dependent upon the pipe ends having been well prepared so they butt up exactly to the pipe stop in the casing. This forms a primary seal and ensures that the pipe is parallel to the movement of the rotating compression nut. An even pressure is then applied to the compression ring so that it does not buckle under the strain of tightening.

What size of pipework and fittings?
Pipework can be sold in metric dimensions, but plumbing in your home may be in imperial sizes. The metric sizes are not exactly the same as their imperial equivalents.

These differences can cause problems. With capillary joints you have to use adaptors when converting pipe from one system to another. Adaptors are also needed for some compression joints.

Adaptors are made with different combinations of metric and imperial outlets to fit most requirements. A supplier will advise on what replacements to use.

Capillary joints
A capillary joint is simply a copper sleeve with socket outlets into which the pipe ends are soldered. It is neater and smaller than a com-

HOW COMPRESSION RINGS MAKE A WATERTIGHT SEAL

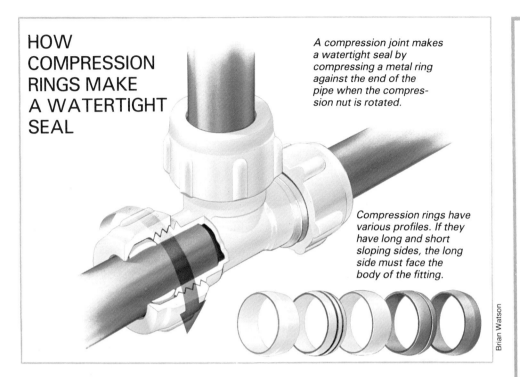

A compression joint makes a watertight seal by compressing a metal ring against the end of the pipe when the compression nut is rotated.

Compression rings have various profiles. If they have long and short sloping sides, the long side must face the body of the fitting.

Brian Watson

Ready Reference

WHICH TYPE OF FITTING?

Capillary fittings are
● cheap to buy
● unobtrusive when fitted
● useful in confined spaces
● very quick to install – and to unmake during alterations, BUT
● using them requires a blow-torch to melt the solder
● if the joint leaks you have to completely remake it.

Compression fittings are
● easy to assemble — you'll only need two wrenches — BUT
● they're much more expensive than capillary fittings
● they are much bulkier and obtrusive on exposed pipe runs
● in awkward places you may not be able to get wrenches in to tighten up the joint. Leaks can sometimes be cured by further tightening.

pression joint and forms a robust connection that will not readily pull apart.

Because it is considerably cheaper than a compression joint it is frequently used when a number of joints have to be made and is particularly useful in awkward positions where it is impossible to use wrenches.

How a capillary joint works

If two pipes to be joined together were just soldered end to end the join would be very weak because the contact area between solder and copper would be small. A capillary fitting makes a secure join because the sleeve increases this contact area and also acts as a brace to strengthen the connection.

Molten solder is sucked into the space between the pipe and fitting by capillary action, and combines with a thin layer of copper at the contact surface thus bonding the pipe to the fitting. To help the solder to

COPPER PIPE SIZES

Copper pipe is available in 12 and 20 foot lengths and three weights — thin-walled, medium-walled and thick-walled.

For most interior home applications, the thin-walled piping can be used, building code permitting. Any underground pipework will require thick-walled piping.

When measuring for a length of copper pipe, you must make allowance for the amount of pipe that slides into a fitting. Measure the distance from each face of the fittings then add twice the distance from the face of one fitting to the fitting's shoulder to determine pipe length.

The diameter sizes of pipes used in a home plumbing system are $1/2$in, $3/4$in, 1in, $11/4$in, 2in, and 3in.

UNDOING A SOLDER JOINT

Make sure water is shut off at the main entry and that water is drained from the pipe.

Heat the joint with your torch and when a bright solder ring appears, tap the pipes apart. Pipe ends can then be cleaned and resoldered.

SAFETY TIPS

When using a torch always
● wear thick heat-resistant gloves
● put down a lighted torch on a firm flat surface with the flame pointing into space
● clear any flammable material from the area where you are working

What happens when solder melts

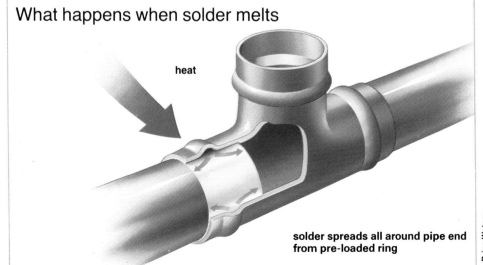

heat

solder spreads all around pipe end from pre-loaded ring

Brian Watson

MAKING A COMPRESSION JOINT

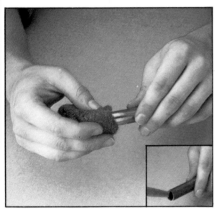

1 *Check that the end of the pipe is square using a file to make any correction and to remove burr. Clean pipe end and compression ring with steel wool.*

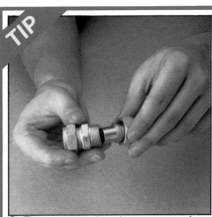

TIP

2 *The compression ring goes on after nut. If it has both long and short sloping sides, make sure the long side faces main body of the compression fitting.*

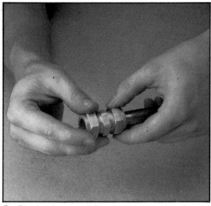

3 *Push pipe end firmly into body of fitting so that it rests squarely against pipe stop. Screw nut tightly with your fingers.*

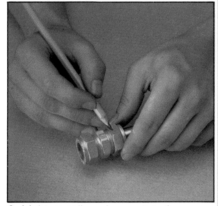

4 *Make pencil mark on nut and another aligning on body of fitting to act as guide when tightening compression nut with wrench.*

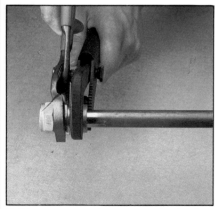

5 *Use one wrench to secure body of fitting and the other to rotate the nut clockwise. About 1½ turns is sufficient to give a watertight seal.*

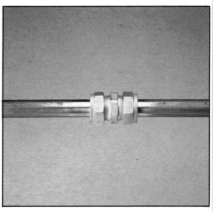

6 *Repeat operation to join other pipe to fitting. If water seeps through when supply is turned on, tighten nut further by half a turn.*

'take' the copper needs to be clean and shining. Therefore flux is applied to prevent oxides forming which would impair the solder-copper bond.

Types of capillary joint

The most common type of capillary joint has a ring of solder pre-loaded into the sleeve. It is known as an integral ring.

The 'end feed' type of capillary joint is virtually the same as an integral ring fitting, but you have to add the solder in a separate operation. The sleeve is slightly larger than the pipe and liquid solder is drawn into the space between by capillary action.

Flux and solder

Essential in the soldering operation, flux is a chemical paste or liquid which cleans the metal surfaces and then protects them from the oxides produced when the blowtorch heats the copper so a good metal-solder bond is formed. Mild non-corrosive flux is easy to use as it can be smeared onto the pipe and fitting with a clean brush or even a finger. Although it is best to remove any residue this will not corrode the metal. There is an acid-corrosive flux which dissolves oxides quickly, but this is mostly used with stainless steel. The corrosive residue must be scrubbed off with soapy water.

Solder is an alloy (mixture) of tin and lead and is bought as a reel of wire. Its advantage in making capillary joints is that it melts at relatively low temperatures and quickly hardens when the heat source (torch) is removed.

Torches

A torch is an essential piece of equipment when making capillary joints. It is easy, clean and safe to use providing you handle it with care. Most modern torches operate off a gas canister which can be unscrewed and inexpensively replaced (larger cans are relatively cheaper than small). Sometimes a range of nozzles can be fitted to give different types of flames, but the standard nozzle is perfectly acceptable for capillary joint work.

Using a torch

When using a blow-torch it's most convenient to work at a bench, but you'll find most jointing work has to be carried out where the pipes are to run. Pipework is usually concealed so this may mean working in an awkward place, such as a roof space, or stretching under floorboards. However, always make sure you are in a comfortable position and there's no danger of you dropping a lighted torch.

MAKING A CAPILLARY FITTING

1   Make sure the pipe end is square, then clean it and the inner rim of the fitting with steel wool or abrasive paper until shining.

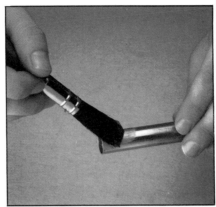

2   Flux can be in liquid or paste form. Use a brush, rather than your finger, to smear it over the end of the pipe and the inner rim of the fitting.

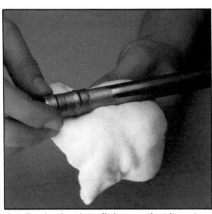

3   Push pipe into fitting so that it rests against pipe stop, twisting a little to help spread the flux. Remove excess flux with a cloth.

TIP

4   When you're making up a whole pipe-run, it helps to make corresponding pencil marks on pipe ends and fittings as a guide for correct lining up.

5   Make other side of joint in same way, then apply blow-torch. Seal is complete when bright ring of solder is visible at ends of fitting.

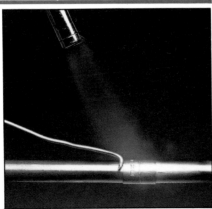

6   For an end feed fitting, heat the pipe, then hold the solder to mouth of joint. A bright ring all the way round signifies a seal.

Jem Grischotti

Ready Reference

WHICH TOOLS?

For cutting pipe:
● rent a **wheel tube cutter** (which ensures perfectly square pipe ends)

or use a **hack saw**
● use a **metal file** for removing ragged burrs of metal and for squaring ends of pipe that have been cut with a hacksaw. A half-round 'second-cut' type is ideal.

For compression joints:
● use two adjustable **pipe wrenches** (one to hold the fitting, the other to tighten the compression nut)

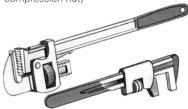

● **steel wool** to clean the surface of pipes before assembling a joint.

For capillary joints:
● a **blow-torch** to melt the solder
● **steel-wool** for cleaning pipe surfaces
● **flux** to ensure a good bond between the solder and copper
● **solder** because even if you're using integral ring fittings (which already have solder in them) you may need a bit extra
● **glass fibre** or **asbestos mat** (or a ceramic tile) to deflect the torch flame from nearby surfaces.

TIP: CUTTING PIPE SQUARELY

For a perfect fit, pipe ends must be cut square. If you're using a hacksaw, hold a strip of paper round the pipe so its edges align and saw parallel to the paper edge. Use the same trick if you have to file an inaccurately-cut end.

TIP: PROTECT NEARBY JOINTS

With capillary fittings, the heat you apply could melt the solder in nearby fittings. To help prevent this, wrap them in wet cloths.

When working near to joists and floorboards, glass, paintwork and other pipework with capillary joints it is important to shield these areas with glass fibre matting or a piece of asbestos.

Applying the heat

When making a capillary joint gradually build up the temperature of the copper by playing the flame up and down and round the pipe and then to the fitting. When the metal is hot enough the solder will melt and you can then take away the flame. The joint is complete when a bright ring of solder appears all round the mouth of the fitting. Stand the torch on a firm level surface and turn it off as soon as you have finished. Where two or more capillary joints are to be made with one fitting, for example the three ends of a tee, they should all be made at the same time. If this is not possible wrap a damp rag round any joints already made.

Repairing a compression joint

If a compression joint is leaking and tightening of the nut doesn't produce a watertight seal, you'll have to disconnect the fitting and look inside — after turning off the water supply. If a nut is impossible to move, run a few drops of penetrating oil onto the thread. If that doesn't do the trick, you'll have to cut it out and replace the fitting and some piping.

Once you have unscrewed one of the nuts there will be enough flexibility in the pipe run to pull the pipe from the casing. Usually the compression ring will be compressed against the pipe. First check that it is the right way round, and if it isn't, replace it with a new one making sure that it is correctly set.

Sometimes the ring is impossible to remove and needs to be cut off with a hacksaw — make the cut diagonally. Reassemble the joint following the procedure on page 218 and repeat the operation for the other end of the pipe. Turn on the water supply to check that the repair is watertight.

Repairing a capillary joint

Poor initial soldering is usually the reason why a capillary fitting leaks. You can try and rectify this by 'sweating' in some more solder but if this doesn't work you'll have to remake the joint.

Play the flame of the blow-torch over the fitting and pipe until the solder begins to run from the joint. At this stage you can pull the pipe ends out of the sockets with gloved hands. You can now reuse the fitting.

If you reuse the fitting, clean the interior surface and the pipe ends with abrasive paper or steel wool and smear them with flux. Then follow the procedure for making a capillary joint.

REPAIRING A COMPRESSION JOINT

1 Unscrew nut using wrenches. There's enough flexibility in pipe run to pull pipe from casing. Check that the ring fits, and isn't damaged.

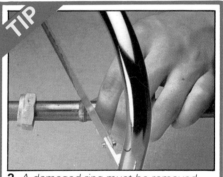

2 A damaged ring must be removed. Use a hacksaw and to make it easier make the cut on the diagonal — but take care not to cut into the pipe itself.

3 Prepare end of pipe with steel wool or abrasive paper. Slip on new ring and finger tighten nut. Rotate nut 1½ turns using wrenches.

REPAIRING A CAPILLARY JOINT

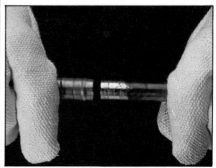

1 Drain pipe and wrap a damp cloth round nearby joints. Play flame on fitting and pull pipe from rim using gloved hands.

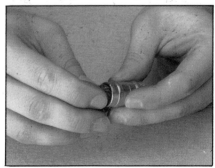

2 If you remake both sides of joint use a new fitting. A spent integral ring fitting, thoroughly cleaned, can be used as an end feed joint.

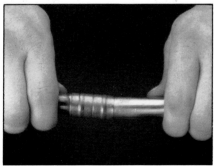

3 Use steel wool to clean end of pipe and inside of fitting. Brush with flux and push pipe into socket. Apply blow-torch to melt solder.

Jem Grischotti

CUTTING & BENDING COPPER PIPE

One of the advantages of domestic copper pipe is that it's easy to cut and bend. Few tools are required and even if you've only a few bends to make in a pipe run, it makes sense to know how it's done. Making accurate bends may need some practice, but it's cheaper than buying specially-shaped fittings.

In all plumbing water has to be carried from a source to a fixture and often then to some type of exit where it can disperse as waste. Basic to all of this is that water must run smoothly with nothing causing resistance to the flow — an important factor when the pressure is low.

Generally the best plumbing practice is to make pipe runs as straight and direct as possible. But sometimes bends are unavoidable (like, for example, when pipe has to go around a room or to turn down into an area below) and if available fittings are neither right for the angle nor attractive to look at, then you'll have to bend the pipe to suit.

Copper piping, because it is both light and resistant to corrosion, is a popular choice for home plumbing work. It can be joined with either capillary or compression fittings (see the techniques on pages 216-220) and when bends are needed you can create the angles in several ways.

The first essential is to accurately work out the pipe lengths you require. Once you've made the measurement double check it — it's quite easy to forget to allow for the pipe that will fit into the socket ends of the joints. You can make the actual marks on the pipe with pencil as this is clearly visible on copper and is a good guide when you come to cutting.

Cutting pipe accurately

For smaller pipe sizes, a sharp-bladed hacksaw is the best tool to use to make the cut. You'll need to hold the pipe firmly, but if you use a vice be careful not to over-tighten the jaws and crush the bore of the pipe (see *Ready Reference*, page 223).

It's important to cut the pipe square so that it butts up exactly to the pipe stop in the joint. This will ensure the pipe is seated squarely in the fitting which is essential for making a watertight seal. It will also help to make that seal. It's surprising how near to square you can get the end just cutting by eye. But the best way to make a really accurate cut is to use a saw guide. This can be made very easily by placing

a small rectangle of paper round the pipe with one long edge against the cut mark. By bringing the two short edges of the paper together and aligning them you effectively make a template that's square to the pipe. All you then have to do is hold the paper in place and keep the saw blade against it as you cut. Any burr that's left on the cut edges can be removed with a file.

If you intend to do a lot of plumbing, or are working mainly in the larger pipe sizes, it may be worthwhile buying (or renting) a wheel tube cutter. Of course using one of these is never absolutely essential, but it does save time if you've more than, say, half a dozen cuts to make. And once you have one you'll use it for even the smallest jobs. It's quick to use and will ensure a square cut without trouble every time. You simply place the pipe in the cutter and tighten the control knob to hold it in place. The cutter is then rotated round the pipe and as it revolves it cuts cleanly into the copper. This circular action removes burr from the outside of the pipe, but burr on the inside can be taken away with the reamer (a scraping edge) which is usually incorporated in the tool.

Bending copper pipe

If a lot of changes of direction are necessary in a pipe run, it's cheaper and quicker to bend the pipe rather than use fittings. This also makes the neatest finish if the pipework is going to be exposed. Under a pedestal wash-basin, for example, the hot and cold supply pipes rise parallel to each other in the pedestal before bending outwards and upwards to connect to the two tap shanks.

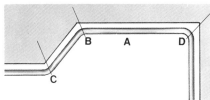

Using fittings in this situation would be more costly as well as possibly being unsightly, while the cheaper alternative, making bends, means the pipework is less conspicuous. The pipe can also be bent to the exact angle required so this method of changing direction is not limited by the angles of the fittings. And with fewer fittings in a pipe system there are fewer places where leaks can occur.

The smaller sizes of copper pipe, those most commonly used in domestic plumbing, can be bent quite easily by hand. The technique of annealing — heating the pipe to red heat in the vicinity of the bend to reduce its temper (strength) and so make bending easier — is unnecessary when working in these pipe sizes. But you will need to support the pipe wall, either internally or externally, as the bend is made. If you don't, you'll flatten the profile of the pipe. Using it in this condition would reduce the flow of water at the outlet point.

For small jobs a bending spring is the ideal tool, supporting the pipe internally. It is a long hardened steel coil which you push into the pipe to the point where the bend will be made. It's best used for bends near the end of the pipe, since the spring can be easily pulled out after the bend is made. However, it can be used further down the pipe if it is attached to a length of stout wire (which helps to push it into place, and is vital for retrieving it afterwards).

Bending techniques

You actually bend the pipe over your knee, overbending slightly and bringing back to the required angle. The spring will now be fixed tightly in the pipe and you won't be able simply to pull it out. However, its removal is quite easy. All you have to do is to insert a bar — a screwdriver will do — through the ring at the end of the spring and twist it. This reduces the spring's diameter and will enable you to withdraw it. It's a good idea to grease the spring before you insert it as this will make pulling it out that much easier (also see *Ready Reference* page 223).

Slight wrinkles may be found on the inside of the bend, but these can be tapped out by gentle hammering. It's wise not to attempt this before taking out the spring. If you do you'll never be able to remove it.

Bending springs are suitable for small diameter pipe. But although it is possible to bend large pipe as well, it's advisable to use a bending machine instead. This is also preferable if you have a lot of bends to make. And if you don't want to go to the expense of buying one, you can probably rent a machine from a tool rental shop.

A bending machine consists of a semi-circular former that supports the pipe externally during the bending operation and a roller that forces the pipe round the curve when the levers of the machine are brought together. The degree of bend depends on how far you move the handles.

Flexible pipe

This is a kind of corrugated copper pipe which can be bent easily by hand without any tools. You can buy it with two plain ends for connection to compression joints or with one end plain and one with a swivel tap connector for connection to a tap or valve.

As it's the most expensive way of making a bend, it's not cost effective to use it when you have to make a number of changes of direction in a pipe run. It's not particularly attractive to look at so it is best used in places where it won't be seen. As such it's most commonly used for connecting the water supply pipes to the bath taps in the very confined space at the head of the bath. And it can make the job of fitting kitchen sink taps easier, particularly when the base unit has a back which restricts access to the supply pipes.

CUTTING COPPER PIPE

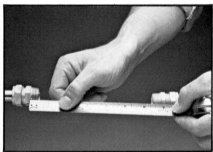

1 *Make an accurate measurement of the proposed pipe run. Don't forget to allow extra for the pipe that will fit inside the joints.*

2 *Use a simple paper template to help you cut pipe squarely. Wrap the paper round the pipe and align the edges.*

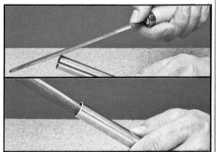

3 *Use the flat side of your file to clean any burr from the outside of the pipe. The curved side of the file can be used to clean the inside.*

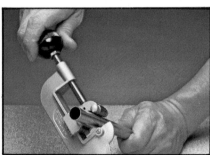

4 *When using a wheel tube cutter, position the cutting mark on the pipe against the edge of the cutting wheel, then tighten the control knob.*

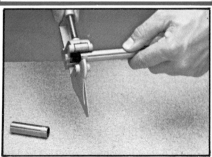

5 *Once the pipe is clamped in place, rotate the cutter so it makes an even cut. The rollers on the tool will keep the blade square to the pipe.*

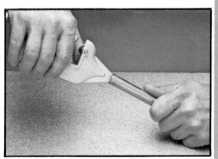

6 *A wheel tube cutter leaves a clean cut on the outside of the pipe, but any burr on the inside can be removed with the reamer (an attachment to the tool).*

BENDING COPPER PIPE

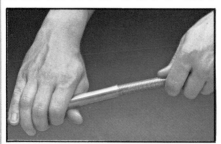

1 *Always use a bending spring which is compatible in size with the pipe. Smear it with petroleum jelly.*

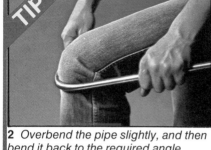

2 *Overbend the pipe slightly, and then bend it back to the required angle.*

3 *Put a screwdriver through the ring at the end of the spring. Twist it, then pull the spring out.*

4 *To use a bending machine, open the levers and position the pipe as shown, then slide the straight former on top.*

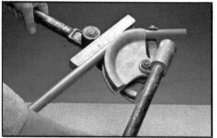

5 *Raise the levers so the wheel runs along the straight edge and the pipe is forced round the circular former.*

6 *Bend the pipe to the required angle, then remove by opening the levers, and taking out the straight former.*

FLEXIBLE COPPER PIPE

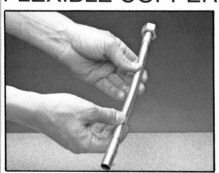

1 *Although relatively expensive, flexible pipe is ideal for making awkward bends in the pipe run to connect to taps.*

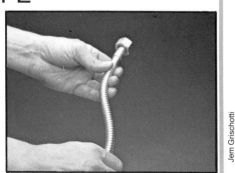

2 *It's easy to hand bend the pipe to the required shape, but don't continually flex it or the thin wall will split.*

Jem Grischotti

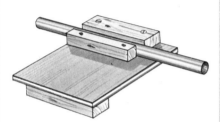

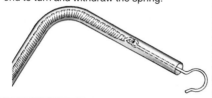

CONNECTIN-- NEW PIPES TO OLD

Improvements or additions to a domestic plumbing system inevitably involve joining new pipework into old. How you do this depends largely on what the existing pipework is made of.

The principle of joining into existing pipework is quite straightforward. You decide where you will need your new water supply — at a new sink or an outside tap, for example — and then pick a convenient point on the plumbing system to connect up your branch line. At this point you have to cut out a small section of the old pipe and insert a tee junction into which the branch pipe will be fitted. That's all there is to it; laying the branch pipe will simply involve routine cutting, bending and joining of new pipe, and final connection to the new tap or appliance at the other end.

Before you can begin the job, however, you have to do some reconnaissance work to identify what sort of existing pipework you have. You might be tempted to relate the plumbing to the age of the house, thinking that an old house will have an old system with lead or iron pipework. But this isn't a reliable guide. Many old properties have been modernized and so may actually have a more up-to-date system than a house built relatively recently.

Until the 1950s the only types of pipe used in domestic plumbing were lead and iron, but then these were superseded by thin-walled copper piping. Today there are other alternatives too: stainless steel is sometimes used as an alternative to copper and PVC (polyvinyl chloride) pipes can be installed for cold water supplies only.

Check the table (see *Ready Reference*, right) for the type of pipe you can use. While copper is the most common one for new work, it must *never* be joined to galvanized iron because of the severe risk of electrolytic corrosion of the iron if the galvanizing is not in perfect condition.

First things first

Before cutting into a pipe run you'll first have to turn off the water supply to the pipe and then drain it by opening any taps or drain cocks connected to it. But this need not be too inconvenient if you make up the complete branch line before you turn the

water off so you are without water only while you make the final branch connection.

Connecting into copper pipe

When taking a branch from a copper pipe it's probably easier to use a compression tee fitting rather than a capillary fitting. A compression fitting can be made even if there is some water in the pipe run – capillary joints need the pipe to be dry – and you won't have to worry about using a blow-torch and possibly damaging other capillary joints nearby (if they are heated up, their solder will soften and the joint will leak).

It's quite easy to work out how much pipe to cut out of the main run in order to insert a tee junction (of either compression or capillary fittings). Push a pencil or stick into the tee until it butts up against the pipe stop. Mark this length with your thumbs, then place the stick on top of the fitting so you can mark the outside to give a guide line. Next you have to cut the pipe at the place where the branch has to be made and prepare one of the cut ends (see the pictures on page 226). Now connect to the pipe the end of the tee that doesn't have the guide line marked on the casing and rest the tee back against the pipe. You will now be able to see where the pipe stop comes to and you can then mark the pipe to give you the second cutting point. Remove the section of pipe with a hacksaw and prepare the pipe end.

With a compression fitting put on the other nut and ring. If you gently push the pipe and

tee sideways to the pipe run, this will give you more room to position the body before you allow the pipe end to spring into place. When this is done the nut can be pushed up to the fitting and can be tightened with your fingers. Both sides of the tee can then be tightened using your wrenches to give the nuts about one-and-a-quarter turns.

Remember that you must use a second wrench to grip the body of the fitting so it stays still as the nut is tightened. If it should turn, other parts of the joint which have already been assembled will be loosened or forced out of position, and leaks will result. The connection into the main pipe run is now complete and you can connect up the branch pipe.

If you are using a capillary tee fitting there are a number of points to bear in mind. It's easiest to use one with integral rings of solder (this saves the bother of using solder wire) and after the pipe ends and the inside rims have been prepared and smeared with flux the fitting can be 'sprung' into place. The branch pipe should also be inserted at this stage so all the joints can be made at the same time.

When using the blow-torch, it is important to protect the surrounding area from the effects of the flame with a piece of glass fibre matting, asbestos or the back of a ceramic tile. It's also worthwhile wrapping damp cloths round any nearby capillary joints to protect them from accidental over-heating and thus 'sweating'.

224

IDENTIFYING YOUR PIPEWORK

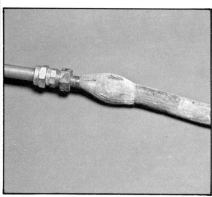

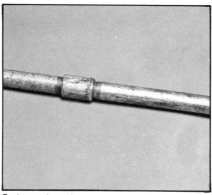

1 *Lead pipes are gray and give a dull thud when knocked. You can nick the surface with a knife. Look for smooth bends and even swellings — these are 'wiped' soldered joints. Repairs are often made using copper pipe.*

2 *Iron pipes have a gray galvanized or black finish and give a clanging sound when knocked. A knife will only scrape along the surface. Look for the large threaded joints which appear as a collar on the pipe or at a bend.*

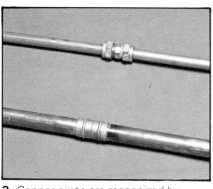

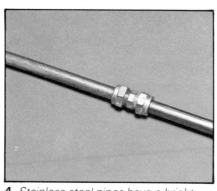

3 *Copper pipes are recognized by their familiar copper color. Changes of direction are often made by bends in the pipe itself or by using angled fittings. The joints will be either the compression or capillary type.*

4 *Stainless steel pipes have a bright silvery surface. They come in the same sizes as copper and can be joined in the same way. Bends are only found in sizes up to 15mm (½in). These pipes are not commonly used in the home.*

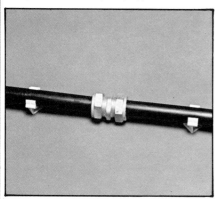

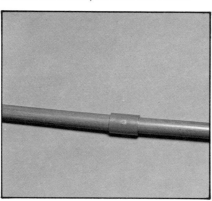

5 *Polyethylene pipes are usually black and are soft enough to be slightly compressed between the fingers. Joints are made with metal compression fittings which require special rings and liners.*

6 *PVC pipes can be white or gray and rigid. Connections and changes in direction are made by angled joints which fit like slim collars over the ends of the pipes. These are fixed in place using solvent weld cement.*

Ready Reference

WHAT JOINS TO WHAT?

Use this table as a guide to choosing new pipework – the first material mentioned is the best or most usual choice.

Existing pipe	New pipework
copper	copper, stainless steel, polyethylene
lead	polyethylene, copper, stainless steel
iron	iron, stainless steel, polyethylene
stainless steel	stainless steel, copper, polyethylene
polyethylene	polyethylene, copper, stainless steel
PVC	copper, stainless steel, polyethylene

CONNECTING OLD TO NEW

Fitting metric to imperial pipework can be complicated by the slight differences in pipe diameters. The problem connections are:

copper to copper (compression fittings)
● some metric fittings can be used directly with imperial-sized pipes (eg, 15mm fittings with ½in pipe and 28mm fittings with 1in pipe)
● with other sizes you need to buy special adaptors or larger rings to replace those inside the fittings, so to connect a 15mm branch into existing ¾in pipe you'll need a tee 22 × 22 × 15mm with special rings for the 22mm ends of the tee.

copper to copper (capillary fittings)
● metric capillary fittings with integral solder rings are not compatible with imperial pipes, but straight adaptors are available to connect the two sizes of pipe
● use these to join in short lengths of metric pipe, the other ends of which are connected to opposite ends of the metric tee
● with end-feed type fittings, extra solder can be added to make a good joint with imperial-sized pipe.

copper to stainless steel – as for copper to copper connections, but usually compression fittings only.

stainless steel to copper – as above for copper to stainless steel.

stainless steel to stainless steel – as for copper to copper.

Connecting into lead pipe

Inserting a tee junction into lead pipe involves joining the run of the tee into two 'wiped' soldered joints. Join short lengths of new copper pipe into opposite ends of a compression tee. Measure the length of this assembly, and cut out 25mm (1in) less of lead pipe. Join the assembly in with wiped soldered joints — a job that takes a lot of practice, and one you may prefer to leave to a professional plumber until you have acquired the skill. You then connect the branch pipe to the third leg of the tee.

Connecting into iron

Existing iron pipework will be at least 25 years old, and likely to be showing signs of corrosion. Extending such a system is not advisable — you would have difficulty connecting into it, and any extension would have to be in stainless steel. The best course is to replace the piping completely with new copper piping.

Connecting into polyethylene pipe

If you have to fit a branch into a polyethylene pipe, it's not a difficult job, especially if you use the same material. Polyethylene pipes are joined by compression fittings similar to those used for copper.

You need to slip a special metal liner inside the end of the pipe before assembling each joint to prevent the pipe from collapsing as the nuts are tightened. In addition, polyethylene rings are used instead of metal rings in brass fittings. Apart from these points, however, inserting a tee in a length of polyethylene pipework follows the same sequence as inserting one into copper.

Connecting into PVC pipe

As with polyethylene it's an easy job to cut in a solvent weld tee — a simple collar fitting over the ends of the pipe and the branch. After you've cut the pipe run with a hacksaw, you have to roughen the outsides of the cut ends and the insides of the tee sockets with abrasive paper and then clean the surfaces with a spirit cleaner and degreaser. Solvent weld cement is smeared on the pipe ends and the insides of the sockets, and the pipe ends are then 'sprung' into the sockets.

You have to work quickly as the solvent begins the welding action as soon as the pipes meet. Wipe surplus cement off immediately, and hold the joint securely for 15 seconds. After this you can fit your branch pipe to the outlet of the tee.

CUTTING INTO METRIC COPPER PIPE

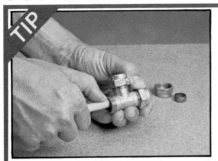

1 On one side of the tee, push a pencil or piece of dowelling along the inside until it butts against the pipe stop. Mark this length with your thumb.

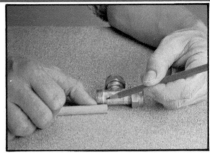

2 Now hold the marked length of dowel against the outside of the fitting so you can see exactly where the pipe stops. Mark this position on the fitting.

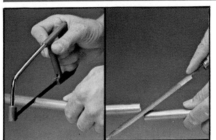

3 Having turned off the water and drained the supply pipe, cut it at the place where you want the branch to join in. Clean one of the ends with steel wool.

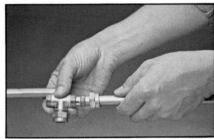

4 Now slip a nut and then a ring over the cleaned pipe end and connect up the unmarked end of the tee fitting to the pipe.

5 Allow the tee to rest alongside the pipe run. The mark on the front of the fitting is your guide to where the pipe has to be cut again.

6 Cut the pipe at this mark, thus taking out a small section. Clean the end and slip a nut and ring into place. Spring the pipe end into the tee.

7 Support the fitting with a wrench while tightening the nuts on both ends of the tee with an adjustable wrench.

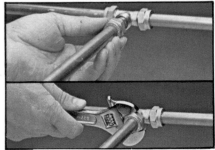

8 Insert the cleaned end of the branch pipe into the tee and tighten the nut 1¼ turns with a wrench, holding the fitting to stop it from twisting.

JOINING METRIC TO IMPERIAL PIPE

1 *Cut two short lengths of metric pipe and prepare the pipe ends, the metric/imperial adaptors and also the tee junction.*

3 *With the water turned off and the pipe drained, cut it where you want to make the connection. Prepare one of the ends with steel wool.*

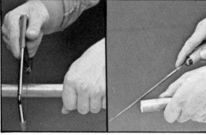

5 *Cut out the section of pipe and prepare the newly-cut end. Don't forget to apply the flux, smearing it on the outside of both pipe ends.*

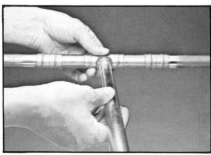

7 *Prepare the end of the branch pipe and push it into the tee. Make sure that all the pipe ends are butting up fully against the pipe stops.*

2 *Smear flux over the ends of the pipe, inside the rims of the adaptors and each opening on the tee. Then assemble the fitting.*

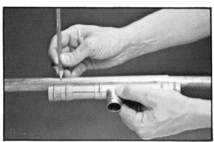

4 *Hold the fitting so the pipe stop of one adaptor rests against the cut. Now you can mark the other pipe stop position on the pipe run.*

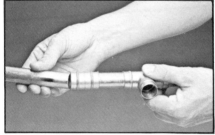

6 *Push the fitting onto one end of the supply run, then gently spring the other end into place so that the tee junction is correctly positioned.*

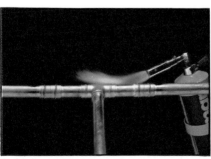

8 *Make all the joints at the same time. Rings of solder round the mouths of the fittings indicate that sound, watertight connections have been made.*

Ready Reference

CONVENIENT CUTTING

Try to join into existing pipework at a point where you have room to maneuver.
If space is very tight
● use a junior hacksaw instead of a full-sized one, or
● use a sawing wire for cutting pipes in corners

THE RIGHT TEE

Your branch line may be the same diameter as the main pipe, or smaller (it should never be larger). Tees are described as having all ends equal, or as having the branch reduced.

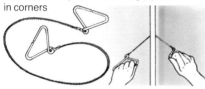

SUPPORTING THE PIPEWORK

All pipework needs supporting at intervals along its length with pipe clips (usually plastic or metal). Fit them at
● 1.2m (4ft) intervals on horizontal pipe runs
● 1.5m (5ft) intervals on vertical pipe runs.

TO SAVE TIME AND TROUBLE

● hold the body of a compression fitting securely with one wrench while doing up the nut with another
● wrap nearby capillary fittings in damp cloths when soldering in new ones
● make up the entire branch line before cutting in the branch tee
● have cloths handy for mopping up when cutting into existing pipework
● if you're using compression fittings on a vertical pipe run, stop the lower nut and ring from slipping down the pipe by clipping a clothes peg or bulldog clip to it
● keep a replacement cartridge for your blow-torch in your tool kit so you don't run out of gas in the middle of a job.

JOINING INTO PLASTIC PIPES

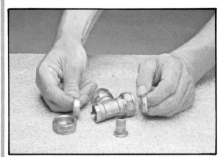

1 Plastic pipe is joined by a compression fitting with a larger ring than usual (right hand) and pipe liners to support the pipe walls.

2 Turn off the water supply and then cut the pipe. Use a file to remove any rough edges and then insert a liner into one end of the pipe.

3 Undo the compression fittings and slip a nut over the pipe end containing the liner; then slip on the ring.

4 Mark the pipe stop on the outside of the tee, join the tee to the prepared end, then mark across the pipe stop to show where the pipe is to be cut.

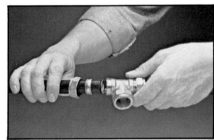

5 Cut out the section of pipe and connect the other end of the tee. Hold the fitting securely while you tighten the nuts 1¼ turns.

6 Insert the branch pipe into the tee fitting and again use a wrench to give the nuts 1¼ turns.

7 With PVC pipe, mark the pipe stops on the outside of the tee. Use these as a gauge to cut out a small section of pipe with a hacksaw.

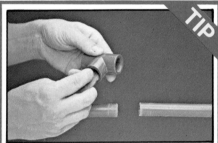

8 Key the ends of the pipe including the branch and the inside of the tee with abrasive paper. This is essential when using solvent-weld cement.

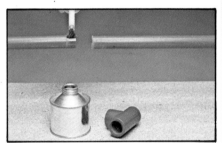

9 Thoroughly clean the ends of the pipes with a degreaser, which you apply with a brush, and leave until completely dry.

10 Once you've done this, spread solvent weld cement on the contact surfaces. Take care not to inhale the fumes as you work.

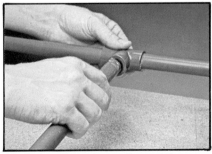

11 Make all the connections at the same time, and check to ensure that all the pipes are pushed right into the tee. Hold for 30 seconds.

12 As soon as you've made all the connections, use a cloth to remove any surplus cement from the pipes. Water shouldn't be turned on for 24 hours.

JOINING PLASTIC PIPING

Most waste pipes installed today are made of plastic, which is cheap, lightweight and easy to work with. A little practice and careful measuring will enable you to replace all parts of your system.

W aste systems draining baths, basins and sinks used to be made of lead, heavy galvanized steel with screwed joints, or copper. Soil pipes from toilets were traditionally cast iron, as was all the outside pipework for both waste and soil disposal. Nowadays waste and soil pipes are made of one or other of a variety of plastic materials, which may be used for repairs, extension work or complete replacement of an existing system.

These plastic pipes are lightweight and easily cut, handled and joined. They are made of materials usually known by the initials of their chemical names — PVC (polyvinyl chloride), ABS (acrylonitrile butadiene styrene) and PP (polypropylene). CPVC (chlorinated polyvinyl chloride) is usually used for hot and cold water supply pipes. Pipes and fittings are available in white, gray or a copper color, depending on type and manufacture.

All these materials are satisfactory for domestic waste systems and — with one exception — can all be joined in the same way: either by push-fit (ring-seal) jointing or by solvent welding.

The exception is PP pipe. This was first developed because of its good resistance to very hot water and chemical wastes, and was therefore extensively used in industry. Nowadays, however, it is frequently used in the home for waste or rainwater drainage. The big difference between PP and other plastic pipes used in waste drainage is that it cannot be solvent-welded. All joints must be push-fit. In most situations this is no great disadvantage but it does make it important to be able to distinguish PP from other plastics. It has a slightly greasy feel and, when cut with a fine toothed saw, leaves fine strands of fibrous material round the cut edges.

Sizes
When buying plastic pipe and components it is wise to stick to one brand only. Pipes and fittings from different makers, though of the same size, are not necessarily interchangeable. Most suppliers stock the systems of only one manufacturer, although the same

PREPARING THE PIPE ENDS

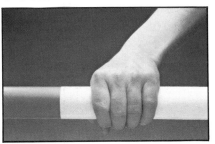

1 *To make sure that you cut the pipe squarely, hold a sheet of paper around it so that the edges meet and overlap each other. This is your cutting line.*

2 *Hold the pipe firmly and cut it with a hacksaw, using gentle strokes. You may find it easier to use a junior hacksaw, which gives a finer cut.*

3 *When you've cut the pipe, use a piece of fine sandpaper to clean off the burr left by sawing.*

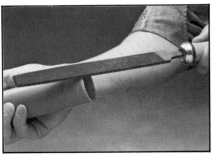

4 *Now take a file and chamfer the end of the pipe all round the edge to a 45° angle. Try to keep the chamfer even.*

Ready Reference

THE TOOLS YOU'LL NEED
● hacksaw – a junior or larger – for cutting the lengths of pipe as you need them
● piece of paper – to help cut the pipe truly square
● tape measure
● file – for chamfering the pipe ends
● sandpaper — to abrade pipes and sockets for solvent-welding, and for cleaning up the ends of pipes where you have cut them
● pencil – for marking the cutting points and socket depths to find the working area of the pipe.

VITAL ACCESSORIES
● solvent cement – for solvent-welding
● cleaning fluid – for cleaning the pipe ends and socket fittings when making solvent-weld joints
● petroleum jelly – for lubrication when inserting the pipe into the socket in push-fit joint assemblies
● tissues or rag for cleaning off excess solvent or petroleum jelly.

TYPES OF PIPE
PVC (PVC) is used for all waste pipe applications.

Chlorinated PVC (CPVC) is used where very hot water discharge occurs, such as washing machine out-flows.

Polypropylene (PP) is an alternative to PVC and can withstand hot water – but it expands a lot and is only suitable on short runs.

Acrylonitrile butadiene styrene (ABS) is used for waste connection moldings.

SAFETY TIPS
● don't smoke when you are solvent-weld jointing – solvent cement and solvent cement cleaner become poisonous when combined with cigarette smoke
● don't inhale the fumes of solvent-weld cement or cleaning fluid – so avoid working in confined spaces
● don't get solvent-weld cement on any part of the pipe you're not joining as this can later lead to cracking and weaknesses, especially inside sockets where the solvent cement can easily trickle down
● hold all solvent-weld joints for 15 seconds after joining and then leave them undisturbed for at least 5 minutes – if hot water is going to flow through the pipe don't use it for 24 hours.

SOLVENT-WELD JOINTING

1 *Push the end of the pipe into the socket of the fitting as far as it will go. Mark the pipe at this point with a pencil as a guide to the length within the joint.*

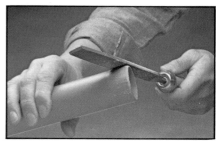

2 *Take the pipe out of the fitting and, with a file, roughen the whole of the end surface that will be inside the fitting up to the pencil mark.*

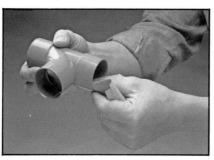

3 *Take the fitting itself and roughen the inside of the socket with fine sandpaper. This will provide a key for the solvent cement.*

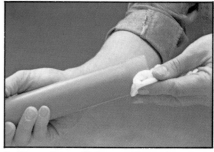

4 *Now clean off the roughened surface of the pipe and socket with turps as recommended by the manufacturer to remove all debris.*

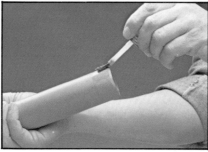

5 *Apply the solvent cement to the roughened end of the pipe, making sure that the whole roughened area is covered. Try and keep it off your fingers.*

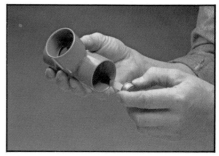

6 *Also apply solvent cement to the socket of the fitting. Try to use brush strokes along the line of the pipe.*

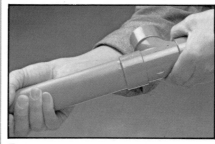

7 *Gently push the pipe fully home into the socket. Some manufacturers suggest a slight twisting action in doing this but check their instructions first.*

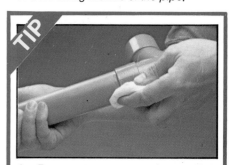

8 *Remove any excess solvent at the edge of the socket with a clean cloth, hold the joint in position for 15 seconds.*

PUSH-FIT JOINTING

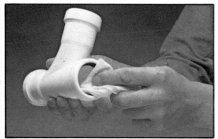

1 Cut the pipe squarely as in solvent-weld jointing and remove the burr, then take the fitting and clean the socket out with the recommended cleaner.

2 Check that the rubber seal is properly seated in the socket. You may find seals are supplied separately and you will have to insert them.

3 Now chamfer the end of the pipe to an angle of 45°, and smooth off the chamfer carefully with fine sandpaper so that no rough edges remain.

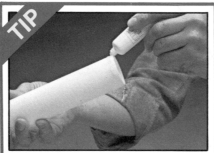

4 Lubricate the end of the pipe with petroleum jelly over a length of about 5mm (3/16in).

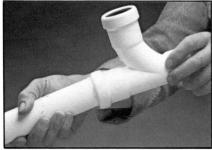

5 Push the pipe into the socket gently but firmly. Then push it fully home and check that all is square, otherwise you may damage the sealing ring.

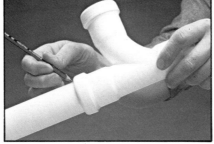

6 Now make a pencil mark on the pipe at the edge of the socket – you can easily rub it off later if you want to – to act as a guide in setting the expansion gap.

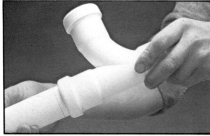

7 Gently pull the pipe out from the fitting so that your pencil mark is about 10mm (3/8in) away from the fitting to allow for expansion when hot water is flowing.

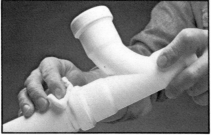

8 The joint is now complete. Wipe off any excess petroleum jelly. Don't lose the expansion allowance when joining the other side of the fitting.

manufacturer may make both PP and either PVC or ABS systems.

It is worth asking the supplier if there is an instruction leaflet supplied by the maker. There are slight variations in the methods of using each particular make of pipe and fitting. The manufacturer's instructions, if available, should be followed to the letter.

Buying new pipe

Existing waste pipe is likely to be imperial in size – 1½in internal diameter for a sink or bath and 1¼in internal diameter for a wash basin.

Metric sized plastic pipes are normally described – like thin-walled copper tubes – by their external diameter, though at least one well-known manufacturer adds to the confusion by using the internal diameter. Both internal and external diameters may vary slightly – usually by less than one millimetre between makes. This is yet another reason for sticking to one make of pipe for any single project.

The outside diameter of a plastic tube that is the equivalent of a 1¼in imperial sized metal tube is likely to be 36mm and the inside diameter 32mm. The outside diameter of the equivalent of a 1½in pipe is likely to be 43mm and the inside diameter 39mm. If in doubt, it is usually sufficient to ask the supplier for waste pipe fittings for a basin waste or – as the case may be – a bath or sink waste. Plain-ended plastic pipe is usually supplied in 3m (10ft) lengths, though a supplier will probably cut you off a shorter piece.

Joining solvent-weld types

Solvent-weld fittings are neater and less obtrusive than push-fit ones and they offer the facility of pre-fabrication before installation. However, making them does demand a little more skill and care and — unlike push-fit joints — they cannot accommodate the expansion (thermal movement) that takes place as hot wastes run through the pipe. A 4m (12ft) length of PVC pipe will expand by about 13mm (just over ½in) when its temperature is raised above 20°C (70°F). For this reason, where a straight length of waste pipe exceeds 1.8m (6ft) in length, expansion couplings must be introduced at 1.8m intervals if other joints are to be solvent-welded. This rarely occurs in domestic design, however, and use of push-fit or solvent-weld is a matter of personal preference.

Although the instructions given by the different manufacturers vary slightly, the steps to making solvent-weld joints follow very similar lines. Of course, the first rule is to measure up all your pipe lengths carefully. Remember to allow for the end of the pipe overlapping the joint. When you've worked out pipe lengths cutting can start.

Ready Reference

TYPES OF FITTINGS

A number of fittings are available in both solvent-weld and push-fit systems – here are just a few of them. Check the complete range before you plan a new system – special bends and branches may exist that will make the job much easier.

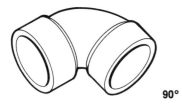

90°

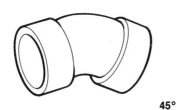

60°

45°

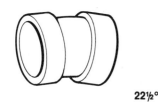

22½°

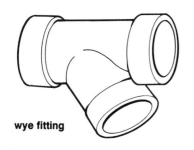

wye fitting

JOINING SOIL PIPES

These are joined in the same way as plastic waste pipes but are much bigger — about 100mm (4in) in diameter — so they take longer to fit. They also have some different fittings, such as a soil branch for use where the outlet pipe joins the stack, and access fittings with bolted removable plates for inspection. There are also special connectors to link to the toilet pan, via a special gasket, and to link to the underground drainage system which is traditionally made of vitrified clay.

The accurate molding of the fittings and the ease of assembly means that you can confidently tackle complete replacement of a soil system.

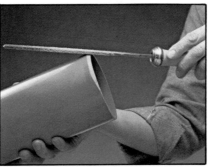

1 Soil pipes are joined in the same way as their narrower waste counterparts, but as they're bigger take special care with cutting and chamfering.

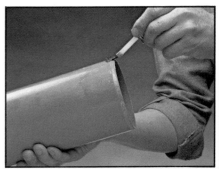

2 You have got a lot more area to cover with the solvent cement so you must work speedily – but don't neglect accurate application.

3 The soil branch pipe has a swept entry into the main stack fitting. This is one of the most important joints in the system, so make sure you get it right.

4 When you finally push the pipe into the fitting socket make quite sure that it goes right home against the pipe stop inside the fitting.

Cut the pipe clean and square with a hacksaw or other fine-toothed saw. A useful tip to ensure a square cut is to fold a piece of newspaper over the pipe and join the edges beneath it. The paper will then act as a template.

Remove all internal and external 'burr' or roughness at the end of the pipe, then use a file to chamfer the outside of the pipe end to about 45°. Not all manufacturers recommend this, but it does provide an extra key for the solvent.

Insert the pipe end into the fitting and mark the depth of insertion with a pencil. Using medium grade abrasive paper, or a light file, lightly roughen the end of the pipe, as far as the pencil mark, and also roughen the interior of the socket. Thoroughly clean the roughened surfaces of the socket and the pipe end using a clean rag moistened with a cleaner recommended by the manufacturer of the fittings.

Select the correct solvent cement (PVC pipes need a different solvent cement from ABS ones; once again, buy all the materials needed at the same time from the same supplier). Read the label on the tin and stir only if instructed.

Using a clean paintbrush apply the solvent cement to the pipe end and to the inside of the fittings, brushing in the direction of the pipe. It is usually necessary to apply two coats to ABS pipes and fittings. The second coat should be brushed on quickly before the first has dried.

Push the pipe fully home into the fitting (some, but not all, manufacturers suggest that this should be done with a slight twisting action). Remove excess solvent cement and hold the assembled joint securely in position for about 30 seconds. If hot water will be flowing through the pipe, don't use it for 24 hours to give time for the joint to set completely.

Joining ring-seal types

Preparation for ring-seal or push-fit jointing is similar to that for solvent welding. The pipe end must be cut absolutely squarely and all the burr removed. You should draw a line round the cut end of the pipe 10mm (³⁄₈in) from its end and chamfer back to this line with a rasp or shaping tool, then clean the recess within the push-fit connector's socket and check that the sealing ring is evenly seated. One manufacturer supplies sealing rings separately, and they should be inserted at this point. The pipe end should now be lubricated with a small amount of petroleum jelly and pushed firmly into the socket past the joint ring. Push it fully home and mark the insertion depth on the pipe with a pencil. Then withdraw it by 10mm (³⁄₈in), which is the allowance made for expansion. The expansion joint that is inserted into long straight lengths of solvent-welded waste pipe consists of a coupling with a solvent-weld joint at one end and a push-fit joint at the other.

As with solvent-weld jointing, individual manufacturers may give varying instructions. Some, for instance, advise the use of their own silicone lubricating jelly. Where the manufacturer supplies instructions it is best to follow these exactly.

Fittings

PVC pipe can be bent by the application of gentle heat from a blow-torch, but this technique needs practice and it is best to rely on special fittings. Sockets are used for joining straight lengths of pipe, tees for right-angled branches, and both 90° and 45° elbows are usually available. If you need to reduce the diameters from one pipe to another you can use reducing sockets. These are really sockets within sockets which can be welded together, one taking the smaller diameter pipe and the other the larger. Soil outlet pipes from toilets are joined in the same way; they are merely bigger — usually 100mm (4in) — in diameter. Sockets work in the same way, but the branch-junction with the main soil stack must be of a specially 'swept' design.

HOW PLASTIC FITTINGS WORK

Solvent-weld joints

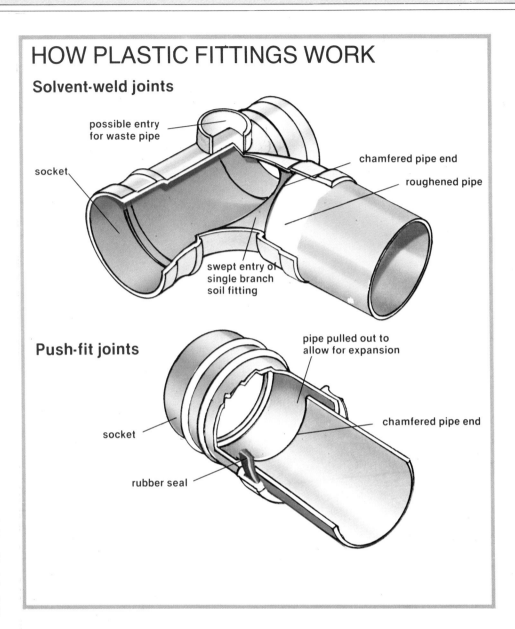

possible entry for waste pipe

chamfered pipe end

roughened pipe

socket

swept entry of single branch soil fitting

Push-fit joints

pipe pulled out to allow for expansion

chamfered pipe end

socket

rubber seal

SPECIAL FITTINGS

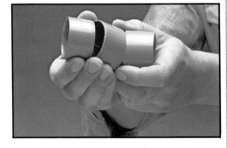

Special fittings are available when pipe fitting is not straightforward. This is a reducing adaptor for push-fit fittings where you need to join a 32mm (1¼in)

pipe to a 40mm (1½in) pipe. You join the relevant pipe to the mating part of the adaptor and then join the two adaptor parts together.

USING PLASTIC PIPE AND FITTINGS

Plastic pipe and fittings can be used for hot water supplies. They are easy to work with and allow the do-it-yourself plumber to tackle a wide range of jobs.

Over the last twenty years plastic has become the most popular plumbing material for above and below ground drainage, for rainwater collection and disposal, and for subsoil drainage. In the form of black polyethylene tubing it has also become a material widely used for water transportation on camping sites and farms. In the home, however, it has not proved popular. Although this lack of interest can partly be attributed to the conservatism of plumbers and householders, the main reason has been that up until now the plastic pipes that have been available have been suitable for cold water supplies only. This has meant that plumbers, who have had no choice but to use copper or some other metal for the hot water system, have almost always tended to use the same material when dealing with the cold water system. Householders have doubted the ability of plastic pipework to do a good, life-long job, and have also tended to resist its use on grounds of taste: quite simply, in places where pipework is exposed to view the combination of plastic and copper (or stainless steel or iron) is not one that is very pleasing to the eye.

Now, however, all this has changed. Polybutylene and chlorinated polyvinyl chloride (CPVC) can both be used for cold *and* hot water supply.

The advantages of plastic pipework

The most obvious advantage is the lightness of the pipework, which makes for ease of handling, but the most important benefit is the ease with which plastic can be cut and joined. This means that the level of skill you require to undertake a particular plumbing task is greatly reduced, as is the amount of time you require to carry it out. Both systems are also strong and durable, more resistant to frost than a traditional plumbing system and, unlike the latter, not subject to corrosion. Last but not least, they are competitively priced.

Plastic pipes are less vulnerable to frost because plastic is a poor conductor of heat compared to metal (which means that, unlike metal, it provides a certain amount of insulation), and because it has greater elasticity. This means that plastic pipes are not only less likely to freeze than metal ones, but also that in the event of their doing so they are much less likely to burst. The greater degree of insulation that plastic provides also brings other benefits: it results in less heat being lost from pipe runs between radiators (or between the hot water tank and the taps), as well as meaning that less insulation is necessary for pipework that needs to be protected against the cold.

Plastic pipes aren't subject to corrosion for the simple reason that plastic isn't attacked by the water supply.

This also means that plastic is a safer material to use for your drinking water supply pipes than metal, the use of which can, under some circumstances, present a health risk.

One final point to be borne in mind before you replace metal pipes with plastic ones is that plastic is a non-conductor of electricity. This means that all-plastic plumbing systems cannot be used to ground a domestic electricity supply (see *Ready Reference*).

You can obtain both polybutylene and CPVC tubing in the 15mm (½in), 22mm (¾ in) and 28mm (1in) diameters commonly used in domestic hot and cold water supply. However, in other respects — particularly as regards the flexibility of the two different types of tubing and methods of cutting and jointing — the two systems differ. So, before you undertake a plumbing task using plastic pipes and fittings, you'd do well to consider which system best suits your particular application.

Polybutylene tubing

Polybutylene tubing is brown or gray in color and naturally flexible; in this respect it differs from CPVC tubing, which is rigid. As well as being available in 3m (10ft) lengths in all three diameters, it is also obtainable as a 100m (390ft) coil in the 15mm (½in) size, and as a 50m (195ft) coil in the 22mm (¾in) size. This flexibility, and the long lengths in which the tubing is available, is particularly useful as it cuts down the time you need to spend on installation, and reduces the number of fittings necessary (which means less cost). You can thread polybutylene pipes under floors and between joists with minimal disturbance, their flexibility also allowing you to take them through apertures and round obstacles that would otherwise present serious difficulties. You can bend the tubing cold to easy bends with a minimum radius of eight times the pipe diameter; 15mm (½in) tube can therefore be bent to a minimum radius of 120mm (4¾in) and 22mm (¾in) to a minimum radius of 176mm (7in). You must, however, provide a clip on either side of the bend to secure it. The flexibility of polybutylene tubing means that you

POLYBUTYLENE PIPE AND FITTINGS

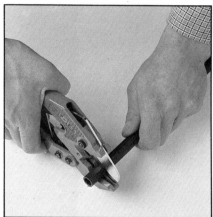

1 The best way to cut polybutylene pipe is with the manufacturer's shears. These are easy to use and ensure that you get a square-cut pipe end every time.

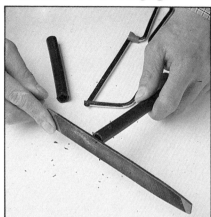

2 Alternatively, you can cut polybutylene pipe with a hacksaw or a sharp knife. If you use this method don't forget to clean off any burr with a file.

3 Before jointing the pipe, insert a stainless steel support sleeve into the pipe end. This prevents the tube end getting crushed within the fitting.

4 Polybutylene pipe can be used with ordinary compression fittings. The joint is made in exactly the same way as one made using ordinary copper pipe.

5 Within a polybutylene fitting a grab ring holds the pipe in place, while an 'O' ring ensures a watertight seal. The two are separated by a spacer washer.

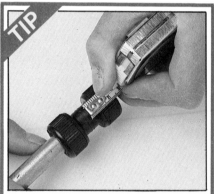

6 The witness lines on the body of the fitting indicate the length of pipe hidden within it when the joint is assembled. Remember to allow for this.

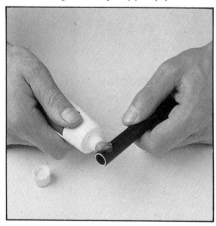

7 Before inserting polybutylene pipe into a polybutylene fitting, apply a special lubricant to both the pipe end and the interior of the socket.

8 Make the joint without unscrewing or even loosening the nuts. Simply thrust the pipe end into the socket until it meets the pipe stop inside.

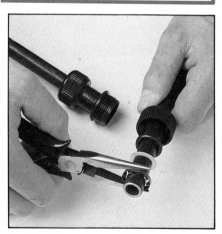

9 The pipe can be withdrawn only if you unscrew the nut. To re-use the joint, crush and discard the grab ring, and then replace it with a new one.

CPVC PIPE AND FITTINGS

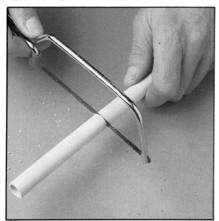

1 You can cut CPVC pipe with either a fine-toothed saw or an ordinary pipe cutter. If using a saw, make sure that you hold it at right-angles to the pipe.

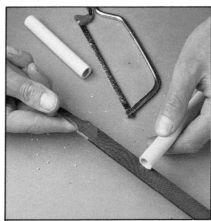

2 Use a file or a knife to remove the burr from the pipe end. Check that the pipe fits snugly in the socket, and that the fitting is free from imperfections.

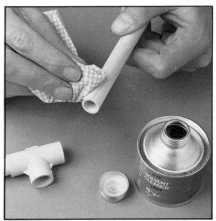

3 Before making a joint with CPVC the surfaces to be solvent-welded must first be cleaned. Use the manufacturer's special solvent cleaner for this purpose.

4 Immediately afterwards, apply the solvent weld cement, brushing this liberally on the tube end and only sparingly in the interior of the fitting socket.

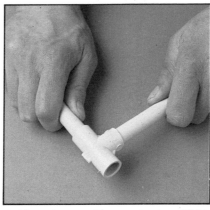

5 The solvent-weld cement goes off fairly rapidly, so you must make the joint as soon as you've applied it. Push the pipe home with a slight twisting motion.

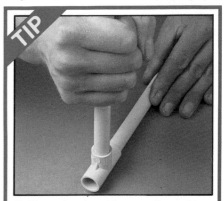

TIP

6 The solvent-weld cement's rapid setting time also means you must make adjustment for alignment immediately. Do not remove surplus cement.

7 You can join CPVC pipe to copper using a compression fitting and a two-part adaptor. Discard the ring as the first part of the adaptor is self-sealing.

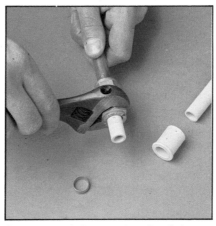

8 Tighten up the compression fitting in the usual way. Use a second wrench to hold the body of the fitting before giving the coupling nut a final turn.

9 Having solvent-welded the two parts of the adaptor together, complete the fitting by solvent-welding the CPVC pipe to the second part of the adaptor.

will have to give continuous support to any visible horizontal pipe runs in order to eliminate the possibility of unsightly sagging (see *Ready Reference*).

You can cut polybutylene tube with a sharp knife or a hacksaw. However, for speed of operation and to ensure an absolutely square cut pipe end every time, the manufacturers recommend that you use their specially designed pipe shears. It would certainly be worthwhile investing in a pair of these shears before embarking on a major project that involved the marking of a large number of joints.

You can join polybutylene tubing by using either compression joints (as used with copper), or else the manufacturer's own patent push-fit connectors. One of the advantages of being able to use compression joints with tubing is that it enables you to replace a length of copper pipe with polybutylene tubing using the existing compression tee or coupling.

When using polybutylene tubing with this type of joint the procedure you follow is identical to that which you adopt with copper pipe (see the techniques on pages 216-220). But in order to prevent the collapse of the tube end when the nut is tightened, you must insert a stainless steel support sleeve into the tube end. And if you use jointing compound to complete a threaded fitting connected to polybutylene pipe, make sure none comes into contact with the polybutylene.

The patent polybutylene joints and fittings are available in the usual range of straight couplings, tees, elbows, reducing fittings and tap and tank connectors, and in appearance they resemble their brass compression counterparts. But there is one important difference — you don't have to loosen or unscrew the nuts to make a joint. To make a connection you simply have to push the prepared pipe end into the fitting (see step-by-step photographs). Polybutylene fittings have one further advantage in that they allow you to rotate a pipe that has been inserted into one of them, even when it is filled with water. This means, for example, that a polybutylene stop-valve can rest neatly against a wall until you need to use it. You then pull the handle away from the wall so you can open and close it easily.

CPVC tubing

CPVC tubing differs from the polybutylene type in two basic ways. First, it is rigid rather than flexible, which means that it is only available in relatively short lengths of 1.8m (6ft) or 3m (10ft). Second, it is joined by a process known as solvent welding, a slightly more involved procedure than making a push-fit or compression connection (see step-by-step

photographs). Superficially, CPVC tubing can be distinguished from polybutylene by its off-white color. An hour after the last joint has been made you can flush through the system and fill it with cold water; before filling with hot water you need to wait at least four hours.

CPVC pipe does expand when hot water passes through it, but this won't cause a problem in most domestic systems unless one of the pipe runs exceeds 10m (33ft), which is unlikely. In this case you will have to create an expansion loop using four 90° elbows and three 150mm (6in) lengths of pipe.

The manufacturers of CPVC tubing provide an exceptionally wide range of fittings to meet every eventuality. There are 90° and 45° elbows, equal and unequal tees, reducing pieces, tap and ball-valve connectors, stop-valves and gate-valves, and provision for connection to existing copper or screwed iron fittings. The connectors for copper tubing have a solvent-weld socket at one end and a conventional compression joint at the other. Those for iron fittings have a solvent-weld fitting at one end and either a male or female threaded joint at the other. If you are connecting a fitting to an existing iron socket, make sure that you render the screwed connection watertight by binding plastic tape round the male thread before screwing home.

What system to use

Neither system is 'better' than the other, and each has its merits and its drawbacks. The polybutylene tubing is flexible and available in extremely long lengths which reduce the number of joints you will have to use, as well as enabling you to get through or round obstacles that might prove difficult were you using the CPVC system. On the other hand the push-fit polybutylene joints are bulkier and more obtrusive than those used with the CPVC system.

Bearing in mind this, and the fact that the rigid CPVC pipes will be less prone to sagging than the flexible polybutylene tubing, the CPVC system is probably the more acceptable one in situations where plumbing is exposed to view. The more complex construction of the polybutylene joints – the cause of their bulkiness – also makes them relatively expensive: which means that the smaller number necessary for carrying out a given plumbing task won't always cost you less than the greater number necessary with CPVC. However, polybutylene joints, unlike CPVC ones, can be used more than once.

Lastly, in case your decision to opt for one system or the other is influenced by the color of the material out of which it is made (dark brown for polybutylene and off-white for CPVC), you can paint both systems with ordinary household paints.

Ready Reference

TIP: CHECK GROUNDING

Metal plumbing systems were often used to ground the domestic electricity supply. Since plastic pipework doesn't conduct electricity, it's vital that the house's grounding arrangements are checked by an electrician if you replace any part of the plumbing system with plastic.

BENDING POLYBUTYLENE PIPE

You can form bends in polybutylene pipe to a minimum radius of eight times the pipe diameter.

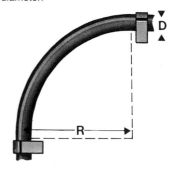

CONNECTING POLYBUTYLENE TO IMPERIAL COPPER PIPES

You can use 15mm (½in) polybutylene fittings with ½in imperial-sized copper pipe without adaptation. If you wish to use 22mm (¾in) fittings with ¾in imperial-sized copper pipe, you have to replace the sealing ring with a purpose-made one of larger size.

SUPPORTING PIPE RUNS

With CPVC pipe, space pipe brackets at 500mm (20in) intervals on horizontal pipe runs, at 1m (39in) intervals on vertical ones. With polybutylene pipe, use the following spacings:

Pipe size	Horizontal run	Vertical run
15mm (½in)	400mm (16in)	800mm (31in)
22mm (¾in)	600mm (24in)	1m (39in)

Reduce these by 25 per cent for pipes carrying water over 60°C (140°F), increase them by 25 per cent for cold pipe runs.

E LACI G A WASHBASIN

Replacing a washbasin is fairly straightforward. It's a job you'll have to undertake if the basin is cracked – but you may also want to change the basin if you're redesigning your bathroom and adding some up-to-date fittings.

Basin and fittings from Royal Doulton

A part from replacing a cracked basin, which you should do immediately, the most common time to install a new basin is when you're improving a bathroom or decorating a separate toilet. The chances are that the basin you'll be removing will be one of the older ceramic types, wall-hung, a pedestal model or built into a vanity unit.

The main advantage of a wall-hung basin is that it doesn't take up any floor space and because of this it is very useful in a small bathroom. You can also set the basin at a comfortable height, unlike a pedestal basin whose height is fixed by the height of the pedestal. However, it's usual to fit a wall-hung basin with the rim 800mm (32in) above the floor.

Vanity units are the descendents of the Edwardian wash-stand, with its marble top, bowl and large water jug. The unit is simply a storage cupboard with a ceramic, enamelled pressed steel or plastic basin set flush in the top. The advantage of vanity units is that you have a counter surface round the basin on which to stand toiletries. There is rarely, if ever, sufficient room for these items behind or above conventional wall-hung or pedestal basins. Usually the top has some form of plastic covering or can be tiled for easy cleaning. A useful storage area is also provided beneath the basin.

Fittings for basins

It's a good idea to choose the taps and waste fittings at the same time you select the basin, so everything matches. You could perhaps re-use the taps from the old basin, but it's doubtful if these will be in keeping with the design of the new appliance. As an alternative to shrouded head or pillar taps, you could fit a mixer, provided the holes at the back of the basin are suitably spaced to take the tap shanks.

Ceramic basins normally have a built-in overflow channel which in most appliances connects into the main outlet above the trap. So if you accidentally let the basin overfill you reduce the risk of water spillage.

PUTTING IN A NEW BASIN

You should have little trouble installing a new washbasin in the same place as the old one. It's also a good opportunity to check the pipe runs. If they're made of lead it's a good idea to replace them.

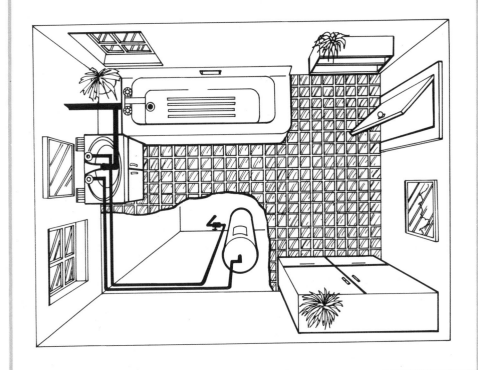

238

Vanity unit basins are usually sold complete with a waste and overflow unit which resembles that of a modern stainless steel sink. A flexible tube connects the overflow outlet of the basin with a sleeve or 'banjo' unit which fits tightly round a slotted waste fitting.

With both types of basin the flange of the waste outlet has to be bedded into the hole provided for it in the basin on a layer of plumber's putty. The thread of the screwed waste must also be smeared with jointing compound to ensure a watertight seal where the 'banjo' connects to it.

Traps

The outlet of the waste must, of course, connect to a trap and branch waste pipe. At one time it was the practice to use 'shallow seal' traps with a 50mm (2in) depth of seal for two-pipe drainage systems, and 'deep seal' traps with a 75mm (3in) depth of seal for single stack systems. Today, however, deep seal traps are always fitted.

Of course, the modern bottle trap is one of the most common types used. It's neater looking and requires less space than a traditional U-trap. Where it's concealed behind a pedestal or in a vanity unit you can use one made of plastic, but there are chromium-plated and brass types if you have a wall-hung basin where trap and waste will be clearly visible. The one drawback with bottle traps is that they discharge water more slowly than a U-trap. You can now also buy traps with telescopic inlets that make it much easier to provide a push-fit connection to an existing copper or plastic branch waste pipe.

Connecting up the water supply

It's unlikely that you'll be able to take out the old basin and install a new one without making some modification to the pipework. It's almost certain that the tap holes will be in a different position. To complicate matters further, taps are now made with shorter shanks so you'll probably have to extend the supply pipes by a short length.

If you're installing new supply pipes, how you run them will depend on the type of basin you're putting in. With a wall-hung basin or the pedestal type, the hot and cold pipes are usually run neatly together up the back wall and then bent round to the tap shanks. But as a vanity unit will conceal the plumbing there's no need to run the pipes together.

You might find it difficult to bend the required angles, so an easy way round the problem is to use flexible corrugated copper pipe which you can bend by hand to the shape you need. You can buy the pipe with a swivel tap connector at one end and a plain connector, on which you can use capillary or

ASSEMBLING A VANITY UNIT

1 *Cut a hole in the vanity unit with the help of the template provided or, if the hole is precut, check the measurement against that of the sink.*

2 *Prop the basin up while you install the mixer unit. Start with the outlet spout which is fixed with a brass nut and packing washers.*

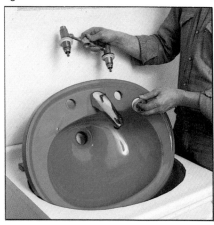

3 *Now take the water inlet assembly and check that the hot and cold spur pipes are the right length so that the tap sub-assemblies are correctly positioned.*

4 *Fix the assembly in position with the brass nuts supplied by the manufacturer. Make sure that all the washers are included otherwise the fitting won't be secure.*

5 *Now complete the tap heads by first sliding on the flange which covers up the securing nut; next put on the headwork and tighten the retaining nut.*

6 *Finish off the tap assembly by fitting the colored markers into place (red for hot is usually on the left), and gently pressing home the chrome cap.*

Ready Reference

BASIN SIZES

On basins, the dimension from side to side is specified as the length, and that from back to front as the width.

Most standard sized basins are between 550 and 700mm (22 and 28in) long, and 450 to 500mm (18 to 20in) wide.

BASIN COMPONENTS

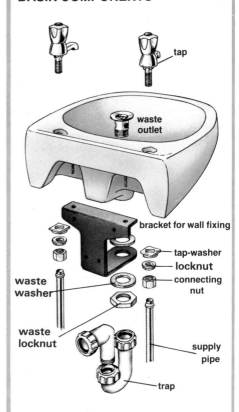

tap

waste outlet

bracket for wall fixing

tap-washer
locknut
connecting nut

waste washer

waste locknut

supply pipe

trap

THE SPACE YOU'LL NEED

2200mm

1000mm

400mm 700mm

Think about the space around your basin particularly if you are installing a new one. You not only need elbow room when you are bending over it, such as when you are washing your hair, but also room in front to stand back – especially if you put a mirror above it. Here are the recommended dimensions for the area around your basin.

PLUMBING IN A VANITY UNIT

7 Now insert the waste outlet. Make sure the rubber flange is fitted properly and seats comfortably into the basin surround.

8 Turn the basin over; secure the outlet and the pop-up waste control rods. These may need shortening depending on clearance inside the vanity unit.

TIP

9 Before you put the basin into its final position put a strip of mastic around the opening in the vanity unit to ensure a watertight seal.

10 Press the basin gently into position and fix it to the underside of the top of the vanity unit. Attach the waste plug to its keeper.

11 Now fix the inlet pipes to the two mixer connections and screw on the waste trap. Take the doors off the vanity unit to make access easier.

12 Turn the water back on and check for leaks. Check the pop-up waste system works, then put the doors of the vanity unit back on.

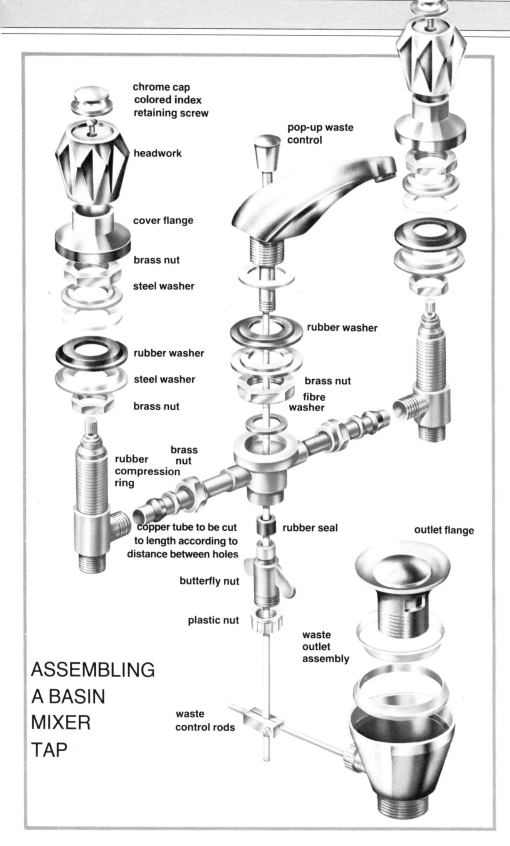

chrome cap
colored index
retaining screw

headwork

cover flange

brass nut

steel washer

rubber washer

steel washer

brass nut

rubber compression ring

brass nut

copper tube to be cut to length according to distance between holes

pop-up waste control

rubber washer

brass nut
fibre washer

rubber seal

butterfly nut

plastic nut

waste control rods

waste outlet assembly

outlet flange

ASSEMBLING A BASIN MIXER TAP

When fitting the taps all you have to do is to remove the locknuts and slip flat plastic washers over the shanks (if they aren't there already). The taps can then be positioned in the holes in the basin. When this has been done more plastic washers have to be slipped over the shanks before the locknuts are replaced. It's important not to over-tighten these as it's quite easy to damage a ceramic basin.

Mixers usually have one large washer or gasket between the base of the mixer and the top of the basin and you fix them in exactly the same way.

When you've fitted the taps you can then fit the waste. With a ceramic basin you'll have to use a slotted waste to enable water from the overflow to escape into the drainage pipe. Getting this in place means first removing the locknut so you can slip it through the outlet hole in the basin — which itself should be coated with a generous layer of plumber's putty. It's essential to make sure that the slot in the waste fitting coincides with the outlet of the basin's built-in overflow. You'll then have to smear jointing compound on the protruding screw thread of the shank, slip on a plastic washer and replace and tighten the locknut. As you do this the waste flange will probably try to turn on its seating, but you can prevent this by holding the grid with pliers as you tighten the nut.

Finally, any excess putty that is squeezed out as the flange is tightened against the basin should be wiped away.

A vanity unit will probably be supplied with a combined waste and overflow unit. This is a flexible hose that has to be fitted (unlike a ceramic basin, where it's an integral part of the appliance). The slotted waste is bedded in in exactly the same way as a waste on a ceramic basin. You then have to fit one end of the overflow to the basin outlet and slip the 'banjo' outlet on the other end over the shank of the waste to cover the slot. It's held in position by a washer and locknut.

Fitting the basin
Once the taps and waste have been fixed in position on the new basin, you should be ready to remove the old basin and fit the new one in its place. First you need to cut off the water supply to the basin, by turning off the main shut-off valve or any valve on the supply line. Then open the taps and leave them until the water ceases to flow. If the existing basin is a pedestal model, you'll have to remove the pedestal which may be screwed to the floor. Take off the nut that connects the basin trap to the threaded waste outlet and unscrew the nuts that connect the water supply pipes to the shanks of the taps. These will either be swivel tap connectors or cap and lining joints. You'll need to be able to lift the

compression fittings at the other. If you're using ordinary copper pipe, the easiest way to start is by bending the pipe to the correct angle first, and then cutting the pipe to the right length at each end afterwards. See techniques on pages 221-223.

Preparing the basin
Before you fix the basin in position, you'll need to fit the taps (or mixer) and the waste. It's much easier to do this at this stage than later when the basin is against the wall because you will have more room to maneuver in.

Ready Reference

TYPES OF BASIN

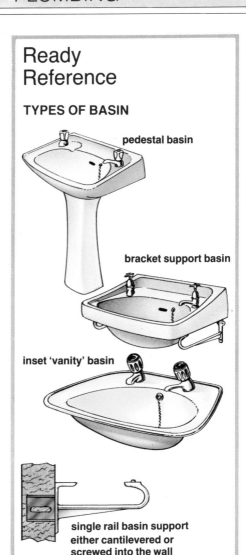

pedestal basin

bracket support basin

inset 'vanity' basin

**single rail basin support
either cantilevered or
screwed into the wall**

**basin support with towel
rail, screwed to the wall**

FITTING A VANITY BASIN

When you buy a vanity basin it should be supplied with a template to guide you in cutting your work surface or vanity unit. This should also include fitting instructions, and necessary fixing screws and mastic strip. It may look like this.

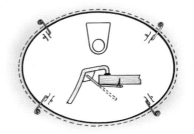

basin clear and then remove the brackets or hangers on which it rests.

You'll probably need some help when installing the new basin as it's much easier to mark the fixing holes if someone else is holding the basin against the wall. With a pedestal basin, the pedestal will determine the level of the basin. The same applies with a vanity unit. But if the basin is set on hangers or brackets, you can adjust the height for convenience.

Once the fixing holes have been drilled and plugged, the basin can be screwed into position and you can deal with the plumbing.

Before you make the connections to the water supply pipes you may have to cut or lengthen them to meet the tap shanks. If you need to lengthen them, you'll find it easier to use corrugated copper pipe. The actual connection between pipe and shank is made with a swivel tap connector — a form of compression fitting.

Finally you have to connect the trap. You may be able to re-use the old one, but it's more likely you'll want to fit a new one. And if its position doesn't coincide with the old one, you can use a bottle trap with an adjustable telescopic inlet.

FITTING A PEDESTAL BASIN

1 *Stand the basin on the pedestal to check the height of the water supply pipe runs and the outlet. Measure the height of the wall fixing points.*

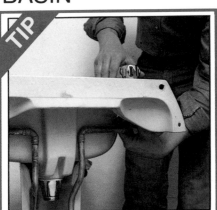

2 *When you're making up the pipe run to connect to the tap shanks, plan it so the pipes are neatly concealed within the body of the pedestal.*

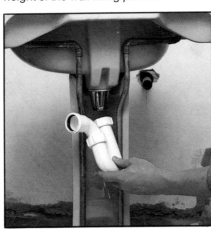

3 *Line up the piped waste outlet and fix the trap to the basin outlet. A telescopic trap may be useful here to adjust for a varying level.*

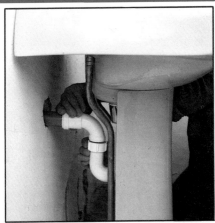

4 *Move the whole unit into its final position, screw the basin to the wall, connect the waste trap to the outlet, and connect up the supply pipes.*

INSTALLING A TOILET

Ensure a water-tight seal when replacing a toilet.

Although toilets are large fixtures, they aren't difficult to replace. If you buy a replacement toilet with the same rough-in measurement as the existing fixture, then you should have little problem connecting the toilet to the existing system.

The rough-in measurement is the distance from the finished wall behind the toilet to the center of the floor flange that holds the toilet bowl in place. The usual measurement for the rough-in is 30cm (12in).

To remove the existing toilet, shut off the water supply and flush the toilet. Remove all the remaining water in the tank and the bowl using a sponge and pail. Disconnect the water supply line that leads from the floor or wall to the flush valve.

If your tank is screwed to the wall, disconnect the couplings on the pipe that join the tank to the bowl. Remove the screws that hold the tank to the wall, remembering to support the tank as you loosen the screws. Most modern tanks are not fastened to the wall and therefore don't need to be removed from the bowl.

Pry off the porcelain or plastic caps that cover the bolts on the base of the bowl. Remove the bolts. The toilet bowl is sealed to the floor with some form of caulking. Loosen this caulking with a putty knife and rock the bowl from side to side and back to front until it comes loose.

Remove the toilet bowl and clean the excess caulking material from the floor. Clean the floor flange well.

To prepare the new toilet for installation, put a new wax, rubber or putty gasket around the bowl horn and place a 25mm (1in) thick ring of putty around the bottom rim of the toilet bowl.

Replace the floor flange bolts. Most new toilets only have two bolts. If your old one had four, remove the extra two.

Lower the toilet bowl with the horn centered over the floor flange, allowing the bolts to rise up through the toilet bowl base. Twist the bowl slightly to form a tight seal on the new gasket but don't raise the bowl. Once the bowl is pressed into place, don't raise it or the gasket seal will be broken. Check the level of the bowl and shim if necessary.

INSTALLING A TOILET

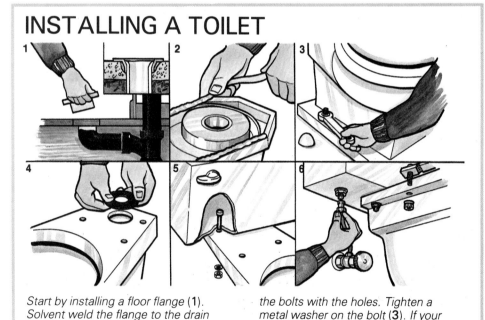

Start by installing a floor flange (1). Solvent weld the flange to the drain pipe (if the pipe is ABS plastic) and also screw the flange to the floor. Fit a wax gasket ring around the toilet horn and a strip of putty around the edges (2). Fit the bowl on the flange aligning the bolts with the holes. Tighten a metal washer on the bolt (3). If your tank sits directly on the bowl, fasten a spud washer over the bowl inlet opening (4). Lower the tank into position and fasten the tank hold down bolt (5). Reconnect the water supply (6).

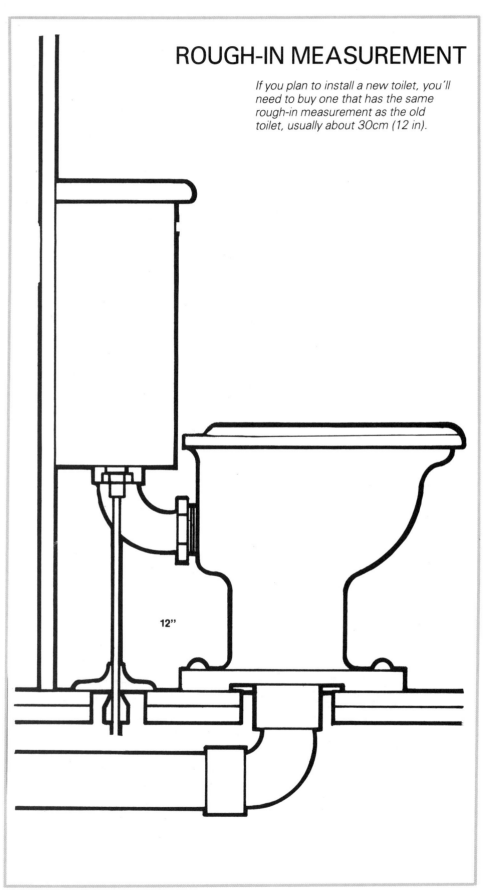

ROUGH-IN MEASUREMENT

If you plan to install a new toilet, you'll need to buy one that has the same rough-in measurement as the old toilet, usually about 30cm (12 in).

12"

If the tank of the toilet comes separate from the bowl, attach the tank according to the manufacturer's directions. Once the tank is aligned with the wall, the bolts on the toilet bowl can be tightened and capped.

Make all the water supply connections and turn on the water. Flush the toilet several times to check for leaks.

CLOTHES WASHERS

Installing a clothes washer is as easy as one, two, three . . .

A clothes washer needs three plumbing connections. It comes equipped with a hot-water hose, cold-water hose and drainage hose. The water hoses have female thread connectors that can be attached directly to the faucets on the laundry sink. However, to minimize damage to the plumbing system caused by the abrupt shut-off of washing machines, it's preferable to connect hoses to their own faucets.

These faucets must be attached to 12mm (½in) water supply pipes that have 60cm (24in) long air chambers to cushion the water shut-off. The air chambers are also one pipe size larger than the water supply pipes. The faucets act as shut-off valves should emergency service be necessary to the clothes washer.

With the drain hose you have a choice. It can be hung over the side of the laundry tub to expel the waste water from the machine through the plumbing system, or a standpipe can be installed, which will direct the waste water directly into the drain and out into the sewer system.

The standpipe must be high enough that when the drain hose is placed in the opening at the top, it is higher than the level of the water in the machine. If the hose is placed lower than the machine's water level, back-siphoning of the drain water can occur. The diameter of the standpipe must also be 12mm (½in) larger than the diameter of the drain hose.

The washer must be electrically grounded into a 120-volt outlet with a 15-amp time-delay fuse or circuit breaker. Do not use an extension cord. This time-delay action will compensate for the immediate surge of power it takes to start up the machine without blowing the fuse.

Once the connections have been made, it's simply a matter of adjusting the bolts at the corners of the machine to level it, and the clothes washer is ready for use.

INSTALLING A WASHING MACHINE

The standpipe should be higher than the water level in the washing machine. Air chambers should be larger than the diameter of the water pipes and 60cm (24in) long.

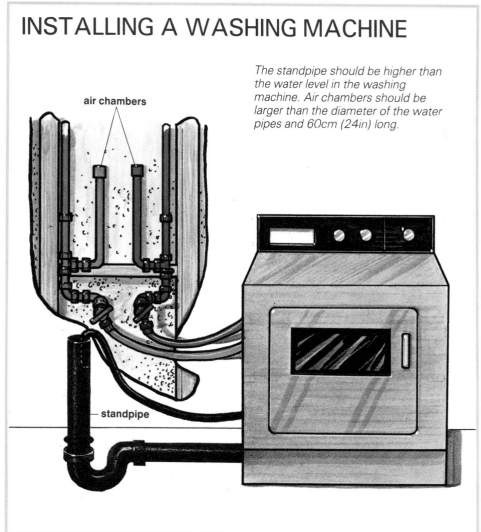

air chambers

standpipe

TUBS AND SHOWERS

Follow these steps to modernize your bathtub and shower.

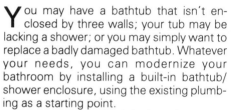

You may have a bathtub that isn't enclosed by three walls; your tub may be lacking a shower; or you may simply want to replace a badly damaged bathtub. Whatever your needs, you can modernize your bathroom by installing a built-in bathtub/shower enclosure, using the existing plumbing as a starting point.

If your current bathtub isn't enclosed and you don't want to replace your tub with a free-standing, cast-iron bathtub, you'll need to build a new wall at the head of the tub. Build a 2 × 4 stud wall the width of the bathtub you plan to install. Notch all the framing members to allow for the pipes. If you're installing a shower where there wasn't one before, you'll need to extend the pipes to create a single water supply pipe to the shower head. And, in some cases, you may even need to extend the water supply pipes to the faucets. The water supply pipes should be attached about 50 to 75cm (20 to 30in) above the floor, with the tub spout centered about 50cm (20in) above the floor. Shower pipes extend 1.5 to 1.8m (5 to 6ft) above the floor and are centered on the width of the tub.

When building a new enclosure wall, you'll need to install a 2 × 4 brace at the tops of the water supply pipe and the shower pipe to support the faucets and shower outlet. A third brace should be installed between the first two to support the long shower pipe.

To remove your old tub, you'll need access to the drain- and overflow pipes. If your tub is freestanding, the job is easy. Shut off the water supply, remove the faucets and disconnect the drain line and overflow pipe. If your bathtub is enclosed, there may be an access panel behind the wall at the head of the tub, which will enable you to make the necessary disconnections. If there's no access panel, you may be able to disconnect the tub from the front. If you plan to install a new shower head where there isn't any existing pipework, you'll need to remove the wallboard anyway, so you may as well re-

move it now to help you make your tub disconnections.

Once the drain- and overflow pipes have been disconnected, you can pull the tub from its 1 × 4 supports. These supports line the three walls and the tub flanges rest on them. You may have to unscrew the tub flanges. After the tub is removed, handle any necessary plumbing work.

To install the new tub, lower the tub onto the 1 × 4 support beams. With luck, the tub will rest on the beams and also sit solidly on the floor. If it doesn't, adjust the wall supports until the bathtub is level and the drain and overflow holes are lined up with the pipes. Most plumbing codes prohibit shimming of the tub. Some manufacturers also recommend sloping the tub toward the drain. With the tub lined up, screw the tub flanges in place.

Connect the drain- and overflow pipes, cover your new wall with waterproof wallboard and matching tiles. Caulk around the tub to prevent water seepage, then turn on the water supply.

Bathtubs are made from steel, cast iron, porcelain or fiberglass, with fiberglass being the most popular in today's homes. Many homeowners, when replacing bathtubs, are installing whirlpool tubs that have jetted water sprays. This type of tub is usually made of molded acrylic. When installing this type of tub, check the manufacturer's directions for plumbing, because jet sprays around the tub require additional plumbing work.

Cast-iron tubs have a historical look that some people desire in their bathrooms. When installing this type of tub, remember that it weighs about 225kg (500lb) and may demand bracing of the joists if the tub is to be installed on the main floor, and may be an impossible installation on a second floor because of its weight.

INSTALLING A BUILT-IN BATHTUB

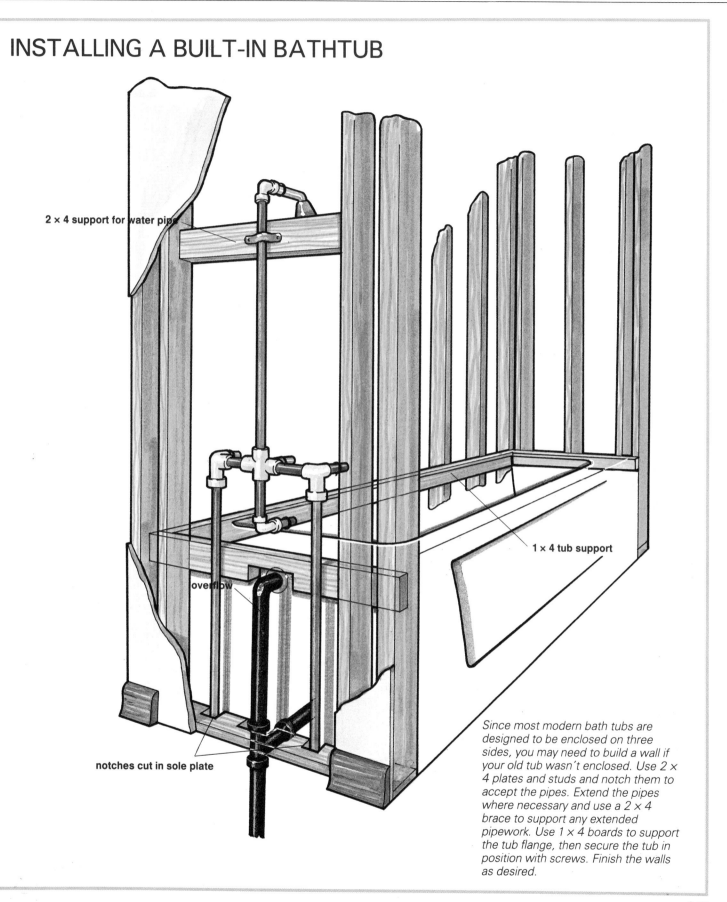

2 × 4 support for water pipe

1 × 4 tub support

overflow

notches cut in sole plate

Since most modern bath tubs are designed to be enclosed on three sides, you may need to build a wall if your old tub wasn't enclosed. Use 2 × 4 plates and studs and notch them to accept the pipes. Extend the pipes where necessary and use a 2 × 4 brace to support any extended pipework. Use 1 × 4 boards to support the tub flange, then secure the tub in position with screws. Finish the walls as desired.

OUTDOOR WATER SUPPLY

Two installations to help make outdoor water use more convenient.

In warm weather, property maintenance requires a ready supply of water and a convenient source for it. Installing extra outdoor faucets makes lawn and garden watering more efficient. You can also go one step further and install an inground sprinkler system.

Installing an outdoor bib tap

Rather than patching two lawn hoses together and running extremely long lengths of hose around your property to water the lawn, fill the pool or wash the car, installing an extra hose bib tap makes for more efficient use of your garden hose.

If you have a cold-water supply pipe running inside the house close to the spot where you wish to place your new bib tap, the installation will be easy. Drill a hole through the wall so that the center of the hole is at the center of the water supply pipe. Tap into the water pipe with a copper tee and solder it in place. Attach a length of pipe long enough to extend about 25mm (1in) beyond the exterior wall, then attach the new bib faucet.

The second installation procedure is to tap a new water supply line into the existing outdoor faucet. Tap a tee into the existing faucet run and attach a new water supply run to where you need your new hose bib. The run can go through the garage, but try to keep the run in as straight a line as possible. Any runs through unheated areas are subject to freezing during the cold months, so make sure the pipes are well insulated and make sure the outdoor taps have been left open during the winter months with the outdoor water shut-off valve closed.

Installing a sprinkler system

A sprinkler system installation isn't a difficult task if you use plastic plumbing and are prepared for all the digging. But once the system is installed, keeping your lawn green is no longer a boring chore.

There are many different types of sprinkler systems on the market; however, all underground systems are polyethylene hoses, which are strong yet flexible and are not subject to damage from water freezing in them during the cold months.

Sprinkler heads come in a variety of sprinkling patterns, from full circle to half circle and quarter circle, squares and waves.

UNDERGROUND SPRINKLER SYSTEM

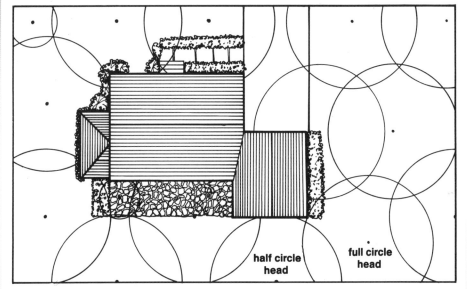

half circle head

full circle head

Before buying your system, make a plan of your lawn and determine where the sprinklers will be necessary, the number of heads you'll need and the sprinkling patterns. Heads are available in full circle, half circle, quarter circle, squares and waves.

SPRINKLER CONNECTIONS

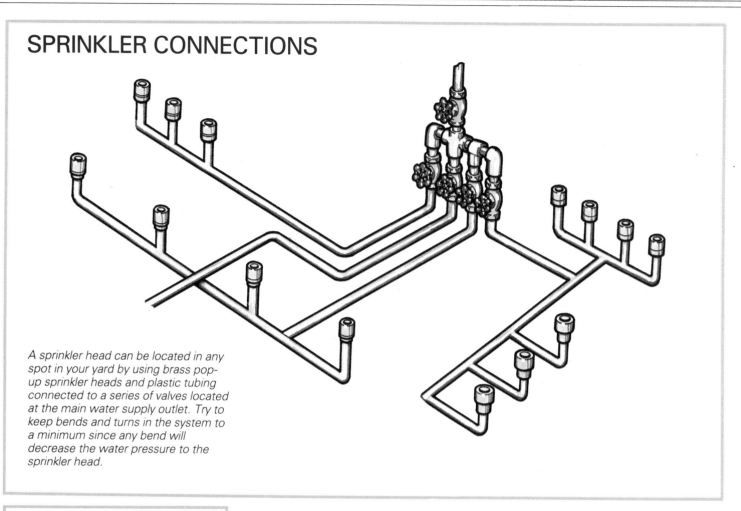

A sprinkler head can be located in any spot in your yard by using brass pop-up sprinkler heads and plastic tubing connected to a series of valves located at the main water supply outlet. Try to keep bends and turns in the system to a minimum since any bend will decrease the water pressure to the sprinkler head.

CLEARING OBSTRUCTIONS

To install a pipe under a walkway, dig a trench under the sidewalk and insert a steel pipe. Use a garden hose to flush out the pipe.

Decide what your needs are first. Make a sketch of the areas to be watered, then check the specifications of the sprinklers to determine how many heads you'll need and the necessary sprinkling patterns.

Before buying your system, you'll also need to know your water pressure, the size of your water meter and the size of the water supply pipe you'll be tapping into. To check the water pressure, you can ask your utilities company or you can check yourself by inserting a pressure gauge into the hose bib, checking to make sure all inside taps are shut off, then turning on the outside tap full force and taking a reading. Sprinkler heads are arranged in groups and each group is controlled by a valve. The number of valves and the amount of piping you'll need will be determined by the number of sprinkler heads you use.

An automatic timer and a distribution control, which makes the most of your water pressure by alternating the flow through various sprinkler heads, are recommended purchases to make your lawn watering completely automatic.

Most plumbing codes require the use of an antisiphon device on the sprinkler system

between the water connection in the house and the system to prevent any back-siphoning of hose water into the house water system.

Your sprinkler system should be connected to the water supply pipes inside the house just past the water meter and the control valves outside the house.

Use a flat spade for digging V-shaped trenches 10 to 15cm (4 to 6in) deep to hold the hose. Save the sod for reuse. Tap the pipe into the trench and backfill.

When laying a pipe under a concrete walkway, dig the trench from both sides, and insert a steel pipe with a wider diameter than your plastic hose under the walk. Cover the end of your plastic piping to keep debris from entering the hose, then slide the plastic hose through the steel pipe to the other side and backfill.

Sprinkler heads that have drain fittings will need a dry well. Dig a hole 30cm (12in) wide and 30cm (12in) deep and fill with coarse gravel for drainage.

Don't bend your plastic piping when installing it, and keep all curves to a minimum to prevent a reduction in water pressure to the sprinkler head.

INSTALLING A DISHWASHER

Proper hookup and an understanding of repair procedures will ensure a long life for your dishwasher.

A dishwasher uses the hot water supply only, and needs to be installed as close as possible to the kitchen sink to be able to tap into the hot-water supply line and the sink's drain.

Be sure of the rough-in dimensions before buying a dishwasher.

With a tee, build a run from the hot-water supply line to the intake valve on the dishwasher. The fittings at this point depend upon the manufacturer's directions. It's advisable also to place a shut-off valve on the run for emergency repairs.

The drain hose is connected to the outlet valve in the back of the washer and brought to the sink, where it is tapped into the sink drainpipe above the trap. Use a gradual bend in the hose to ensure adequate drainage pressure.

Hook up the wiring and test your dishwasher.

Make sure the temperature of the water entering the dishwasher is at least 60°C (140°F). Anything cooler will prevent your dishes from coming clean. If the temperature is cooler, adjust the temperature gauge on the hot-water heater.

If small children are in the house and the hot water supply is at a lower temperature (48°C/120°F) to prevent scaulding accidents, you may wish to install a small electric step-up water heater. This heater is installed under the sink to increase only the temperature of the hot water entering the dishwasher.

Dishwashers can develop a number of problems over time. The rubber gasket around the door can deteriorate, causing leaks around the door during the wash cycle. To repair, simply replace with a new gasket, following the manufacturer's directions for installation.

If your machine won't start and the fuses or circuit breaker are in operation, or if your machine goes through one or more cycles then stops without proceeding to the next cycle, you could have a faulty timer switch. Buy a new switch of the appropriate model. Disconnect the power before touching the timer. Then remove the wires one by one from the old switch and attach to the new one.

If your tank doesn't fill high enough with water, check the water pressure in your system. If water doesn't stay in the tank, tighten the drain valve flange.

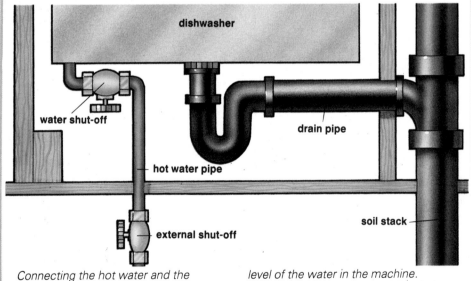

Connecting the hot water and the drain are the only two plumbing connections necessary for a dishwasher. Be sure to follow the manufacturer's instructions for the drain installation. Some models require the drain pipe to be raised above the level of the water in the machine. Others allow you to connect the drain through the floor and along the joists in the basement. Make sure you attach an external shutoff valve on your line in case of emergency.

250

CHAPTER 8

Wiring

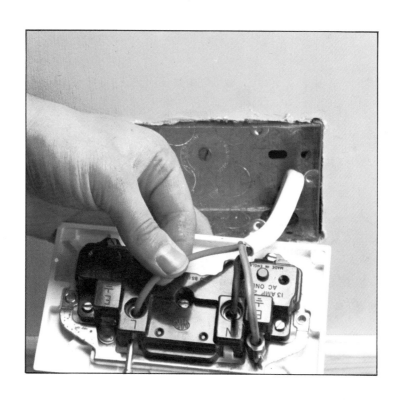

TRACING ELECTRICAL FAULTS

When the lights go out or an electrical appliance won't work, the reason is often obvious. But when it isn't, it helps to know how to locate the fault and put it right.

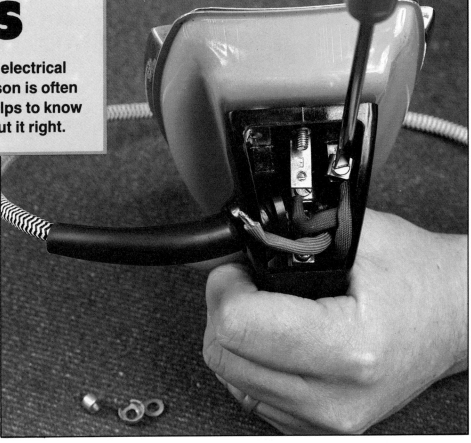

Most people's immediate reaction to something going wrong with their electricity supply is to head for the fuse panel, muttering darkly about another blown fuse. Fuses do blow occasionally for no immediately obvious reason, but usually there is a problem that needs to be pin-pointed and put right before the power can be restored. It's no use mending a blown fuse, only to find that when the power is restored the fuse blows again because the fault is still present.

Tracing everyday electrical faults is not particularly difficult. You simply have to be methodical in checking the various possible causes, and eliminating options until you find the culprit. More serious faults on the house's wiring system can be more difficult to track down, but again some careful investigation can often locate the source of the trouble, even if professional help has to be called in to put it right.

Safety first
Before you start investigating any electrical faults, remember the cardinal rule and switch off the power at the main switch. When fuses blow, it is all too easy to forget that other parts of the system may still be live and therefore dangerous, and even if you know precisely how your house has been wired up it is foolish to take risks. If the fault appears to be on an electrical appliance, the same rules apply: always switch off the appliance *and* pull out the plug before attempting to investigate. Don't rely on the switch to isolate it; the fault may be in the switch itself.

It's also important to be prepared for things to go wrong with your electrics; even new systems can develop faults, and in fact a modern installation using circuit breakers will detect faults more readily than one with cartridge fuses, so giving more regular cause for investigation. Make sure that you keep a small emergency electrical tool kit in an accessible place where it won't get raided for other jobs; it should include one or two screwdrivers, a pair of pliers, a handyman's knife, spare fuses and, above all, a *working* flashlight. There is nothing more annoying when the lights go out than finding the flashlight does not work.

Check the obvious
When something electrical fails to operate, always check the obvious first — replace the bulb when a light doesn't work, or glance outside to see if everyone in the street has been blacked out by a power cut before panicking that all your fuses have blown. Having satisfied yourself that you may have a genuine fault, start a methodical check of all possibilities.

A fault can occur in a number of places. It may be on an appliance, within the cord or plug linking it to the main circuit, on the main circuitry itself or at the fusebox. Let's start at the appliance end of things. If something went bang as you switched the appliance on, unplug it immediately; the fault is probably on the appliance itself. If it simply stopped working, try plugging it in at another socket; if it goes, there's a fault on the circuit feeding the original socket. If it doesn't go, either the second socket is on the same faulty circuit as the first one (which we'll come to later) or there may be a fault in the link between appliance and the socket — loose connections where the cores are connected to either the plug or the appliance itself, or a damaged cord (both these electrical problems are caused by abuse of the cord in use).

Plug and cord connections
The next step is to check the cord connections within the plug and the appliance. The connections at plug terminals are particularly prone to damage if the plug's cord grip is not doing its job; a tug on the cord can then break the cores, cutting the power and possibly causing a short circuit. If the connections are weak or damaged, disconnect them, cut back the sheathing and insulation and remake the connections. Make sure that the cord is correctly anchored within the body of the plug before replacing the cover.

If the plug contains a fuse, test that it has not blown by using a continuity tester, or by holding it across the open end of a switched-on metal-cased flashlight — see *Ready Reference*. Replace a blown fuse with a new one of the correct current rating.

Next, check the cord connections within the appliance itself. Always unplug an appliance before opening it up to gain access to the terminal block, and then remake any doubtful-looking connections by cutting off the end of the cord and stripping back the outer and inner insulation carefully to expose fresh conductor strands. If the cord itself is worn or damaged, take this opportunity to fit new cord of the correct type and current rating. Make sure you re-use any grommets,

REWIRING A PLUG

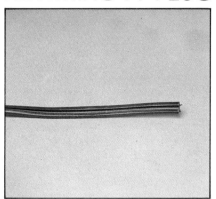

Should the plug on your cord become frayed or the prongs broken, a repair is simple with some of the modern plugs. First cut the cord straight. Don't slit or strip wire.

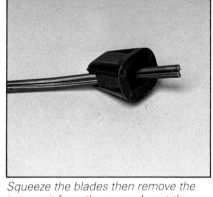

Squeeze the blades then remove the inner unit from the cover. Insert the wire through the hole in the back of the cover.

Spread the blades apart with your fingers. Push the wire as far as possible into the opening at the back of the inner unit.

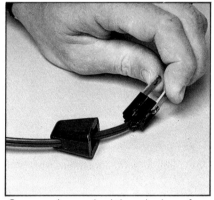

Once you've pushed the wire in as far as it can go, squeeze the blades together. This action forces the blades to pierce through the wire.

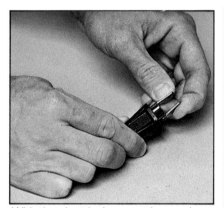

With the electrical connection made by forcing a section of the blades through the wire, push the inner unit back into the cover.

Ready Reference

COMMON FAULTS

Many electrical breakdowns in the home are caused by only a few common faults. These include:

● overloading of circuits, causing the circuit fuse to blow or the circuit breakers to trip
● short circuits, where the current by-passes its proper route because of failed insulation or contact between cable or cord cores; the resulting high current flow creates heat and blows the fuse
● grounding faults, where insulation breaks down and allows the metal body of an appliance to become live, causing a shock to the user if the appliance is not properly grounded, and blowing a fuse
● poor connections causing overheating that can lead to a fire and to short circuits and grounding faults.

TIP: TESTING FUSES

You can test suspect cartridge fuses by holding them across the open end of a switched-on metal-cased flashlight, with one end on the casing and the other on the battery. A sound fuse will light the flashlight.

CHOOSE THE RIGHT CORD

When fitting new cord to an appliance, it's important to choose the correct type and current rating.

---

heat-resistant sleeving, special captive washers and the like that were fitted to the appliance.

Lastly, check the cord continuity; it is possible that damage to the cord itself has broken one of the cores within the outer sheathing. Again use a continuity tester for this, holding the two probes against opposite ends of each core in turn, or use your metal-cased flashlight again, touching one core to the case and the other to the battery. Replace the cord if *any* core fails the test; the appliance may still work if the ground core is damaged, but the grounding will be lost and the appliance could become live and dangerous to anyone using it in the event of another fault developing in the future.

Lighting problems

Similar problems to these can also occur on lighting circuits, where the pendant cord link-ing ceiling caps to lampholders can become disconnected or faulty through accidental damage or old age. If replacing the bulb doesn't work, switch off the power at the main circuit and examine the condition of the cord. Look especially for bad or broken connections at the ceiling cap and within the lampholder. Replace the cord if the core insulation has become brittle, and fit a new lampholder if the plastic is discolored (both these problems are caused by heat from the light bulb). If the lampshade ring will not turn, you will have to cut this with a hacksaw.

Mending blown fuses

A circuit fuse will blow for two main reasons, overloading and short circuits — see *Ready Reference*. Too many appliances connected to a circuit will demand too much current, and this will melt the fuse. Similarly, a short circuit — where, for example, bare live and neutral wires touch — causes a current surge that blows the fuse.

If overloading caused the fuse to blow, the remedy is simple: disconnect all the equipment on the circuit, mend the fuse and avoid using too many high-wattage appliances at the same time in future. If a short circuit was to blame, you will have to hunt for the cause and rectify it before mending the fuse.

When a circuit breaker blows, after finding the cause of the overloading, simply move the lever back into position.

If you have cartridge fuses, all you have to do is find which cartridge has blown by removing the fuseholder and testing the cartridge with a continuity tester or metal-cased flashlight. A blown cartridge fuse should be replaced by a new one of the same current rating. Again, if the new fuse blows immediately, suspect a circuit fault.

Tracing circuit faults

If you have checked appliances, cords, plug connections and pendant lights, and a fault is still present, it is likely to be in the fixed wiring. Here, it is possible to track down one or two faults, but you may in the end have to call in a professional electrician.

The likeliest causes of circuit faults are damage to cables (perhaps caused by drilling holes in walls or by nailing down floorboards where cables run), ageing of cables (leading to insulation breakdown, and overheating) and faults at wiring accessories (light switches, socket outlets and so on). Let's look at the last one first, simply because such items are at least easily accessible.

If the cable cores are not properly stripped and connected within the accessory, short circuits or ground faults can develop. To check a suspect accessory such as a socket outlet, isolate the circuit, unscrew the faceplate and examine the terminal connections and the insulation. Ensure that each core is firmly held in its correct terminal, and that each core has insulation right up to the terminal, so that it cannot touch another core or any bare metal. There is usually enough slack on the main circuit cable to allow you to trim over-long cores back slightly. Try not to double over the cable as you ease the faceplate back into position; over-full boxes can lead to short circuits and damage to cable and core insulation ... and more trouble. You can carry out similar checks at light switches and ceiling caps. Any damaged accessories you find should be replaced immediately with new ones.

Damage to cables is relatively easy to cure provided that you can find where the damage is. If you drilled or nailed through a cable, you will of course be able to pin-point it immediately. Cable beneath floorboards can be repaired simply by isolating the cir-

REPLACING CORD

1 To replace damaged cord, remove the appropriate cover plate or panel from the appliance. Make a note of which core goes where before undoing it.

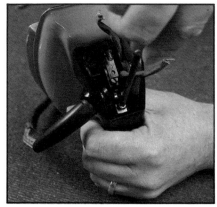

2 Loosen the cord grip within the appliance and withdraw the old cord. Here heat-resisting sleeving has been fitted; save this for re-use.

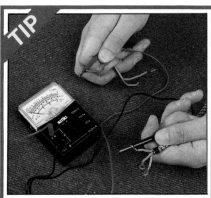

3 If you suspect that the cores within apparently undamaged cord are broken, test each core in turn with a continuity tester.

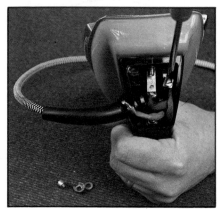

4 Connect in the new cord by reversing the disconnection sequence, re-using grommets, sleeving and washers. Make sure each connection is secure.

cuit, cutting the cable completely at the point of damage and using a three-terminal junction box to link the cut ends. Cable buried in plaster must be cut out and a new length of cable inserted between adjacent accessories to replace the damaged length. Where this would involve a long length of cable (on a run to a remote socket, for example) it is acceptable to use junction boxes in nearby floor or ceiling voids to connect in the new length of cable.

If you are unable to trace an electrical fault after checking all the points already described, call in a professional electrician who will be able to use specialist test equipment to locate the fault. Do *not* attempt to bypass a fault with a makeshift wiring arrangement,

and NEVER use any conducting foreign body such as a nail to restore power to a circuit whose fuse keeps blowing. Such tricks can kill.

Regular maintenance

You will find that a little common-sense maintenance work will help to prevent a lot of minor electrical faults from occurring at all. For example, it's well worth spending a couple of hours every so often checking the condition of the cord on portable appliances (especially those heavily used, such as kettles, irons, hair driers and the like) and the connections within plugs. Also, make a point of replacing immediately any electrical accessory that is in any way damaged.

FUSE TYPES

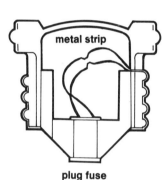

plug fuse

A break in the metal strip that shows at the top of the fuse means a blown fuse.

metal strip

time delay fuse

Similar to a plug fuse but the spring allows for a temporary overload of power.

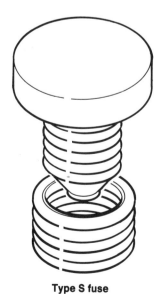

Type S fuse

cartridge fuses

Ready Reference

CHECKLIST FOR ACTION

When something goes wrong with your electrics, use this checklist to identify or eliminate the commonest potential causes of trouble.

Fault 1
Pendant light doesn't work
Action·
● replace bulb
● check lighting circuit fuse
● check cord connections at lampholder and ceiling cap
● check wire continuity.

Fault 2
● check wire continuity
● check power circuit fuse

Fault 3
Whole circuit is dead
Action
● switch off all lights/disconnect all appliances on circuit
● replace fuse
● switch on lights/plug in appliances one by one and note which blows fuse again
● isolate offending light/appliance, and see Faults 1 and 2 (above)
● check wiring accessories on circuit for causes of short circuits
● replace damaged cable if pierced by nail or drill
● call qualified electrician for help.

Fault 4
Whole system is dead
Action
● check for local power cut
● reset ELCB if fitted to system (and see Faults 1, 2 and 3 if ELCB cannot be reset)
● call electricity board (main service fuse may have blown).

Fault 5
Electric shock received
Action
● try to turn off the power
● use wooden broom handle or stick to push victim away from electrical contact
● keep victim warm
● if victim is conscious, keep warm and call a doctor; don't give brandy or food
● if breathing or heartbeat has stopped, CALL AN AMBULANCE and give artificial respiration or cardiac massage.

RUNNING CABLE

The hardest part of the average electrical job is running the cables: it takes up a lot of time and a lot of effort. But there are certain techniques used by experts which can make it much easier.

Before you get involved in the details of how to install the wiring, there's one simple question you must answer. Does it matter if the cable runs show? This is because there are only two approaches to the job of running cable. Either you fix the cable to the surface of the wall, or you conceal it. The first option is far quicker and easier but doesn't look particularly attractive; it's good enough for use in, say, an understairs cupboard. For a neater finish, using this method, you can smarten up the cable runs by boxing them in with some trunking. Many people, however, prefer to conceal the wiring completely by taking it under the floor, over the ceiling, or in walls.

TYPICAL CABLE RUNS

More and more electrical equipment is now being used in the home. And the chances are that sooner or later you will want to install a new receptacle, wall or ceiling light, or another switch. In which case you will have to get power to your new accessory. To do that will involve running cable from an existing circuit or installing a completely new one. Running cable to a new appliance can be the hardest part of any job and, as the illustration on the right shows, you will be involved in trailing cable across the roof space or ceiling void, channelling it down walls and threading it behind partitions as well as taking it under floorboards. But it's much easier than it seems. There are a number of tricks of the trade that will make any electrical job simpler and less time consuming. For example, once you can 'fish' cable, the daunting task of running it under a floor is simple.

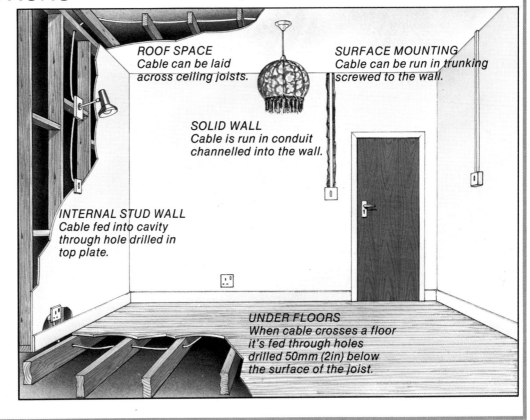

ROOF SPACE
Cable can be laid across ceiling joists.

SURFACE MOUNTING
Cable can be run in trunking screwed to the wall.

SOLID WALL
Cable is run in conduit channelled into the wall.

INTERNAL STUD WALL
Cable fed into cavity through hole drilled in top plate.

UNDER FLOORS
When cable crosses a floor it's fed through holes drilled 50mm (2in) below the surface of the joist.

SURFACE MOUNTING CABLE

1 To run cable in trunking, cut the trunking to length and fix the channel half to the wall with screws and wall plugs at 450mm (18in) centers.

2 Run the cable and press it firmly into the channel as far as it will go, carefully smoothing it out to avoid kinks and twists.

3 Next, snap the trunking's capping piece over the channelling, tapping it firmly along its length with your hand to lock it into place.

4 If the cable is to be on show, merely secure it every 225mm (9in) with cable clips. Fit them over the cable and drive home the fixing pins.

Ready Reference

RUNNING CABLE

You can mount cable:
● on the surface of a wall or ceiling
● concealed within the wall, above the ceiling or below the floor.

SURFACE-MOUNTED CABLE

This should be run above baseboards, round window and door frames and in the corners of rooms to disguise the run and protect the cable. Never run cable across a floor.

Fix the cable in place every 225mm (9in) with cable clips. Make sure the cable isn't kinked or twisted.

For a neater finish run the cable in PVC trunking, which you can cut to length using a hacksaw. Fix the channel part of the trunking to the wall first with screws and wall plugs at roughly 450mm (18in) centers. Then lay in the cable and clip the cover in position — tap it with your fist to ensure a tight fixing.

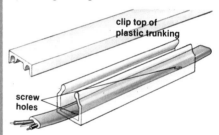

clip top of
plastic trunking

screw
holes

CONCEALED WIRING

To conceal a cable in a solid wall run it down a channel (chase) chopped in the surface and plaster over it. Run the cable in conduit and plaster this into the channel.

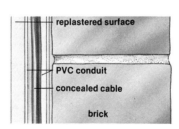

replastered surface

PVC conduit

concealed cable

brick

Concealed wiring should always be run vertically or horizontally from the fitting it supplies; never run it diagonally. This makes it easier to trace the runs in the future, when the wall has been decorated, and will prevent you drilling into the cable.

Planning the route

Having made your decision you must now work out a suitable route for the cable to follow.

If it is to be surface-mounted — with or without trunking — run the cable around window and door frames, just above base-boards and picture rails, down the corners of the room, or along the angle between wall and ceiling. This not only helps conceal the cable's presence, but also protects it against accidental damage. This last point is most important, and is the reason why you must never run cable over a floor.

With concealed wiring, the position is more complicated. When running cable under a floor or above a ceiling, you must allow for the direction in which the joists run — normally at right angles to the floorboards — and use an indirect route, taking it parallel to the joists and/or at right angles to them.

When running cable within a wall, the cable should *always* run vertically or horizontally from whatever it supplies, *never* diagonally.

Surface-mounting techniques

If you are leaving the cable on show, all you need do is cut it to length, and fix it to the surface with a cable clip about every 225mm (9in), making sure it is free from kinks and twists. With modern cable clips, simply fit the groove in the plastic block over the cable and drive home the small pin provided.

Surface mounting cable within trunking involves a bit more work. Having obtained the right size of PVC trunking, build up the run a section at a time, cutting the trunking to length with a hacksaw. Once each piece is cut, separate it into its two parts – the channelling and capping – and fix the channel to the wall with screws and wall plugs at roughly 450mm (18in) intervals (you may have to drill screw clearance holes in the channelling yourself).

Continue in this way until the run is complete. Turn corners by using store-bought fittings or by angling the ends of two pieces of trunking to form a neatly mitred joint, then run the cable. Press this firmly into the channel, and finish off by snapping the capping pieces firmly into place.

Concealing cables in walls

There are two ways to conceal cable in a wall. With a solid wall, chop a channel (called a 'chase') out of the plaster using a hammer and chisel, carefully continuing this behind any baseboards, picture rails, and coverings. Fit a length of conduit into the chase and run the cable through this before replastering.

To continue the run either above the ceiling or through the floor before you position the conduit, use a long drill bit so you can drill through the floor behind the baseboard. If a joist blocks the hole, angle the drill sufficiently to avoid it.

With a hollow internal partition wall, the job is rather easier, because you can run the cable within the cavity.

First drill a hole in the wall where the cable is to emerge, making sure you go right through into the cavity. Your next step is to gain access to the timber 'plate' at the very top of the wall, either by going up into the attic, or by lifting floorboards in the room above. Drill a 19mm (3/4in) hole through the plate, at a point vertically above the first hole, or as near vertically above it as possible.

All that remains is to tie the cable you wish to run to a length of wire — and then to tie the free end of this wire to a length of string. To the free end of the string, tie a small weight, and drop the weight through the hole at the top of the wall. Then all you do is make a hook in a piece of stout wire, insert it in the cavity, catch hold of the string and pull it (and in turn the draw wire and cable) through the hole in the room below.

What are the snags? There are two. You may find that, at some point between the two holes, the cavity is blocked by a horizontal board. If this happens, try to reach the board from above with a long auger bit (you should be able to rent one) and drill through it. Failing that, chisel through the wall surface, cut a notch in the side of the board, pass the cable through the notch, and then make good.

The second snag is that you may not be able to reach the top plate to drill it. In which case, either give up the ideas of having concealed wiring, or try a variation on the second method used to run cable into the cavity from below the floor.

CHASING OUT SOLID WALLS

1 *Mark out the cable run using a length of conduit, and chop a channel ('chase') in the wall to receive it, using a hammer and a chisel.*

2 *Continue the chase behind any coving, baseboard, or picture rail by chipping out the plaster there with a long, narrow cold chisel.*

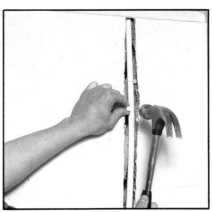

3 *Cut a length of conduit to fit, and lay it in the chase, securing it temporarily with nails driven into the wall's mortar joints.*

4 *Pull the cable through the conduit, then make good the wall by filling in over the conduit with plaster or cellulose filler.*

Here, it is sometimes possible to lift a couple of floorboards and drill up through the plate forming the bottom of the wall. Failing that you have to take a very long drill bit, drill through the wall into the cavity, then continue drilling through into the wooden plate. You can now use the weighted string trick to feed the cable in through the hole in the wall, and out under the floor.

Running cable beneath a floor

The technique for running cable beneath a suspended wood floor depends on whether the floor is on an upper storey and so has a ceiling underneath, or is on a ground floor with empty space below. If it's a ground floor, it may be possible to crawl underneath and secure the cable to the sides of the joists with cable clips, or to pass it through 19mm (3/4in) diameter holes drilled in the joists at

least 50mm (2in) below their top edge. This prevents anyone nailing into the floor and hitting the cable.

If you cannot crawl underneath, then the cable can be left loose in the void. But how do you run it without lifting the entire floor? The answer is you use another trick, called 'fishing'.

For this, you need a piece of stiff but reasonably flexible galvanized wire, say 14 standard wire gauge (swg), rather longer than the intended cable run, and a piece of thicker, more rigid wire, about 1m (3ft) in length. Each piece should have one end bent to form a hook.

Lift a floorboard at each end of the proposed cable run and feed the longer piece of wire, hook end first, into the void through one of the resulting gaps in the floor. Hook it out through the second gap using the shorter

COPING WITH STUD WALLS

1 *Drill a hole in the wall where the cable is to emerge, then bore a second hole in the wooden plate forming the top of the wall.*

2 *Tie a weight to a length of string and lower this through the hole in the wall plate. Tie the free end of the string to a wire.*

3 *If the weight gets blocked on its way to the hole in the wall, use a long auger bit to drill through the board obstructing it.*

4 *Fish out the weighted string through the hole in the wall, using a piece of wire bent to form a hook. Now, pull through the draw wire.*

5 *Tie the draw wire to the cable you wish to run, then return to the hole in the wall's top plate, and use the string to pull up the draw wire.*

6 *Then use the draw wire to pull the length of cable through. Remember, do this smoothly and don't use force if there's an obstruction.*

Ready Reference

TRICKS OF THE TRADE

Hollow internal partition wall

Drill a hole in the top or bottom plate, then drill another in the wall where the cable is to emerge. Drop a weighted piece of string through one of the holes and hook it out through the other. Use this to pull through a wire which is attached to the cable.

● if the weighted piece of string gets obstructed on its way to the hole in the wall, use a long auger bit to drill through the board.

● don't pull the cable through with the weighted string – the string tends to snap

● never run cable down the cavity of an external wall– treat these as solid walls.

Under floors

Use a technique known as fishing:
● lift the floorboards at either end of the run
● thread stiff wire beneath the floor through one hole and hook it out of the other with another piece of wire
● use the longer piece of wire to pull the cable through.

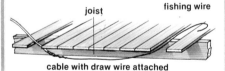

joist   fishing wire

cable with draw wire attached

cable pulled through

● if there's a gap beneath a ground floor you can 'fish' the cable diagonally across the room under the joist

● if the gap under the joists is large enough you can crawl in the space clipping the cable to the joists

● where the cable crosses the joists at right angles, run it through holes drilled 50mm (2in) below their top edges.

Over ceilings

If you can get above the ceiling into a loft, you can clip the cables to the joists. Otherwise you'll have to 'fish' the cable across (see above).

If you can't get above the ceiling and fishing doesn't work you'll have to surface-mount the cable.

piece of wire, and use it to pull through the cable in the same way as the wire used to pull cable through a hollow wall.

This technique is also used where there is a ceiling below the floor, and where you wish to run cable parallel to the joists, but in this case, check for any ribs and struts between the joists which might stop the fish wire getting through. Do this with the aid of a small mirror and a flashlight. If there is an obstruction, lift the floorboard above it, and drill a hole through which the cable can pass.

If the cable is to run at right angles to the joists, lift the floorboard above the line of the cable run, and feed the cable through holes drilled in the joists, 50mm (2in) below their top edge.

And what about solid floors? Obviously there is no way to run cable beneath these. Instead run the cable around the walls of the room, surface-mounting it just above the baseboard.

Running cable above a ceiling
Running cable above a ceiling is essentially the same as running it below a suspended wood floor. In fact, if there is a floor above the ceiling, it is generally easier to tackle the job from there, rather than from the room below.

If running the cable above the ceiling means taking it into the attic, then you can tackle it in much the same way as if you were running it below a suspended ground floor. If you cannot gain access to the attic, fish the cable through. If you can get into the attic, run the cable by hand, clipping it to the sides of the joists where it runs parallel to them.

You can run the cable at right angles to the joists by passing it through holes as already described.

Unfortunately, there are situations in which running cable above a ceiling is almost impossible. The main ones are where the ceiling is solid concrete, as in many modern apartments; where the ceiling is below a flat roof; and where, although there is a floor above the ceiling, you can't get at it (again this applies mainly to apartments).

In the last two instances, if you intend the cable to run parallel to the joists, you may be able to fish it through. If not, you will have to treat the ceiling as if it were solid, and that means surface mounting the cable.

ELECTRICAL SYSTEM LAYOUT

Understanding how your electrical system works will provide you with a healthy respect for electricity while minimizing your fear of any improvement or repair work.

Working with electricity need not be hazardous as long as strict safety practices are followed. Electrical work must be done to code. Government electrical codes regulate the materials that can be used and how those materials should be used. Some municipalities prohibit anyone but a qualified electrician from handling any electrical work, while others demand an electrical inspection before your repairs or improvement can begin.

Always make sure the power is shut off before handling any wires. Test the outlet to make sure there's no electrical feed before beginning any work. And always use only approved parts for an electrical system.

Electricity is powerful and deserves respect. Should you doubt your abilities to handle any electrical repair, call in a licensed electrician. However, your fear of electricity shouldn't be so great that it will prevent you from changing a blown fuse.

Electricity travels into the home under pressure, measured in voltage. Most homes have an electrical power pressure of 120/240 volts. The electricity enters the home from electrical wiring outside through the meter, which measures a home's electrical service use, and into the service panel, usually located in the basement. From the panel, charged power surges through a series of circuits to the various outlets in your home. Spent power returns through a different wire on the same circuit and out into the service entrance wires or to the earth by means of a ground.

While electrical pressure is measured in volts, the rate at which the power is distributed to an outlet is measured in amperes. The number of amps is limited by the size of the wire the power flows through. A larger wire allows a larger amperage to travel to an outlet. However, excess power in a wire can cause that wire to overheat. Therefore the fuse size must match the wire size to prevent fires. A 15-amp fuse must be used with wire meant to carry 15 amps of power. Any excess amperage running through the cable will cause the fuse to blow. A larger fuse on a 15-amp service will allow excess power through the wire, creating a fire hazard.

Most home appliances operate on a 120-volt service, although some heavy-duty appliances such as stoves and driers need a 240-volt service. These heavy-duty appliances have their own circuits.

A circuit is a length of wire that carries a current to a number of outlets in the house.

Each circuit is safeguarded by a fuse or a circuit breaker which will blow or trip if excess power is admitted to the circuit. Too many outlets in use on one circuit will create excess power. For example, in a 15-amp circuit, the amperage of all the appliances in use on that circuit cannot exceed 15. If the

ELECTRICAL CIRCUITS

A series of circuits supply electricity to the outlets in your home. If fuses constantly blow, lights flicker, or you use too many extension cords, you *should consider installing extra circuits to spread the electrical load. Circuits should be designed so that only 1650 watts are carried on a 15 amp fuse.*

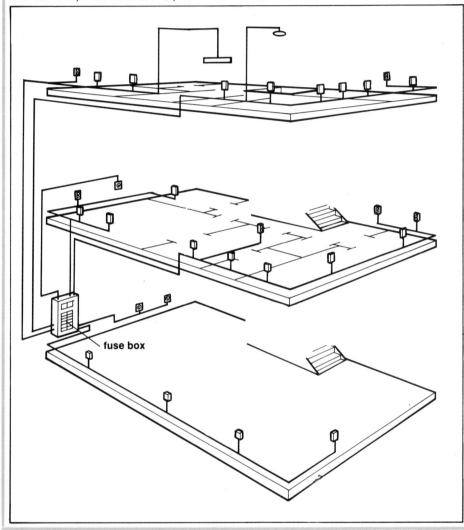

fuse box

number exceeds 15 amps and the appliances are turned on, a fuse will blow every time.

Different appliances have different amperage ratings, and all it takes to blow a fuse is to turn on two high-amperage appliances. Should you find your fuses blow frequently, an improved electrical service is in order. A kitchen, for example, needs at least two circuits, other than those for the stove and refrigerator, since several small appliances are often in operation at the same time.

Older homes, particularly those over 20 years old, usually need an updated wiring service to handle the electrical draw of all our modern appliances.

The ideal electrical service in today's homes is a 200-amp service. This should be plenty to handle all your electrical needs.

Other than frequently blown fuses, a poor electrical service can be recognized by lights flickering when appliances are turned on, appliances that don't operate at full power, and the use of too many extension cords.

If your house displays any of these symptoms, improvement to your electrical system is in order.

GROUNDED WIRING

All electrical codes require grounded wiring to prevent fatal shocks from faulty switches.

Faulty switches, outlets and motors can leak electrical current without affecting the fuse or circuit breaker. Since power continues to surge through the wires, the leak needs an outlet. Pulled by the earth's magnetic force, this leaking current will search for the quickest route to the earth. If you happen to be touching the faulty switch as the current is leaking, you become the route to the earth and serious injury can result.

This is why all codes require equipment needing a powerful current to be grounded, so that any leaking current will find a safe route to the earth.

The service panel in your home is grounded by a wire connecting the panel to a rod in the earth. Frequently, the ground wire is attached to a water supply pipe leading into the ground. If your wiring system is grounded, then all metal outlets, switches and cables are connected to the grounding terminals in the fuse box. The use of a three-prong cord on an appliance continues the grounding right into the appliance.

To check to see if your system is grounded, look at the wiring in your house. Non-metallic cable wiring should have an unsheathed third wire connected to electrical outlet boxes. The use of BX cable means your system is grounded, since the metallic sheathing on this type of cable acts as a grounding conductor, as does any metal conduit that holds your wiring system. Three-prong electrical outlets should also be installed in the house, to carry the grounding into the appliances. Never use a grounded three-prong plug in an outlet that doesn't allow for the grounding prong. Never remove the third prong from the appliance plug.

In household wiring systems, the wires are coded for safety. In a 120-volt system, the neutral wire is white, the hot wire is a color other than white. Both wires are live. In a 240-volt system two different-colored wires are used but neither should be white. The ground wire in your system should be bare.

HOW THE INTERRUPTER WORKS

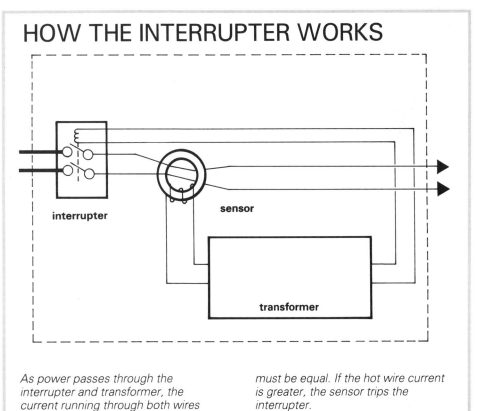

As power passes through the interrupter and transformer, the current running through both wires must be equal. If the hot wire current is greater, the sensor trips the interrupter.

OUTDOOR WIRING

Installing outdoor outlets is no more difficult than indoor wiring. However, there are extra safety regulations that must be followed.

We're a nation equipped with electronic gizmos. While at one time the interior of the house was the domain of electricity, there's an increasing need for power outdoors to handle our lawn mowers, lights and power tools.

If you're living in an older home without an electrical outlet outdoors, or if you want to add more outlets in your garden, outdoor wiring is simply a variation of the techniques used indoors. However, there are a few regulations unique to outdoor wiring that must be followed for safety considerations.

Outdoor receptacles must be waterproof, with a spring-loaded cover sealing the outlets, to prevent moisture penetration when not in use. The perimeter of the outlet must be sealed against the weather by a caulking compound.

Although grounding and wiring connections are the same for outdoor outlets as they are for indoor ones, all outdoor outlets must have a ground fault interrupter to protect against shock from a defective outlet. And all fixtures and wiring must be approved for outdoor wiring. All cords plugged into an electrical outlet must be the three-prong grounded type.

A new outdoor line can be tapped into an existing wire, code permitting, or can be run directly from the service panel. It's preferable to run your outdoor wiring on a new circuit, but you can tap into an existing general-purpose circuit that has a light electrical load on it. Remember that most electrical standards allow for a maximum of 12 outlets on a circuit. Always make sure the power is off before you work on a circuit.

When deciding on the placement of your new outlets, always consider the most advantageous location. Install an outlet on the side of the house to allow a cord to reach the front and back yards; put an outlet near the front door to handle Christmas lights; and, of course, outlets in the garage will provide power for block heaters or power tools. Freestanding outlets, those connected to posts in the ground, with wiring running underground to the service panel in your house, are most frequently located near patios or in gardens where you want some outdoor lighting.

Whichever outlet you decide to install, try to place it in an area that is protected from the elements. Don't position it in a spot that constantly floods or drifts with snow, and try to keep it out of a direct wind path.

Plan the number of outlets you'll need so you can avoid the use of extension cords, which can reduce the amount of current travelling to your electrical equipment. For safety considerations, install an indoor switch to turn your outdoor power on and off.

Number 12 or 14 gauge wire is used for outdoor wiring installations. The wire is run from the service panel to a junction box located on the inside wall at the spot where you'll install the outdoor receptacle. Do not hook up the wire to the service panel until all wiring is completed.

Since most service panels are in the basement, you can run the wire along the ceiling joists either parallel to the joists, using cable clips to support the wire, or at right angles to the joists through predrilled holes. Locate your wire at least 7.5cm (3in) from the top and bottom of the joist, to avoid damage from any nails that might be driven into the floor above or the ceiling below at some point in the future. Make sure your wiring isn't touching any plumbing or heating pipes or any other wires that could create a hazardous situation.

Drill a hole through the foundation or

OUTDOOR WIRING

To determine where you might need outdoor electrical wiring, draw a sketch of your lot and plot in patio receptacles or lights, garage receptacles, front sidewalk lighting or garden lighting.

through the wall surface above the foundation. If drilling through the wall surface, make sure you drill between studs and make sure there's no wiring or plumbing in that spot.

The hole you drill needs to be large enough to contain the conduit through which the wire will run. The conduit should be long enough to attach to both the junction box inside the house and the receptacle on the outside.

The outlet box should be flush with the wall surface. Chip and cut away an area large enough to contain the box. Attach the conduit to the outlet box and the junction box inside the house, then caulk your outlet box in place.

You're now ready to make your wiring connections to the receptacle and the service panel. Remember that many electrical codes require a permit and inspection for any type of house wiring. Before you make your final electrical hook-up, you'll need to call an inspector.

Installing a freestanding outlet follows similar hook-up techniques, but you need to bury the cable below the ground, and the conduit pipe holding the outlet will need to be sup-

ported in a cement footing.

Check your electrical code to see how deep the wiring needs to be buried. In some areas you may have to dig a trench 60cm (24in) deep.

Try to dig your trench in a straight line from the hole in your wall to the outlet to avoid conduit joints. Dig your trench with a flat spade so that you can save the sod.

The conduit pipe supporting the outlet will have to be buried in a gravel-based concrete footing. Slope the concrete away from the conduit to help water drainage.

Your wiring may have to run through a conduit underground, or you may be able to use plastic-sheathed wiring approved for underground applications. The type you use depends on your electrical code.

Install the wiring, remembering the need for a ground fault interrupter, and refill your trench. The electrical hook-up is the same as for a wall-mounted outlet.

A wall-mounted light fixture is handled in the same manner as the wall receptacle, and a post-mounted light at the end of a driveway or sidewalk or in the garden uses the same techniques as a freestanding receptacle.

Exterior freestanding electrical outlets should be placed 45 to 50 cm (18 to 20 in) above the ground on a galvanized conduit supported in concrete.

INSTALLING AN OUTDOOR RECEPTACLE

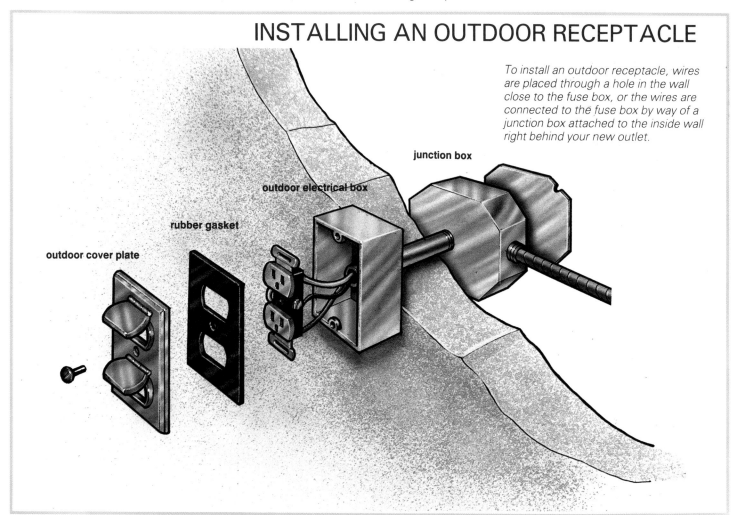

To install an outdoor receptacle, wires are placed through a hole in the wall close to the fuse box, or the wires are connected to the fuse box by way of a junction box attached to the inside wall right behind your new outlet.

junction box

outdoor electrical box

rubber gasket

outdoor cover plate

DOOR CHIMES

By following a few basic steps, you can install or repair door chime units.

Door chimes operate off low voltage. Power from 6 to 30 volts is enough to make your chimes ring. The normal 120-volt household current is stepped down to this low voltage by means of a transformer.

To install a new door chime, the transformer is first connected to a junction box close to the chime unit's location. Although the low voltage in door chimes will not give you a deadly shock, the power should be turned off before making any repairs. The connection of the transformer must be done with the power shut off. There are still 120 volts of current running through the junction box.

The transformer is mounted outside the junction box with the wires entering the box. White wires are attached to white wires, black wires to black.

The bell wire is connected to the transformer and runs through the house to the chime unit. The wires for the push button are connected to the chime unit and the transformer. All wires must be connected to the correct terminals on the chime unit.

Should the chimes fail to ring, start your troubleshooting with the push button. Unscrew the push button and jump the terminals. If the chimes ring, you need a new button. If the chimes fail to ring, the trouble is elsewhere in the system. Disconnect the wires from the push button and twist them together. This makes a connection that will allow the chimes to ring without the need of running to the door to push the button, saving you some time on your repair work.

Test the transformer next. Make sure the wires are connected properly. A faulty connection will prevent the chimes from sounding.

If there is no faulty connection, disconnect both wires from the transformer terminal and use a voltmeter to touch each terminal. If the voltmeter registers no reading, the transformer needs replacing.

Check the chime unit next for faulty connections. Test the chime terminals with a voltmeter. If there is a reading, you'll need to replace the chimes. If the chimes check out okay, as do all the other parts of the system, then you could have a broken wire that needs replacing.

INSTALLATION

Install a transformer at the nearest junction box. The transformer steps down the voltage from the house current to a 6 to 24 volt system to operate your chimes. Run the wires from the transformer to the chimes and to the exterior buttons. Make sure you install a transformer with enough voltage to operate your system.

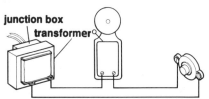

junction box
transformer

single button unit wiring diagram

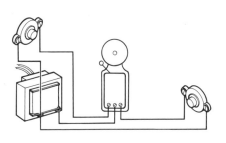

two button unit wiring diagram

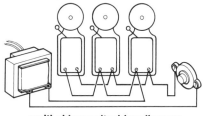

multi-chime unit wiring diagram

CHAPTER 9

Outdoor Improvements

BUILDING A DECK

A well-planned deck is simply an outdoor addition to your home and should provide both privacy and convenience.

A deck is a part of the house and must be as comfortable as any other room in your home. Although the deck is built for outdoor living, you want it to afford some privacy so you can either relax undisturbed or have a private outdoor spot for entertaining.

The first step in building a deck is the planning. Although this may seem obvious, there are several factors other than the structural techniques that need to be considered before you start to saw and hammer.

The location of the deck should be your first consideration. Will it be used as an extension of your living room for outdoor entertaining, or do you plan to use the deck as an eating area where it would be best located off the dining room or kitchen? Do you want to create an outdoor sitting room off the master bedroom, or will the deck be used for a play area and for sunbathing?

Your second consideration should be the solar orientation of the deck. You may want to use the deck for entertaining, but if it's a sunny spot your guests may find the heat unbearable. Conversely, if you want to use the deck for sunbathing, a shady location is less than ideal. In the summer, a deck on the west side of your house will gather the most sun. A southern exposure for your deck also means a warm spot but is the ideal location for an enclosed deck you can use all year round. Even in the winter, although the sun is low, it still shines from the south, allowing you to pick up some of the sun's warm winter rays through a glassed-in deck enclosure. A deck on the north side of your house will rarely receive warm sunlight, and a deck on the east will only receive the cooler morning sun.

The ideal situation for a deck then is to site it around your house on the north and west side or the east and south sides. This L-shaped deck will provide both sunny and shady spots to handle almost all your deck requirements. If your building code doesn't permit an L-shaped deck, or if you simply want a deck on one side of your house, you'll have to decide on the major use of your deck before you can determine its solar orientation.

Wind will also affect your comfort on the deck. Try to choose a location that is sheltered from wind. If you can't find a sheltered area, build a windscreen next to your deck, using trees or latticework fencing.

The size of your deck is an important consideration. Too small a deck won't give you the necessary room to handle large outdoor furniture, and too large a deck may be out of scale with your house and property. To get a feel for the size of deck you need, arrange your patio furniture in the spot you've chosen for the deck. Is there enough room to allow for both the furniture and for traffic patterns around the furniture?

A second way of determining the size of your deck is to draw the deck to scale. Start with some lined graph paper and use a scale of 25mm (½in) to 7.5cm (1ft). Draw the boundaries of your lot and add the outline of your house. Put in any trees, shrubs, gardens and walkways. Mark the location of doors and windows on your house outline.

Once everything is in place in the drawing, cut a piece of cardboard (to scale) the size you'd like your deck to be. Move this cardboard around the perimeter of the house outline on your drawing to find a suitable location. Remember that a door from the interior of the house to the deck is ideal, so you'll have to place your deck where there is an existing door or be prepared to install a new door in the location.

Once you have found a location, cut out cardboard to scale to represent your current outdoor furniture and possible future purchases. Place them on the deck to see if it will be large enough to accommodate everything that will be required of it. Built-in seating can be handled around the perimeter of the deck without wasting a lot of floor space.

Now is the time to consider the options for your deck. If you build your deck around trees or other plantings, you can give the appearance of a larger deck without the need of building one. You may also want to consider a multilevel deck with separate areas for eating and relaxing. Building in a barbecue or a sandbox are other options. The choice is up to you, and you should decide based on your needs and the size of the deck that can be accommodated on your lot.

Once you've arranged all the pieces on your drawing, you can then set up the actual boundaries of your deck to get a feel for the actual size. Pound a wood stake into the ground at the proposed four corners of your deck. Link the stakes with some heavy string and you'll have the perimeter. Make any adjustments to the size that you feel are necessary and transfer these changes to your drawing.

The final step in planning is to determine the look of your deck — multilevel, single level, on grade, raised, steps if necessary, built-in seating, planters, boards laid flat or on end, sides on the deck or not and the appearance these sides will take, and type and amount of wood. Check your neighbors' decks for ideas or search through books at the library. Some lumber companies offer special deck design services or will provide pamphlets with decking ideas. You can pull ideas from various deck designs to suit your purposes and have your lumber supplier help you with the quantities of wood you'll need.

Before starting construction, visit your local building permit department to see if a building permit is necessary. If it is, you'll have to present your plans to ensure that they're 'up to code', and your construction will require inspection along the way.

Building the deck

Although you can build decks from other material, wood is most commonly used. The

When planning your deck, consider the options. You can build a deck around a tree or you can have a multi- *level deck with separate areas for dining and relaxing. Decide on your needs – do you want privacy; large* *areas for entertaining; or a small, private outdoor room in which you can relax?*

wood you buy must be rot-resistant and impervious to termites and other insects. The most common choices for decking material are redwood, cedar and pressure-treated wood, although you may find cedar and redwood hard to come by and certainly more expensive than the pretreated wood. Should you use redwood or cedar on your deck, they can be left unstained to age naturally. Pressure-treated wood usually has a green cast and, unless you like the green look of the wood, it would be best to stain the deck with a waterproof semitransparent stain. The water-repellent stain offers a bit more protection against the weather.

Wood is sized in nominal measurements that are slightly larger than the actual measurements. For example, a 2 × 4 is actually 1½ by 3½. Be aware of these sizing differences when purchasing your wood so that you'll buy enough to handle your deck measurements. Use a construction-grade lumber for your deck. Anything less will be inadequate to handle the loads a deck must carry.

When buying your wood at the lumberyard, insist on selecting your own lumber. The wood you select should be free from defects such as knots, warps, cups or checking. You want straight, sturdy wood, and if you leave the choice of wood up to the lumberyard, there's no guarantee you'll get the best wood for your purposes.

Wood has a maximum stress point. This point is the weight the wood can bear without cracking. You'll need to know this weight-bearing load before you can determine the size of wood you need to buy and the post and beam structural configuration you'll need to support the deck. You won't need a course in engineering, however. Most local building departments will supply structural tables to make your decision easier.

We'll start our deck construction techniques with an on-grade deck. This is the easiest type of deck to build, because it doesn't require the digging of post holes or the pouring of concrete.

Your first step is to outline the area of your

deck by driving stakes into the ground at the corners of the deck. Join the stakes with some heavy string. Make sure your outline is square and true. Use a framing square for checking or use the following mathematical calculation. Measure exactly 91cm (3ft) from the corner along one of the strings and mark the spot. Measure exactly 121cm (4ft) from the corner along the second string and mark. Measure the distance between the two marks. If the distance is exactly 152cm (5ft), your corner is square.

Dig out the earth within your outline to a depth of 10 or 12cm (4 or 5in) to provide a drainage layer. Tamp the soil firm. Add a 5cm (2in) layer of gravel for drainage and rake the gravel level. On top of the gravel add a 5 or 7.5cm (2 or 3in) layer of sand and rake level.

You'll want to control weed growth under your deck, and this can be done at this stage following one of two methods. The first is to apply a chemical weed-killer to the area within your outline. The second method, and one that will ensure you won't destroy the

MODULAR DECK

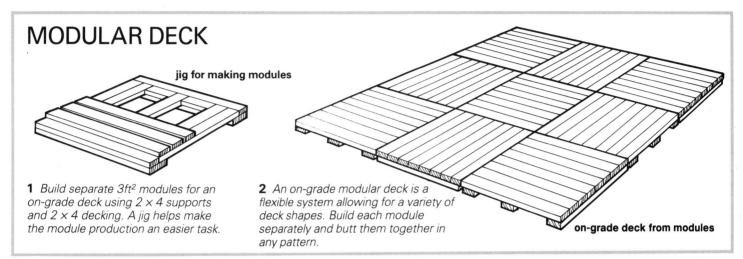

jig for making modules

1 *Build separate 3ft² modules for an on-grade deck using 2 × 4 supports and 2 × 4 decking. A jig helps make the module production an easier task.*

2 *An on-grade modular deck is a flexible system allowing for a variety of deck shapes. Build each module separately and butt them together in any pattern.*

on-grade deck from modules

lawn surrounding the deck with a chemical, is to apply a layer of polyethylene over the sand to fill the entire outline of your deck area. You'll need to perforate the plastic to allow for drainage and to prevent runoff. You can build your on-grade deck directly over this plastic or add another layer of gravel and sand, again making sure the surface is level.

An on-grade deck can be placed directly on top of this ground surface. Start the deck by installing 1 × 8s on edge around the perimeter of the deck. Make sure the board extends above grade even with the top surface of your planking. Ensure that the boards are square and true, then backfill the outside area to provide support.

On-grade decks without footings are usually made in .29m² (3ft²) modular units, which can rest directly on the ground. In cold climates where the ground shifts, modular units can move without a complete break-up of the decking.

To build a modular unit, construct a jig of four pieces of lumber, making sure the corners are square. Lay two pieces of 2 × 4 on opposite sides of the jig for runners, the base to which you'll nail your planking. Cut enough 2 × 4 planking to cover the runners either laid flat or on edge. Leave at least 60mm (¼in) between the planks for drainage and to allow for the expansion and contraction of wood. Nail the planks to the runners and you have your first module. Continue building modules in this manner until you have enough to fill your deck area.

Once all the units have been constructed, start laying them in place from one corner of the deck area. For a more attractive appearance, lay the modules with planking at right angles to each other. Make sure each unit is flat and level before proceeding to the next. Each unit should be butted firmly to the adjacent units.

Fill the area below the planks and between the runners with sand for additional support.

If the door leading from the house to your deck is above the ground, you can install

steps down to your on-grade deck or you can build a raised deck so that the deck floor sits flush with the door threshold, giving it the appearance of an extension of your house.

Raised decks are more difficult to build than on-grade decks. This is where the structural rules come into play.

The deck is made up of 2 × 4 or 2 × 6 planking nailed at right angles to 2 × 8 joists. The joists are secured at right angles across 2 × 12 beams, 2 × 8 braces can be nailed between the joists for support. One beam is bolted to each side of a 4 × 4 post, which is anchored in a concrete footing sitting below the frost line. The number of posts and beams needed will usually be dictated by building code specifications.

The raised deck is usually fastened to the house on one side by means of a 2 × 8 ledger rather than post and beam construction. The ledger is fastened into the studs of the house by means of lag screws or expansion bolts.

To build a raised deck, start by forming the outline of the deck with batter boards. Make sure the corner of the batter board is square, then attach string to the batter board so that the corner of the deck will be where the two strings intersect. Check for squareness, then drive a short stake into the ground at the corner. This will be where you dig your first post hole to accommodate the concrete footing, pillar and post. Mark the locations for the required number of posts along the strings.

You'll need to dig your holes deep enough to satisfy your building code requirements for footings. Remember that the holes need to be dug below the frost line. A firm base of earth is also required for the footings. Dig to tight, firm soil or tamp your soil to ensure solidity.

Footings are poured concrete 15 to 20cm (6 to 8in) thick and 30 to 60cm (1 to 2ft) in diameter placed 30 cm (1ft) below the frost line. Concrete piers are poured on top of the footings to extend 15 to 20cm (6 to 8in) above ground level. While the pier concrete

is still wet, a post anchor is embedded in the concrete, which will later support the wood post. A concrete pier eliminates the need to bury the post in the ground and will prevent wood rot.

The convenient way to handle your concrete is to buy premixed bags, to which you add water following the instructions on the bag. One 18kg (40lb) bag of premix will provide about 1 cubic yard of concrete. Buy footing and pillar concrete molds at your building supply dealer.

Once the concrete has set with the post anchor in place, fit your posts into the anchors, level them, and nail the boards in place. Attach braces to support the posts while you construct the deck.

Next, install the ledger board to your house. This 2 × 8 board is fastened into the studs or masonry of your house, eliminating the need for a row of footings and posts. The ledger is levelled and fastened securely to the house. Make sure the ledger is fastened below the door threshold at a distance equal to the width of your deck planking.

Once the ledger is fastened, you can accurately measure for the height of your posts. The posts you've already attached to the pillars should have enough excess height on them to allow cutting. This will ensure a level deck over the uneven ground. Place a nail at the bottom of the ledger board, in line with the row of posts. Run a string from the nail to the last post, levelling the string with a line level. Mark the posts at the string.

Before you cut your posts, you'll need to determine the method you'll use to attach the beams. The first method is to attach a 2 × 12 beam to each side of the post, bolting the beams together through the post. If this method is used, the mark you've just placed on your post will be the cut line and is also the placement line for the top of the beams. The other method is to place the two beams together, fitting them into post caps at the top of each post, then nailing through the post cap into the beams. If you choose this method, a new cut line will have to be established on the post, down from your original mark the width of the beams.

To prevent lateral movement of the deck, brace the post and beams using a 2 × 4 nailed at a 45° angle between the post and the beam.

Measure and mark where the joists will cross the beams and butt against the ledger. These marks will indicate where the joist hangers will need to be nailed to the ledger and where the beam saddles will be nailed to support the joists over the beams. Use the beam saddles and joist hangers for securing the joists instead of toenailing the boards. Nailing will provide a weaker fastening than the hangers and saddles. Make sure your building code has been followed for the proper joist spans.

Each end of the deck has a joist fitted to it, and another joist header or deck skirting board is attached to the open end of the deck to hide the joist ends.

You're now ready to lay your deck planking. Start at the ledger, laying the first board over the top edge of the ledger then proceeding along the deck, spacing the boards about 60mm (¼in) apart for drainage. Use two nails to fasten each plank at each joist.

Building codes will often require a railing around the deck. This railing is usually about 91cm (3ft) high and can be built by adding posts and rails after the main deck is finished or, in the original construction, by extending the posts from the concrete pillar up through the deck to a height 91cm (3ft) above the deck floor. Railings added after the deck has been built should have the posts bolted into place.

If you need to add a stairway to your deck, make sure the treads are at least 22cm (9in) wide and the distance between the risers is no more than 20cm (8in). Whatever size you select, make sure the size remains the same for each step. Pour a concrete slab about 12cm (5in) thick the width of your stairway at the bottom of the steps. The bottom of the stringers will rest on this slab, while the top of the stringers are attached to the deck with framing anchors. Bolt 2 × 2 cleats to the stringers for the treads to rest on. Measure and level carefully before fastening the cleats. Cut the 2 × 12 treads and nail them to the cleats. The deck railing should also be continued down the steps for safety.

Maintaining the deck

The use of pressure-treated wood will guarantee that your wood will be resistant to rot and decay, the natural enemies of wood. Redwood or cedar is also rot-resistant but, as mentioned earlier, these types of wood are more expensive than pressure-treated wood and more difficult to find now that lumberyards seem to prefer stocking the treated wood.

RAILINGS

Railings are often required by building codes and usually the railings must be 1m (3ft) high. A railing can be added during or after original construction.

DECK STAIRWAY

The bottom of a deck stairway sits on a 12cm (5in) thick concrete slab while the top is attached to the deck. Treads rest on cleats fastened to the stringers.

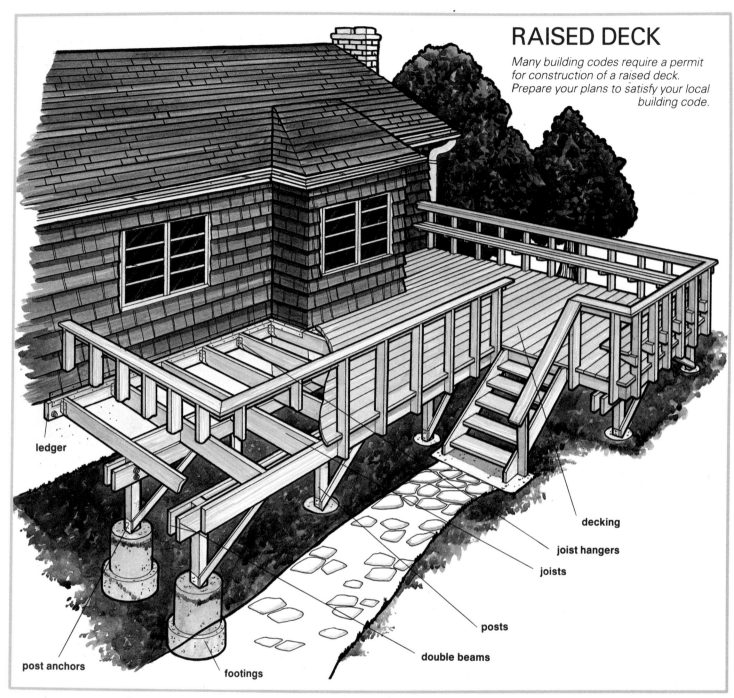

RAISED DECK

Many building codes require a permit for construction of a raised deck. Prepare your plans to satisfy your local building code.

ledger

decking

joist hangers

joists

posts

double beams

post anchors

footings

If you like the green cast of the pressure-treated wood, no further finish need be added to the deck. However, for extra protection, or to change the color of the wood, you could either spray or brush on some stain. Never paint a deck. Paint will not stand up to the wear that a deck receives and will soon crack and chip, creating the need for frequent repainting. Besides, if you've gone to all the trouble of building a deck out of wood, why not show off the beautiful grain?

You can finish your deck with an opaque stain which penetrates the wood and reveals the wood texture. However, the wood grain will be covered up by the solid pigments of the opaque stain. If you want both the texture and the grain of the wood to show through, use a semi-transparent stain.

Make sure the stain you buy is a penetrating water-repellent stain suitable for outdoor deck use. And try to buy a stain that resists mildew as well.

Unlike paint, which will likely need to be recoated annually and will also need to have the damaged paint coat scraped off before applying a new finish, stains will last from two to three years, perhaps longer depending on use, and can be renewed simply by washing the deck and restaining. Never use a varnish on a deck, for the same reasons that you wouldn't want to use paint. The varnish will chip, blister and peel and would need to be removed completely before you could restain.

To keep your deck clean, especially if you've stained with a dark color (footprints tend to leave gray marks on a dark-colored deck) use a stiff-bristled brush and scrub with a mild detergent. Hose the deck down to rinse off the detergent.

PATIOS

Garden seating areas can be formal with mortared joints, or informal with the bricks or stones resting on sand.

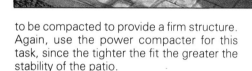

P atios are individual. They are designed to suit the needs of the user. They can be built close to the house for dining and entertaining. They can be built in the middle of the yard, surrounded by plants and shrubs for a relaxing conversation area. They can be small for intimate seating or large to handle a party. And they can be made from a variety of materials: brick, smooth concrete, textured concrete, stones, blocks, precast concrete tiles and even ceramic tiles.

Mortarless paving

One of the easiest types of patios to build is the mortarless paver patio. Bricks, precast concrete tiles and stones can be used for this type of patio. The paving stones are set on a bed of crushed limestone, which restricts weed growth and allows for proper drainage.

To build a mortarless patio, outline the perimeter of your area by driving stakes into the ground and joining the stakes with string. Dig the patio area to a depth of 12cm (5in) plus the thickness of the paver you'll be using. To allow for drainage, the patio should slope away from the house 3 to 6mm (⅛ to ¼in) for every 30cm (1ft). Should your patio not be located near the house, make the center of your patio the highest point and slope all sides away from the center. Place roofing felt on the area to inhibit plant growth. Overlap the seams by 15cm (6in).

You'll need to add an edging around your patio to prevent shifting of the pavers. Use treated wood or, if using brick, turn the bricks on end and bury them in a trench the perimeter of the patio. Make sure the top of the wood or brick edging will be flush with the surface of your patio.

Next add a 10cm (4in) layer of gravel covered with a 25mm (1in) layer of small stone screenings. Level the fill and compact it with a power compacter. These machines can be rented from most rental shops.

Cover the screenings with at least a 25mm (1in) layer of sand. Dampen the sand with spray from a garden hose.

Lay your bricks or stones in the chosen pattern, placing the pavers close together. You'll inevitably need to cut some of the pavers to fit the patio area. Cutters can be rented from rental shops to make light work of this task.

Once the bricks have been laid, they need to be compacted to provide a firm structure. Again, use the power compacter for this task, since the tighter the fit the greater the stability of the patio.

The last step is to sweep sand into all the small cracks between the pavers to fill the gaps and to provide extra support. Hose the patio clean and it's ready for use.

A word of caution: should you use clay bricks for your patio pavers, don't use limestone screenings for the base. The salts from the limestone will migrate through the brick, creating a discoloring and haze on the surface of the brick.

Pavers with mortar

A more formal look to your patio can be created by again using pavers, but this time setting the pavers in mortar to provide a smooth, strong surface.

If you live in a cold climate where the ground freezes and thaws, creating the potential for ground heaving, you'll need to provide a firm concrete base, with good drainage underneath, for your patio. Should you live in a milder climate, you can follow the same method as for the mortarless paving.

To create a patio in cold climates, you'll need to dig your patio area deep enough to allow for a 10cm (4in) concrete base and a 15cm (6in) layer of gravel underneath the concrete.

Dig your excavation, fasten a permanent or temporary edging around the perimeter, and apply a 15cm (6in) layer of crushed stone. Level the stone and pack it down firmly. Remember to pitch the surface for drainage. Place polyethylene sheeting over the stone, overlapping the seams of the sheeting by 15cm (6in). The plastic prevents moisture from seeping into the concrete. Next, apply wire reinforcement mesh. This

welded wire mesh reinforces the 10cm (4in) concrete layer that is poured directly on the mesh. Strike the concrete surface level. Use a flat 2 × 4 to strike off the concrete, moving the board back and forth as you advance. Let the concrete cure for several days.

Dry-lay your stones onto the concrete, starting in one corner. Leave about 6mm (¼ in) of space between the stone for the mortar. Make any necessary cuts, then remove a small section of stone and start applying mortar. Apply a layer of mortar (2 parts sand to 1 part cement), lay your stones and tamp them level. Once they're level, fill the joints with mortar and smooth with a jointing tool.

If you're not using a concrete slab base, apply a 50mm (2in) layer of sand to the gravel base, lay your stones, then tamp each stone into place, making sure it's level. Once the stones have been levelled, apply a dry mortar mixture of 4 parts sand and 1 part cement to the gaps between the stones. Use the edge of a board to tamp down the mortar, pressing firmly to ensure a good fill. Sweep the stones carefully then wet the surface with a fine spray keeping the area damp for 2 to 3 hours. Tool the joints. Once the mortar has hardened, rub off the excess from the stones using a stiff brush. Then, using a wet sponge, clean each stone, being careful not to touch the mortar.

When laying a brick patio with mortar, it's best to butter the edges of each brick with wet mortar as you lay them. Then shove the brick toward the previous one laid, leaving a distance of 6 to 12mm (¼ to ½ in) between bricks. Make sure you butter the edges with enough mortar to fill the gap. Keep laying the bricks, but after about an hour go back and tool the joints. Remember that mortar starts to set in about two hours. You can slice off the mortar to leave a flush joint or you can

BOND PATTERNS

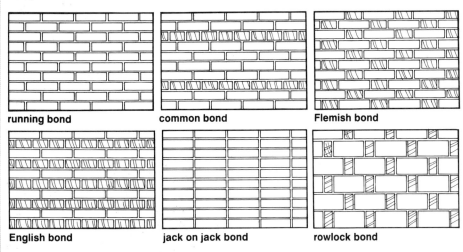

running bond   common bond   Flemish bond

English bond   jack on jack bond   rowlock bond

Several bond patterns can be used in laying a brick patio. The running bond is the most common, but you can also use the others shown in the illustration along with herringbone and square patterns.

PATIO FOUNDATION

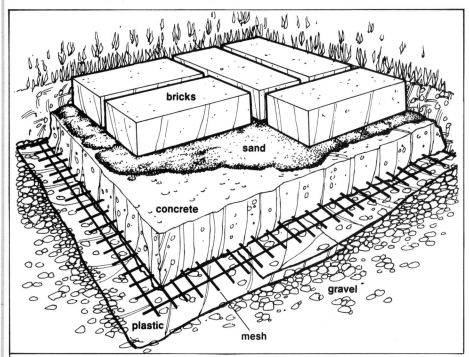

bricks

sand

concrete

gravel

plastic   mesh

For a stone or brick patio to be durable, care must be taken in building the foundation. In cold climates, you'll need to add a concrete base to prevent heaving. Dig deep enough to allow for a layer of gravel on a firm soil base, plastic, concrete, sand and bricks.

PATIO BORDER

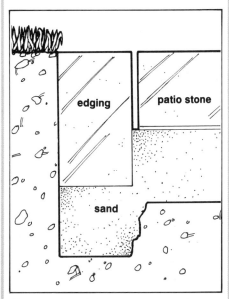

edging   patio stone

sand

To keep the bricks on your mortarless patio from shifting, you'll need to install a border or edging. You can use wood or a row of bricks placed on end. Dig a trench about 15cm (6in) wide to allow for the width of the brick plus a 5cm (2in) layer of sand. Make sure edging is flush with the top of the patio.

draw a dowel along the mortar to make a concave joint.

Mortar stains on the brick can be removed with a mixture of 10 parts water to 1 part muriatic acid. Scrub the acid solution over the brick with a stiff brush. Wear rubber gloves, goggles and old clothes to protect yourself against acid burns. Don't use muriatic acid on stone patios; the acid could stain the stones.

WORKING WITH CONCRETE

Knowing how to handle concrete will ensure a long life for your concrete driveway, sidewalk or patio.

Concrete is a mixture of Portland cement, sand, gravel and water, mixed in measured proportions to form a durable and fairly inexpensive building material. Portland cement is a fine powder which, when mixed with water, forms a cement paste that binds the gravel and sand (aggregates) together to form concrete. The aggregates form about 75 percent of the concrete, and the ratio of the aggregates used in the mixture determines the strength of the concrete.

The fine aggregate (sand) must be clean and free of clay or vegetable matter, which will prevent the cement paste from bonding the aggregates. To test for clean sand, place an inch or two of your sand in a jar and fill it with water. Shake the contents and let the jar sit overnight. If the silt at the top of the jar is more than 3mm (⅛in) thick, the sand is not clean enough to use; it will need to be washed. Sand used for mortar is too fine for concrete work.

The coarse aggregate (gravel or stone) should be 6 to 37mm (¼ to 1½in) thick and must be clean.

The fine aggregate fills the spaces around the coarse aggregate for a tight bond.

Mixing concrete

You can buy ready-mixed concrete or you can buy the aggregates and cement to mix your own. In either case, the addition of the right amount of water is essential to ensure the durability and strength of the concrete. Too much water will make the concrete weak and porous; too little will make the concrete too stiff to work.

Air-entrained concrete is only available as a ready mix. This concrete contains millions of tiny bubbles, which protect against scaling from the freezing and thawing cycle in cold climates, as well as providing protection from damage caused by rock salt. This concrete should be used on sidewalks and driveways in cold climates.

The concrete mixture should be dry enough to stick together without crumbling but should be a mushy consistency. The mixture should never be runny.

For concrete that doesn't demand water tightness and abrasion resistance, such as footings, foundation walls or retaining walls, the ratio of your dry mix should be 1 part cement to 3 parts sand and 4 parts gravel.

For a more critical concrete, use 1 part cement to 2 parts sand and 3 parts gravel.

To mix your ingredients, use a bucket as a measure. Fill the bucket with sand and level with a flat piece of wood. Dump the contents of the bucket onto a concrete slab or into a wheelbarrow, then fill, level and dump another bucket of sand. Fill and level a bucket of cement and add to the sand. Mix the two ingredients together then add three buckets of gravel and mix again. Make a depression in the center of your mixture and add water from a garden hose a little at a time, mixing the ingredients as you go. If you've added too much water, add more of the dry mixture in the same proportions as you originally mixed. Never add just cement, or sand or gravel. The proportions must be maintained in the concrete mixture.

To determine the amount of concrete you'll need to mix, measure the length and width of the area you plan to concrete and determine the thickness of the concrete. Measurements should be in feet, with the thickness measurement expressed in fractions of a foot. Multiply the numbers and divide by 27, which is the number of cubic feet in a cubic yard, and you have a figure that represents the number of cubic yards of concrete you'll need. For example, if the length of your area is 3ft, the width 4ft and the thickness of the concrete 3in (¼ft), then multiply 3 × 4 × ¼ and divide by 27. This gives you .12 cubic yards.

Building forms

Although building forms is an essential and exacting step in the pouring of concrete, it is also one of the most frustrating.

The form you use to brace the cement for the pour must be accurately constructed. It must be level, plumb and square. Your finished concrete will only be as accurate as your form. The form must also be braced solidly or it may collapse in mid-pour, creating a messy clean-up job and a waste of concrete.

But the frustrating part about the forms is that they're only temporary. You must take the time to create some exacting carpentry and structural components, then, once the concrete sets, the forms must be dismantled.

WALL BUILDING FORM

Use ¾in plywood for wall building forms supported every 60cm (2ft) with 2 × 4 stakes. Brace each stake with 2 × 4 to support the considerable weight of the concrete. Use 1 × 2 spacers between the two wall boards to provide equal spacing along the length of the wall form. At 60cm (2ft) intervals, tie the forms together with iron wire.

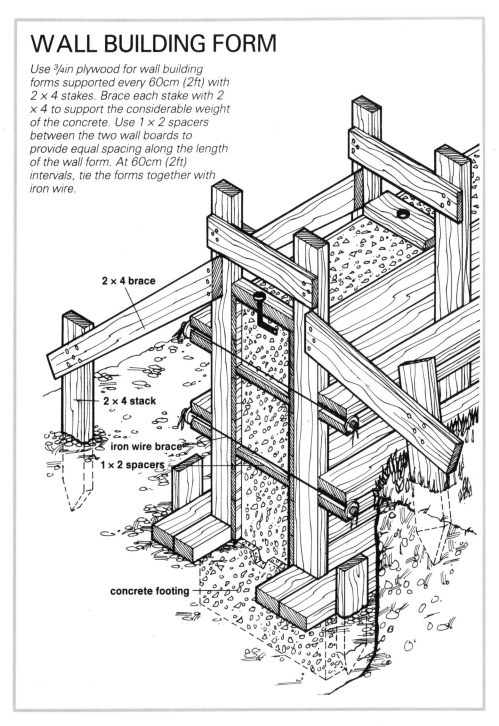

2 × 4 brace

2 × 4 stack

iron wire brace

1 × 2 spacers

concrete footing

Sidewalk forms are constructed in the same way as forms for driveways, except 2 × 4 wood is used for the boards rather than 2 × 6 because the sidewalk concrete only needs to be 10cm (4in) thick. Forms for sidewalks, paths and patios can be made from redwood or treated wood and left in place permanently for a decorative effect.

To pour a porch and steps combination, you'll need some substantial forms well braced to prevent bulging. Step risers should be no more than 20cm (8in) high, while treads are 23 to 27cm (9 to 11in) wide. Any larger and the steps would be difficult to negotiate. Use 2 × 8s for the frame. The actual width of the 2 × 8 is 7½ in, which will make an adequate riser height. Brace the form with 2 × 4s and anchor the form to the foundation wall with metal anchors.

Make sure all forms are well oiled, to allow for easy removal.

Laying concrete

Outline your area with stakes and string, then begin your excavation. Dig deep enough to allow for a 10 to 15cm (4 to 6in) compacted gravel fill plus the thickness of your concrete. Allow for a pitch of 6mm (¼in) per 30cm (12in) for drainage. A sidewalk or driveway should also be raised about 5cm (2in) above the surrounding land to allow for drainage.

Build your forms, making sure they're level and well braced. Dampen the compacted gravel and then lay a wire-mesh reinforcement. Although the mesh isn't essential for driveways or sidewalks, it does spread the stresses throughout the concrete when the ground heaves during the winter months, helping to prevent cracking.

Pour your concrete into the form. Try to place the concrete as close as possible to its final location. Excessive movement of the damp concrete can lead to scaling and dusting later.

Rake the concrete to the level of the forms, then, as soon as possible, strike off the concrete to level it. Use a flat 2 × 4 to strike off by resting the board on the forms and moving it back and forth as you advance.

Immediately after striking off, use a bull float — a short board on a long handle — to bring the surface level.

Immediately after using the bull float, run a trowel between the concrete and the forms. This helps free the forms later. The next steps must wait until the concrete has begun to set. There should be no water sheen on the surface and the concrete should be slightly stiff.

Run an edging tool around the edges to round them off, then use the jointing tool to cut the control joints. Control joints help eliminate cracking and should be cut across the width of driveways at 3m (10ft) intervals and up the middle of a double-car driveway.

Forms require different strengths depending on the project. A concrete footing, for example, can be poured into laminated fibre forms, while a foundation wall requires an elaborate structure.

We'll deal with form construction for driveways, sidewalks and steps in this chapter.

For all the above concrete projects you'll need a firm, compacted base. If your soil meets these requirements, simply remove grass and weeds and level the area. If not, you'll need to excavate an area 10 to 15cm (4 to 6in) deep to fill with gravel. Compact the gravel thoroughly.

For driveways, your forms should be made from 2 × 6 boards. Concrete should be 15cm (6in) thick for heavy loads, 10cm (4in) thick for cars. Support your forms with 2 × 4 stakes about 30cm (12in) long. Drive the stakes into the ground every 60cm (2ft) along the form. Use duplex nails to fix the forms to the stakes. Drive the nail through the stake into the form. Use double stakes wherever 2 × 6s butt.

PORCH BUILDING FORM

To make a concrete porch, place footings 15cm (6in) below the frost line then build a strong form, anchoring it to the wall with metal anchors. You'll need to apply an isolation joint between the foundation wall and your new porch. Slope the treads .6cm (¼in) forward for runoff. Make sure you broom your concrete for a non-skid surface.

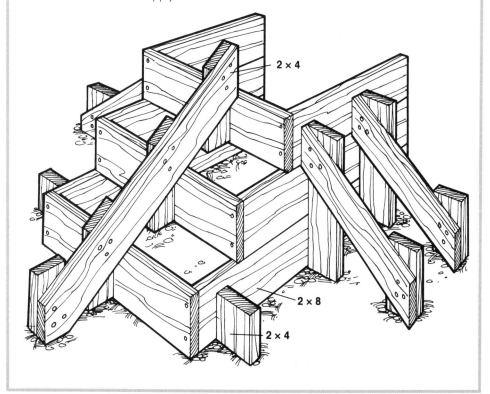

2 × 4

2 × 8

2 × 4

On sidewalks, the control joints should be cut every 1.2m (4ft).

Use a wood float next to flatten and smooth the surface. This step will produce a slight texture in the concrete that is suitable for driveways and sidewalks.

If you need a very smooth surface, you'll have to take the final step of steel trowelling. You may need to trowel two or three times for a smooth surface. The trowel is arched back and forth across the concrete, with the leading edge of the trowel slightly raised above the surface.

For the concrete to be durable, it must be cured over a period of days. Cover the concrete with plastic sheeting to keep the moisture in, and leave the sheeting in place, anchoring it with stones, for a period of 5 to 7 days.

Texturing concrete

The above method of pouring concrete offers a utilitarian cement slab. If you want to cast your own slab to make stepping stones or if you want to create a decorative garden path or patio, there are several texturing effects that can be done to concrete to create a more attractive finish.

A basic texture that creates a non-skid surface especially suitable on pool decks is handled by a stiff-bristled broom. After steel trowelling, run the broom through the concrete to create wavy lines. The broom can be dragged lightly to produce a soft finish or heavily to produce a richer texture that also helps eliminate glare off the concrete.

You can produce swirled effects at the trowelling stage by holding the steel trowel flat against the concrete and making small or large swirling motions with your hand.

A wonderful texture can be created in the concrete by exposing the aggregate on the surface. When you trowel the cement you're smoothing the cement paste over the top. If you remove that cement, you expose the aggregate, creating a rough stone surface. When mixing your concrete, try to use aggregate that is rounded rather than sharp edged. Pour the concrete in the same manner and trowel smooth. Then, with a garden hose and a stiff broom, spray the concrete with water to wash away the cement. The broom will help move the cement, exposing the rocks underneath. Use a gentle spray on the hose and only expose the top surface of the stones.

Pebble concrete produces a similar effect to the exposed aggregate concrete, but the pebbles are added after the pour, the stones are smoother and a variety of colors can be inserted into the concrete.

After pouring and striking off your concrete, place pebbles over the entire surface of your pour. Use the strike-off board to press the pebbles firmly into the concrete surface. Use a wood float to force pebbles lower into the surface and to smooth the cement over the stones.

Once the concrete has begun to set, you can start exposing the pebbles. To test the concrete, hose a gentle spray of water in one spot on the concrete and use a stiff brush to scrub the area clean. If this work doesn't dislodge or overexpose the pebbles, the concrete is ready to work. Use the same treatment over the entire concrete, exposing as many of the pebbles as you can while still maintaining a smooth surface.

Coloring concrete

Although textured surfaces help detract from the plain dull gray color of concrete, you still have that flat color. If your plans call for something a little more daring, you can change the look of your concrete by adding colored pigment prepared especially for use in concrete.

If white is your choice of color, you can buy white Portland cement to use in your mixture. However, this cement is considerably more expensive than the regular Portland. And white concrete will show every stain, as well as help create a blinding glare on the concrete surface.

The white cement can be used with colored pigments, however, to give you cleaner, brighter, concrete colors.

There are three ways to color concrete. You can add pigments when you mix the concrete ingredients. This will mean a thorough mixing of the ingredients so that the color will be evenly blended. You can trowel the color in during the finishing stages. Or, after the concrete has set, you can use concrete paint or stain to provide the color you want.

You can never really predict the final color of concrete, but, as a rule, if you want a strong color, add about 3kg (7lb) of pigment to each bag of cement; if you like pastel colors, use 1kg (2lb) of pigment for each bag of cement.

When adding color directly to the mix, you can eliminate great quantities of pigment if you use a two-step method. Lay a level of ordinary concrete to about an inch below the top of the form. Once the surface water has disappeared, complete the pour with a layer

USING CONCRETE

1 *You can buy ready mixed concrete where all you need to do is add the water or you can mix your own ingredients. This is an example of an undersanded mixture.*

2 *This properly sanded mixture has the right proportions of sand (fine aggregates), gravel (coarse aggregates) and Portland cement.*

3 *Portland cement, fine aggregate (sand) and coarse aggregate (gravel from ¼'' to 1½'' thick) are used in varying proportions to make concrete.*

4 *After pouring the concrete, rake it to the level of the forms then strike off using a flat 2 × 4. Rest the board on the forms and move it back and forth.*

5 *Use a plank as a guide when cutting control joints. Control joints are placed where stresses accumulate to control cracks. Space control joints 10 to 20 ft. apart.*

6 *A series of floats and trowels are used to smooth the concrete surface both while the surface is wet and after the water sheen has disappeared.*

7 *Concrete must be cured for five to seven days for it to be durable. Cover the concrete with plastic to keep moisture in.*

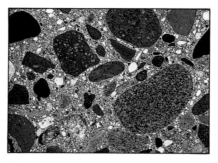

8 *For a decorative effect in concrete, expose the aggregate on the surface. After trowelling smooth, use a hose and broom to wash away the surface cement.*

9 *To create a non-skid surface in the concrete, run a stiff broom through the concrete after steel trowelling to create wavy lines.*

of colored concrete mixed without the coarse aggregate. The finishing techniques are the same as for ordinary concrete.

A second method of applying color is to trowel it in during the finishing. Pour your concrete as usual and level it with the strike-off board and bull float. Shake the dry mineral-oxide pigments over the surface of the concrete as evenly as possible. Allow it to rest for a few minutes to soak up some moisture, then trowel it into the surface thoroughly. Repeat if necessary, then follow up with the steel trowelling.

Staining and painting concrete is handled in the same way you would stain or paint any other surface. Make sure you buy stain or paint specially formulated for concrete.

APPENDIX

HAND TOOLS

Owning, and knowing how to use, a core group of hand tools is the first step in repairing any damage to your home.

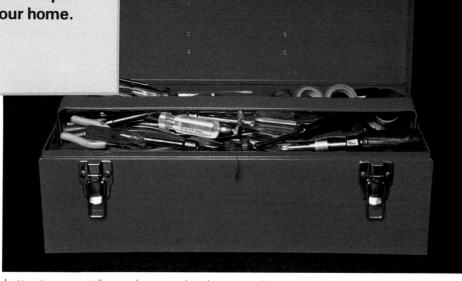

A lthough there's a tool for every need, they're not all essential for you to handle most of the repair jobs around your house.

Stock your toolbox with the basic hand tools and proceed from there as your needs and skills develop. A few key tools will help you out in most emergency repair situations, and if you buy good quality they will last a lifetime.

Saws

The two major handsaws are the crosscut and rip saw. A crosscut saw is used to cut across the grain of wood; the rip saw cuts with the grain.

In a crosscut saw, the number of teeth per 2.5cm (1in) ranges from 7 to 12 with 8 teeth, or points, per 2.5cm (1in) being enough for average work. The higher the number, the smoother the cut, but the saw also works slower. In better-quality saws the teeth are precision-ground, to provide tiny points for sharper, smoother cutting.

Alternate saw teeth are set outward from the blade to create a cut that is wider than the blade thickness, allowing the saw to cut the wood freely.

To start a cut: after marking your cut line with a square or rule, place the end of the saw closest to the handle on a corner edge of the wood on the waste side of your marked line. (The waste is the side of the wood that will not be used.) Use several pulling strokes to start your groove, then continue with full strokes at a cutting angle of 45° between the saw's edge and the work surface.

The crosscut saw cuts on both the forward and back strokes, so light pressure is needed when sawing.

A rip saw cuts parallel to the wood grain. The blade usually has 5½ teeth per 2.5cm (1in) and cuts on the forward stroke.

To start a cut: since the teeth are usually one point finer at the tip of the blade, a few pulling strokes using the tip will start your groove.

If you're making a long cut in a board, drive a wedge into the starting end of the saw cut, which will keep the two sides separated and prevent the saw from jamming.

If the saw starts to veer off course, twist the saw slightly toward the line to set the blade back on course. If you're sawing a long ripping cut, it would be helpful to clamp a

batten to your cut line and saw against it to keep the saw blade straight. A bench hook is also useful for this purpose (see page 000).

When cutting with either type of saw, use long easy strokes to ensure an even distribution of teeth wear along the blade. On nearing the end of your cut, support the waste piece to prevent splintering on the underside of your cut.

The backsaw is smaller than either the rip or crosscut saw, about 25 to 40cm (10 to 16in), and usually has 12 or 13 teeth per 2.5cm (1in) for smooth cuts with or against the grain.

The backsaw is designed for joinery work and has a reinforced back to ensure a stiff blade for smooth, straight cuts. To make a cut with a backsaw: hold the tool at a slight angle to the wood, and with a few backward strokes start your cut. Gradually level the blade so that it's straight along the surface of the wood.

A coping saw is used for ornamental and curved cuts. The blade is very fine and can have from 10 to 20 teeth per 2.5cm (1in). The blades are 15 to 16.5cm (6 to 6½in) long and are usually replaceable.

The blade should be mounted on the handle with the teeth pointing in the direction you'll be cutting. If you'll be cutting on the push stroke, the teeth should point away from the saw handle. A pull stroke should have the teeth facing the handle. A pull stroke is used for more delicate work.

A coping saw is limited to working near the edge of a board or into a board as far as the throat of the saw will allow, whereas a compass or keyhole saw can cut curved or straight lines from a bored hole without having to be near an edge. This makes them useful for cutting holes in walls or floors.

Use vertical strokes to start your cut then gradually bring the saw to an angle as the cut progresses.

Hammers

The claw hammer is a basic in any toolbox, and there are two types you can buy to serve specific purposes.

The curved claw hammer is the one found in most homes for nailing and nail-pulling. It usually has a domed face, which minimizes marring of the surface when a nail is driven flush and helps reduce nail deflection if the hammer doesn't hit the nail square.

The straight claw hammer, as its name implies, has a straight claw which maneuvers easily under boards for dismantling or ripping apart.

Hammer weights range from 140 to 560g (5 to 20oz), with the average weight for general work being around 450g (16oz). However, buy a hammer that feels most comfortable to you. Test the weight in your hand and try a few swings to get the feel of the hammer. But remember that one that is too light will require a great amount of muscle power and one that is too heavy will tire your arm quickly.

Buy a high-quality hammer and it will last a lifetime. A steel or fibreglass handle is best, but a wooden handle will suffice with proper care. High humidity can swell the fibres inside the head of the handle, which crushes them and loosens the head. Dryness, on the other hand, will shrink the handle. Both situations can create dangerous operating problems if not looked after right away.

To replace a handle, saw off the old handle at the base of the head and force out the remaining wood from inside the head. Shape your handle to ensure the fit will be snug,

SAND TEETH

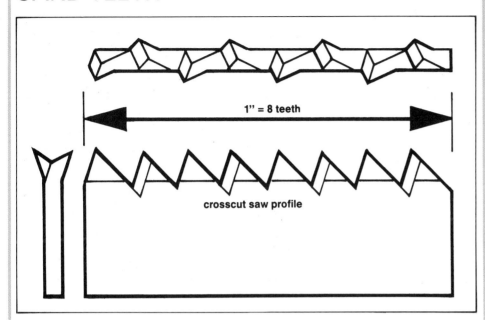

1" = 8 teeth

crosscut saw profile

A crosscut saw usually has 8 teeth, or points per inch and a rip saw 5½. A lower number of teeth cuts faster but leaves a rougher surface.

then cut two slots in the top of the handle. They should be no more than two-thirds the depth of the hammer head. Push the new handle into the head, trim off excess wood and let sit in a dry atmosphere for several hours to ensure a tight fit. An oven can help – – set the temperature at 37°C (100°F) and leave the hammer in the oven for about an hour.

Make metal or hardwood wedges and drive them into the slots at the top of the handle. This forces the pieces of the handle into the sides of the hammer head for a tight fit. File the top flush then cover the wood with a sealer to prevent moisture intake.

Metal can rust if left in an unheated area where temperature changes occur. The metal surfaces of hammers left in a garage, for example, will be exposed to condensation caused by temperature changes and will start to rust. To help prevent corrosion, cover the metal surfaces with a film of oil before storing the hammer.

To use a hammer, grasp the handle near the end, position the nail on the surface to be fastened by holding it between your thumb and forefinger, then tap the nail lightly until it stands in the wood on its own. Remove your fingers and drive the nail home. You can drive a nail flush to the surface, which might mar it, or you can stop driving slightly above the surface then use a nailset to drive the nail head below the surface of the wood for later concealment.

If the hammer head is at the same angle as the head of the nail, the nail will be driven straight and surface marring will be unlikely.

When pulling nails, place a scrap of wood under the claw of the hammer to prevent marring the surface. A claw also becomes useful when the hammer is in one hand, the other hand is being used for positioning the work, and you need to drive a nail. Place the nail head into the V of the claw, which will hold the nail in place for a few light taps that will get the nail started.

Remember never to use the hammer to strike anything harder than the hammer face, to prevent damage to the tool.

Files

Files are used to remove, shape and smooth material, and there are a number of file shapes that will suit almost any need you have.

A file shape is classified by its cross-section shape and the coarseness of the teeth. Common shapes are flat, half round, round, square, pillar and triangular; and the coarseness designations, starting with the roughest, are coarse, bastard, second cut and smooth cut. File size affects the coarseness of the cut as well, since the longer the file, the larger the tooth.

The common cuts of the teeth are: single, which can produce a smooth finish; double-cut, which produces a rougher finish but with heavy pressure can remove material quickly;

Ready Reference

THE BASIC TOOL KIT

For a basic tool kit, the following pieces are recommended:
● a flexible steel tape measure — since there's no end to the use this tool receives, buy a tape measure with a heavy-duty casing, a coated tape and a lock button.
● a crosscut saw — although there are several different types of saws, the 8-point crosscut saw will probably see the most use in your workshop. This is an indispensable tool even after you've upgraded to a power saw.
● a hammer — buy a 450g (16oz) curved claw hammer for driving and removing nails.
● a hand drill and bits — if you're a novice carpenter, the hand drill will provide all the drilling action you'll need. But the first power tool you should buy should be an electric drill.
● a backsaw and mitre box — for handling mitre joints in door casings and moldings.
● screwdrivers — at least one slot and one Phillips or Robertson screwdriver.
● an assortment of nails and screws.
● clamps — a few C-clamps will help you hold work while sawing, drilling or joining.
● an adjustable wrench — for fastening nuts and bolts.
● slip-joint pliers.
● a nailset — for burying a nail head below a surface.
● a level.
● a combination square — for squaring up small pieces and marking 45° angles.
● a chalk line — to establish vertical lines.
● wood chisels — to cut and smooth wood joints.
● an assortment of sandpaper for smoothing wood.
● a wood file and rasp for shaping wood.
● an oilstone or whetstone for sharpening tools.
● an awl for making pilot holes and marking cut lines.
● a utility knife.
● wood glue.
● safety glasses for eye protection when cutting or hammering.
● a first-aid kit.
● a marking gauge for scribing cutting lines on wood.

These tools will take care of most of your repairs. As the need arises, start adding to your toolbox with an electric drill and an assortment of bits, including countersink masonry and screwdriver bits, a power saw, an electric sander, framing square, planes and vise, on up to the more sophisticated power tools such as a jointer or radial-arm saw. Of course, if you plan to continue to add to your toolbox and to develop your do-it-yourself skills, a workbench will become essential.

BASIC HAND TOOL KIT

Basic hand tool kit: (1) level (2) cross cut saw (3) hand drill (4) screwdrivers (5) nail and screw assortment (6) hammer (7) mitre box and saw (8) wood glue (9) first aid kit (10) sandpaper (11) C clamps (12) wrench (13) pliers (14) awl (15) nailset (16) chalk line (17) chisel (18) file (19) combination square (20) oilstone (21) utility knife (22) marking gauge (23) measuring tape.

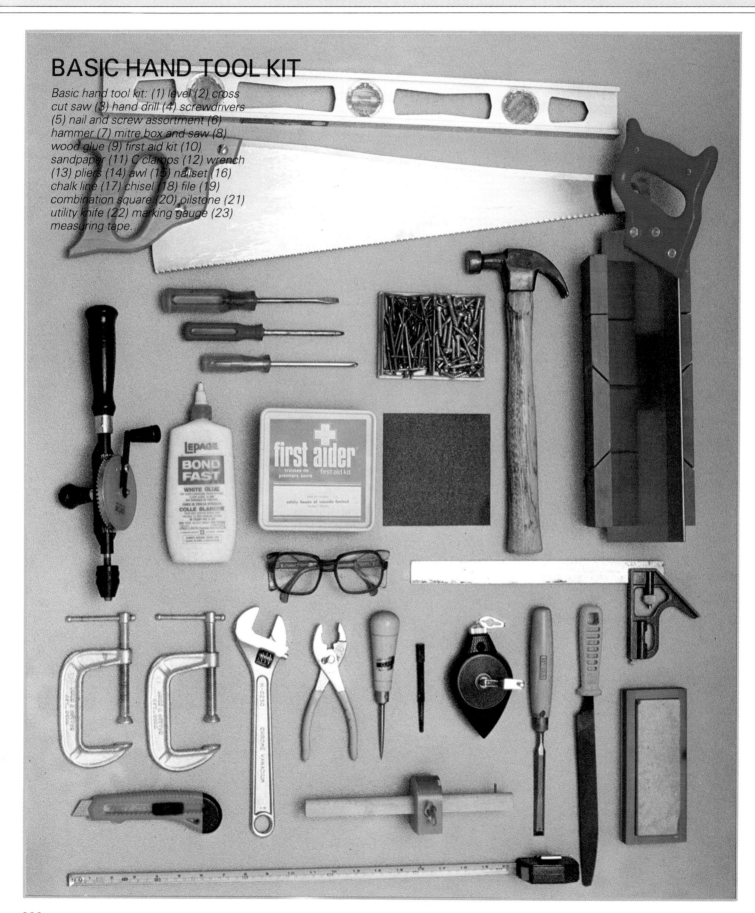

HAMMERS

Hammers are the basic workshop tool with the curved claw hammer being the one found in most homes. It's used for nailing and nail pulling. Ball peen hammers are used for metal work such as riveting; wood and plastic mallets shape metal and drive chisels; tack hammers are used for tacking and sledge hammers for heavy work.

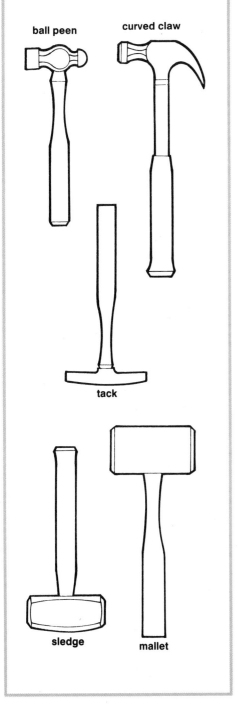

ball peen   curved claw

tack

sledge   mallet

rasp, which allows for fast material removal in woodworking; and curved cut, which is best for filing metal.

For delicate work, tight corners and small holes, needle files can be used. These files are small, thin versions of their larger cousins and will perform the same tasks on metal or wood.

If you use your files on metal, use a file card and brush on the teeth after each use to remove metal particles from the space between the teeth.

Store your files in a rack to prevent the teeth from touching other files or hard surfaces that will chip them.

To use a file, hold it at both ends and file in one direction, away from your body, holding the file either flat or at a slight angle to the piece you're working on. The piece should be held in a vise when filing. To protect your hands while filing, make sure a handle is on one end of the file and wrap a cloth around the other end.

Vises and clamps

Clamps and vises are versatile tools for the workshop. They hold pieces for gluing, fastening, tightening and sharpening.

The basic clamp that should be found in every workshop is the C-clamp. These C-shaped clamps have a range in opening sizes from 2.5 to 20cm (1 to 8in) and a throat depth from 2.5cm (1in) up to 25cm (10in) or 30cm (12in) on some clamps.

When using C-clamps, place a scrap of wood between the jaws and the work surface to prevent marring and to distribute pressure evenly. Don't overtighten the clamps.

For fast, light-pressure work, spring clamps can be used. Many can be applied quickly if you're using a fast-setting glue. The jaw openings of these clamps range from 2.5cm (1in) to 7.5cm (3in).

Although C- and spring clamps will handle many of the gluing jobs around the house, larger clamping jobs require the services of bar, pipe or web clamps.

Bar clamps are jaws mounted to flat steel pipes that range up to a length of 1.2m (4ft). Pipe clamps have separate jaws that can be mounted to a pipe cut to the length you need. Both types have a fixed jaw at one end and a movable jaw at the other for positioning against your work. These clamps are particularly useful for gluing the edges of boards. Web clamps are designed to hold irregular shapes or several joints at one time. They work by tightening a fabric band that is placed around the work being glued and pulled snug at the clamp.

For holding work that is to be shaped, filed or planed, a bench or woodworking vise is the tool to use.

Bench vises can be bolted to the top of your woodworking bench or, for lighter duty,

clamp-on models can be purchased for easy removal from the bench top. For practical purposes, the jaw opening should be at least 7.5cm (3in) wide.

Again make sure your work surface is protected from marring by placing wood scraps between the jaws and the surface.

Woodworkers' vises are bolted to the side of a bench with the top of the jaws flush to the bench top. The jaws are covered with wood to protect the work piece.

Screwdrivers

There are three types of screwdriver — slot, Phillips and Robertson, and each type is meant to fit a specific screw.

Unfortunately, each type of screwdriver also has a series of different sizes in its family, and so the size must be matched to the screw or there could be damage to the screwdriver blade or the screw head.

The standard screwdriver type is the slot head. The blade is ground flat to fit both the thickness and the width of a slot in the screw head.

The Phillips screwdriver is made to fit Phillips screws, which contain a cross-slot on the head. The fit of the screwdriver into the screw helps eliminate the tendency for the screwdriver to slide out of the slot, as can happen with the common slot screwdriver. There are a number of sizes of Phillips screwdrivers, but if you stock a size 1 and size 3 you should be adequately equipped for driving most screws.

The Robertson screwdriver has a square tip that matches up to the square hole in the screw. A number 1 and number 2 Robertson screwdriver should be sufficient for your toolbox needs. This type of screwdriver is most familiar in Canada.

There are also some specialized screwdrivers on the market to handle a variety of tasks.

For awkward areas where it becomes almost impossible to turn the screw, there are offset screwdrivers to handle the task, or square-shanked screwdrivers on which a wrench can be used to tighten the screw.

There are screwdrivers available that will hold a screw in the tip of the blade if you need to drive a screw into an area where your hand won't fit to hold the screw.

And if you need to drive many screws rapidly and you prefer a hand tool to a screwdriver drill bit, a spiral-ratchet screwdriver will save some muscle power. These screwdrivers are operated by depressing the handle, which rotates the blade and twists the screw.

Chisels

Although there are a number of chisel types in the woodworking chisel family, most do-it-yourselfers can get by with four — the mor-

FILES

The half-round (1), round (2), flat (3), pillar (4), triangular (5) and square (6)

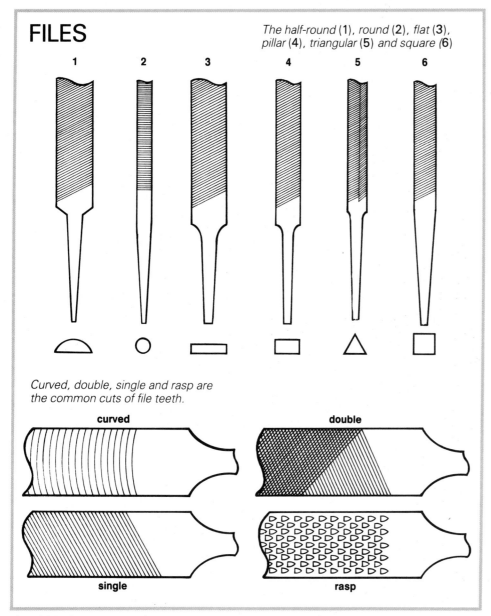

Curved, double, single and rasp are the common cuts of file teeth.

curved

double

single

rasp

tise chisel, bevel-edged firmer chisel, paring chisel and a paring gouge.

The mortise chisel is a single-purpose tool used for cutting strike plate mortises in door frames, or the mortise of a mortise and tenon joint. To cut a mortise, outline the mortise area with a knife cut, place the chisel in the center of the area and, with a mallet, strike the chisel to start the cut. By working from the center toward the sides, cut small slivers of wood away from the mortise area. Continue until desired depth is reached. A second way to cut a mortise is to bore holes in the mortise area with an electric drill, then use the chisel to clean up the mortise by removing the waste wood.

The bevel-edged firmer chisel is a heavy-duty chisel driven by a mallet and used for the bulk of your cutting work.

The paring chisel is a long, thin-bladed

chisel with a bevel. It's driven by hand for smooth, precise shave cuts in wood.

The paring gouge has a bowl-shaped blade and is most useful for smoothing holes in wood.

Use a chisel when other tools will not handle the job, and always make sure the blade of your chisel is sharp (see chapter on sharpening tools).

Chisel handles are available in both plastic and wood. Whichever one you choose, it must be able to withstand repeated blows from a mallet without danger of splitting.

Cold chisels are manufactured to withstand the heavy-impact demands of cutting into stone or metal.

The flat chisel is the most useful for the do-it-yourselfer. This type of cold chisel can be used for cutting chain, shearing metal or cutting into brick and stone for repair work.

There is a danger of bits of stone and metal flying off from your chisel cuts. To protect your eyes, make sure you wear safety glasses whenever you use a cold chisel.

Wrenches

Although the number of wrenches available is almost infinite, the one wrench you should have in your workshop is a smooth-jawed adjustable wrench. These wrenches are adjusted by a knurled knob on the handle to grip tightly any nut or bolt head.

As you add to your collection of wrenches, you can purchase specific-use tools such as socket wrenches or open-end wrenches, which are thinner than an adjustable wrench and so can operate in tighter quarters; Allen ('L') wrenches, which are essential for working Allen screws; and pipe (Stillson) wrenches, which are grooved-jaw wrenches worked in pairs to handle pipe work.

Pliers

Pliers are one of the most versatile tools in the home workshop. Although there are a number of special-purpose pliers available, five different sets of pliers will be enough to enable you to handle most jobs around the home.

The most popular and versatile are slip-joint pliers, which have a two-position pivot to allow for normal and wide jaw opening.

Long-nosed, or needle-nosed, pliers, as the name implies, have long faces that offer maneuverability in tight working quarters. These pliers are used for shaping and bending sheet metal and thin wire, and are also useful in taking the place of your fingers when holding brads for nailing.

Diagonal-cutting pliers (wire cutters) have hardened, tapered edges useful for cutting wire or small nails.

Channel pliers offer a wider jaw opening than other pliers and can be used to grip almost any shape.

Side-cutting pliers have large square jaws that will grip flat metal for bending or cutting. The side cutters on these pliers are designed for more heavy-duty wire-cutting work than can be handled by the diagonal-cutting pliers.

Sandpaper

Sandpaper comes in a range of grades, from very fine to extra coarse. The work determines the grade to use.

Very fine (No. 600) gives a smooth final finish to wood and is useful for sanding between coats of paint or varnish where you don't want to see scratch marks.

Fine-grade sandpaper is useful for removing scratches from metal or wood and as a final sanding before applying a primer to the wood surface.

Use medium, coarse and extra-coarse grades of sandpaper for stock removal and

CLAMPS

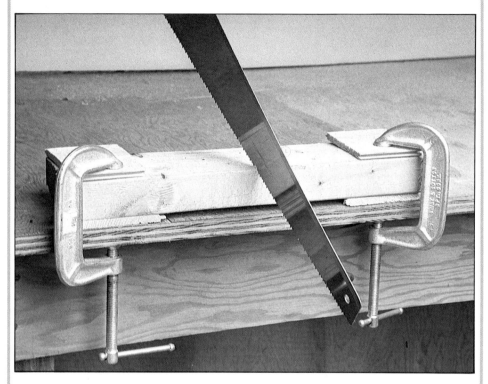

When using C clamps to hold wood, place scrap of wood between the jaws of the clamp and the work

surface to prevent marring of your work.

smoothing of deep scratches or imperfections.

If a wood or metal surface has deep scratches or imperfections, start sanding with a coarse abrasive then sand with increasingly finer grades of sandpaper until the surface is smooth and free from scratches.

Abrasive materials include silicon carbide (the hardest abrasive available), aluminum oxide, garnet flint and emery, on cloth or paper backings, with normal or wet sanding capabilities.

To sand large imperfections or heavy coats of paint and varnish, use an inexpensive grit such as flint or emery which can be discarded when the grit clogs.

For sanding harder surfaces such as metal, plastic or hardwood, use aluminum oxide or silicon carbide. Silicon carbide used wet also gives a fine smooth finish to metal or varnish.

Measuring and marking tools

The difference between a professional- and amateur-looking job can be in the measuring. For pieces to fit perfectly, accurate measurements are essential. An eighth of an inch can throw off the whole balance of a job.

No matter what tool you use to measure, take your time and follow the adage, "Measure twice, cut once."

The steel tape measure is the most common measuring tool used by do-it-yourselfers. It offers the flexibility of making inside and outside measurements as well as measuring round objects.

The folding wooden rule is used in place of the flexible steel rule when rigidity is of con-

WRENCHES

The smooth-jawed adjustable wrench is the most useful workshop wrench of the many types available. Open-end wrenches are used where it's impossible to apply the wrench over the end of the work. Socket wrenches can be worked in tighter areas.

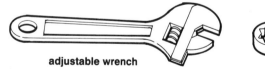
adjustable wrench

box wrench

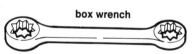
socket wrenches with rachet handle

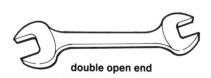
double open end

open end and box combo

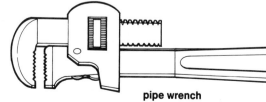
pipe wrench

MEASURING TOOLS

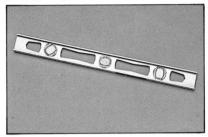

1 *Levels are used for checking vertical and horizontal surfaces and are available in a range of sizes from the tiny line level to the 1.2m (4ft) mason's level.*

2 *The steel tape is the most common measuring tool. Its flexibility allows the do-it-yourselfer to make inside and outside measurements.*

3 *The framing square (also called the rafter square) is a large carpenter's measuring tool that is used for marking rafter cuts.*

4 *The folding wooden rule is preferable to the flexible steel tape when rigidity is of concern. Use it to measure across wide openings such as stairways.*

5 *To aid in making an accurate cut line, mark your cut points with a V. The point of the V is the exact measurement from which you draw your cut line.*

6 *The try square is used for right-angle marking and for testing the squareness of adjoining surfaces to ensure a tight fit when joined.*

7 *The combination square is also used for right-angle marking and for testing squareness in adjoining surfaces, but it can also be used for mitre marking.*

8 *Use a T bevel to duplicate an angle cut from one object to another. Line up the bevel with the angle. Tighten the wing nut and transfer the angle.*

cern. If you need to measure across wide openings, then it's preferable to use the wooden rule.

To ensure accurate marking when using the steel or wooden rule, mark your cut points with a V. The point of the V is the exact measurement from which you draw your cut line, using a square or T-bevel.

The try square is used to test for squareness in adjoining surfaces and is also used for right-angle marking.

The combination square tests for squareness, can be used for right-angle marking or mitre marking.

The framing square is a large carpenter's marking tool.

The T-bevel is used to duplicate an angle cut from one object to another.

Levels, which are used for checking vertical and horizontal surfaces, are available in a range of sizes from the smallest, the line level, which is suspended on a string for long-span levelling, to the mason's level, which is 1.2m (4ft) long. The most practical level for home use is a 60cm (2ft) long carpenter's level, which provides level, plumb and 45° tubes that check horizontals, verticals and angles respectively.

For accurate marking, make sure one end of the board you're cutting is square. To do this, hold the body of a combination or try square firmly against a machined edge of the board. The blade of the square then lays flat across the width of the board to show the true 90° edge. Scribe or draw a line along the blade of the square and cut the board at this line. Use the new cut edge to measure your length, mark the cut line with a V, then, holding the body of the square firmly against the side of the board, draw or scribe your measured line. Remember to cut on the waste side of the line for accurate fittings. If you don't plan on cutting the board right away, mark the waste side of the wood with an X so you'll know where to cut when you come back to it.

If you need to mark for a lengthwise cut on a board, a marking gauge can be used. These tools have an adjustable ruled gauge which is locked in place for marking. The body of the gauge is held firmly to the side of the board and drawn down the length of the wood. A scriber on the tip of the ruled gauge then scratches a line in the wood parallel to the side of the board. A chalk line can also be used for lengthwise marking.

For marking small circles, use metal dividers. For large circles, trammel points can be used with a wood strip. Simply hammer one metal trammel through the strip to indicate the center of the circle. The second trammel is hammered through the strip at a distance equal to the radius of your circle. The center trammel point is held firmly against the wood while the circle is scribed using the trammel at the end of the wood strip.

SHARPENING TOOLS

Spending some time to create a finely honed cutting edge will help extend the life of your tools and make your tasks more pleasurable as well.

Cutting with your hand tools should be effortless. If you find you're using a lot of force, your tools are probably dull and are damaging your materials.

Sharpening saws

If cutting speed slows down, saw teeth usually just need to be filed sharp. But after several sharpenings, the teeth may need to be reset to ensure a cut that is slightly wider than the blade.

SHARPENING SAWS

Use a triangular file to sharpen saws, keeping the file level and angled properly. For rip saws, the file is moved straight across and at right angles to the blade. For sharpening cross cut saws, hold the file against the bevel of the teeth. To prevent chattering, clamp the saw in a vise just below the gullets.

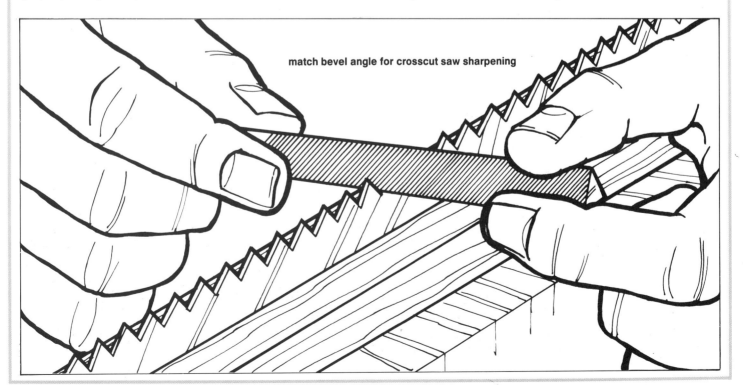

match bevel angle for crosscut saw sharpening

SHARPENING CHISELS

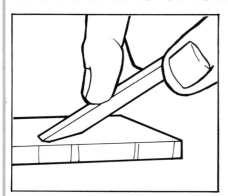

1 *To sharpen a chisel, hold the blade on a whetstone at a 30° angle to the stone. Move the blade in a figure 8 motion. Coat the stone with oil first.*

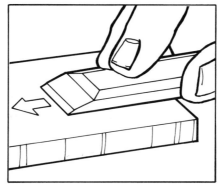

2 *A burr will be formed on the flat side of the chisel which can be removed by placing the flat side on the whetstone and moving it in a circular motion.*

3 *The angle of the cutting edge in a chisel is important. To help ensure the correct angle, sharpening jigs can be purchased.*

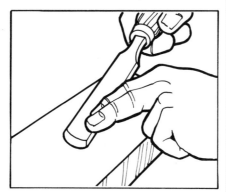

4 *To sharpen the round surface on a gouge, you can purchase round and tapered whetstones which can be rubbed over the edge of the gouge.*

around in a figure-eight motion. When a burr appears along the entire edge of the opposite side of the chisel, flip the tool over, lay it flat on the stone and stroke it up and down the stone surface to remove the burr. Apply only light pressure.

To sharpen a crosscut saw, clamp the saw blade between two pieces of hardwood in a vise. The wood should be the length of the blade and only the teeth should show above the wood surface.

Run a flat file lightly along the top of the teeth, making sure the file is held absolutely level. This creates a base on the teeth to guide you in your sharpening.

Rest a small triangular file in the gullet to the left of the first tooth that is set toward you. Move the file until it rests against the bevel of the tooth, then file down into the gullet. Continue down one side of the blade, reverse the saw and repeat the process.

To file a rip saw, follow the same procedure but draw the file straight across the blade at right angles.

To reset teeth, buy or rent a saw set that will bend saw teeth to the correct, predetermined angle.

If filing and setting saw teeth seems like a tedious task, most hardware stores or home centers offer an inexpensive sawblade sharpening service. A sharp blade will add years of life to your saw while creating smoother cuts and less strain on your arm muscles.

Sharpening chisels

A dull chisel is useless, a sharp one a joy to use.

To return the cutting edge of a chisel to its original sharpness, use a whetstone with some light machine oil applied to the top. The oil keeps the stone clean and the tool cool.

Hold the ground face of the chisel at a 30° angle to the stone and move the chisel

POWER TOOLS

Although power tools are more expensive than most hand tools, the increased cost is more than outweighed by the speed with which any power tool does the job.

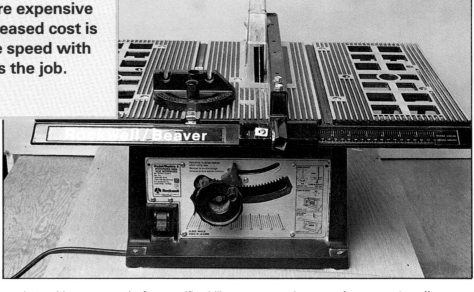

Power tools will handle any job with the same accuracy as hand tools, but they have the extra advantage of speed. A table saw will cut a board in seconds providing a straight, clean cut. And a drill can cut, sand or shape in far less time than the job can be done by hand.

Drills
The portable electric drill should be the first power tool in any do-it-yourselfer's toolbox. The machine is inexpensive and versatile. It can drill wood, stone, metal and plastic; it can cut, sand, shape, grind, mix paint and serve as an electric screwdriver.

Drills commonly come in sizes of 6mm, 9mm, 12mm (¼in, ⅜in and ½in). The size refers to the maximum shank diameter the chuck will hold. However, that doesn't mean you're limited to drilling with bits only as large as your chuck. Oversize bits will have shanks milled down to 6mm (¼in) to allow them to be used in homeowners' drills.

The speed of the drill is usually determined by the size. As size increases, speed decreases. However, the slower speeds provide greater torque to drive oversize bits and hole saws.

Some drill models offer variable speed and some are reversible. A variable speed drill offers you the option of drilling through glass or ceramic at the slow speeds necessary for these materials, while also being able to function as a sander at high speeds. The reverse option means you can back out screws from a hole or alternate the rotation when using sanding or shaping bits.

There are several accessories available to make drilling tasks easier.

For hard-to-reach areas there are flexible shafts, extension bits and right-angle attachments. A flexible shaft is a long flexible tube with a chuck on the end. The tube is attached to the drill and the bit placed in the chuck on the shaft. Extension bits are long enough to allow for hole drilling in areas beyond the reach of a normal drill bit. Right-angle attachments allow for right-angle drilling without the awkwardness of working in a confined space.

Stands are available to turn your portable drill into a stationary drill press. The drill fastens quickly into the stand to allow for vertical cutting. There are a variety of stands on the market, with some made for specific drills only. Check with your drill manufacturer to see if a drill-press stand is available for your model.

Grinding wheels, disks and stones, sanding drums and disks, circle cutters, hole cutters, circular saw blades for metal cutting, paint stirrers and screwdriver attachments are also available to turn your portable drill into a versatile tool in your home workshop.

Routers
The router is an uncomplicated tool that operates at high speeds (around 20,000 to 30,000 rpm) to cut, groove, recess or shape wood.

Although a router is perhaps best known for cutting moldings or fancy edges on workpieces, the machine can also handle dados, stopped dados, grooves, rabbets, dovetails, lap-and-mortise and tenon joints.

Router bits are inserted into the collet chuck at the bottom of the router. The machine is gripped with two hands and moved into the work with the bit in operation.

To insert a bit, unplug the router, grip the lower nut with a wrench to prevent the motor shaft from moving, and loosen or tighten the collet nut with a second wrench. Some machines have a locking device that prevents motor shaft movement, so you'll need only one wrench to insert a bit.

The bit should move easily through the work with only slight reduction in motor speed. Moving it too slowly can burn the wood and damage the bit, moving it too fast can damage the motor. Too much motor reduction means you're trying to force the cut.

The bit moves clockwise in the router, so try to keep the router positioned so that the router tends to pull into the wood. This will prevent the router from wavering off course.

Keep bits sharp and buy nothing less than high-speed steel bits. If you plan on using your router frequently, it may be worth investing in carbide-tipped cutters, especially if you'll be cutting plywood, plastic or laminates which contain abrasives that will dull your cutters quickly.

Work security and safety is important when using a router.

Since initial torque is high when starting the router, it must be gripped firmly in both hands before being turned on. Once in operation, guide the cutter into the top of the work and move it along a path to cut or shape; or guide the router into the work from an edge.

Make sure all work is clamped firmly and the base of the router has enough support. If cutting narrow stock, it would be wise to fasten a block of wood to the base of the router for support.

Routers can also be operated from the underside of a special router table, which can be either purchased or made. The machine is fastened to the underside of the table with the router bit extending through a hole in the table surface. This frees your hands to control the work being cut. Use a fence clamped to the tabletop to guide the work.

Remember to keep fingers clear of router bits, and always wear goggles when operating any equipment.

Circular saws
Although a circular saw won't replace a table saw or radial-arm saw in terms of accuracy of cut, it does have one advantage over the stationary tools — it's portable.

The circular saw was originally developed so that sizing of lumber could be done

DRILL ATTACHMENTS

Hole cutters, which are available in several different sizes, can be attached to your drill to cut holes for door handles or dowel inserts.

DRILL STANDS

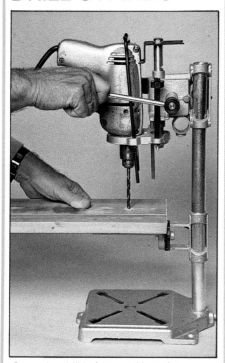

Once the drill is fastened into the stand, a hand-operated lever lowers the drill into the wood for straight, accurate boring or countersinking.

speedily on the construction site. Since then the saw has become popular with do-it-yourselfers where portability is of concern. It can be used in the yard when you're building a deck or a sandbox. But it can also be used in

the shop to make rough cuts in large sheets of plywood or panelling.

The size of the saw is indicated by the diameter of the blade. Since you won't be cutting through 12mm (½in) wood all the time, make sure the blade size of the saw you decide to purchase will, at the least, handle cuts in 5cm (2in) stock at a 45° angle. Blade sizes of 18 or 20cm (7 or 8in) will handle the job.

The blades on a circular saw turn counter-clockwise. The top of the blade is covered by a permanent casing, the bottom by a retractable housing that moves up and out of the way as you cut but immediately moves back to cover the blade once the cut is complete.

When cutting, don't feed the saw into the wood until full speed is obtained. Don't force the saw, and keep a steady, straight course. Cutting off the line can create a bind in the blade, which will cause kickback.

When setting the blade for cutting, make sure that a full tooth of the blade extends beyond the bottom of the work for efficient cutting.

Straight cuts should be made using a guide clamped to the work to keep the saw from veering off course. If you need to cut thick pieces of stock, adjust the blade depth to maximum level, make your cut, flip the stock over and make a matching cut through the other side. Accuracy in marking the cutting line and in saw placement is important in handling this procedure.

Remember to keep your blades clean (by wiping dirt off with turpentine) and sharp so you won't have to force the saw and damage the motor. Keep the base of the saw lightly waxed for smooth gliding. Always wear goggles when cutting.

Portable jigsaw
In addition to making crosscuts or rip cuts in stock up to 5cm (2in) thick, the jigsaw or saber saw is an ideal tool for cutting curves or making pocket cuts for receptacles or light switches. It will cut through wood, metal, glass or tile.

Pocket cuts can be made by piercing a start hole with a drill. Place the blade of the jigsaw through the starter hole and saw according to your layout. The blade cuts with a forward, vertical motion. Angle cuts can be created by using the tilt adjustment on the saw.

The jigsaw's main feature is its ability to cut curves, but it is also a good tool to use for light-duty cutting in or out of the workshop.

Table saws
If you've used a handsaw for a task and then followed that task by using a table saw, you'll see why table saws have become the most important stationary power tool in any home workshop. The speed and accuracy with which they cut will let you handle any task

with greater efficiency.

Blade diameters range from 19 to 25cm (7½ to 10in) with a maximum cutting depth of 3.8 to 8.6cm (1½ to 3⅜in) respectively. The most common size found in home workshops is the 25cm (10in) table saw. The 20cm (8in) has the added advantages of being slightly more portable and less expensive than the larger version, making it easier on the budget for those who don't plan to make considerable use of it.

In all types of table saws, the blade is mounted on an arbor which is turned by a motor. The blade projects through a slot in the top of the table, and is adjustable to create different depths of cut. All machines come equipped with mitre gauges for cross- or mitre cutting and laterally adjustable rip fences.

The blade rotates toward you as you stand in front of the saw, and the work is fed into the blade from the front of the table.

The blade is covered with a pivoted blade guard, which should be kept in position at all times as a safety precaution. There are some cuts, however, such as dados, grooves or shaping, that can't be made with the guard in position. Know this when you're making these cuts and keep your mind focused on your cutting activity. Remember, these machines can hurt.

Keep fingers at least 15cm (6in) away from the blade. To move narrow stock past the blade, use a push stick instead of your fingers.

Table saws are capable of producing smooth, accurate and straight cuts. But these saws are only as good as their users, so learn how to make the fullest use of them. And make sure you measure and mark accurately without relying on the calibrations on the tool. Tool calibrations are not always perfect, and measuring accurately with a protractor can mean the difference between a perfect mitre or one that gaps.

Sanders
You can make fast work of sanding with two of the most common power sanders found in home workshops — the belt sander and the pad sander.

The belt sander is the workhorse, removing old finishes, taking down stock, polishing metal and re-edging some of your garden tools. The wide selection of abrasives and grits means a number of rough sanding tasks can be handled quickly by this tool.

The belt sander uses a continuous belt of coated abrasive that runs over two drums, one located at each end of the machine. The motor powers the rear drum and the front drum adjusts tension and tracking. The most common belt sizes are 7.5 or 10cm (3 or 4in) width, with a length of about 60cm (24in).

A coarse grit belt moving at high speeds will remove stock the fastest if that's your

USING POWER SAWS

When using a circular saw, adjust the blade to ensure that one full tooth will penetrate the work to ensure maximum efficiency in cutting.

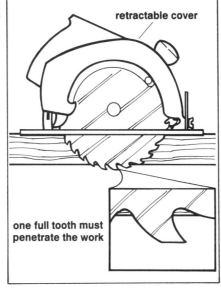

retractable cover

one full tooth must penetrate the work

When using a table saw, make sure your fingers are always at least 15cm (6in) away from the blade. Use a push stick to move thin stock past the blade.

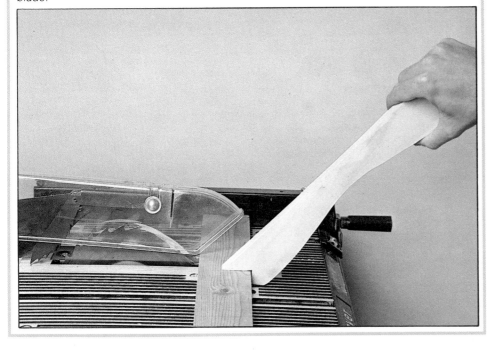

aim. Finer grits and slower speeds allow for smoother work.

Since the belt sander removes a considerable amount of material, the inevitable sanding dust can float and land anywhere. Check out the sanders that come with built-in dust-collecting systems or attachments to allow the use of your home vacuum cleaner while sanding. You'll keep the air free of dust and your workshop cleaner.

To operate the belt sander, start the motor, then lower the tool to the work. Always keep the sander in motion or you'll create depressions in your work.

Move the sander back and forth, working in the direction of the grain. Cross-grain sanding will raise considerable nap on the wood, which creates a rougher surface.

Light-weight material should be clamped when sanding, since the tool has enough force to cause kickback.

Remember to watch the edges of wood when sanding. Keep the base of the sander firmly on the wood so that the edges don't become rounded.

The pad sander, which has a straight-line sanding action, or the orbital sander, which cuts in circular movements, are considered to be finishing sanders. They don't remove stock; they smooth it to create a scratch-free surface either in varnish and lacquer or on wood.

The sanders come with a soft flat pad wrapped with a rectangle of sandpaper. The abrasive material is pulled taut over the pad and clamped tight at both ends of the sander.

A front knob is a feature on most machines and it permits two-hand operation. However, two-hand operation is meant only for guiding the machine, not for extra pressure. In most instances, the abrasive will cut the surface simply by the weight of the tool. A heavier pressure is likely to inflict deep scratches in the stock.

Watch your sandpaper and as the grit becomes clogged, replace it. Clogged paper won't abrade stock and you'll end up wasting a lot of time and effort.

INDEX

Home Repair Record

Address:

Repair	Date	Supplies	Cost

Home Repair Record

Address:

Repair	Date	Supplies	Cost

Home Repair Record

Address:

Repair	Date	Supplies	Cost

Home Repair Record

Address:

Repair	Date	Supplies	Cost

Home Repair Record

Address:

Repair	Date	Supplies	Cost